ANNALS of
DYSLEXIA

VOLUME XLIX   1999

Annals of Dyslexia is listed in *Current Contents / Social and Behavioral Sciences* (CC/ S&BS), the Social Sciences Citations Index ©(SSCI™), and *Chicoral Abstracts to Reading and Learning Disabilities*. Microfilm and photocopies are available from University Microfilms International.

Annotated and indexed by the ERIC Clearinghouse on Handicapped and Gifted Children for publication in the monthly print index *Current Index to Journals in Education* (CIJE) and the quarterly index, *Exceptional Child Education Resources* (ECER).

The International Dyslexia Association
Chester Building/Suite 382
8600 LaSalle Road
Baltimore, MD 21286-2044

Printed in the United States of America

Notice

Members of The International Dyslexia Association® receive *Annals of Dyslexia* without charge. Additional copies of this issue are available from The International Dyslexia Association® at $15.00 each for members and $18.00 each for nonmembers plus 20% for postage and handling. Send orders prepaid to the address above.

Cover design: Joseph M. Dieter, Jr.
Compositor: Type Shoppe II Productions, Ltd.
Printer: Port City Press

ISSN 0736-9387

ANNALS OF DYSLEXIA

Volume XLIX   1999

Contents

FOREWORD

The *Annals of Dyslexia* is an interdisciplinary peer-reviewed journal published by The International Dyslexia Association. The focus of the journal is on the understanding, prevention, and remediation of reading disability. Although primary emphasis is placed on original research articles, we also publish significant reviews and well-documented reports of effective practice. We invite submissions to the journal from members of the Association as well as from other researchers, educators, and clinicians concerned with reading acquisition and reading disability.

Each year, the combination of papers published in *Annals* seems to take on a life of its own. This year, what is most striking is the critical attention paid to empirical evidence in refining theoretical explanations and creating practical solutions for those questions that have long challenged the student of dyslexia. As the tools we have available to address these important questions become increasingly sophisticated, it is reassuring that the findings obtained do not refute prior research, but rather help us to understand how to reconcile what has previously seemed contradictory.

On the theoretical side, a major focus this year is on rapid serial naming. Martha Denckla and Maryanne Wolf each provide a rich and thoughtful discussion (and new data) on what underlies rapid serial naming deficits and how naming might intersect with well-documented phonological aspects of reading disability. (You will also want to look to chapters 5 and 9 for relevant data on RAN).

The basic research papers in this year's volume all seek to place phonological weaknesses within the context of other contributions to difficulties with reading, spelling, and other aspects of school achievement. The first set (chapters 3 through 5) focus on how phonological dyslexia fits within the larger context of reading and/or learning disabilities. They have very different emphases and use quite different approaches, but each comes up with the same answer: phonological weaknesses do not account for all of the difficulties of struggling students, and perhaps not all of the difficulties of students with dyslexia face, but they do account for the lion's share of reading difficulties. The second set (chapters 4 through 6) all look at the the role of phonology in accounting for spelling difficulties. There too,

despite quite different techniques and emphases, the over-
whelming conclusion is that spelling difficulties are strongly associated with sensitivity to the alphabetic system.

As is our intention, intervention research remains a central
focus of this journal. I am particularly pleased with the scope
and specificity of the strategies and goals addressed by this
year's authors—from morpheme analysis to speech recognition
technology to repeated readings for fluency and and interest-
driven activities. Each paper emphasizes the many components
to reading success; each also includes phonology as a central
piece (or result) of the intervention.

For their assistance in reviewing manuscripts, I am grateful
to my dedicated Editorial Associates and recently expanded
Editorial Advisory Board; additional and much appreciated
input was provided by P. Cornelissen, S. Gathercole, A. Jenner,
A. Pollatsek, R. Treiman, and F. Vellutino. The Publications
Committee of the IDA has provided guidance and support to
the journal, as have Cindy Ciresi and Tom Viall from the
Baltimore office. Sharon Ringgold and Abigail Struthers have
been flexible, gracious, prompt, and thoughtful through the
many stages of the editorial process. As in years past, Type
Shoppe II has committed itself to a timely and accurate product.

Finally, I want to thank the many authors who make the
Annals what it is. This includes not only those whose papers are
represented in this volume, but all who put their work forth to
be judged. I am terribly proud of the quality of research and
writing I have witnessed over the six years I have been Editor.
As we celebrate the 50th meeting of the IDA and, in the year
2000, the 50th volume of the *Annals of Dyslexia*, we should all
feel proud of the major contributions that this society has made
to our understanding and treatment of dyslexia.

—Editor

To submit a manuscript to the *Annals of Dyslexia*, you must do so by
January 15 to receive consideration for publication in the following
year. A copy of Information for Contributors is included in the back of
this volume or may be obtained by writing to: The International
Dyslexia Association®, Chester Building/Suite 382, 8600 LaSalle Road,
Baltimore, Maryland 21286-2044. Individual copies of papers in the
current or prior issues (including those from the *Bulletin of the Orton
Society*) are available at the same address. The cost is $4.00, including
postage and handling.

THE 1998 SAMUEL T. ORTON AWARD PRESENTED TO PRISCILLA LUKE VAIL

by Sylvia O. Richardson

It was 1977. The Orton Dyslexia Society (now the International Dyslexia Association) was meeting in Dallas. Drake Duane was President and I was on the old Executive Council, some committees, and gave a couple of presentations. Those of us with such pervasive occupations were hard pressed to attend many sessions. However, I shall never forget one that I missed, after I read it in the 1978 *Bulletin of the Orton Society* (now the *Annals of Dyslexia*) and rued the day that I didn't hear it. The paper was "Limerence, Language, and Literature: An Essay" by Priscilla L. Vail.

At the start of the article Priscilla wrote that limerence "means being in love, or falling in love. I have a feeling of limerence for language and I want my students to feel the same way." Priscilla Vail's limerence for language is obvious to all who hear her and read her work. She is not only a miracle worker with words, but also an inspiring, dedicated teacher and staunch advocate for children and literacy.

For many years Priscilla was the Reading Specialist for Rippowam-Cisqua School in her hometown of Bedford, N.Y. (That she could teach the children to pronounce and to spell the school's name attests to her ability as a teacher!) The children there have profited from her wit and wisdom, and her effervescent encouragement. Drawing from decades of experience as an elementary school teacher and learning specialist, and always including humor and insightful case studies, she has also taught countless teachers and parents to help students achieve success in the language arts.

During this past year, along with continuing to write and attending her many speaking engagements, Priscilla has collaborated with the Allen-Stevenson School. In the words of the headmaster, they "have invited Ms. Vail to help us pull together how we teach, think about, understand, and develop the use of language, especially oral and written language, in the ten years boys spend with us." I can think of no better person to provide that kind of assistance, and to help them apply current research about learning to their curriculum.

Priscilla has been a popular Guest Lecturer at the Graduate School of Education, Manhattanville College in Purchase, N.Y., which brings up an interesting point. This paragon of priceless prose was, believe it or not, a prototypical dropout, who received her Bachelor's degree from that same college in 1973, 24 years after she entered Vassar. This was indeed a road less traveled and a stoly that needs telling.

Priscilla entered Vassar in 1949, but fell madly in love and married Donald Vail after her sophomore year, prepared in heart and mind to become a good corporate attorney's wife and mother, which indeed she was. Soon, in rather quick succession, came her first three children to whom she devoted her fullest love and attention.

In 1960 Sarah Lawrence College received a grant to establish a program which was designed to determine if thirty-year-old women could still learn! She was encouraged to enroll by her very supportive husband, who said, "You go. I can learn to take my suits to the cleaners myself." Priscilla applied, was interviewed by the President of the College, and was accepted. However, after a couple of years of study, the stork dropped in and Priscilla dropped out to nurture the new little Vail.

Then came a stroke of luck: New York University offered courses for college credit on TV, which could be taken at home. Once again our heroine resumed serious study, now accruing knowledge and credits from 3 colleges. By this time, Priscilla had developed an avid interest in children who had difficulty learning. She became a member of the Orton Dyslexia Society and literally soaked up information on dyslexia. Again, Donald Vail, who was now an expert in taking his suits to the cleaners, urged her to get her B.A. She knew she wanted to teach children, to put into practice all she was learning, but that necessitated getting the degree.

Priscilla now went to Manhattanville College, but found that the education courses offered for the B.A. degree did not meet her needs. In fact, at that time very few colleges of education included courses on learning disabilities, let alone dyslexia. In her inimitable, persuasive, and rather persistent manner she convinced the Dean to let her take the necessary requisites plus a variety of independent studies that she wanted. She essentially invented her own program to study learning disabilities and dyslexia. It is not surprising that, after a lot of finagling, the Dean agreed, on condition that Priscilla would leave the College when she had completed her studies!

She received her B.A. in 1973, and her M.A.T. (Master of Arts in Teaching) in 1974. This was a pattern of continuing education that lasted 25 years! Of note, she received the B.A. three weeks before her oldest daughter received hers! But then Priscilla comes from a rare group of women indeed. She is proud that her grandmother, a widow who raised six daughters and a son, was in the eighth class to graduate from Wellesley. Three of these daughters graduated from Vassar, three from Smith. Priscilla's own three daughters comprise the fourth successive generation of college graduates. Her equally accomplished son received his B.A. from Denison University and is presently working on his Ph.D.at the University of Connecticut at Storrs.

Priscilla's professional affiliations are numerous and varied. She is well known to all in the International Dyslexia Association as one of our most popular speakers, and her columns written for the Newsletter of the New York Branch (since 1980) are veritable treasures. She has been active in the National Association of Independent Schools, the American Association of Gifted Children, the World Association for Gifted and Talented, the Author's Guild, the Hallowell Clinic for Cognitive and Emotional Health, and is even on the education committee of the Mystic Seaport Museum.

Organizations such as NAIS, the Bank Street College of Education, the Bryn Mawr Child Study Institute, Teacher's College of Columbia University, the Principal's Center at Harvard Graduate School of Education, and Cambridge University, England have benefited from her work.

Priscilla has spoken all over the United States, as well as in England, Canada, Spain, and Saudi Arabia. How she keeps up with her speaking schedu}e alone is mind-boggling, yet she has also found time to publish 11 books. She states that they are not "big" books, but I have found them to be enormous in content and importance. In a review of her book, *Smart Kids with School Problems*, I wrote that it was "a sumptuous feast providing much food for thought, laced with examples that add both spice and nourishment. It should be required reading for all educators and parents." Equally high praise could be given to the majority of her output, both written and spoken.

Much of Priscilla's effectiveness is due to her greatly varied experiences and reading, to her limerence for language, and to that gifted mind which has such a wonderful propensity for parable and allegory. The value of her endowment to us of knowledge, wisdom, and humor has been immeasurable.

The noted theologian, Soren Kierkegaard, described a man as a "Knight of faith" in beautiful language. I have taken the liberty of converting the "Knight of faith" to a "Lady of faith." The following is from Kierkegaard, with a change of gender:

"This figure is the woman who lives in faith, who has given over the meaning of her life to her creator, and who lives centered on the energies of her maker. She accepts whatever happens in this visible dimension without complaint, lives her life as a duty. . . . No pettiness is so petty that it threatens her meaning, no task is too frightening to be beyond her courage. She is fully in the world on its terms and wholly beyond the world in her trust of the invisible dimension."

This, to me, is Priscilla Luke Vail, a "Lady of faith", whose existence has been a constant expression of her faith in life, in love, and in the gifts and talents of children with dyslexia.

Tonight, Priscilla, it pleasures and honors me to have the privilege of presenting to you, the 1998 Samuel T. Orton Award on behalf of the members of this Association and of the innumerable children and teachers you have taught.

The Citation:

The Samuel T. Orton Award
to Priscilla Luke Vail

Teacher, learning specialist, consultant, author, silver-tongued wordsmith, Priscilla L. Vail has devoted her life, her vigor and her gifted mind to children with dyslexia and to their teachers. She has influenced the program of many schools in this country and abroad through her insightful workshops and writings. In recognition of her gifts, her wisdom, her humor and character, and with deep affection, the Association presents the 1998 Samuel T. Orton Award to Priscilla Luke Vail.

ACCEPTANCE OF THE SAMUEL TORRY ORTON AWARD
NOVEMBER 14, 1997, MINNEAPOLIS

Priscilla Luke Vail

ACCEPTANCE
On Many Levels

Thank you more than I can express. Thanks to the Society for this unbelievable honor, thanks to Sylvia for knowing me so well and still being able to say good things about me, thanks to those who have helped me . . . those who are here and those who are here in spirit . . . thanks to my colleagues, thanks to my students, thanks to Bob Schneider for keeping me in the glorious health that teaching requires, thanks to the Baseball Hall of Famer who said "Thanks for making this occasion necessary", and thanks to E. B. White for his honest comment on human vanity when he wrote in *Charlotte's Web* "It is deeply satisfying to win a big prize in front of a lot of people."

But my deepest thanks go to the individuals with dyslexia, young and old, who have opened their lives to our explorations and who have so much to contribute to our world.

I have a story I want to tell you. No. I don't really want to tell you this story, but honesty is forcing me.

Embarrassment hardened into a problem the day I told the lie.

This was no ordinary lie . . . not a permissible social self-protection lie such as "No, I'm sorry I can't come for dinner three weeks from tonight to see the two hour home video of your kindergartner's school play, I think there's going to be a funeral that night." (Mine if I don't avoid this ghastly scene). No, this lie was a whopper, and I didn't just lie to a friend). I lied to kids. And not just strangers' kids in the supermarket. I lied to my grandchildren two of whom are here tonight. Here's the skinny.

Our family has a motor boat we use for going to a nearby island for summer picnics. My husband used to manage the anchoring and going-ashore procedure with such skill that it looked easy. So I asked him to show me how. For the most part, he's a noble fellow, but as a teacher he belongs to the school of "Watch out. Look what you're doing. STOP! Quick! Here . . . I'll take over."

The first summer he wasn't there to run the boat, I did my best. We'd take off from the dock on moderate harbor tours These I could manage. But then came the day when we all went off to the island on a picnic with me at the helm. I didn't confess that I was terrified, and that I had no idea how to anchor and unload. I was the Chicken of the Sea to the 100th power. Although no lives were actually lost, it was not a pretty sight, and I did what embarrassed adults do . . . I yelled at everybody. In the aftermath, first I felt guilty, then my self-protective instincts surged, finally I turned devious.

The sun would be shining, the waters sparkling, the gulls calling and arcing gently, the trusting children would say, "Granny, will you take us to Sandy Point?" I would stall, change the subject, vanish on my bike, or invent supermarket errands One day, when my ruses and excuses were all used up, I told the whopper. "I've just heard the weather. Bad thunderstorms and squalls are coming." The kids believed me! I was off the hook. But I didn't like myself.

As the summer unfolded, my sleep was tortured with boat/island/anchoring nightmares. I would dream of tuna fish sandwiches dismembered by an errant propeller, or of tangling my foot in the line and dropping overboard, attached to the anchor, to thrash around in my watery grave.

Storms, shipwrecks, maritime disasters of all sorts and dimensions wrung the adrenaline out of my system night after night. But during the day my tongue kept on lying. "I wish we could but I hear the wind may gust all the way to seven."

Like people everywhere . . . teachers and students in particular . . . I couldn't face up to the problem until I realized there might be a solution.

Over the following winter I mulled. Should I sell the boat? No. The kids would divorce me. However, maintaining a sham is a high-energy activity. Then one day in March? in what Yogi Berra might call a "Déjà vu all over again" moment, it came to me. I was thinking about a kid I had taught who had arrived in my classroom as an ornery, prickle-pear, mulish, crabby-appleton fibber. He'd grumble, "This is boring" or "This looks stupid." I'd say, "Sit right down. I'm going to show you how." Once he'd had a few lessons, he couldn't wait to keep going

LESSONS! The light bulb! That was it. I'd find myself a teacher . . . maybe on the QT . . . in case I flunked or had dys-anchor-ia. People take lessons to play the clarinet or to figure skate, but I'd never heard of anchoring/beaching lessons for a small outboard motorboat, sort of coaching for water-borne parallel parking 105. Maybe I was the only person in the world who didn't know how. Maybe I would be incapable of learning.

I called my friend Matt at the boatyard and asked him if he would try to teach me. I chose him carefully. I wanted someone skillful, quiet, and kind He said, "Sure. We'll start at the easiest place. First we'll do it together while I talk you through the process, then you'll do it again while I watch, then you'll do it again pretending I'm not here. By then you won't need me but I'll be here anyway. Then we'll go to a harder place and do the same thing We're going to use eight rules."

"The first is this: there is no need for urgency."

"No urgency?" I thought back to my nightmares, and my first attempt. "No urgency?"

"That's right? " he said, "No urgency."

"Rule 2," he continued, "Have full gas tanks, a fire extinguisher, a compass, and your navigation chart.

Rule 3. Anchor bow out. That way you'll never get swamped.

Rule 4. Keep your engine running while you set your bow anchor. No urgency. Fool around as long as you want till you're sure it's holding Once *it's* set, *you're* set.

Rule 5. Pay out extra line for scope so tides and currents don't make trouble.

Rule 6. Put in a stern anchor on the beach. Then you can reel yourself out or pull yourself in.

Rule 7. Turn off your engine. Then help your passenger ashore.

Rule 8. Watch the weather while you're having your picnic. Return to the mainland before a squall or thunderstorm arrives. Remember, no urgency."

After the lesson I practiced and I improved. I took passengers. They survived and everyone had fun. Using the boat for what it offers, we found delicious combinations of adventure and safety. We read the heavens and rode the waters. Far and wide, I praised my teacher, Matt.

And I knew I was an initiate when one fine day a cool-dude Boomer sidled up to me at a party. "Say," he leaned down over me from his 6'4" height and said, "I've got a new picnic boat. Do you . . . I mean . . . do I understand that you know how to anchor?"

"Yes. I know how to anchor," I said proudly, and probably loudly.

"Well," he said, dropping his voice conspiratorially, "Do you think you could . . . teach *me*?"

"Sure, I'd love to."

"Could we go out, you know, really early in the morning?"

Sensing the power-lunch fellow's need for privacy and his horror of being seen getting hot boating tips from a chubby old lady, I suggested 7:00 AM. We went. I chanted Matt's script. He learned. And now he can do it too. So I sent Matt a check for royalties.

What's this story all about? Switch a few nouns and verbs and we coast right up on to approaches to dyslexia.

To start with, teachers who haven't been shown how to teach dyslexics while simultaneously maintaining high standards in their disciplines (those who say "I teach history, I don't teach dyslexics") need to be shown by someone, perhaps someone in this room, how to reach their students so their joint voyages are safe, productive, and joyful, and so neither teachers nor students get caught in the fibbety of denial.

We all, parents, educators, physicians, and students, need Matt's eight rules.

1. *No urgency.* Panic is contagious. Established, effective, proven methods and materials exist. Fixes don't come fast but reliable procedures are trustworthy anchors.

2. *Have full gas tanks, a fire extinguisher, a compass and a chart.* Dyslexic students can't afford to run out of fuel (or stamina) by mistake. Neither can the adults they trust. Put out fires fast to avoid an explosion. And with help, each student must lay out an academic course according to a personal compass, charting passages to avoid intellectual shoals and emotional reefs while traveling safe, buoyed channels, and exploring new waters of learning, literature, and laughter.

3. *Anchor bow out.* The bow of a boat is designed to cut through or ride over waves. Understanding, compassion, thorough training, self awareness and self acceptance mold the hull of the dyslexic's vessel. Well shaped, such a craft will carry a student across calm or turbulent waters, and will give safe rest in chosen harbors.

4. *Keep your engine running until the bow anchor is set.* The dyslexic's engine is powered by the well maintained spark plugs, fuel pumps, and cooling systems of solid training, willingness to engage, and personal courage. Our job and privilege as concerned adults, no matter our discipline, is to help kids maintain and fine-tune their engines.

5. *Pay out the extra line for scope.* Many dyslexics need extra time for reading, for integrating new concepts, for orga-

nizing their spoken or written output, or for exploring their gifts and expanding their original insights. Sometimes institutions provide accommodations, but often students have to engineer their own ways to meet such needs. Without extra line, or scope, tides or currents can trip an anchor, allowing a boat to break loose, run aground, or fetch up on the rocks. Parents, educators, and physicians are lengths of line.

6. *Put a stern anchor on the beach.* With the boat anchored to the sea bottom in the front (or the bow) and attached to the land from the back (or the stern), the student can reel him or herself in and out from deep to shallow water, controlling the boat's destiny and responding safely to shifts in tide and current. The stern anchor represents familiarity with curriculum, requirements, expectations, and the student's and teacher's optimistic acceptance of the job at hand.

7. *Cut the engine first and then help the passengers ashore.* Stop the motor so the propeller doesn't slash the ankles of partygoers. Dyslexics, as much as (or perhaps more than) others need times of relaxation, metamorphic snoozes in the sun, games of conceptual Frisbee, or symbolically and actually, chances to gather beautiful shells.

8. *Watch the weather.* Strong winds blow across dyslexics' academic "courses" and extracurricular lives. Rain may pelt down on dreams. Thunder and lightning may strike from outside or from inner turbulence. Alertness to warning signs are a part of safe journeying. Preparation, by adults and by students themselves, can change a tempest from a disaster into an inconvenience.

All this said, we can see that we who work with and for dyslexics, or who are ourselves dyslexic, have both complexity of challenge and clarity of mission.

After the plates and dishes and pots and pans of this wonderful Hyatt Regency dinner have been washed and put away, when this 49th annual conference is history, researchers need to keep on researching; parents need to keep understanding loving and supporting, educators need to continue learning and teaching; students need to keep moving forward with courage and with pride. The jobs are as big as they are important. They matter in history and in human lives.

My wish is for all of us to receive and share the blessing Peter Gomes, Chaplain of Memorial Church and Plummer Professor of Human Morals at Harvard gave to the senior class in June 1998 just before they processed into the Yard to receive their degrees. His words span age as well as geography. The said to them, as I hope we may say to one another, "God grant you life until your work is done, and work until your life is over."

Thank you. Godspeed.

Priscilla Luke Vail
San Francisco, California
November 13, 1998

PART I
Rapid Serial Naming and the Double-Deficit Hypothesis

Understanding why some children experience inordinate difficulties in sequentially labeling an array of familiar symbols is a question that fascinates theorists and clinicians alike. (And isn't there a bit of both in most of us?) As evident in previous research published in *Annals* and elsewhere this phenomenon is not perfectly related to either intelligence or phonological awareness, and persists over time even as other aspects of reading difficulty succumb to treatment.

If you have known a student with severe naming deficits and have tried to relate their difficulties to other features of their reading disability, you will appreciate the two papers in this section. Two very central figures share their views on how to reconcile rapid serial naming deficits with what we have learned about phonological problems—without giving short shrift to either.

Maryanne Wolf provides a lucid introduction to the whole topic of rapid serial naming and the theories that have attempted to account for it. Her discussion will benefit not only students well versed in this literature, but also those new to the issues.

In the second chapter, Martha Denckla and Laurie Cutting provide a historical overview of rapid automatized naming with thoughtful insights gleaned from a quarter century of work with this task since Denckla first brought it to our attention in 1976. Their ongoing interest in and keen understanding of this phenomenon make it a paper that will you read more than once.

What Time May Tell: Towards a New Conceptualization of Developmental Dyslexia

Maryanne Wolf

Center for Reading and Language Research, Tufts University
Medford, Massachusetts

This paper is a written version of the Norman Geschwind Lecture delivered to the International Dyslexia Association on November 13, 1998. The first purpose is a theoretical one: to describe a new conceptualization of reading disabilities, the double-deficit hypothesis, that depicts and integrates work on two core deficits in the phonological system and in processes underlying naming speed. Implications for subtyping, diagnosis, and, in particular, intervention are described. The second purpose is to thank the women and men whose commitment to children with reading disabilities has transformed our field over the last century. Within that double set of purposes, I wish to dedicate this paper to five research teachers whose insights have been the foundation for my work and the efforts of many of us in the field of reading disabilities research: Jeanne Chall, Carol Chomsky, Martha Bridge Denckla, Helen Popp, and especially, Norman Geschwind.

INTRODUCTION

In writing this paper, I depart somewhat from a conventional neuroscience paper to construct a bridge between a body of theory in the cognitive neurosciences and applied work in our clinics and classrooms. To do so, I have structured this paper in three parts. The first section is about the rich cognitive puzzle

Annals of Dyslexia, Vol. 49, 1999
ISSN 0736-9387

concerning the nature of the processes underlying naming speed. In this section, I provide evidence that slow naming speed constitutes its own core deficit in developmental dyslexia and consider why serial naming has proven such an extraordinary predictor of reading disabilities across many ages, languages, and reader subtypes.

Part II focuses on the double-deficit hypothesis, developed by Patricia Bowers and myself. Here I attempt to integrate the naming-speed literature with the large and successful body of work on the phonological core deficits of children with dyslexia (Blachman 1997; Bradley and Bryant 1983; Brady and Shankweiler 1991; Bruck and Treiman 1990; Catts 1996; Foorman, Francis, Shaywitz, Shaywitz, and Fletcher 1997; Fowler 1991; Kamhi and Catts 1989; Liberman, Shankweiler, and Liberman 1989; Lyon 1995; Olson, Wise, Connors, Rack, and Fulker 1989; Perfetti 1985; Shankweiler and Liberman 1972; Siegel and Ryan 1988; Stanovich 1986, 1992; Stanovich and Siegel 1994; Tunmer 1995; Vellutino and Scanlon 1987; Wagner, Torgesen, and Rashotte 1994). There is no question that the research in this area comprises what Stanovich has called "a true success story in science." The double-deficit hypothesis represents not a refuting of the phonological core-deficit hypothesis, but rather a new theoretical integration of what we have learned about phonology in reading, with what we are learning about naming-speed processes.

In the third part of this paper, I present the most recent undertakings from our laboratory with an emphasis on an innovative reading intervention program designed by us. This program, RAVE-O, is one of the first, comprehensive approaches to fluency-based reading treatments for children with reading disabilities. Finally, I end with a coda, where I discuss some of the implications of this conceptualization for new directions in dyslexia research.

PART I:

Let us begin with the question, "Why does the field of dyslexia need a second-core deficit?" The punch line of this paper is the following: Despite some of the best work in the field on phonological-based explanations and interventions, there remain aspects of dyslexia unexplained by our theories; there remain reading-impaired children who slip through our diagnostic batteries with adequate decoding and phonological awareness skills but poor comprehension; and there remain dyslexic children who resist our best phonological-based treatments, children whom Blachman (1994) and Torgesen (1998) call the "treatment resisters." Who are these children? And what will push them from halting decoding to fluency to comprehension?

The conceptualization presented here is not intended to serve as a comprehensive explanation for all reading disabilities. The history of dyslexia research, the heterogeneity of our dyslexic children, and the very complexity of the reading process argue against any single-factor, two-factor, or even three-factor explanation. Rather, the work described here is meant to provide a compelling argument why a new dual emphasis on both phonological processes and the fluency-related processes underlying naming speed will push our understanding, both of the heterogeneity in the reading-disabled population, and of the treatment resisters who do not fit solely phonological-based theories. Most important, we believe this new conceptualization will add a new dimension to our diagnosis, our intervention, and possibly our definitions of developmental dyslexia.

The early history of naming-speed deficits has at least two sets of roots. One set of roots was set within the reading research in the 1960s and 1970s and emphasized the powerful prediction capacity of a child's letter-naming ability. This work included a group of esteemed researchers who helped shape our field: Jeanne Chall, Jeanette Jansky and Katrina deHirsch, Doris Johnson and Helmut Myklebust, and Richard and Sally Masland. This work provided fertile ground for the later work on naming speed, as did the work on naming processes in acquired aphasia and alexia by Harold Goodglass and Edith Kaplan (see Goodglass 1980; Goodglass and Kaplan 1972); and in developmental language disorders by Anthony Bashir (1976).

The second and direct set of roots of what we now call rapid or serial naming speed is found in the middle of Norman Geschwind's most important monograph, *The Disconnexion Syndrome in Animals and Man* (1965). Although most people in our field are aware of the profound influence Geschwind's early work had on the cytoarchitectonic studies of dyslexic brains by Al Galaburda, Thomas Kemper, Gordon Sherman, Glen Rosen, and others (see, for example, Galaburda, Menard, and Rosen 1994; Sherman 1998), very few are aware that it was yet another of Geschwind's now infamous, slightly misdirected insights that began this line of research. Based in part on Dejerine's classic alexia case in 1896, Geschwind hypothesized that the best predictor of reading readiness would be a child's color naming ability. His logic was a precursor to many cognitive models to come: both color naming and reading require many of the same cognitive, linguistic, and perceptual processes involved in retrieving a verbal match for an abstract visual stimulus; therefore, color naming, Geschwind reasoned, should be a good early predictor of later reading.

This notion lay obscured and hidden in the folds of Geschwind's thinking until his then student, Martha Denckla, put it together with Dejerine's case and pursued the hypothesis with children. What she discovered was the beginning of naming-speed research. She found that color-naming speed, rather than color-naming accuracy, differentiated dyslexic reading groups from other children. Based on this finding, Denckla designed the Rapid Automatized Naming (RAN) tasks (see figure 1), in which the child names 50 stimuli as rapidly as possible (for example, 5 common letters, 5 digits, 5 colors, or 5 pictured objects, repeated randomly 10 times on a board). Denckla and Rudel (1974, 1976a,b) found that naming speed for basic symbols differentiated dyslexic children from average readers as well as other learning-disabled children, a conclusion also reached early on by Spring and Capps (1974). The daunting question was *why*.

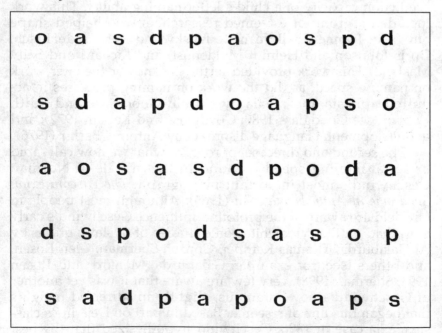

Figure 1.   Rapid Automatized Naming (RAN) test for letters.

From this point, the evidence began to increase from many researchers (Ackerman and Dykman 1993; Badian 1995, 1996a, b; Bowers, Steffy, and Tate 1988; Denckla and Rudel 1976a, b; Grigorenko, Wood, Meyer, Hart, Speed, Shuster, and Pauls,1997; Lovett 1992, 1995; McBride-Chang and Manis 1996; Meyer, Wood, Hart, and Felton 1998; Snyder and Downey 1995; Spring and Capps 1974; Spring and Davis 1988; Swanson 1989; Wolf 1979; Wolf, Bally, and Morris 1986; Wolff, Michel, and Ovrut 1990a, b; Wood and Felton 1994). In this paper, I consider myself the representative of this body of researchers in chronicling naming-speed history.

My own work, rooted in the cognitive neurosciences, began with an exploration of the developmental course of naming speed in children with and without developmental dyslexia. Results from a five-year longitudinal study indicated that differences in naming speed for children with reading disabilities were visible from the first day of kindergarten (Wolf, Bally, and Morris 1986). Further, differences were most dramatic for letters. In other words, children with dyslexia began their school years with both a general naming-speed problem and a particular difficulty with speed for letter naming. These differences were maintained through the last year of our study in grade 4 for all categories, but especially for the more automatized categories, letters and numbers. We now know from researchers like Meyer, Wood, Hart, and Felton (1998) that these differences continue through grade 8 into adulthood (see also Scarborough 1998; Wolff 1993).

Hard on the heels of these data came a challenge by Stanovich (1986). He suggested that if one sought to prove that the processes in serial naming speed represented a truly different cognitive core deficit in children with severe reading disabilities, there would need to be several kinds of evidence. For example, naming-speed differences should distinguish dyslexic from reading-age match children in order to eliminate external factors like exposure to reading. He suggested that we might also expect to see differences between dyslexic readers and nondiscrepant poor readers, the putative "garden-variety poor readers" characterized by poor reading that is commensurate with their intelligence or achievement measures (Gough and Tunmer 1986). This second comparison is important because there appear no significant differences on phonological awareness measures between discrepant and nondiscrepant readers. Should such differences be found for naming-speed tasks, there would be additional support for differentiating naming speed from phonology.

In response to Stanovich's remarks, we analyzed our longitudinal data in two ways. First, we compared older dyslexic readers with children two years younger, matched on reading level. We found highly significant group differences: grade 4 dyslexic readers were significantly slower than grade 2 average readers; and grade 3 dyslexic readers were significantly slower than grade 1 average readers. These results demonstrated that it cannot be greater exposure to print that explains naming-speed differences because the older dyslexic children had considerably more exposure than the younger average-reading children.

In the second effort, we compared discrepant dyslexic and nondiscrepant poor readers and found that the nondiscrepant poor reader group was similar by grades 3 and 4 to average readers, a finding also shown by Biddle (1996). In other words, there appeared to be essential cognitive-based differences in how discrepant dyslexic and nondiscrepant dyslexic readers named letters and numbers in this sample. In a recent study, Scarborough and Domgaard (1998) indicated that although they also found no differences for nondiscrepant readers in letter and number naming, there were differences in object naming related to IQ. Because the implications of this finding are so important, Morris, Lovett and I are now attempting to replicate this result using a much larger sample.

My next question concerned the relative universality of naming-speed deficits. Specifically, I wished to know whether naming speed was equally predictive in languages that have orthographies that are more regular than English, and, thus, place fewer phonological based demands in areas like phonemic analysis and grapheme-phoneme correspondence rules. In a Fulbright Research Study in Berlin, my students and I (Wolf, Pfeil, Lotz, and Biddle 1994) studied German-speaking poor readers and found not only that naming-speed deficits differentiated reader groups in that language, but that naming-speed performance was a better predictor of later reading than phoneme deletion tasks, also a finding by Wimmer (1993). We now know across German (Näslund and Schneider 1991; Wimmer and Hummer 1990; Wimmer 1993; Wolf, Pfeil, Lotz, and Biddle 1994), Dutch (Van den Bos 1998; Yap and Van der Leij 1993, 1994), Finnish (Korhonen 1995), and Spanish (Novoa and Wolf 1984; Novoa 1988) that serial naming speed is a powerful predictor in many transparent languages. The point of this work is that it demonstrates that when phonological skills play a somewhat more reduced role in languages with more regular orthographies than English, naming-speed performance becomes an even stronger, more important diagnostic indicator and predictor of reading performance. We will return to this point in the following section.

The third challenge was, and continues to be, a daunting one. Members of my lab and I wished to know at which point in the act of naming stimuli in seriation that dyslexic children were impeded. In so doing, we wished to confront three potential explanations offered by various other researchers about the origins of naming-speed deficits: (1) articulation; (2) end-of-line scanning; and (3) fatigue toward the end of lines or task. Mateo Obregón (1994) in our lab designed a sophisticated computer program to digitize the speech stream of children on the RAN, and to analyze where in the speech stream dyslexics differed. The results of these investigations indicated that there were *no* group differences for articulation, end-of-line scanning, or fatigue-related effects, but rather only for the interstimulus intervals (ISIs)—that is, the gap of time between the response to one stimulus and the response to the next. Within this interstimulus gap are found multiple processes that include inhibiting the response towards the previous stimuli, perceiving the next stimulus, directing the access and retrieval of a label, and moving the system onto the next stimulus.

Obregón's finding is an important one, but future work remains before a full understanding of the role of articulation in naming speed is resolved. Snyder and Downey (1995), for example, came to a different conclusion in a similarly sophisticated study that found significant differences in dyslexic children's performance on a variety of access and post-access measures, including categorical verbal fluency, naming speed, and articulatory speed. Other researchers (e.g., Ackerman, Dykman, and Gardner 1990) have found mixed results on articulatory rate measures with interactions between counting speed and severity of reading disability. It is of note that only counting rate, and not general naming speed, correlated with phonological measures in the Ackerman et al. (1990) study. Obregón's ISI findings, when connected to the others cited, led us to consider the multiple ways that naming speed might be impeded in different children. This consideration, in turn, led us back to an examination of the underlying component processes of naming and naming speed.

In confronting this complex issue, I was haunted by a statement much earlier by Andrew Ellis (1985): "Whatever dyslexia may ultimately turn out to be, it is not a reading disorder." Was the same thing true about naming-speed deficits? During the first phases of my work, like the rest of my field, I had conceptualized naming speed under the rubric of a phonological process. The reading-age match comparisons and the preliminary data on discrepant and nondiscrepant readers gave some evidence for a different, separate categorization. The crosslinguistic data, however, went further. If, as these data suggest, naming-speed measures are even more predictive of reading disability in orthographies that make fewer phonological demands, then it is unlikely that naming should be thought of as a phonological process. Data from Obregón (1994) pointing to longer delays between stimuli in RAN tasks do not refute the presence of phonological processes but increase the importance of studying other factors contributing to lengthy interstimulus intervals.

The cumulative results of these studies convinced us of the necessity to look beyond previous notions of naming speed as a phonological retrieval process in order to consider all the other processes that comprise it, including nonlinguistic processes that might have little to do with reading, *sensu* Ellis (1985). We began to conceive of naming speed as a small behavioral window on the brain's ability to inhibit, activate, and integrate discrete constellations of neurons within a very small period of time (Wolf and Bowers 1999). With this shift of lenses, naming speed was no longer to be categorized as a phonological task but rather thought of as a complex ensemble of multiple processes that included, but was not limited to, phonological processes. Most important, if naming speed should no longer be subsumed under phonology, then there were other processes that were also impeding the acquisition of reading in our dyslexic children that had to be understood.

To push forward our understanding of naming speed and to disentangle it from its phonological components, we undertook two different directions: first, the construction of cognitive models of letter-naming speed; and second, the beginning of multiple regression studies to examine the hypothesized independence of the two variables in reading prediction (described in next section). Depicted in figure 2, a model of letter naming illustrates the primary principle I wish to stress in the present paper; that is, the multiple-componential nature of letter-naming speed (for a broader discussion of figure 2, see Wolf and Bowers 1999). These components include a range of attentional, perceptual, cognitive, phonological, semantic, and articulatory processes, each of which is necessary for a letter to be named quickly. The model depicted in figure 2 underscores three points: (1) that phonological processes are one set of processes

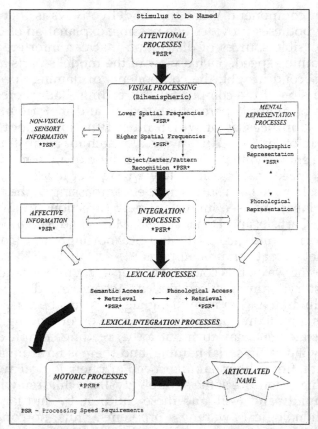

Figure 2.   A model depicting major components in letter naming. Re-
printed permission from the American Psychological Assn.

of many, albeit a most critical set; (2) that the underlying components of naming speed have great overlap with the underlying components of reading, as Geschwind (1965) early on
surmised; and (3) that with multiple component parts, there can
be different possible sources of breakdown resulting in different
kinds of poor namers and poor readers.

    An examination of the individual components in this model
also provides an interesting overview of the various hypotheses
raised about the nature of naming-speed deficits. For example,
most reading researchers have looked at naming speed as "part
of the phonological family" (Torgesen et al. 1997); Pat Bowers
and I have emphasized the centrality of speed of processing factors; Wood and Eden (1995; Eden and Zeffiro 1998) have stressed
the importance of understanding visual and visual motion
processes; and Denckla (1998) has emphasized the executive

function component. What the model conveys is that each of these hypotheses provides one possible explanation of the multiple, possible sources of disruption that can interfere with or delay naming speed. Such a view of the model's parts also conveys a second insight: the components of naming speed are a microversion of the components of reading. Both represent ensembles of multiple perceptual, lexical, and motoric processes, all the subprocesses of which must function smoothly and rapidly in order to produce a verbal match for an abstract, visually presented symbol. Thus, there is no explanation to date of naming speed that is completely wrong; yet few of us, including myself, have been sufficiently encompassing of the whole in our explanations (see important new directions in studies by Cutting, Carlisle, and Denckla 1998; Manis and Seidenberg, personal correspondence 1998; and Scarborough and Domgaard 1998, that look at component parts.)

In some ways, this could be a logical, cognitive denouement of my story: naming-speed deficits accompany dyslexia in so many children and in many language systems because naming speed is a mini, multicomponential version of reading. As true as this statement may turn out to be, reading complexity goes well beyond rapid serial naming, and there is far from a perfect prediction from either naming speed or phonological awareness to reading. There are some severely dyslexic children who name quite rapidly and well, and these children, by and large, have clear phonological awareness problems. Thus, no conceptualization that attempts to explain the relationship of naming-speed processes to reading failure can leave out the contributions of phonology to reading failure.

PART II: THE DOUBLE-DEFICIT HYPOTHESIS

It is the work of Bowers and her colleagues that offered a new window on what the combined study of naming speed and phonology can teach us about reading breakdown (Bowers et al. 1988; Bowers and Swanson 1991). Bowers' research provided a set of axes for looking at the separate contributions of phonology and naming speed to particular aspects of reading, specifically word attack, word identification, and comprehension. Her work showed that phonological awareness contributed significantly to word attack skills in reading, whereas naming speed contributed more to the orthographic aspects in word identification, a conclusion also reached by Manis and Doi and their colleagues

(Manis, Doi, and Bhadha in press; McBride-Chang and Manis 1996). This important distinction has recently been replicated by Lovett, Morris, and myself (Wolf, Goldberg, Gidney, Cirino, Lovett, and Morris 1999) in a population with severe reading impairments. Phonological awareness tasks predict significant portions of the variance in word attack; naming speed best predicts word identification (Bowers and Swanson 1991).

Most important, Bowers suggested we seek other forms of evidence for a double dissociation between the two variables to demonstrate that naming speed and phonology make separate contributions to reading failure. The concept was the following: if some poor readers have slow naming speed and good phonological awareness, and others have average naming speed and poor phonological awareness, then it is unlikely that the two variables should be considered within the same family of processes. Together, Bowers and I reanalyzed our previous databases in Canada and Boston, and indeed, four discrete groups of children emerged in each sample (see table 1). The first subgroup of average readers had no deficits. The second and third groups were composed of children with single deficits. That is, there were children with only naming-speed deficits who had adequate decoding/word attack skills, and children with only phonological-based problems who had poor decoding. Both school-based, single-deficit groups had modest comprehension deficits. The most impaired readers had both naming-speed and phonological awareness problems and pervasive problems in word attack, word identification, and comprehension. The term, *double deficit*, emerged as a concrete metaphor to convey at once the critical blow that the combination of both deficits represents. Just as naming-speed skills predicted word identification, and phonological skills

TABLE 1 Classification of subtypes according to the Double-Deficit Hypothesis.	
Average Group	**Rate Group**
Average phonological awareness	Naming-speed deficit
Average naming-speed skills	Intact phonological awareness
Average reading	Impaired comprehension
Phonology	**Double-Deficit**
Phonological-awareness deficit	Naming-speed deficit
Intact naming speed	Phonological-awareness deficit
Impaired comprehension	Severe comprehension deficit

predicted word attack, deficits in both variables would impede both aspects of reading, leaving no compensatory route easily available.

The means of average readers and each of the single and double-deficit subgroups in my longitudinal data are graphed in figures 3 to 6. This sample represents a group of unselected children from the Boston area who began in kindergarten and were studied until grade 4. At the end of grade 4, they were classified retrospectively on the basis of grade 4 performance on a battery of tasks and divided into the double-deficit subtypes. Figure 3 shows the performance of the four groups on naming speed, figure 4 on nonsense word decoding, figure 5 on oral reading, and figure 6 on comprehension.

The two single-deficit subtypes would be considered modestly reading impaired and were not significantly different from each other on overall reading performance. Nevertheless, the phonological deficit subtype was consistently more impaired than the rate group. The double-deficit group would be categorized as classic dyslexic children according to almost any known criteria. Their performances were the lowest across all naming, phonological, and reading categories in every year from kindergarten though grade 4. Note, however, their early

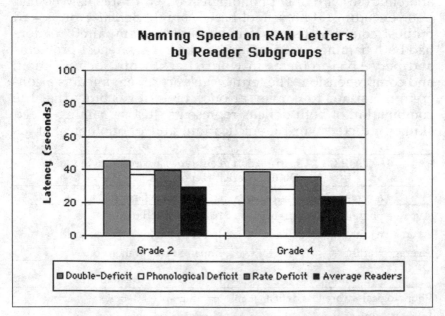

Figure 3.   Mean naming-speed latency of three impaired reader subtypes (n = 6 for each group) and average readers.

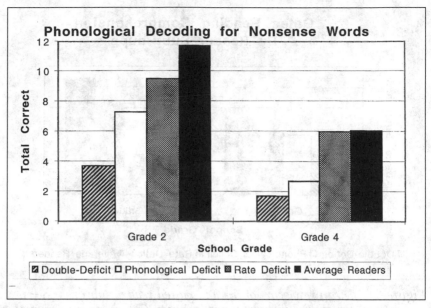

Figure 4.   *Mean accuracy of three impaired reader subtypes (n = 6 for each) and average readers (n = 61) for phonological decoding of nonsense words.*

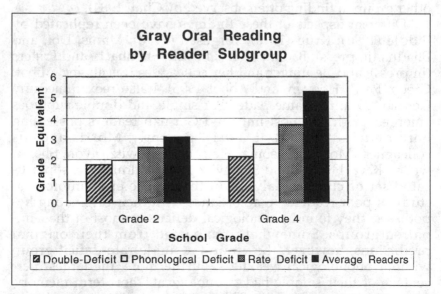

Figure 5.   *Mean raw score of three impaired reader subtypes (n = 6 for each) and average readers (n = 61) on oral reading (Gray Oral Reading Test).*

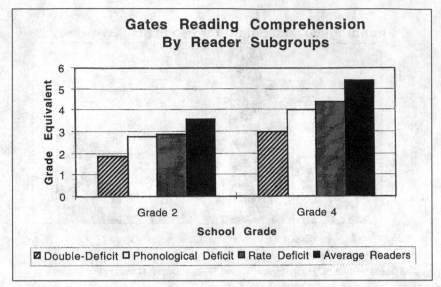

Figure 6.   Mean raw score of three impaired reader subtypes (n = 6
for each) and average readers (n = 61) on reading comprehension (Gates-McGinitie Reading Comprehension Test).

receptive vocabulary was not significantly different from any
other group (a finding often observed by Chall 1984).

Different aspects of these findings have been replicated by
Biddle (1996); Krug (1996); Torgesen (1998); Manis, Doi, and
Bhadha (in press); Badian (1996); Lovett, Steinbach, and Frijters
(in press); and Berninger and her colleagues (Berninger, Abbot,
Greep, Reed, Hooven, and Abbot 1995). I also reexamined my
German data: the same pattern of single and double subtypes
emerged, with the most impaired German readers possessing
both deficits (Wolf et al. 1994). Recently, Morris and his
colleagues (Morris, Stuebing, Fletcher, Shaywitz, Lyon, Shankweiler, Katz, Francis, and Shaywitz 1998) conducted a sophisticated set of cluster analyses on their large epidemiological
study of poor readers. In accordance with their originating hypotheses, they found phonological deficits in most of their impaired groups. Somewhat unexpected from their original
predictions, however, they found a single rate-deficit group
without phonological weakness. Furthermore, the largest percentage of their sample had phonological, short-term memory,
and naming-speed deficits. This latter group was most similar
to our double-deficit subgroup and these children had pervasive reading failure.

The question that remains unresolved in this chronicling of naming-speed deficits continues to be *why*. Why should deficits in the speed of naming familiar stimuli affect reading performance? For the last several years, Bowers and I have been working on two nonexclusive, speculative hypotheses that attempt to explain the different possible effects of naming-speed deficits on reading failure, based on behavioral and neurophysiological evidence. In our first hypothesis, cytoarchitectonic findings by Galaburda (Galaburda et al. 1994; Livingstone et al. 1991) and psychophysical data by Chase (1997) were integrated in the following ways. Galaburda and his colleagues demonstrated that the magnocellular system, that is, those groups of cells responsible for rapid processing, is aberrant in the subcortical center in the thalamus responsible for coordinating visual areas (the lateral geniculate nucleus). Chase (1997) has shown through visual flicker-fusion studies that dyslexic children have much longer ISIs in order to be able to see single visual images that are flashed in rapid succession. Chase used these data to argue that the visual processing of lower spatial-frequency components is slowed in children with reading disabilities. These component processes are necessary for extracting the global shapes of letter, objects, or words within 60–80 ms (Legge 1978), and they are believed to be governed by the magnocellular system within the lateral geniculate nucleus. Based on Chase (1997) and Galaburda's findings, we argue that slower rates of processing and the concomitant decreased quality of visual information could potentially lead to: (1) slower letter-pattern identification; (2) slower naming speed for visual stimuli; (3) delayed induction of common orthographic patterns in written language; and (4) the need for multiple exposures before a letter pattern is adequately represented in the child's repertoire. Naming-speed performance in this first hypothesis is viewed as an index of slowing in lower-level processes that ultimately contribute to the disruption of fluency, particularly in the reading and understanding of connected text (see elaborated description in Wolf and Bowers 1999). The reader with a single, naming-speed deficit would present an example of one such sequence of problems.

In hypothesis two, naming speed is potentially both an index of dysfunction in lower-level processes and a contributing factor to a more pervasive rate-of-processing problem that affects varied aspects of reading (see Wolf et al. 1999). Several types of sources for timing problems are considered: a central time-keeping mechanism; multiple systems; and a notion of timing as a consequence of other factors like seriation and memory (see Cohen 1999; Rosenbaum and Collyer 1998; Wolf, Bowers, and Biddle in press). Within this scenario, naming speed is conceptualized as the midpoint in a cascading system of rate deficits—be they domain-general or involve multiple, more specific areas—that implicate a range of perceptual, lexical, and motoric processes. Such general processing-speed impairments could potentially affect both orthographic and phonological input. The reader with a double deficit and pervasive reading difficulties would present an example of this profile.

PART III:
DEVELOPING FLUENCY-BASED INTERVENTION

The single most important implication of the findings and speculations introduced in Part I and Part II is that they provide a whole new dimension to both diagnosis and intervention. Although the phonological subtype would be amply treated by current emphases on phonological-based treatments that emphasize systematic decoding skills, the rate-deficit subtype children with their adequate, but slow decoding skills would require a different emphasis to enhance automaticity and fluency. The children with double deficits would need both phonological and fluency intervention. But how does one treat deficits in rate of processing? Are they amenable to treatment? Given the multiple sources possible for slowed processing rates, should intervention focus on the overt behaviors of reading (e.g., word attack, word identification, and comprehension), the underlying processes, or a comprehensive attack on both the behaviors of reading and the individual processes beneath them?

In 1996, Morris, Lovett and I began a three-city, four-year reading intervention project sponsored by NICHD to test the effects of different treatments, when combined with Lovett's well-documented phonological analysis and blending program, PHAB (see Lovett et al. 1994). Three treatment packages were studied: the PHAB program; PHAB plus a metacognitive strategy program; and PHAB plus our new program on fluency, RAVE-O. Therefore, the NICHD study represents the first prospective test of the implications of the double-deficit hypothesis for intervention.

The RAVE-O program (Retrieval, Automaticity, Vocabulary, or Elaboration and Orthography, Wolf and Miller 1997; Wolf,

Miller, and Donnelly in press) is a comprehensive, fluency-based intervention that is a direct outgrowth of the double-deficit hypothesis and a connectionist view of reading (Adams 1990; Foorman 1994). It directly addresses the need for automaticity in phonological, orthographic, and semantic systems and the connections between these systems. To address the multiple possible sources of dysfluency in readers, it specifically works to increase processing speed, both in underlying components (visual and auditory recognition, orthographic pattern recognition, lexical-retrieval, and vocabulary processes) and also in three reading outcome behaviors (word identification, word attack, and comprehension). A central emphasis is placed on quick recognition of the most frequent orthographic letter patterns in English. Toward that end, the first step in the program is to connect the early phoneme analysis skills (taught in Lovett's PHAB program) with the training of orthographic patterns in RAVE-O. For example, children are taught individual phonemes in PHAB (like /a/, /t/, and /m/) and orthographic chunks with the same phonemes in RAVE-O (*at* and *am* and their word families). A special set of computerized games (see Speed Wizards, Wolf and Goodman 1996) has been designed to increase the speed of orthographic pattern recognition (onset and rime) and also the multiple underlying components like visual scanning; auditory discrimination at the phoneme and phoneme cluster levels, and letter and word identification (see description in Wolf, Miller, and Donnelly in press).

A further emphasis in the program involves the incorporation and integration of vocabulary development and increased lexical retrieval skills. Combining these two areas addresses several clinical and theoretical issues much discussed in reading disabilities research. Clinically, it has been noted that, although many dyslexic children begin school with adequate to superb vocabularies, vocabulary levels fall behind those of average readers exposed to literacy-based vocabulary in increasingly sophisticated texts. Moreover, although children with reading disabilities may well know a given word, they often cannot retrieve it (Katz 1986; Wolf and Goodglass 1986; Wolf and Obregón 1992). Finally, whether an antecedent or consequence of reading and fluency problems, a less flexible understanding of multiple word meanings is evident in some children with reading disabilities. They simply may not be able to allocate more time to processing more than one meaning to a known word, thereby affecting comprehension.

RAVE-O sets out through its daily structure to combat flagging vocabulary development, word-retrieval problems, and inflexibility by teaching a whimsical, imaginative approach to language from the start. For example, every core word in the program has at least three possible meanings. "Word-webs" are created for many of the words and bring to life the principle that "if you know one word, you know a hundred." To enhance the speed of lexical retrieval, a series of metacognitive strategies for word retrieval are taught in RAVE-O, alongside a systematic approach to enriched semantic development (see earlier RAVE program in Wolf and Segal 1999).

From a theoretical perspective, the dual emphasis on vocabulary and retrieval is based on earlier work in vocabulary development by others that suggests that one retrieves fastest what one knows best (see Beck, Perfetti, and McKeown 1982; German 1992; Kameenui, Dixon, and Carnine 1987). Vocabulary growth is conceptualized as essential to both rapid retrieval in oral *and* written language and also to improved comprehension, a critical goal in the program. A series of timed and untimed comprehension stories such as *Minute Mysteries* accompany each week of RAVE-O. The controlled vocabulary in the stories incorporates the week's particular rime patterns and also emphasizes the multiple meanings and semantically related words of the week's core words. In addition, the stories provide a good vehicle for repeated reading practice that facilitates fluency in connected text. Thus, the *Minute Mysteries* facilitate fluency in phonological, orthographic, and semantic systems at the same time that they push forward comprehension.

In sum, the RAVE-O program represents a first, systematic step toward a more comprehensive approach to fluency programs. This evolving program offers no complete remediation; there are none that do (see review of fluency programs in Meyer and Felton 1998). Rather, it offers a theoretically based beginning to the field's new emphasis on fluency. As Torgesen (1998) recently noted, we have done our work well on teaching decoding skills; now it is a true empirical question for the field whether the factors underlying fluency will prove amenable to treatment. Within this large question are numerous other issues, particularly how best to treat fluency. At the level of connected text? Word level? Sublexical level? Will emphases on different levels be important to particular subgroups? Using very different methods, Steven Stahl, Zvia Breznitz, Betty Ann Levy, Pat Bowers, and others have begun to work in this frontier (see review in Meyer and Felton this volume).

CODA

I will now respond to the implicit question(s) in the title of this paper, "What Time May Tell," as a way of summarizing this new conceptualization of dyslexia and what it can and cannot contribute to our understanding of reading failure. There are three main contributions that have structured this paper. First, I believe that there is now sufficient evidence across all languages and ages tested that the processes underlying naming speed represent a second-core deficit in developmental dyslexia. Not only does this distinction point our research toward additional areas of disruption that are key to understand; it also sharpens our understanding of phonological processes, the centrality of which in reading breakdown is unquestioned in the perspective presented here. What it does not do is resolve the broader issue of timing and dyslexia: that is, does naming-speed represent a language-specific weakness in processing speed? Or is it the linguistic tip of a systemic iceberg of temporal problems? My best guess (summarized in Wolf et al. in press) is that it can be either, depending on the child, and several other sources as well such as early visual pattern recognition problems.

The movement toward multiple dimensions in our explanations for naming speed and reading failure leads to the second major contribution of this reconceptualization. The dissociation of phonological and naming-speed deficits, and also the combination of these two deficits, provides an important, albeit temporary aid in classification efforts in reading disabilities. The primary advantage of the double-deficit subtype classification is that it places critical, equal emphases on the dimensions of processing speed and phonology. In this way, some children who have adequate decoding but later developing comprehension problems, do not slip through our early screening batteries. The temporary drawback of such a taxonomy is that the heterogeneity of our children with reading disabilities will never be captured by any single-, double-, or triple-deficit theory. It is, therefore, essential that the double-deficit hypothesis is thought of as a means, not an end, toward a more comprehensive, multidimensional model of reading failure. It is, in fact, the systematic examination of the multiple components in both naming speed and reading that may ultimately prove more important than the present focus on naming speed. Such an approach ensures attention to the various possible sources of disruption in both processing speed and fluent, accurate reading.

The third, and to my mind, most important contribution of the double-deficit hypothesis regards new forms of intervention that stress automaticity and fluency. Preliminary data that are just being analyzed for the RAVE-O program package (consisting of RAVE-O plus a phonological analysis and blending program) indicate significant gains in almost every aspect of reading when compared to either a math control group or a program that emphasizes only phonological decoding principles (Morris, Lovett, and Wolf 1999). We interpret these data as evidence that the combined emphases on phonological decoding, orthographic pattern fluency, semantic facilitation, and retrieval strategies enhance the acquisition of fluent decoding and reading comprehension.

Pre- and postintervention analyses of a current case study of a poor reader named BH, who typifies the single naming-speed deficit subtype (Deeney, Wolf, and Goldberg 1999), provides a first indication to us that the naming-speed deficit may be, at least in part, amenable to change. BH's composite preintervention naming-speed performance on four RAN measures for letters, objects, numbers, and colors was three standard deviations below the mean; at posttesting one year later, his scores were still well below average but had changed greatly along with significant improvement in comprehension. This is a hopeful result, but we will need considerable data before resolving whether such changes in underlying speed and comprehension can be effected for other children with processing-speed issues. Perhaps equally important, we need to know whether RAVE-O's more comprehensive approach to fluency in reading behaviors and to automaticity in underlying components is the appropriate course or whether some children are better helped by single-word level or connected-text level approaches. These are questions we need to pursue.

Two final areas that are as yet inadequately addressed by the double-deficit hypothesis are the following. First, we have only begun in our curricular work to address the potentially critical importance of linguistic differences between children who speak Standard English and those who speak either African-American English or another language. I believe that more collaborative efforts across other disciplines like speech-language pathology and sociolinguistics are necessary for us to progress in this area. New work in our lab (Gidney, Deeney, Wolf et al. 1999) indicates no differences in naming speed, but significant differences in some phonological processes for poor readers who speak African-American English. These initial studies must be refined and replicated, but already have begun to push our work in this direction.

Second, this new conceptualization of reading disabilities was, ironically, named too quickly. To be sure, double deficit captures the phenomenon of study—that is, the importance of understanding the separate and combined effects of two core deficits—but it fails miserably in redirecting our simultaneous attention as a field to the entire profile of strengths and limitations manifest in children with reading disabilities. Only when we develop truly multi-dimensional models of deficits *and* strengths will our diagnostic and remedial efforts be best matched to individual children. Thus, in the last analysis we look at the double-deficit reconceptualization as an evolving set of bridges: between two important bodies of research on phonology and naming speed; between the cognitive neurosciences and the classroom; and between the twentieth century's emphasis on understanding deficits and the next century's efforts to encompass the multiple aspects of all our children.

ACKNOWLEDGMENTS

The author wishes to thank past and present members of the Center for Reading and Language Research group Heidi Bally, Kathleen Biddle, Charles Borden, Tami Katzir-Cohen, Theresa Deeney, Katharine Donnelly, Katherine Feinberg, Wendy Galante, Calvin Gidney, Alyssa Goldberg, Julie Jeffery, Terry Joffe, Cynthia Krug, Ruth Lotz, Lynne Miller, Mateo Obregón, Claudia Pfeil, Denise Segal, and Catherine Stoodley. The work cited in this paper could never have been done without their efforts. I also am indebted to my colleagues Pat Bowers, Robin Morris, and Maureen Lovett for their intellectual collaborations over many years of our work together. I also wish to acknowledge the support of the Stratford Foundation, Educational Foundation of America, Biomedical Support Grants, Fulbright Research Fellowship, and Tufts Eliot-Pearson Department of Child Development Fund for the first phases of this work, and NICHD grant OD30970-01A1 for support during ongoing intervention phases.

Address correspondence to Maryanne Wolf, Eliot-Pearson Department of Child Development, Tufts University, Medford, MA 02155. Electronic mail may be sent to MWolf@Emerald.Tufts.EDU.

References

Ackerman, P. T., Dykman, R. A., and Gardner, M. V. 1990. Counting rate, naming rate, phonological sensitivity and memory span: Major factors in dyslexia. *Journal of Learning Disabilities* 23:325–37.

Ackerman, P. T., and Dykman, R. A. 1993. Phonological processes, confrontation naming, and immediate memory in dyslexia. *Journal of Learning Disabilities* 26:597–609.

Adams, M. J. 1990. *Beginning to Read: Thinking and Learning About Print*. Cambridge, MA: MIT Press.

Badian, N. 1995 Predicting reading ability over the long-term: The changing roles of letter naming, phonological awareness and orthographic processing. *Annals of Dyslexia: An Interdisciplinary Journal XLV*:79–86.

Badian, N. A. November, 1996a. *Dyslexia: Does it exist? Dyslexia, garden-variety poor reading, and the double-deficit hypothesis*. Paper presented at Orton Dyslexia Society. Boston, MA.

Badian, N. 1996b. Dyslexia: A validation of the concept at two age levels. *Journal of Learning Disabilities* 29(1):102–12.

Bashir, A. 1976. Presentation at Conference of New York Orton Society, New York, NY.

Beck, I. L., Perfetti, C. A., and McKeown, M. G. 1982. Effects of long-term vocabulary instruction on lexical access and reading comprehension. *Journal of Educational Psychology* 74:506–21.

Berninger, V. W., Abbot, S. P., Greep, K., Reed, E., Hooven, C., and Abbot, R. D. March, 1995. *Single, double, and triple deficits in impaired readers at the end of first grade: Individual differences in learner characteristics and response to intervention*. Paper presented at the Society for Research in Child Development, Indianapolis, IN.

Biddle, K. R. 1996. *The development of visual naming speed and verbal fluency in average and impaired readers: The implications for assessment, intervention, and theory*. Unpublished doctoral dissertation. Boston: Tufts University.

Blachman, B. A. 1994. What we have learned from longitudinal studies of phonological processing and reading, *and* some unanswered questions: A response to Torgesen, Wagner, and Rashotte. *Journal of Learning Disabilities* 27:287–91.

Bowers, P. G., Steffy, R., and Tate, E. 1988. Comparison of the effects of IQ control methods on memory and naming speed predictors of reading disability. *Reading Research Quarterly* 23:304–09.

Bowers, P. G., and Swanson, L. B. 1991. Naming speed deficits in reading disability: Multiple measures of a singular process. *Journal of Experimental Child Psychology* 51:195–219.

Bradley, L., and Bryant, P. E. 1983. Categorizing sounds and learning to read: A causal connection. *Nature 301*:419–21.

Brady, S., and Shankweiler, D. (Eds.). 1991. *Phonological Processes in Literacy: A Tribute to Isabelle Y. Liberman*. Hillsdale, NJ: Lawrence Erlbaum Associates.

Bruck, M., and Treiman, R. 1990. Phonological awareness and spelling in normal children and dyslexics: The case of initial consonant clusters. *Journal of Experimental Child Psychology* 50(1):156–78.

Catts, H. W. 1996. Defining dyslexia as a developmental language disorder: An expanded view. *Topics in Language Disorders* 16(2):14–29.

Chall, J. S. 1983. *Stages of Reading Development*. New York: McGraw-Hill.

Chase, C. 1997. A visual deficit model of developmental dyslexia. In *Developmental Dyslexia: Neural, Cognitive, and Genetic Mechanisms*, C. Chase, G. Rosen, and G. Sherman, eds. Baltimore: York Press.

Chukovsky, K. 1963. *From Two to Five*. Berkeley and Los Angeles, CA: University of California Press.

Cutting, L., Carlisle, J., and Denckla, M. B. April, 1998. *A model of the relationships among RAN and other predictors of word reading*. Poster presented at Society for Scientific Study of Reading, San Diego, CA.

Deeney, T., Gidney, C., Wolf, M., and Morris, R. 1999. *Phonological and naming-speed skills of African-American reading disabled students*. Paper presented at the Annual Meeting of the Society for the Scientific Study of Reading, Montreal, Canada.

Deeney, T., Wolf, M., and Goldberg, A. 1999. *"I like to take my own sweet time": Case study of a child with naming-speed deficits and reading disability*. Exceptional Child (Special Issue on Case Studies in Dyslexia; Special Issue Editor: R. Felton).

Denckla, M. B., and Rudel, R. G. 1974. "Rapid automatized naming" of pictured objects, colors, letters, and numbers by normal children. *Cortex* 10:186–202.

Denckla, M. B., and Rudel, R. G. 1976a. Naming of objects by dyslexic and other learning-disabled children. *Brain and Language* 3:1–15.

Denckla, M. B., and Rudel, R. G. 1976b. Rapid automatized naming (R.A.N.): Dyslexia differentiated from other learning disabilities. *Neuropsychologia* 14:471–79.

Denckla, M. B. 1998. *Research Symposium*. Presentation at the meeting of New York Orton Society. New York, NY.

Eden, G., and Zeffiro, T. 1998. Neural systems affected in developmental dyslexia revealed by functional neuroimaging. *Neuron* 21:279–82.

Ellis, A. W. 1985. The production of spoken words: A cognitive neuropsychological perspective. In *Progress in the Psychology of Language, Vol. 2*, A. W. Ellis, ed. Hillsdale, NJ: Lawrence Erlbaum Associates.

Foorman, B. 1994. Phonological and orthographic processing: Separate but equal? In *The Varieties of Orthographic Knowledge*, V. Berninger, ed. Dordrecht, The Netherlands: Kluwer.

Foorman, B., Francis, D., Shaywitz, S., Shaywitz, B., and Fletcher, J. 1997. The case for early reading intervention. In *Foundations of Reading Acquisition*, B. Blachman, ed. Mahwah, NJ: Lawrence Erlbaum Associates.

Fowler, A. 1991. How early phonological development might set the stage for phoneme awareness. In *Phonological Processes in Literacy*, S. Brady and D. Shankweiler, eds. Hillsdale, NJ: Lawrence Erlbaum Associates.

Galaburda, A. M., Menard, M. T., and Rosen, G. D. 1994. Evidence for aberrant auditory anatomy in developmental dyslexia. *Proceedings of the National Academy of Sciences* 91:8010–13.

Geschwind, N. 1965. Disconnection syndrome in animals and man (Parts I, II). *Brain* 88:237–94, 585–644.

Goodglass, H. 1980. Disorders of naming following brain injury. *American Scientist* 68:647–55.

Goodglass, H., and Kaplan, E. 1972. *The Assessment of Aphasia and Related Disorders*. London: Lea and Febiger.

Gough, P., and Tunmer, W. 1986. Decoding, reading, and reading disability. *Remedial and Special Education* 7:6–10.

Grigorenko, E., Wood, F., Meyer, M., Hart, L., Speed, W., Shuster, A., and Pauls, D. 1997. Susceptibility loci for distinct components of developmental dyslexia on chromosomes 6 and 15. *American Journal of Human Genetics* 60:27–39.

Kamhi, A., and Catts, H. 1989. *Reading Disabilities: A Developmental Language Perspective*. Austin, TX: PRO-ED.

Kamhi, A., Pollack, K., and Harris, J. 1996 (Eds.). *Communication Development and Disorders in African American Children*. Baltimore, MD: Paul M Brookes.

Korhonen, T. 1995. The persistence of rapid naming problems in children with reading disabilities: A nine-year follow-up. *Journal of Learning Disabilities* 28:232–39.

Krug, C. 1996. *The diagnostic implications of the "Double Deficit Hypothesis": An investigation of fifth grade readers classified by decoding skill and visual naming speed*. Unpublished doctoral dissertation. Boston: Tufts University.

Liberman, I. Y., Shankweiler, D., and Liberman, A. M. 1989. The alphabetic principle and learning to read. In *Phonology and Reading Disability*, Vol. IARLD Monograph Series, D. Shankweiler and I. Y. Liberman, eds. Ann Arbor, MI: University of Michigan Press.

Livingstone, M. S., Rosen, G. D., Drislane, F. W., and Galaburda, A. M. 1991. Physiological and anatomical evidence for a magnocellular defect in developmental dyslexia. *Proceeds of the National Academy of Science* 88:7943–47.

Lovett, M. W. 1984. A developmental perspective on reading dysfunction: Accuracy and rate criteria in the subtyping of dyslexic children. *Brain and Language* 22:67–91.

Lovett, M. W. 1992. Developmental dyslexia. In *Handbook of Neuropsychology*, Vol. 7, F. Boller and J. Grafman, eds. Amsterdam: Elsevier.

Lovett, M. W. 1995. *Remediating dyslexic children's word identification deficits: Are the core deficits of developmental dyslexia amenable to treatment?* Symposium paper presented at Society for Research in Child Development, Indianapolis, IN.

Lovett, M. W., Borden, S., DeLuca, T., Lacerenza, L., Benson, N., and Brackstone, D. 1994. Treating the core deficits of developmental dyslexia: Evidence of transfer of learning after phonologically and strategy-based reading training programs. *Developmental Psychology* 30:805–22.

Lovett, M., Steinbach, K., and Frijters, J. in press. Remediating the core deficits of developmental reading disability: A double-deficit perspective. *Journal of Learning Disabilities*.

Lyon, G. R. 1995. Toward a definition of dyslexia. *Annals of Dyslexia: An interdisciplinary Journal*, XLV, 3–27.

Manis, F., Doi, L., and Bhadha, B. in press. Naming speed, phonological awareness and orthographic knowledge in second graders. *Journal of Learning Disabilities*.

McBride-Chang, C., and Manis, F. 1996. Structural invariance in the associations of naming speed, phonological awareness, and verbal reasoning in good and poor readers: A test of the double deficit hypothesis. *Reading and Writing* 8:323–39.

Meyer, M. S., and Felton, R. H. 1998. *Evolution of fluency training: Old approaches and new directions*. Paper presented at meeting of International Dyslexia Association, San Francisco, CA.

Meyer, M. S., Wood, F. B., Hart, L. A., and Felton, R. H. in press. Longitudinal course of rapid naming in disabled and nondisabled readers. *Annals of Dyslexia*.

Meyer, M. S., Wood, F. B., Hart, L. A., and Felton, R. H. 1998. The selective predictive values in rapid automatized naming within poor readers. *Journal of Learning Disabilities* 31:106–17.

Morris, R., Stuebing, K., Fletcher, J., Shaywitz, S., Lyon, R., Shankweiler, D., Katz, L., Francis, D., and Shaywitz, B. 1998. Subtypes of reading disability: A phonological core with cognitive variability. *Journal of Educational Psychology* 90:347–73.

Morris, R., Lovett, M., and Wolf, M. 1995. *Treatment of developmental reading disabilities.* Proposal to the National Institute of Child Health and Human Development (Grant 1R55HD/OD30970-01A1).

Näslund, J. C., and Schneider, W. 1991. Longitudinal effects of verbal ability, memory capacity, and phonological awareness on reading performance. *European Journal of Psychology of Education* 4:375–92.

Novoa, L. 1988. *Word-retrieval process and reading acquisition and development in bilingual and monolingual children.* Unpublished doctoral dissertation. Cambridge, MA: Harvard University.

Novoa, L., and Wolf, M. 1984. *Word-retrieval and reading in bilingual children.* Paper presented at Boston University Language Conference, Boston, MA.

Obregón, M. 1994. *Exploring naming timing patterns by dyslexic and normal readers on the serial RAN task.* Unpublished Master's thesis. Boston: Tufts University.

Olson, R. K., Wise, B., Connors, F., Rack, J. P., and Fulker, D. 1989. Specific deficits in component reading and language skills: Genetic and environmental influences. *Journal of Learning Disabilities* 22:339–48.

Perfetti, C. A. 1985. *Reading Ability.* New York: Oxford Press.

Scarborough, H. 1998. Predicting the future achievement of second graders with reading disabilities: Contributions of phonemic awareness, verbal memory, rapid naming, and IQ. *Annals of Dyslexia* 48:115–36.

Scarborough, H. S., and Domgaard, R. M. 1998. *An exploration of the relationship between reading and rapid serial naming.* Poster presented at meeting of Society for Scientific Study of Reading. San Diego, CA.

Shankweiler, D., and Liberman, I. Y. 1972. Misreading: A search for causes. In *Language by Ear and by Eye*, J. F. Kavanagh and I. G. Mattingly, eds. Cambridge, MA: MIT Press.

Sherman, G. 1998. *Research Symposium.* Presentation at meeting of New York Orton Society. New York, NY.

Siegel, L. S., and Ryan, E. B. 1988. Development of grammatical-sensitivity, phonological, and short-term memory skills in normally achieving and learning disabled children. *Developmental Psychology* 24(1):28–37.

Snyder, L., and Downey, D. 1995. Serial rapid naming skills in children with reading disabilities. *Annals of Dyslexia, XLV*, 31–50.

Spring, C., and Capps, C. 1974. Encoding speed, rehearsal, and probed recall of dyslexic boys. *Journal of Educational Psychology* 66:780–86.

Spring, C., and Davis, J. 1988. Relations of digit naming speed with three components of reading. *Applied Psycholinguistics* 9:315–34.

Stanovich, K. 1986. "Matthew effects" in reading: Some consequences of individual differences in acquisition of literacy. *Reading Research Quarterly* 4:360–407.

Stanovich, K. E. 1992. Speculations on the causes and consequences of individual differences in early reading acquisition. In *Reading Acquisition*, P. B. Gough, L. C. Ehri, and R. Treiman, eds. Hillsdale, NJ: Lawrence Erlbaum Associates.

Stanovich, K. E., and Siegel, L. S. 1994. Phenotypic performance profile of children with reading disabilities: A regression based test of the phonological-core variable difference model. *Journal of Educational Psychology* 86(1):24–53.

Swanson, L. B. 1989. *Analyzing naming speed-reading relationships in children.* Unpublished doctoral dissertation. University of Waterloo, Waterloo, Ontario, Canada.

Torgesen, J. K., Wagner, R. K., Rashotte, C. A., Burgess, S., and Hecht, S. 1997. Contributions of phonological awareness and rapid automatic naming ability to the growth of word-reading skills in second- to fifth-grade children. *Scientific Studies of Reading* 1(2):161–85; Torgesen, J.K. (Personal correspondence, 1998).

Tunmer, W. 1995. *Intervention strategies for developing onset-rime sensitivity and analogical transfer in reading disabled children.* Paper presented at the Extraordinary Brain III Conference. Kauai, Hawaii.

Van den Bos, K. 1998. IQ, phonological awareness, and continuous-naming speed related to Dutch children's poor decoding performance on two word identification tests. *Dyslexia* 4:73–89.

Vellutino, F., and Scanlon, P. 1987. Phonological coding, phonological awareness, and reading ability: Evidence from a longitudinal and experimental study. *Merrill Palmer Quarterly* 33:321–63.

Wagner, R. K., Torgesen, J. K., and Rashotte, C. A. 1994. The development of reading-related phonological processing abilities: New evidence of bi-directional causality from a latent variable longitudinal study. *Developmental Psychology* 30:73–87.

West, T. 1998. Presentation at the National Dyslexia Research Foundation Conference. Kona, Hawaii.

Wimmer, H. 1993. Characteristics of developmental dyslexia in a regular writing system. *Applied Psycholinguistics* 14:1–34.

Wimmer, H., and Hummer, P. 1990. How German-speaking first graders read and spell: Doubts on the importance of the logographic stage. *Applied Psycholinguistics* 11:349–68.

Wolf, M. 1979. *The relationship of disorders of word-finding and reading in children and apha-sics*. Unpublished doctoral dissertation. Cambridge, MA: Harvard University.

Wolf, M., and Bowers, P. in press. The question of naming-speed deficits in developmental reading disabilities: An introduction to the double-deficit hypothesis. *Journal of Learning Disabilities*.

Wolf, M., and Goodglass, H. 1986. Dyslexia, dysnomia, and lexical retrieval. *Brain and Language* 28:154–68.

Wolf, M., and Goodman, G. 1996. *Speed Wizards*. Computerized reading program. Tufts University and Rochester Institute of Technology.

Wolf, M., and Miller, L. 1997. *The Retrieval, Automaticity, Vocabulary-Elaboration-Orthography (RAVE-O) reading intervention manual*. An unpublished manual for NICHD grant #1R55HD/OD30970-01A1.

Wolf, M., and Obregón, M. 1992. Early naming deficits, developmental dyslexia, and a specific deficit hypothesis. *Brain and Language* 42:219–47.

Wolf, M., and Segal, D. 1999. Retrieval-rate, Accuracy, and Vocabulary Elaboration (RAVE) in reading-impaired children: A pilot intervention program. *Dyslexia: An International Journal of Theory and Practice* 5:1–27.

Wolf, M., Bally, H., and Morris, R. 1986. Automaticity, retrieval processes, and reading: A longitudinal study in average and impaired readers. *Child Development* 57:988–1000.

Wolf, M., Bowers, P., and Biddle, K. in press. Naming-speed processes, timing, and reading: A conceptual review. *Journal of Learning Disabilities*.

Wolf, M., Miller, L., and Donnelly, K. in press. Retrieval, automaticity, vocabulary elaboration-orthography (RAVE-O): A comprehensive, fluency-based reading intervention program. *Journal of Learning Disabilities*.

Wolf, M., Pfeil, C., Lotz, R., and Biddle, K. 1994. Towards a more universal understanding of the developmental dyslexias: The contribution of orthographic factors. In *The Varieties of Orthographic Knowledge I: Theoretical and Developmental Issues*, V. W. Berninger, ed. Dordrecht, The Netherlands: Kluwer.

Wolf, M., Goldberg, A., Gidney, C., Lovett, M., Cirino, P., and Morris, R. 1999. *The second deficit: An investigation of the independence of phonological and naming-speed deficits in developmental dyslexia*. Invited, submitted manuscript. *Reading and Writing*.

Wolff, P., Michel, G., and Ovrut, M. 1990a. Rate variables and automatized naming in developmental dyslexia. *Brain and Language* 39:556–75.

Wolff, P., Michel, G., and Ovrut, M. 1990b. The timing of syllable repetitions in developmental dyslexia. *Journal of Speech and Hearing Research* 33:281–89.

Wolff, P. 1993. Impaired temporal resolution in developmental dyslexia: Temporal information processing in the nervous system. In *Annals of the New York Academy of Sciences*, P. Tallal, A. Galaburda, R. Llinas, and C. von Euler, eds. 682:87–103.

Wood, F. B., and Felton, R. H. 1994. Separate linguistic and developmental factors in the development of reading. *Topics in Language Disorders* 14(4):42–57.

Wood, F. B., and Eden, G. 1995. Paper presented at meetings of Society for Research in Child Development. Indianapolis, IN.

Yap, R., and van der Leij, A. 1993. Word processing in dyslexics: An automatic decoding deficit? *Reading and Writing: An Interdisciplinary Journal* 5(3):261–79.

Yap, R. L., and van der Leij, A. 1994. Testing the automatization deficit hypothesis of dyslexia via a dual-task paradigm. *Journal of Learning Disabilities* 27(10):660–65.

History and Significance of Rapid Automatized Naming

Martha Bridge Denckla, M.D.

Kennedy Krieger Institute
Baltimore, Maryland

Laurie E. Cutting, Ph.D.

Kennedy Krieger Institute
Baltimore, Maryland

In this review, the origins and history of a test of rapid automatized naming (RAN) are traced from nineteenth-century classical brain-behavior analyses of cases of acquired "alexia without agraphia" through adaptations to studies of normal and reading disabled children. The element of speed (of responding verbally to a visual stimulus) was derived from a test of color naming developed over 50 years ago as a bedside measure of recovery from brain injuries. Merging the "visual-verbal" connection essential to reading (specific) with the response time element (general), RAN turned out to be a useful correlate and predictor of reading competence, accounting even for variance beyond that accounted for by timed tests of discrete naming. As one of the two deficits highlighted in the Double Deficit hypothesis with phonological awareness, RAN has emerged as something more than a particularly difficult challenge to a unitary phonological retrieval deficit, and has itself been subjected to further dissection. Coming full circle to its origins, recent research suggests that RAN taps both visual-verbal (language domain) and processing speed (executive domain) contributions to reading.

Annals of Dyslexia, Vol. 49, 1999
Copyright© 1999 by The International Dyslexia Association®
ISSN 0736-9387

HISTORY AND SIGNIFICANCE OF RAPID AUTOMATIZED NAMING

The Rapid Automatized Naming (RAN) test can be traced to Norman Geschwind's description of Dejerine's case of "pure alexia without agraphia." Indeed, the analytic beauty of Geschwind's description of the disconnection syndrome not only led to the RAN but also inspired many of us to pursue neurology. The finding that an adult-acquired lesion could result in a "visual-verbal" disconnection that rendered reading impossible was the seed of an approach to understanding children who could not read. The color-naming connection and its parallel with word reading was elucidated by a predictable outcome of visual-verbal disconnection.

A neurological connection model based on the adult brain was the starting point for the RAN. The concept behind the color-naming test, in particular, was a paper by Geschwind and Fusillo (1966). That paper describes an adult whose "stroke" not only led to "pure alexia without agraphia," (Dejerine's term) but who was also unable to name colors despite normal color matching and no evidence of color blindness. The fact that there was no "agraphia" (inability to spell and write words) indicates that the adult could generate the pathway from spoken words to visual and kinesthetic representations. The discussion of color naming as a marker for visual-verbal disconnection led to a search for children with unexpected reading failure in first grade who might be unable to name colors. In fact, what was found was not the dramatic inability to name colors but long latencies, a hesitancy described as "lack of automaticity" (Denckla, 1972). What next occurred was a search for a timed challenge to color naming. This turned out to be but one instance of a general principle: the need to become subtle in developmental research and to look for "pastel" versions of adult-acquired deficits. Where the adult "loses" a capacity, it appears the child both (1) acquires the capacity more slowly, and (2) performs the task tapping that capacity "on-line" more slowly. For reading, this principle turns out to have profound and practical implications.

At that time, most neurologists owned copies of the Ruesch and Wells *Mental Examiner's Handbook*. Because the handbook was recommended to all medical students by Professor of Neurology Derek Denny-Brown, who also trained Norman Geschwind, Denny-Brown gets ancestral credit in the RAN story. In the *Mental Examiner's Handbook* was a page on which was printed in color a series of 50 squares, five primary colors repeated in random order ten times. This was meant to be administered at the bedside as a timed "continuous performance" color-naming task, used to measure recovery from head injury. The status of rapid color-naming as a test of "continuous performance" was not to reemerge until the very recent past. Colors were chosen because they are learned early, named often, and updated in daily life, and because examiners themselves often master color names in quite a few foreign languages. As a first step, large "oak tag" copies of the color-naming task were constructed and used to collect norms on kindergarten children (Denckla 1972). In subsequent research, using color-naming as a "template," and guided by the collegial psychological know-how of Rita G. Rudel, three additional RAN tasks were created. The Objects RAN used "four-year-old" vocabulary from the then-current Stanford Binet and was conceived of as a downward extension of the Colors RAN. The symbol cards (five numerals and five lower-case letters) were conceived of as an upward extension of the Colors RAN.

Thus it happened that beginner's luck gave rise to the RAN. The concept of a basic circuit in the brain, the link to child development through color naming as a kindergarten milestone, and the availability of a template for testing speed of naming, added together to yield a test that has, like a child one rears, gone out into the world and done better than one ever would have dreamed.

RESEARCH FOLLOWING THE INVENTION OF THE RAN AND THE DISCRETE VERSUS CONTINUOUS DEBATE

The research that established RAN as a predictor of reading success (Denckla and Rudel 1972; 1974; 1976) initiated an entire area of inquiry within the educational field. Many subsequent research studies (e.g., Blachman 1984; Stanovich 1981; Vellutino et al. 1996; Wagner, Torgesen, and Rashotte 1994; Wolf, Bally, and Morris 1986) both extended and duplicated Denckla and Rudel's findings that RAN was a correlate of reading. However, early on there were some methodological debates that centered around whether or not RAN would still contribute to reading success if the items were presented in a discrete format rather than in the continuous format used by Denckla and Rudel. In the discrete format, the items are presented individually and the latencies for the 50 items are averaged, whereas in the continuous format, all 50 items are presented on a board and the child's score is the total time to name *all* items consecutively. Advocates of a discrete-trial format have argued that it eliminates those processes of scanning, sequencing, and motoric requirements, or extraneous sources of variance that are present in continuous trial formats (Wolf 1991, p.128); advocates of continuous formats argue that it is these very components (i.e., scanning, sequencing, and so on) that reflect those processes important for textual reading. As an added component, the continuous format may also place more demands on executive functioning than the discrete format; this may explain why continuous formats are better predictors of reading than discrete formats.

There are conflicting research findings as to whether or not discrete trial format discriminates good and poor readers. Some researchers (e.g., Perfetti, Finger, and Hogaboam 1978; Stanovich 1981) have found that the discrete trial RAN does not discriminate good and poor readers, whereas others have found the opposite (e.g., Bowers and Swanson 1991). In addition, Walsh, Price, and Gillingham (1988) found that discrete-trial RAN correlates with reading in the early grades, although in their study, second grade discrete-trial RAN did not predict third grade reading. As Wolf (1991) has noted, some of these conflicting findings may have to do with the severity of disability in different samples of poor readers. Nonetheless, research on the discrete-trial RAN has not yielded consistent differences between good and poor readers.

In contrast to discrete-trial research, continuous-trial research, most prominently conducted by Bowers, Wolf, and colleagues (e.g., Bowers 1989; Bowers, Steffy, and Tate 1988; Wolf, Bally, and Morris 1986; see Wolf 1997), has consistently found that the RAN discriminates between good and poor readers, even among adults (Felton, Naylor, and Wood 1990). On the other hand, RAN does not predict individual variation in word identification skill among *normal* readers past the elementary grades (Meyer, Wood, Hart, and Felton 1998). Significantly, the continuous-trial format appears to have features, distinctly different from the discrete-trial format, that make it a more powerful discriminator of good and poor readers. In their 1991 study, Bowers and Swanson found that even after entering discrete-trial format first in a regression equation, the continuous-format RAN added uniquely to reading ability. Thus, they confirmed that continuous-format RAN involves more demands than the discrete-trial format. As pointed out by Wolf (1991), Spring and Davis (1988) have hypothesized that discrete-trial RAN may be a "precursor of automaticity, [but] is not a measure of automaticity itself."

The added cognitive demands of the continuous RAN highlight why the slowness and inefficiency observed in poor readers may overlap with the executive dysfunction characteristic of children with ADHD. As discussed in greater detail below, the cognitive demands of continuous RAN may heavily tax executive control of those language systems in the brain (e.g., scanning and sequencing) that lie at the "intersection" of the neurological domains hypothesized to underlie ADHD and RD.

RELATIONSHIP OF RAN TO OTHER PREDICTORS OF READING AND THE DOUBLE-DEFICIT HYPOTHESIS

Aside from the debates that surround the continuous-versus discrete-trial formats of RAN, there are numerous debates as to what exactly RAN measures. Many research studies have demonstrated that RAN makes a contribution to reading that is independent of the contribution of other predictors of reading ability such as phonological awareness and memory (e.g., Blachman 1984; Bowers 1989; Bowers, Steffy, and Tate 1988; McBride-Chang and Manis 1996). Nonetheless, RAN has often been placed within the phonological processing domain, along with phonological awareness (both synthesis and analysis) and memory (both memory span and working memory) (Wagner, Torgesen, Laughon, Simmons, and Rashotte 1993; Wagner and Torgesen 1998). Those who believe that RAN is a component of phonological processing, alongside phonological awareness and memory, define RAN as the "efficiency of phonological code retrieval" (Wagner et al. 1993; Vellutino et al. 1996). However, there are some (see Wolf 1997 for a review) who have argued that RAN is not a subsidiary component of phonological processing. The argument that RAN represents functions separate from the phonological processing domain stems from the facts that (1) RAN consistently makes a unique contribution to reading beyond phonological awareness and memory, and (2) poor readers can be subtyped into those with RAN deficits only, phonological deficits only, or those who have both phonological and RAN deficits (i.e., Wolf's double-deficit readers). RAN-impaired readers are accurate, albeit slow, decoders; phonologically impaired readers are poor decoders; and double-deficit readers are the poorest readers overall (Wolf 1997).

The double-deficit hypothesis led us (Cutting, Carlisle, and Denckla 1998) to try to design a study that would explain RAN. Our general questions were: (1) what is the relationship of RAN to other predictors of word reading? and (2) what is going on "behind the scenes," or what "goes into" RAN? In an attempt to answer these questions, a preliminary model of word reading was developed and tested on 79 *normal* readers in first, second, and third grade who were not diagnosed with any type of learning disability or ADHD. This model (presented in Figure 1) attempted to test several integrated theories (e.g., Bowers, Golden, Kennedy, and Young 1994; Bowers and Wolf 1993; Wagner et al. 1993; Wolf 1997) of the relation of RAN to other predictors of word reading such as phonological awareness (measured by a phoneme deletion task), memory span (measured by memory for increasingly longer series of digits; i.e., "digits forward"), and orthographic awareness (a word likeness task)[1]. The model also included two hypothesized behind the scenes predictors of RAN: processing speed (measured by the processing speed cluster from the Woodcock Johnson Psychoeducational Battery - Revised, Woodcock and Johnson 1989); and articulation (measured by speed of repetition of letters and numbers).

Results of the model indicated that RAN made a unique contribution to word reading alongside phonological awareness and orthographic awareness. Memory span did not contribute uniquely to word reading because it overlapped with phonological awareness. Processing speed had an impact on RAN speed, as well as on phonological awareness and on memory span. It also had marginally significant effects on orthographic awareness. Articulation had an impact only on phonological awareness. Thus, no variable included in the model was able to fully explain RAN, as RAN still contributed uniquely to word reading, even with all the other variables included in the model.

In summary, while RAN could in large part be accounted for by processing speed (called "rapid efficient responding" in figure 2), it could not fully be explained by it. Therefore, whatever RAN represents, it is in part subsumed under the domain educators call processing speed.

It should be emphasized that our model is only preliminary in nature; there may be different results when the model is tested with a larger sample size and/or dyslexic readers.

---

[1]It has been hypothesized that RAN contributes to the development of orthographic awareness/knowledge (see Bowers et al. 1994), a topic that is beyond the scope of this article.

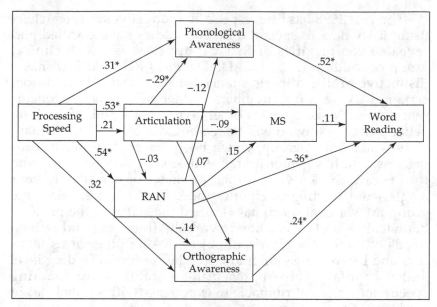

Figure 1. Model of Word Reading with Significant Path
Coefficients (GFI = .96, *p < .5).

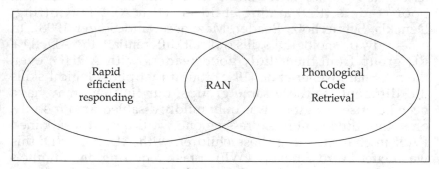

Figure 2. RAN in the overlap of two domains

Perhaps even a different model may be suggested altogether.
However, this model does provide some interesting initial results and beginning thoughts as to some of the potential relationships between RAN and other predictors of word reading, as
well as some of the possible behind the scenes processes thought
to contribute to RAN. It should be noted that Scarborough and
Domgaard (1998) have also analyzed various hypothesized subskills of RAN in an effort to further understand the complex set
of skills required for the RAN.

The year 1998 has been especially productive for researchers using RAN data as several different studies have clarified and revealed complexities of RAN. It appears that each clinical group of children (i.e., RD, ADHD versus RD + ADHD) has a distinctive profile of performance on RAN tasks. In addition, certain RAN tasks (i.e., numbers and letters) are better concurrent *discriminators*, whereas others (i.e., colors and objects) are better *predictors* of who will be reading disabled. The Bowman-Gray/Wake Forest group, which has pioneered so much reading research, has demonstrated that among third-graders who read poorly, the RAN is a strong predictor of persistently poor single-word reading in eighth grade. Furthermore, this same group (Meyer et al. 1998) has clarified the status of the presymbolic (colors and objects) and symbolic (numbers and letters) dyads of the RAN; colors and objects RAN outperforms numbers and letters across all grades in relationship to reading level and vocabulary, thus representing a stable factor (naming speed) not simply attributable to experience with symbols (as in reading itself).

Our own group (Kennedy Krieger Institute/Johns Hopkins University School of Medicine) has found RAN (numbers and letters) to be a key factor in discriminating between good and poor readers (RD) among children with ADHD (Cutting, Denckla, Schuerholz, Reader, Mazzocco, and Singer 1998). In our study, phonological skills did not differentiate the ADHD + RD group from the solidly good readers with ADHD; even though Shankweiler et al. (1995) found that phonological skills did differentiate these same groups, our findings may have been because our group was only mildly disabled. In our study, one other time-limited expressive one-word output task joined RAN in characterizing those children with ADHD + RD; this was Letter Word Fluency (LWF), a task requiring one minute's work. For example, the child is asked to "say all the words [you] can think of that begin with the letter 'A,' but no proper names." Traditionally listed as an executive function probe, LWF demands efficient rule-governed, self-monitored search of the lexicon. Does LWF have something in common with RAN?

Serendipitously for us, also in 1998, we encountered evidence for RAN as a task related to LWF presented in a poster at the October 1998 meeting of the Academy of Child and Adolescent Psychiatry by Tannock and her colleagues from Toronto. Tannock reported that slow color naming characterized a group of children who were diagnosed with ADHD but read well; that is, were not comorbid for RD. When treated with methylphenidate (Ritalin), these children with ADHD (but no RD) became somewhat faster on color RAN but did not become normal in speed.

These 1998 findings, bringing the diagnosis of ADHD (and its related cognitive characteristics) into the conceptual field of functions probed by RAN, shed a new light on the double-deficit theory of dyslexia, but also add a complicating factor. Now we have to ask whether slowness, inefficiency, and lack of fluency and automaticity in reading may in some cases be attributable to the brain dysfunction underlying ADHD, suggesting that the very common comorbidity of RD and ADHD may require reanalysis. From a neurologist's perspective, it would seem that ADHD is even more neurologically heterogeneous in origins than RD, allowing ample opportunities for the two to intersect. Many ADHD-related characteristics involve slowness, such as slow and variable reaction time and slow-for-age timed motor coordination (Denckla and Rudel 1978). It is often necessary to pause and explain to students, or parents in the clinic, how it is that hyperactive children should perform slowly; it makes sense if one recalls that the shortest distance between two points is a straight line, with no deflections or diversions!

The reading-relevant zone of convergence within language-related skills, linking ADHD to RD, concerns the executive aspects of language. One of these is letter-word fluency which has already been described. Certain error types within word list learning tasks also link "dyslexic" and "dysexecutive" errors because such errors reflect (1) impaired phonological working memory, as in self-repetitions, and (2) impaired specific word retrieval, as when over-categorical recall leads to some random fruit being recalled instead of the listed fruit, a "paraphasia-in-kind." Our research focussed on children with ADHD and associated cognitive dysfunctions collectively referred to as "executive" (Reader, Harris, Schuerholz, and Denckla 1994). The ADHD plus RD subgroup was not language-impaired except when RAN, LWF, or qualitative error analysis on word list learning revealed a problem at the nodal point where the "phonological slave system" feeds into the central executive (in the original Baddeley 1986 terminology in the field of cognitive psychology). Although in theory a neurologist would like to dichotomize within the executive system so that children with RD-free-of-ADHD would show phonological-but-not-central dysexecutive features, and those with ADHD-free-of-RD would show the reverse, as yet no such splendid double dissociation has been consistently demonstrated. Our group with ADHD plus RD shows both motor-related and language-related dysex-ecutive characteristics. Phonological inputs to the central work-ing memory system may be necessary very broadly for academic success, most particularly in every phase of reading. In addition to the working memory connection, reading re-quires other executive aspects such as recall and application of rules, looking ahead for that silent "e" while recalling the rule thereof, or searching the mental lexicon and monitoring the match between what is sounded out and blended and some re-called word. If such executive skills are called on in the de-coding process, how much more demanding of executive aspects of cognition is that mysterious process we call "reading comprehension!"

This language/executive crossroads is exemplified by the RAN, at least in our current state of understanding. Starting with the neurologically (but not fully developmentally) grounded concept of a visual-verbal connection, experienced re-searchers are forced to add to that circuit the influence of other, possibly parallel (or at least nonlinear) circuitry that drives the search for the name and the speed of repeated responses, oculo-motor and oral-motor. The surface simplicity of RAN is subject to complications, although the visual-verbal (symbol-sound) re-mains at the core of the significant sensitivity of the RAN. The specificity of RAN is still remarkable with respect to the skill of single word reading, but the specificity with respect to the brain, in terms of an underlying localizing diagnosis, has been called into question. We need to ask, "who is slow on RAN and why?" Visual perception is an unlikely candidate, but connec-tions between and among several systems leave open to explo-ration several RAN pathologies. In typical neurological localizing logic, the double-deficit dyslexic many be the easiest to pinpoint, since it is at the phonology intercept that both deficits may exist. Yet, even with such a language-system local-ization, the double deficit might be in the temporal lobe (the posterior part of the system) or in the frontal lobe (the anterior part of the system). Heilman's formulation of speech-motor on-togeny of "phonological awareness" is one of the most intrigu-ing topics of current reading research (in neurological context); thus, if slowing comes at the speaking end of RAN process, in such cases the double deficit would emanate from the Broca's area. Nonetheless, it is important to keep in mind that it is not possible to assign each deficit of the double-deficit hypothesis neatly to one neuropsychological domain or the other. This is because a more extensive linguistic impairment may cause deficits in both phonological awareness and RAN. Similarly, the executive demands implicit in both "awareness" of phonological components and sustained efficient response preparation on RAN may underlie double deficits in some cases of ADHD + RD. In summary, clean distinctions are probably incorrect; a variety of mix and match linguistic/executive profiles can underlie reading-related deficits.

In fact, oversimplification of phonological competence endangers the future of truly prescriptive individualized remediation. The phoneme is not a simple unitary perceptual unit susceptible to observation as a psychophysical event (e.g., on an acoustic spectrograph). Rather, as its neurological basis has been elucidated by researchers (e.g., Heilman, Voeller, and Alexander 1996; Liberman, Cooper, Shankweiler, and Studdert-Kennedy 1967; Studdert-Kennedy 1987), the phoneme is constructed from the connection between auditory percept and mouth position (itself constructed from movement and its kinesthetic "e" perception). The phoneme is no more accurately described as auditory than water (H_2O) would be if described as "H" or "O." By analogy to the chemical compound (H_2O), the phoneme exists in the human brain as the bond, the connection, between nearly simultaneous auditory and kinesthetic experiences. Such an analysis opens up the possibility that multiple forms of phonological disorder(s) exist, since a two-way loop with three way-stations (i.e., connecting auditory, motor, and kinesthetic processes) must be intact in order for there to be adequate phonological awareness.

As for awareness, the very term escalates the complexity of this central issue in dyslexia. Awareness implies an explicit, conscious capacity to cleave words into auditory-kinesthetic compounds called phonemes, in order to perform an active manipulation of the word heard or spoken. This is an executive function.

In future research, the RAN must be combined with other tasks to help us find our way along and among its several connections. Slowing could (and probably does) arise from any one of several key connections or combinations thereof. There is no central timer or pacer mechanism to be sought; slowing is specific to, and resides in, each component-connection. Slowing can be one sign of that fundamental aspect of executive function known as response preparation. The domain executive function is so broad that in addition to response preparation, it also encompasses search/retrieval processes. Executive function cannot be substituted for phonological awareness in terms of importance for reading, nor can executive function be considered a mere compensatory strategy secondary to slow processing manifested in RAN performance. Rather, a blended multifactorial hypothesis is put forward in which phonological factors, visual-verbal connections, and the executive aspects intrinsic to and within each task are interwoven. Thus, the present state of RAN research raises interesting questions rather than reach explanatory closure.

Wherever slowing occurs, however, it probably implies that remediation will require one or more detour(s). Some research by Horwitz, Rumsey, and Donohue (1998) has recently shown, using Positron Emission Tomography (PET), that those who are successfully compensated dyslexic adults do use detours when phonological processing is asked of them. Research will in all probability demonstrate that such detours are effective except where speed is concerned. More sophisticated elaborations and variations of RAN will make legitimate our advocacy, as clinicians, for lifelong extended-time accommodations for compensated yet residually slow readers.

ACKNOWLEDGMENTS

This work was supported in part by the following: NINDS-funded P50 NS 35359 (Learning Disabilities Research Center) and NICHD Post-doctoral Fellowship ND 07414-07, a Northwestern University Dissertation Fellowship Award and a Council for Exceptional Children Division of Learning Disabilities dissertation award. The authors acknowledge Mrs. Pamula D. Yerby-Hammack for her help in the preparation of this manuscript.

Address Correspondence to: Martha Bridge Denckla, M.D., or Laurie E. Cutting, Ph.D., Kennedy Krieger Institute, 707 North Broadway, Suite 516, Baltimore, Maryland 21205, telephone (410) 502-9399, fax (410) 502-9101, e-mail denckla@kennedykrieger.org. or cutting@kennedykrieger.org.

References

Baddeley, A. 1986. *Working Memory*. Oxford: Oxford University Press.

Blachman, B. A. 1984. Relationship of rapid naming ability and language analysis skills to kindergarten and first-grade reading achievement. *Journal of Educational Psychology* 76:610–22.

Bowers, P. G. 1989. Naming speed and phonological awareness: Independent contributors to reading disabilities. In *Cognitive and Social Perspectives for Literacy Research and Instruction: 38th Yearbook of the National Reading Conference*, S. McCormick and J. Zutell, eds. Chicago: National Reading Conference, Inc.

Bowers, P. G., Golden, J., Kennedy, A., and Young, A. 1994. Limits upon orthographic knowledge due to processes indexed by naming speed. In *The Varieties of Orthographic Knowledge I: Theoretical and Developmental Issues*, V. W. Berninger, ed. Dordrecht, The Netherlands: Kluwer Academic Press.

Bowers, P. G., Steffi, R. A., and Tate, E. 1988. Comparison of the effects of IQ control methods on memory and naming speed predictors of reading disability. *Reading Research Quarterly* 23:304–19.

Bowers, P. G., and Swanson, L. B. 1991. Naming speed deficits in reading disability: Multiple measures of a singular process. *Journal of Experimental Child Psychology* 51:195–219.

Bowers, P. G., and Wolf, M. 1993b. Theoretical links between naming speed, precise timing mechanisms and orthographic skill in dyslexia. *Reading and Writing: An Interdisciplinary Journal* 5:69–85.

Cutting, L. E., Carlisle, J. F., and Denckla, M. B. 1998. A model of the relationships between Rapid Automatized Naming and other predictors of word reading. Poster presentation at the Society for Scientific Study of Reading, April 1998, San Diego.

Cutting, L. E., Denckla, M. B., Schuerholz, L. J., Reader, M. J., Mazzocco, M. M., and Singer, H. S. in preparation. Rapid Automatized Naming in children with and without attention deficit hyperactivity disorder.

Denckla, M. B., and Rudel, R. G. 1972. Color-naming in dyslexic boys. *Cortex* 8:164–76.

Denckla, M. B., and Rudel, R. G. 1974. Rapid "Automatized" Naming of pictured objects, colors, letters, and numbers by normal children. *Cortex* 10:186–202.

Denckla, M. B., and Rudel, R. G. 1976. Naming of objects by dyslexic and other learning-disabled children. *Brain and Language* 3:1–15.

Denckla, M. B., and Rudel, R. G. 1978. Anomalies of motor development in hyperactive boys. *Annals of Neurology* 3:231–33.

Felton, R. H., Naylor, C. E., and Wood, F. B. 1990. Neuropsychological profile of adult dyslexics. *Brain and Language* 39:485–97.

Geschwind, N., and Fusillo, M. 1966. Color-naming defects in association with Alexia. *Archives of Neurology* 15:137–46.

Heilman K. M., Voeller K., and Alexander, A. W. 1996. Developmental dyslexia: A motor-articulatory feedback hypothesis. *Annals of Neurology* 39:407–12.

Horwitz, B., Rumsey, J. M., and Donohue, B. C. 1998. Functional connectivity of the angular gyrus in normal reading and dyslexia. *Proceedings of the National Academy of Sciences of the United States of America*, 95:8939–44.

Liberman, A. M., Cooper, F. S., Shankweiler, D. P., and Studdert-Kennedy, M. 1967. Perception of the speech code. *Psychological Review* 74:431–61.

McBride-Chang, C., and Manis, F. 1996. Structural invariance in the associations of naming speed, phonological awareness, and verbal reasoning in good and poor readers: A test of the double-deficit hypothesis. *Reading and Writing: an Interdisciplinary Journal* 8:323–39.

Meyer, M. S., Wood, F. B., Hart, L. A., and Felton, R. H. 1998. Selective predictive value of Rapid Automatized Naming in poor readers. *Journal of Learning Disabilities* 31:106–17.

Perfetti, C. A., Finger, E., and Hogabaum, T. 1978. Sources of vocalization latency differences between skilled and less skilled young readers. *Journal of Educational Psychology* 70:730–39.

Reader, M. J., Harris, E. L., Schuerholz, L. J., and Denckla, M. B. 1994. Attention Deficit Hyperactivity Disorder and executive dysfunction. *Developmental Neuropsychology* 10:493–512.

Scarborough, H. S., and Domgaard, R. M. 1998. An exploration of the relationship between reading and rapid serial naming speed. Paper presented at the Society for Scientific Study of Reading, San Diego.

Shankweiler, D. P., Crain, S., Katz, L., Fowler, A. E., Liberman, A., Brady, S., Thornton, R., Lundquist, E., Dreyer, L., Fletcher, J., Stuebing, K., Shaywitz, S., and Shaywitz, B. 1995. Cognitive profiles of reading-disabled children: Comparison of language skills in phonology, morphology, and syntax. *Psychological Science* 6:149–56.

Spring, C., and Davis, J. M. 1988. Relations of digit naming speed with three components of reading. *Applied Psycholinguistics* 9:315–34.

Stanovich, K. E. 1981. Relationships between word decoding speed, general name-retrieval ability, and reading progress in first-grade children. *Journal of Educational Psychology* 73:809–15.

Studdert-Kennedy, M. 1987. The phoneme as a perceptuomotor structure. In *Language Perception and Production*, A. Alloport, D. Mackay, W. Prinz, and E. Scheerer, eds. London: Academic Press.

Tannock, R. October, 1998. Poster presentation at the Academy of Child and Adolescent Psychiatry, Anaheim, California.

Vellutino, F. R., Scanlon, D. M., Sipay, E. R., Small, S. G., Pratt, A., Chen, R., and Denckla, M. B. 1996. Cognitive profiles of difficult-to-remediate and readily remediated poor readers: Early intervention as a vehicle for distinguishing between cognitive and experiential deficits as basic causes of specific reading disability. *Journal of Educational Psychology* 88:601–38.

Wagner, R. K., Torgesen, J. K., Laughon, P., Simmons, K., and Rashotte, C. A. 1993. Development of young readers' phonological processing abilities. *Journal of Educational Psychology* 85:83–103.

Wagner, R. K., Torgesen, J. K., and Rashotte, C. A. 1994. Development of reading-related phonological processing abilities: New evidence of bidirectional causality from a latent variable longitudinal study. *Developmental Psychology* 30:73–87.

Walsh, D., Price, G., and Gilllingham, M. 1988. The critical but transitory importance of letter naming. *Reading Research Quarterly* 23:108–22.

Wells, F. L., and Ruesch, J. 1945. Color naming and reading. In *The Mental Examiners' Handbook - Second Edition*. New York: Psychological Corporation.

Wolf, M. 1991. Naming speed and reading: The contribution of the cognitive neurosciences. *Reading Research Quarterly* 26:123–41.

Wolf, M. 1997. A provisional, integrative account of phonological and naming-speed deficits in dyslexia: Implications for diagnosis and intervention. In *Foundations of Reading Acquisition and Dyslexia*, B. Blachman, ed. Mahwah, NJ: Lawrence Erlbaum Associates.

Wolf, M., Bally, H., and Morris, R. 1986. Automaticity, retrieval processes, and reading: A longitudinal study in average and impaired readers. *Child Development* 57:988–1005.

PART II
Classification Issues Pertaining to Dyslexia and Other Learning Weaknesses

One of the most contentious issues in the field of dyslexia concerns the question of subtyping. Are there multiple "kinds" of dyslexics? Do some children have dyslexia *plus* some other deficit or do the difficulties interact to create some whole new syndrome? Further, although reading disability is evident in 80% of all students with a diagnosed learning disability, what are the attributes of those children who present different learning problems.

The three papers in this section provide some balance on the issue of subtyping by taking a careful empirical look at how specific difficulties with word recognition fit within the larger context of learning difficulties. Two of the papers (chapters 3 and 4) involve large samples of schoolchildren; two are longitudinal in scope (chapters 3 and 5) and all provide data on analytic measures of reading and nonreading measures that bear on theoretical questions that have challenged the reading community.

In chapter 3, Nathlie Badian provides a definitive account of what is known about math disability to date, including some benchmark figures on the incidence of persistent math, reading, and reading-plus-math disability in an extremely well-defined sample. The paper is comprehensive in the manner in which participants were selected, in the extent of the data included, and in terms of its attention to how these data fit within what has been learned about math disability from other labs over the last 25 years. It provides a wealth of information that will be referred to often by researchers, practitioners, and policy makers.

When researchers obtain differing results regarding what are and are not central characteristics of dyslexia, it is often hypothesized (but rarely proven) that the differences derive from

43

different standards used to exclude or include research participants. In chapter 4, Victor Van Daal and Aryan van der Leij
provide data on a large number of theoretically critical measures on a representative cross-section of 12-year olds who
qualify as learning disabled. These investigators identify those
children with "pure" dyslexia, but provide equally detailed information on the full spectrum of children that special educators work with daily, but who rarely figure in analytic studies of
dyslexia.

Van Daal and van der Leij's results corroborate what many
other studies have found: when defined as word recognition
difficulties combined with good listening comprehension,
dyslexia is specifically associated with weaknesses in phonological decoding naming speed. The data provide no support for
hypotheses that suggest that dyslexia is also associated with
cognitive and motor skills outside the language domain.

In chapter 5, Frank Manis and his colleagues at the University of Southern California take up the very difficult challenge of defining subgroups among normally intelligent
children with weak word recognition skills They provide evidence that only a subset of such children also present extreme
weaknesses in phoneme awareness and pseudoword decoding;
these "phonological" dyslexics are also weak on sentence repetition and persist in their pattern of weaknesses over the year of
testing covered in this paper. Manis et al. acknowledge that the
greater challenge is in accounting for those poor readers ("delayed" dyslexics) whose skills in phoneme awareness and pseudoword decoding are comparable to those of younger normal
readers matched on word recognition skill. Although it would
be "elegant" to account for this group in terms of slow speed on
rapid serial naming, limited sensitivity to orthographic patterns, or even weak prit exposure, Manis points out the limitations in each of these accounts to leave us with a quandary that
warrants further investigation. There is much to ponder over in
this very thoughtful paper.

Persistent Arithmetic, Reading, or Arithmetic and Reading Disability

Nathlie A. Badian

Holbrook Public Schools
Holbrook, Massachusetts
and
Harvard Medical School
Boston, MA

The achievement of 1,075 school children was followed to the end of grade 7 or 8. Retrospective details of birth, medical history, and infant adaptive behavior, as well as current information about preschool behavior, were provided by parents before kindergarten entry when their children were ages four to five. At that time, each child was given language, preacademic, and visual-motor tests, and a short-form verbal IQ was obtained. For grades 1 to 8, a mean 6.9 percent qualified as low in arithmetic (including 3.9 percent low only in arithmetic) and 9 percent as low in reading (including 6 percent low only in reading). Groups of children with persistent disability in arithmetic only (2.3 percent), reading only (6.6 percent), and arithmetic plus reading (3.4 percent) were compared on all variables, and gender differences were examined. The specific arithmetic group was superior to the other two groups in preschool verbal IQ and language, and had suffered more birth problems and illness. As found by Rourke and his colleagues (e.g., Rourke and Finlayson 1978) for older children, boys with a specific arithmetic disability showed a preschool profile with high verbal scores and low nonverbal scores. Many gender differences were found for the total sample, but few for the learning disability subgroups.

Annals of Dyslexia, Vol. 49, 1999
Copyright© 1999 by The International Dyslexia Association®
ISSN 0736-9387

INTRODUCTION

Twenty years ago, Rutter (1978, p. 15) commented on the absence of systematic studies of any large group of children with arithmetic disability. Even today, the trend to concentrate research on reading disability continues (Ginsburg 1997; Rourke and Conway 1997). Although a disability in mathematics may have a less pervasive effect on ability to function in society than a disability in reading, mathematical competency is important for many basic aspects of adult daily life such as telling time, counting change (Rivera 1997), planning within a time frame, and balancing a checkbook. According to Paulos (1988), the consequences of mathematical illiteracy, or innumeracy, are very widespread and may include misinformed governmental policies and confused personal decisions. During the school years, poor achievement in mathematics stigmatizes a child and, like a reading disability, contributes to feelings of low self-esteem.

DEFINING MATHEMATICS

Mathematics is a vague, global term that has different meanings at different educational levels. In the later school years mathematics may include algebra, geometry, calculus, trigonometry, and so on, but in the early grades it refers primarily to computation or arithmetic, at least in the United States, and for many people the term mathematics is synonymous with arithmetic. When a child is described as having a mathematics disability, it is not immediately apparent whether the disability is in arithmetic or in other aspects of mathematics. Mathematics has been shown by factor analyses to comprise several factors (Barakat 1951; Wrigley 1958), and even among younger children, a different set of skills may be involved in understanding mathematical concepts and verbal problem-solving than that involved in computation.

Because a disability in understanding mathematical concepts or in verbal problem-solving may stem from language or reading deficits, the study reported here focuses on mathematical computation rather than on other aspects of elementary mathematics.The term "arithmetic" will be used here to refer to computational ability.

PREVALENCE OF MATHEMATICS DISABILITY

Relatively little is known about the prevalence of a disability in mathematics. Earlier estimates (Badian 1983; Kosc 1974), which continue to be quoted (Ginsburg 1997; Rourke and Conway 1997), give a prevalence of approximately 6 percent. Weinstein (1980) also reported that 6 percent of children have developmental dyscalculia. However, for both reading and mathematics disability, the percentage of poor achievers will vary according to how the term disability is operationalized and as a function of the cutoff point for low achievement. Although a learning disability is usually defined as achievement that is significantly below the level expected from IQ, reading researchers in recent years have argued forcefully that the concept of IQ should not enter into the definition of reading disability, and that a learning disability should mean achievement that is low for age or grade placement (see, for example, Siegel 1989, 1992; Stanovich 1991).

It is surprising that Kosc (1974) and Badian (1983) both reported that 6.4 percent of their samples were poor in mathematics. Kosc, who tested 375 eleven-year-old children in Bratislava, defined mathematics disability or developmental dyscalculia by their performance on several mathematical tasks and used a ratio formula to determine low achievement. Badian reported the percentage of a total school population in the northeastern United States in grades 1 to 8 who scored at or below the 20th percentile on a composite measure including computation, numerical concepts, and verbal problem-solving. A somewhat higher figure was obtained by Share, Moffitt, and Silva (1988) who gave tests of reading and arithmetic to 459 New Zealand eleven-year-old children, followed from birth. Share et al. reported that 8.5 percent were low in both arithmetic and reading, and 6.5 percent had a specific arithmetic disability, a total of 15 percent (69/459) poor in arithmetic. This relatively high percentage is due to the high cutoff point for low achievement: the 30th percentile for boys and the 35th percentile for girls.

Age or grade level also may contribute to variability in prevalence figures. In a large-scale study of students in Iowa, special education services for mathematical problems tended to begin in the upper elementary grades. By contrast, services for reading and spelling occurred more frequently in the early school years (Cone et al. 1985).

DIFFERENCES BETWEEN CHILDREN WITH ARITHMETIC *OR* READING DISABILITY AND *BOTH* ARITHMETIC AND READING DISABILITY

There is strong research evidence that children with a disability only in arithmetic differ in some respects from children with a disability in both reading and arithmetic, and that these two groups differ from children with a specific reading disability (Rourke and Finlayson 1978; Rourke and Strang 1978; Shafrir and Siegel 1994; Share et al. 1988).

In the past 20 years or so, much of the research on the neuropsychological aspects of arithmetic disability has been carried out by Rourke and his colleagues. Rourke and Finlayson (1978), looking at the performance of children with learning disabilities aged 9 to 14 on the Wide Range Achievement Test (WRAT) (Jastak and Jastak 1965) found three groups. Group 1 was uniformly low in reading, spelling, and arithmetic. Group 2 was higher in arithmetic than in reading and spelling, and group 3 was impaired only in arithmetic. Rourke and his colleagues reported that the three groups differed in verbal/performance IQ patterns; on neuropsychological measures of visual, auditory, and tactile perception; and in verbal skills (Rourke and Finlayson 1978; Rourke and Strang 1978; Strang and Rourke 1983). Rourke concluded that groups 1 and 2 were deficient on tasks subserved primarily by the left cerebral hemisphere, whereas group 3 was deficient primarily on right cerebral hemispheric tasks.

Others also have found differences between children or adults low in arithmetic or low in reading (Davis, Parr, and Lan 1997; Shafrir and Siegel 1994; Share et al. 1988). Share et al. (1988) attempted to confirm Rourke's hypothesis that children with pure arithmetic disability and those with arithmetic plus reading disability show reverse patterns of strengths and weaknesses on measures of verbal and nonverbal skills. They found support for Rourke's hypothesis among boys but not among girls. Girls with reading plus arithmetic disability showed a general verbal and nonverbal deficit, whereas those with specific arithmetic disability did not differ from controls. Share pointed out the dangers of drawing conclusions from investigations confined to referred populations and of generalizing findings from predominantly male samples. In the Rourke and Finlayson (1978) and Rourke and Strang (1978) studies, only 13 percent of the children were girls.

Davis et al. (1997), who compared 30 children with a pure arithmetic disability with the same number who showed only a reading/spelling disability, found that the low arithmetic group was weaker than the low reading/spelling group on nonverbal tasks, whereas the low reading/spelling group was stronger on nonverbal than on verbal tasks. There were also indications of greater socioemotional problems in the low arithmetic group.

Shafrir and Siegel (1994) also found many differences between groups in their study of 331 adolescents and adults ages 16 to 72, defined as low specifically in arithmetic or reading, in both arithmetic and reading, or in neither. The most impaired was the reading plus arithmetic disability group. Poor arithmetic, with or without a reading disability, was associated with a visual-spatial deficit, but a pure reading disability was not. A reading disability, with or without an arithmetic problem, was associated with deficits in phonological processing, vocabulary, spelling, and short-term memory.

ETIOLOGY OF MATHEMATICAL AND READING DISABILITIES

There has been considerable research into the antecedents of reading disability, but sparse research into the antecedents of mathematics disability. There is, for example, a volume of evidence that reading disability is due primarily to phonological deficits (Liberman and Shankweiler 1985; Share et al. 1984; Wagner and Torgesen 1987). Whereas earlier research suggested that the inherited element in reading disability is a phonological deficit (Olson et al. 1989), recent twin research indicates that there is also a strong genetic influence for orthographic coding (Olson et al. 1997).

Light and DeFries (1995) conducted a twin study to assess the extent to which comorbidity of reading and mathematical deficits is due to environmental and genetic factors. However, as the participants were selected on the basis of a reading deficit in at least one twin member, there was no pure mathematics disability group; only reading disability and reading plus mathematics disability groups. Another limitation of that study was that the two mathematics measures were primarily verbal in nature. Results suggested that both genetic and environmental influences contribute to comorbid reading and mathematics disability.

In another recent twin study, it was concluded that mathematics disability is significantly heritable, but that environmental factors also contribute importantly to mathematical deficits (Alarcón et al. 1997). Results also suggested that the mathematics deficits of the subgroup with comorbid reading deficits were somewhat more heritable than those of the subgroup with pure mathematics disability.

From their review of the literature, Rourke and Conway (1997) hypothesized that early damage or dysfunction in either cerebral hemisphere disrupts arithmetic learning in the child, with very profound effects to be expected from early right hemisphere damage. Rourke (1993) quoted many studies indicating that a serious deficit in arithmetic, relative to reading, is characteristic of children with neurological diseases and a wide range of developmental disabilities associated with brain impairment.

RATIONALE FOR THE CURRENT STUDY

One aim of the present study was to determine the percentage of children in a total school population over a period of 14 years who displayed poor achievement either in arithmetic or reading only, or in both arithmetic and reading. Children studied in greater depth were those defined as having a persistent disability in arithmetic, reading, or both, with persistence defined as lasting over seven to eight school years. This contrasts with studies of children at one point in time (for example, at a specific age or grade level) which include children who did poorly one year because of environmental or chance factors. Many children who are poor readers in the early school years catch up later, whereas other children are average readers early on, but underachieve later (Cox 1987; McGee, Williams, and Silva 1988; Wright, Fields, and Newman 1996). It is not known whether this phenomenon is also true of mathematical achievement, but there is reason to believe that a similar lack of stability characterizes mathematical disability (Ginsburg, 1997).

A question this study sought to answer was whether children with persistent disability in arithmetic, or reading, or in both, differ in birth and medical history, in infant behavior, and in preschool cognitive and behavioral characteristics. The study also examined the prediction of arithmetic and reading achievement in an unselected population of school children.

METHOD

Participants.   Participants were all the children ($N = 1,075$) who began kindergarten in a small school district over 14 consecutive years (1976–1989), continued in the schools of that district through the end of grade 7 or 8 (mean age 13.7 years, *SD* 0.5), and were tested with a screening battery approximately six months before kindergarten entry (mean age: 4.8 years, *SD* 0.3). There were 547 boys and 528 girls.

On a 5-point parental occupational scale (1 = professional; 2 = management, sales, and office workers; 3 = skilled manual workers; 4 = semiskilled workers; 5 = laborers), the mean socio-economic status (SES) before kindergarten entry was 2.72 (*SD* 1.0). Ethnicity comprised white (96.3 percent), black or Hispanic (2.9 percent), and Asian (0.8 percent).

Procedure. As preschoolers, the participants were tested individually by each member of a team of five trained professionals with the Holbrook Screening Battery (Badian 1990). As part of the screening, all but 22 parents filled out a detailed questionnaire that included medical and family history, retrospective information about birth history and infant temperament, and current information about behavioral characteristics at ages four to five.

From grades 1 to 8, participants were administered standardized school achievement tests by their schools in the spring of each year. Seven of the 14 cohorts were tested every year from grade 1 to 8, and two cohorts were tested every year from grade 1 to 7. The other five cohorts were tested through grade 8, but testing was omitted in one earlier grade (1, 2, 4, 5, or 7). For all children included as participants, we had achievement test scores for at least six years. Additional children, who were tested but not in the study, included four with limited English proficiency as preschoolers, and one with a serious sensory impairment.

Instruments.
1. Developmental Questionnaire (DQ)
   Birth problems including
   - *Prenatal:* poor health, medication, toxemia, bleeding, accidents or injury during pregnancy
   - *Labor and delivery:* long labor (> 24 hours), atypical birth presentation, cord around neck, child rotated, placenta previa
   - *Neonatal:* low birth weight (< 6 lbs), breathing problems, bruising, jaundice, transfusions, incubation, hyaline membrane disease, birth defect

   Infant adaptability problems (first 6 months of life)
   - child overactive, irritable, hardly slept or slept restlessly; sucking or feeding difficulties

   Serious illness in the first 5 years of life
   - illness requiring hospitalization, fever > 105°F, seizures or febrile convulsions, concussion, meningitis, pneumonia, leukemia, anoxia or respiratory arrest, frequent or prolonged ear infections, major surgery, lead poisoning

Preschool inattention
- short attention span, overactive, rushes into things too fast, spends little time in any one activity, gets bored easily

Preschool behavioral problems
- angers easily, prone to temper tantrums or mood swings, difficult to handle, easily upset, very resistant to change, needs someone present or gets into trouble

The number of problems reported by parents in the DQ were totalled to give scores for birth problems, infant adaptability problems, and illness. Preschool inattention and behavioral problem scores were the total of observations made by parents in the DQ and the observations made by the examiners. At the time of the prekindergarten testing, examiners checked off any problems with attention, activity level, impulsivity, or cooperation on a list on the front of the test booklet.

2. Preschool Screening Battery
   Verbal IQ short-form (Wechsler 1963): Scores from two Wechsler Preschool and Primary Scale of Intelligence (WPPSI) subtests (Information, Arithmetic) were converted into a short-form verbal IQ (M 100, SD 15). The validity of this short form is .83 (Sattler 1974, p.456).
   Language measures
   - verbal concept formation: Similarities (Wechsler 1963).
   - sentence memory: Sentences (Wechsler 1963).
   - spoken language sample: The child tells a story about a picture. The story is scored by a trained language therapist, in terms of vocabulary, syntax, semantics, articulation, and so forth (M 10, SD 3).
   Preacademic skills
   - naming 13 letters (BOSERTHPIVZMA), five shapes (circle, cross, square, triangle, diamond), eight colors (red, blue, yellow, green, orange, brown, black, white). Letters and shapes are shown one by one on cards. Crayons and chalk are used for color naming. Scores are the number correctly named in each category.
   Visual matching (1981–1989 only): The child points to the one of four stimuli that matches the item on the extreme left of the line. These 10 items are u, d, j, ((, 38, bo, NAZ, 369, saw, drop. The response stimuli deviate from the target items mainly in terms of sequencing or

spatial orientation. The score is the number correct. Split-half reliability is .82.

Visual-Motor Skills

- name writing: The child writes his/her first and last names (maximum score = 6).
- form copying: The child copies the five geometric shapes listed above with a pencil. Each form is scored as fail (0), pass (1), or superior (2) by the same examiner.
- draw-a-person: The child's pencil drawing of a person is scored using Koppitz's (1968) system in which points are added to or subtracted from a base score of 5 for exceptional details included or essential details omitted.
- pencil use and cutting with scissors: The child is rated on a 3-point scale for pencil use and on a 4-point scale for cutting along a straight line.

Hand usage on the visual-motor tasks was recorded by the examiners as right, left, or mixed.

Total scores for Language, Preacademic Skills, and Visual-Motor Skills were converted to standard scores (M 100, SD 15) based on the performance of the 1981–1982 cohorts (n = 274). Because Preacademic Skills for the 1976–1980 cohorts did not include Visual Matching, the Preacademic Skills normative mean for these cohorts was based on the performance of the 1978–1979 year groups (n = 308).

3. School Achievement Measures

In the spring of each year, participants were administered the Stanford Achievement Test (Gardner et al. 1982) at the appropriate level for grade placement. The subtests used in this study for the total sample were Reading Comprehension, Mathematics Computation, and Concepts of Number, Spelling, and Listening Comprehension. These subtests are included in the Stanford battery at every grade level. Word Reading, tested only at grades 1 to 2, was used as a measure for a subset of the sample. For each subtest at every grade level, the national percentile rank of each participant was converted to a standard score (M 100, SD 15). A mean score for each subtest based on performance over all 7 or 8 grade levels was then computed. Therefore, for each participant, there was a mean score for reading, arithmetic, number concepts, spelling, and listening.

To update information concerning the number of children in a total school population who are poor achievers in reading or arithmetic only, or in both reading and arithmetic, the mean percentage of children (by gender) in the 14 consecutive cohorts who scored below the 20th percentile in grades 1 to 8 was determined.

Prediction of mean reading comprehension and arithmetic scores was examined, using as predictors preschool verbal IQ, screening subtotals, inattention and behavior problems, number of illnesses, birth problems, infant adaptability problems, socioeconomic status, and age.

Persistent Low School Achievement or Learning Disability. Persistent low achievement was defined as a mean standard score for the 7-to-8-year period below the 25th percentile (< 90) in reading or arithmetic or in both. In this study, the term "learning disability" refers to achievement that is low for age or grade placement as advocated by Siegel (1989, 1992) and Stanovich (1991), unless otherwise specified. Three groups were formed from participants who met criteria for persistent low achievement: Low Arithmetic (LA), Low Reading (LR), and Low Arithmetic and Reading (LAR). For some comparisons, a control (C) group of 107 participants (10 percent of sample) who did not meet criteria for low achievement was randomly drawn from the total group of normal achievers in the same gender ratio as that observed in the low achievers.

The four groups were compared on the number of birth and infant adaptability problems, the number of serious illnesses from birth to age five, and on preschool inattention and behavioral problems. The groups were also compared on the three preschool screening battery subtotals (language, preacademic, and visual-motor skills), on preschool short-form WPPSI verbal IQ, on the mean Stanford reading, arithmetic, number concepts, spelling, and listening standard scores, and on grade 2 word reading standard scores.

Data were analyzed by gender, as well as by group, and gender differences in the total population were also investigated.

RESULTS

Low Achievement in Grades 1 to 8. The percentage of children who scored below the 20th percentile in reading or arithmetic only, or in both reading and arithmetic, is shown by grade level and gender in Table I.

Table I. Percentages of children in 14 year-groups scoring below the 20th percentile in arithmetic*, reading**, or in arithmetic and reading.

Grade	n	Arithmetic Only Boys %	Girls %	Total %	Reading Only Boys %	Girls %	Total %	Arithmetic and Reading Boys %	Girls %	Total %
1	948	4.1	3.7	3.9	7.4	3.0	5.3	2.7	2.6	2.6
2	984	5.6	7.4	6.5	6.8	3.5	5.2	3.0	1.7	2.3
3	1,056	5.6	5.4	5.5	5.4	2.5	4.0	3.4	1.7	2.6
4	958	3.1	1.5	2.3	7.6	3.9	5.7	3.7	2.1	2.9
5	974	4.2	1.1	2.7	8.5	5.0	6.8	4.2	1.1	2.7
6	1,063	4.1	4.0	4.1	6.9	2.9	4.9	5.0	2.1	3.6
7	999	4.7	2.0	3.4	9.1	5.9	7.5	4.7	1.4	3.1
8	883	3.1	2.6	2.8	11.1	5.3	8.3	6.9	2.3	4.6
1 to 3		5.1	5.5	5.3	6.5	3.0	4.8	3.0	2.0	2.5
4 to 6		3.8	2.2	3.0	7.7	3.9	5.8	4.3	1.8	3.1
7 to 8		3.9	2.3	3.1	10.1	5.6	7.9	5.8	1.9	3.9
M		4.3	3.5	3.9	7.9	4.0	6.0	4.2	1.9	3.0

*Arithmetic: Stanford Achievement Test (SAT) Mathematics Computation Subtest. **Reading: SAT Reading Comprehension Subtest.

When the percentages were averaged across the eight grades, 6.0 percent were low only in reading (M:F ratio 2:1), 3.9 percent only in arithmetic (M:F ratio 1.2:1), and 3 percent were low in both arithmetic and reading (M:F ratio 2.2:1). Therefore, a mean 6.9 percent were low achievers in arithmetic (mean gender ratio 1.6:1) and 9 percent were low in reading (mean gender ratio 2.1:1). In the early grades (1 to 3), a mean 7.3 percent were low in reading and 7.8 percent in arithmetic. In grades 4 to 6, 8.9 percent were low in reading and 6.1 percent in arithmetic, and in grades 7 to 8, 11.8 percent were low in reading and 7 percent in arithmetic. The gender ratio for poor reading was fairly consistent over the grades, but changed for arithmetic. Although a nearly equal proportion of boys and girls were low in arithmetic in the early grades, approximately twice as many boys were low in arithmetic in grade 4 and beyond.

In all comparisons involving the total sample, the level for significance was set at $p < .01$. Because of the large sample size, very small differences reached significance with the alpha level set at .05. When boys and girls were compared on the school achievement mean scores, girls were superior in reading comprehension: $F(1,1073) = 27.1$, $p < .0001$; arithmetic: $F(1,1073) = 16.18$, $p < .0001$; and spelling: $F(1,1073) = 62.94$, $p < .0001$. Mean scores for listening comprehension and number concepts were virtually identical.

Persistent Learning Disability Groups: School Achievement. Ten percent of the population (108/1,075) had a persistent disability in reading and 5.7 percent (62/1,075) in arithmetic. The number in each of the low achieving groups was LA 25 (2.3 percent), LR 71 (6.6 percent), LAR 37 (3.4 percent). Therefore, a total of 12.3 percent (133/1,075) of the children in this population were persistent low achievers in reading, in arithmetic, or in both. The percentage of males in each group was: LA 56 percent, LR 63.4 percent, LAR 73 percent, C 64.5 percent.[1]

The mean school achievement standard scores of these four groups and of the total sample for the 7-to-8-year period and ANOVA results are given in Table II.

In a two-way ANOVA, with group and gender as factors, there was a significant group difference on all measures. Posthoc tests (Duncan's Multiple Range Test) on Listening Com-

Table II.   Mean school achievement standard scores for the persistent low achievement and control groups and for the total sample.

| | Groups | | | | | | | Total | |
| | LA* | | LR | | LAR | | C | | F | Sample | |
Measure	M	SD	M	SD	M	SD	M	SD	(3,232)**p <	M	SD
Arithmetic	87.2	(2.8)	96.9	(4.5)	84.6	(4.0)	109.0	(8.6)	153.0 .0001	107.0	(10.5)
No. Concepts	88.5	(5.3)	94.3	(6.8)	85.7	(7.3)	108.5	(9.4)	106.5 .0001	106.6	(11.3)
Reading Compr.	97.2	(3.6)	86.6	(2.7)	81.8	(5.3)	106.4	(8.1)	196.7 .0001	105.0	(11.0)
Spelling	94.1	(7.4)	88.3	(5.9)	81.8	(5.8)	104.2	(9.2)	94.3 .0001	104.0	(12.0)
Listening Compr.	100.5	(8.2)	94.6	(7.7)	90.0	(9.2)	109.1	(7.8)	69.6 .0001	107.2	(10.1)
Word Reading	99.4	(10.4)	88.9	(8.0)	83.0	(8.9)	108.7	(13.3)	55.5 .0001	107.1	(14.5)

*LA = Low Arithmetic, LR = Low Reading, LAR = Low Arithmetic and Reading, C = Controls. **F ratios for group differences are based on a two-way ANOVA with group and gender as factors. All scores are the means for grades 1 to 8 except for Word Reading which is the score for grade 2.

---

[1] If a criterion of a mean standard score below the 20th percentile is used, these percentages change to: LA 43%, LR 68%, LAR 69%. Thus, with more stringent criteria there was a trend toward a higher proportion of females in the LA group.

prehension showed that the C group was superior to all other groups and that the LA group was significantly higher than the LR and LAR groups, which did not differ. For the two reading measures and spelling, there was a significant difference between each group, with the C group higher than the LA group which surpassed the LR group and which was higher than the LAR group. For both the mathematical subtests, there was again a significant difference between each group (C > LR > LA > LAR). There were significant gender differences for number concepts: $F(1,237) = 15.67$, $p < .0001$, listening comprehension $F(1,237) = 9.19$, $p < .003$), and spelling $F(1,237) = 4.28$, $p < .039$). Males were higher for number concepts and listening comprehension, and females for spelling. There were no significant group by gender interactions. When further ANOVAs were carried out with the C group excluded, these gender differences persisted.

Birth Problems and Infant Adaptability. Details of the birth history and characteristics in infancy were known for 1,033 participants. Birth history and characteristics in early infancy were not usually known for children who were adopted and for those whose parents failed to fill out the DQ. In the low achievement groups, this information was missing for four children (two adopted, two no DQ).

For the total sample, the mean birth problem score which included problems in pregnancy, labor or delivery, and the neonatal period was 0.85 (*SD* 1.34, range 0 to 10), and the mean for infant adaptability problems was 0.31 (*SD* 0.66, range 0 to 4). Males and females of the total sample did not differ in birth problems or in infant adaptability problems.

The percentages of children in the low achieving and control groups who had a specific birth or neonatal problem or who demonstrated one or more adaptability problems in infancy are shown in Table III.

Bleeding in pregnancy tended to occur more frequently among children low in reading than among those with arithmetic problems only. Toxemia in pregnancy, however, occurred more frequently among children low in arithmetic and was very infrequent among children low only in reading and in the controls. Low birth weight occurred more than three times as often among children poor in arithmetic than among children low in reading or controls, and problems in the neonatal period were also more prevalent among children of the LA group. More children in the three disability groups than in the control group tended to have adaptability problems as infants.

Table III. Percentages of children in the persistent low achievement and control groups with specific prenatal, neonatal, and infant adaptability problems.

Problem	Groups			
	LA* $n = 25$	LR $n = 71$	LAR $n = 37$	C $n = 107$
	%	%	%	%
Bleeding in pregnancy	0.0	11.9	10.8	6.5
Toxemia in pregnancy	17.4	4.5	10.8	1.9
Labor/delivery difficulties	21.7	16.4	8.1	16.8
Birth weight < 6 pounds	34.8	10.6	13.5	9.6
Neonatal complications	56.5	29.9	35.1	21.5
Infant adaptability problems	39.1	36.8	27.0	16.8

*LA = Low Arithmetic, LR = Low Reading, LAR = Low Arithmetic and Reading, C = Controls.

In a two-way ANOVA, with group and gender as factors, there was no gender difference in birth problem scores, but there was a significant group difference: $F(3,226) = 5.17$, $p < .002$. The LR, LAR, and C groups did not differ, but all had significantly fewer birth problems than the LA group. There was no group or gender difference for the number of infant adaptability problems: $F(3,226) = 1.56$, $p < .20$. The mean numbers of birth problems and infant adaptability problems in each group are shown in Table IV, and also the number of serious illness each group suffered in the preschool years.

Table IV. Mean numbers of birth problems, infant adaptability problems, and preschool illnesses for the persistent low achievement and control groups.

Problem	Groups							
	LA* $n = 25$		LR $n = 71$		LAR $n = 37$		C $n = 107$	
	M	SD	M	SD	M	SD	M	SD
Birth Problems	2.3	(2.8)	1.1	(1.3)	1.1	(1.5)	0.8	(1.3)
Infant Adaptability	0.5	(0.7)	0.5	(0.8)	0.4	(0.7)	0.3	(0.6)
Preschool Illness	1.5	(1.6)	0.7	(0.9)	1.0	(1.3)	0.6	(0.9)

*LA = Low Arithmetic, LR = Low Reading, LAR = Low Arithmetic and Reading, C = Controls.

Serious Illness. The mean number of illnesses in the preschool years for the total sample was 0.6 (*SD* 0.9, range 0 to 6). Males had suffered significantly more illnesses than females: Males, 0.71 (1.0); Females, = 0.47 (*SD* 0.8): $F(1,1050) = 18.07, p < .0001$. In a disability group by gender comparison, there was significant group difference in the number of serious illnesses: $F(3,230) = 5.50, p < .002$ (see table V). The LA group had suffered significantly more illness than the LR and C groups. There was no gender difference for illness, but there was a significant group by gender interaction: $F(3,230) = 3.59, p < .014$, which persisted even when the C group was omitted from the analysis. In the LA and C groups, females suffered less illness than males, but females with a reading disability (LR, LAR groups) suffered more illness, and this gender difference was more pronounced for the LAR group. The percentages of children in the three low achieving and control groups who had suffered two or more illnesses were: LA 43.5 percent, LR 18.8 percent, LAR 27 percent, and C 15.9 percent. In the LA group, 21.7 percent suffered one or more seizures compared to 5.9 percent in the LR group, 5.4 percent in the LAR group, and 4.7 percent in the C group. More in the LA group

Table V. Mean scores on preschool variables for the persistent low achievement and control groups.

	Groups									
	LA* (1) $n = 25$		LR (2) $n = 71$		LAR (3) $n = 37$		C (4) $n = 107$		F	Group
Measure	M	SD	M	SD	M	SD	M	SD	(3,232)** $p <$	Differences
Age (years)	4.7	(0.3)	4.9	(0.3)	4.8	(0.3)	4.8	(0.3)	1.5	.211
Socioeconomic Status	3.0	(1.0)	3.0	(1.0)	3.2	(1.1)	2.7	(1.1)	1.5	.210
Attentional Problems	0.96	(1.2)	1.29	(1.3)	1.24	(1.4)	0.61	(1.0)	5.0	.002 2 > 4
Behavioral Problems	0.36	(0.6)	0.64	(0.9)	0.59	(1.0)	0.36	(0.7)	2.2	.089
Verbal IQ	104.0	(12.6)	98.0	(11.6)	93.6	(11.8)	107.5	(11.7)	19.9	.0001 4 = 1 > 2 = 3
Language	96.8	(12.5)	89.3	(13.7)	87.3	(13.4)	101.1	(13.4)	16.4	.0001 4 = 1 > 2 = 3
Preacademic	91.6	(15.1)	87.3	(17.2)	78.7	(12.8)	101.3	(13.4)	22.5	.0001 4 > 1 = 2 > 3
Visual-Motor	0.0	(14.4)	91.2	(13.5)	88.0	(13.1)	100.0	(14.2)	11.7	.0001 4 > 1 = 2 = 3

*LA = Low Arithmetic, LR = Low Reading, LAR = Low Arithmetic and Reading, C = Controls. **F ratios for group differences are based on a two-way ANOVA with group and gender as factors.

suffered one or more episodes of anoxia or respiratory arrest: LA 17.4 percent, LR 7.4 percent, LAR 5.4 percent, C 8.4 percent.

Preschool Cognitive and Behavioral Variables. Boys and girls in the total sample did not differ in terms of SES or in their age at preschool testing. For inattention, the mean score of the total sample was 0.73 (*SD* 1.1, range 0 to 6); for behavior problems the mean score was 0.37 (*SD* 0.7, range 0 to 5). Boys of the total sample had significantly higher scores (more problems) on the two preschool behavioral variables: Inattention: Boys, $M = 0.85$ (*SD* 1.2), Girls, $M = 0.61$ (*SD* 1.0), $F(1,1049) = 8.93$, $p < .003$; Behavioral problems: Boys, $M = 0.46$ (*SD* 0.8), Girls, $M = 0.28$ (*SD* 0.6), $F(1,1049) = 14.7$, $p < .001$.

Girls of the total sample scored significantly higher than boys on verbal IQ: Girls, $M = 108.2$ (*SD* 12.3); Boys, $M = 105.6$ (*SD* 12.1), $F (1,1073) = 11.9$, $p < .001$. Girls also scored higher on the three screening subtotals: Language: Girls, $M = 102.4$ (*SD* 13.8); Boys, $M = 98.8$ (*SD* 12.7), $F(1,1073) = 18.9$, $p < .0001$; Preacademic Skills: Girls, $M = 101.7$ (*SD* 14.6); Boys, $M = 97.8$ (*SD* 15.9), $F(1,1073) = 14.4$ $p < .0002$; Visual-Motor Skills: Girls, $M = 103.0$ (*SD* 14.0); Boys, $M = 98.7$ (*SD* 15.2), $F(1,1073) = 19.4$, $p <. 0001$.

Mean scores for preschool age, SES, and the cognitive and behavioral variables are shown for the three disability groups and controls in table V. The three disability groups and controls did not differ in the percentage of nonrighthanded children (left- and mixed-handed): LA 16.0 percent, LR 18.3 percent, LAR 16.2 percent, C, 14.0 percent.

In the group by gender ANOVA, the groups did not differ in age, SES, or behavioral problems, but they did differ in inattention. The LR group had significantly more attentional problems than the C group. The C and LA groups did not differ in verbal IQ or language and both were significantly higher than the LR and LAR groups which did not differ. All disability groups were lower than the C group in preacademic skills. The LA and LR groups did not differ and both were significantly higher than the LAR group. The three disability groups did not differ in visual-motor skills, but all were significantly lower than the C group.

The only gender difference that approached significance was for verbal IQ, and the group gender interaction was significant. In all disability groups, girls were lower than boys in verbal IQ, but the C group girls were higher than the boys of their group. When a further analysis was carried out for the three disability groups only, boys were significantly higher than girls: $F(1,131) = 6.5$, $p < .012$ (Boys: $M = 100.7$, Girls: $M = 94.7$). Boys

Table VI. Partial correlations between variables, with socioeconomic status as a covariate.

Variable	1	2	3	4	5	6	7	8	9	10	11	12	13
1. Birth Problems													
2. Infant Adaptability	.23**												
3. Inattention	.09*	.20**											
4. Behavior Problems	.04	.15**	.20**										
5. Illness	.26**	.09*	.13**	.09*									
6. Verbal IQ	−.03	.01	−.17**	−.12**	.09*								
7. Language	−.03	−.03	−.19**	−.14**	−.05	.62**							
8. Preacademic	−.01	−.01	−.20**	−.06	−.07	.52**	.46**						
9. Visual-Motor	−.02	.02	−.20**	−.06	−.09*	.32**	.32**	.54**					
10. Arithmetic	−.10*	−.06	−.22**	−.11**	−.17**	.42**	.36**	.47**	.41**				
11. No. Concepts	−.08	−.05	−.21**	−.10**	−.13**	.50**	.43**	.50**	.39**	.88**			
12. Reading Comp.	−.02	−.05	−.21**	−.11**	−.11**	.53**	.53**	.56**	.39**	.74**	.77**		
13. Spelling	−.06	−.07	−.19**	−.07	−.14**	.37**	.34**	.49**	.34**	.71**	.68**	.81**	
14. Listening Compr.	−.00	−.02	−.15**	−.13**	−.06	.55**	.59**	.46**	.30**	.63**	.73**	.79**	.52**

Numbers 3 to 9 are preschool variables. Numbers 10 to 14 are the mean achievement scores for grades 1 to 8. *$p < .01$ **$p < .001$.

of the disability groups were 7 points below the total sample mean for boys in verbal IQ, but girls with a learning disability were 13 points below the girls' mean. Girls of each disability group were approximately 6 points lower than boys of their group. Boys of the LA group were slightly above the total sample mean for boys in verbal IQ and language, whereas girls of the LA group were more than 7 points below the verbal IQ mean for girls and 10 points below in language.

Boys of the LA group showed a strength in language, compared with visual-motor skills. Their mean language score (100.1) was 10 points higher than their visual-motor score, but language was only 2.6 points higher for the girls of this group. Boys of the LR group and both boys and girls of the LAR group showed minimal differences between language and visual-motor scores, but girls of the LR group were 6.3 points higher in visual-motor skills than in language.

Prediction of Mean School Achievement.   Intercorrelations among the variables are given in table VI for the total sample, with SES entered as a covariate. SES was covaried because it had significant negative correlations with all preschool cognitive variables, except visual-motor skills, and with all school achievement measures. Because of the large size of the sample, small correlations were statistically significant. Therefore, the level for significance was set at $p < .01$.

Birth problems were significantly and positively correlated with infant adaptability problems, as well as with preschool inattention and illness. The only school achievement measure predicted by birth problems was arithmetic. The negative correlation (more birth problems associated with lower arithmetic scores), though small, was significant. Infant adaptability problems predicted inattention and behavior problems and illness, but not the screening test subtotals or school achievement.

Preschool inattention was positively correlated with behavior problems and with illness, and negatively correlated with all screening test subtotals, verbal IQ, and all school achievement measures. Preschool behavior problems correlated positively with illness, and negatively with verbal IQ and language, and with all school achievement measures, except spelling. Illness had significant negative correlations with verbal IQ, visual-motor skills, and with all school achievement variables except listening. All preschool test scores predicted all school achievement measures, and all these variables were significantly intercorrelated. The highest predictive correlations were those of listening with verbal IQ ($r = .55$)and with language ($r = .59$). Preacademic skills were the best predictor of reading ($r = .56$) and arithmetic ($r = .47$).

Multiple regression analyses were computed to predict mean arithmetic and reading scores of the total sample using birth problems, infant adaptability problems, illness, preschool inattention and behavior problems, preschool chronological age, SES, verbal IQ, and the screening subtotals as predictive variables. In stepwise regression analyses, preacademic skills accounted for 24 percent of the variance in arithmetic, verbal IQ added 4 percent, visual-motor skills 3 percent, and illness (in a negative direction) 1.3 percent. The total amount of variance accounted for was 34 percent. For reading, preacademic skills accounted for 32 percent of variance, with language adding a further 9 percent, and verbal IQ approximately 2 percent. The total variance accounted for was 45 percent.

Hierarchical regression analyses were also carried out for arithmetic and reading, with verbal IQ, preschool age, and SES entered first, in that fixed order. These analyses are shown in table VII.

The three fixed variables accounted for 21 percent of the variance in arithmetic, with preacademic skills, visual-motor skills, and illness adding a further 11.4 percent. The three fixed variables accounted for 30 percent of the variance in reading, and preacademic skills, language, and inattention added a further 13.4 percent.

DISCUSSION

The school achievement of 1,075 children, who were tested as preschoolers, was followed to the end of grade 7 or 8. Details of birth and medical history and of behavior of the children as infants and as preschoolers were obtained from parents at the time of preschool testing. Main aims of the study were to determine the prevalence of low achievement in arithmetic, reading, and in both arithmetic and reading, and to examine differences in groups of children with a persistent disability in arithmetic, reading, or in both.

Prevalence Rates and Gender Differences. The prevalence rates reported in this study are based on reading and arithmetic scores in grades 1 to 8 for 14 consecutive cohorts. As the mean prevalence figures are derived from many year-groups and are based on approximately 900 to 1000 children per grade, they are likely to be more reliable than figures for a specific year that may not be representative of the population from which it was drawn.

Table VII. Hierarchical regression analyses of preschool variables predicting mean arithmetic and reading comprehension (Grades 1 to 8).

	Arithmetic					Reading Comprehension			
	Cumulative					Cumulative			
Variable	R^2	t	$p <$	R^2 Change	Variable	R^2	t	$p <$	R^2 Change
Verbal IQ	.178	14.7	.0001	.178	Verbal IQ	.279	19.6	.0001	.279
Age	.202	5.4	.0001	.024	Age	.299	5.3	.0001	.020
SES	.212	−3.5	.0005	.010	SES	.304	−2.8	.005	.005
Pre-academic	.284	10.0	.0001	.072	Pre-academic	.400	12.6	.0001	.096
Visual-Motor	.312	6.3	.0001	.028	Language	.438	8.2	.0001	.038
Illness	.326	−4.5	.0001	.014	Inattention	.443	−3.1	.002	.005

The prevalence rate of 6.9 percent for children low in arithmetic included 3.9 percent low only in arithmetic and 3 percent low in both arithmetic and reading. This figure is very similar to the 6.4 percent reported by both Kosc (1974) for dyscalculia and Badian (1983) for a composite mathematics score that included arithmetic. Older (grades 7 to 8) and younger (grades 1 to 3) children did not differ in the percentages low in arithmetic in the current study. Nine percent of the children were poor readers, including 6 percent low only in reading. A trend toward an increase in poor reading with age was observed.

Gender ratios in poor reading or dyslexia have been a subject of some controversy (Finucci and Child 1981). In their Connecticut Longitudinal Study, Shaywitz et al. (1990) reported no difference in gender ratios for reading disability as defined by a discrepancy from intelligence at grades 2 and 3. They attributed the higher male-to-female ratio in school-identified reading disability to referral bias.

In this study of a total population of children over many years in which referral bias played no part, boys at all grade levels were approximately twice as likely to be poor readers for their grade placement. In the lower grades, boys and girls were almost equally likely to be poor in arithmetic, but from the fourth grade, boys were twice as likely to have an arithmetic deficit.

When school achievement test scores for grades 1 to 8 were averaged to obtain mean achievement scores for each child, girls were significantly higher than boys in reading comprehension, spelling, and arithmetic, but there was no gender difference for number concepts and listening comprehension.

Males and females in the total sample also differed on a number of early variables. They did not differ in the number of birth or infant adaptability problems, but males suffered significantly more illness in the preschool years. As preschoolers, males were significantly more inattentive and exhibited more behavior problems. Females scored significantly higher on all preschool cognitive measures, including verbal IQ.

Persistent Low Achievement or Learning Disability. This study did not differentiate between children whose achievement level was significantly below the level expected from IQ or listening comprehension, and those who showed no such discrepancy. The term learning disability (or reading or arithmetic disability) is used here to refer to persistent low school achievement for grade or age over the eight grades. Siegel (1989, 1992) and Stanovich (1991) advocate that IQ not enter into a definition of a learning disability. The percentages of children with a persistent learning disability were 2.3 percent for arithmetic only, 6.6 percent for reading only, and 3.5 percent for arithmetic plus reading. Therefore, only a small percentage of this school population had a persistent and specific disability in arithmetic.

Children with a reading disability only and those comorbid for arithmetic plus reading deficits were similar in early characteristics. They did not differ in SES, number of birth or infant adaptability problems, or in the number of serious illnesses in the preschool years. These two groups exhibited a similar degree of inattentiveness and did not differ in the number of behavior problems as preschoolers. On the preschool cognitive measures, including verbal IQ, they differed only in preacademic skills with the comorbid group significantly lower. The specific reading disability group was significantly higher than the arithmetic plus reading disability group, not only in mean arithmetic and number concepts, but also in mean reading comprehension and spelling and in grade 2 word reading. The two groups did not differ in mean listening comprehension.

Children with a specific disability in arithmetic differed in several respects from the two groups of poor readers. They had suffered significantly more birth problems and illness than either of the low reading groups (or controls), and were approximately four times more likely to have suffered one or more seizures in the preschool years. As preschoolers, they were significantly higher than the two groups of poor readers (and equal to the nondisabled controls) in verbal IQ and language. The specific arithmetic disability group did not differ from the specific reading disability group in preacademic and visual-motor skills, and like the reading disability group, was superior to the arithmetic plus reading deficit group in preacademic skills. In the school years, the low arithmetic group was significantly higher than the two groups of poor readers, not only in reading and spelling but also in listening comprehension. The low arithmetic group was less impaired in arithmetic and number concepts than the arithmetic plus reading disability group.

In Rourke's studies of referred children with reading and/or arithmetic disability, those with a specific arithmetic disability had a strength in verbal skills, but were poor in nonverbal skills (Rourke 1993). Although we tested language, verbal IQ, and visual-motor skills only at age 4 to 5 years of age, our results provide some support for Rourke's findings of a verbal strength and a nonverbal weakness in arithmetic disability: the low arithmetic group was strong (equal to controls) in language, but significantly lower in visual-motor skills. These effects were due primarily to the boys of the low arithmetic group who showed a strength in language compared with visual-motor skills. This pattern was not obtained in the girls of the group. This gender specificity was also made evident by Share et al. (1988) who found that it was only boys (ages 11) with arithmetic disability who showed the high verbal, low nonverbal profile reported in the Rourke studies. It is notable that most of the children in Rourke's studies were boys.

Our participants with specific reading disability did not, however, show the low verbal/high nonverbal profile reported by Rourke. Boys with reading disability obtained virtually identical scores on language and visual-motor measures, and girls with reading disability were only a little higher in visual-motor skills than in language. This lack of a nonverbal advantage may be because this testing was done only in preschool. It is possible that a nonverbal strength will develop later, and/or that verbal ability will decrease as a result of the restricted access to language imposed by the reading deficit (Stanovich 1986).

Boys and girls with persistent deficits in both arithmetic and reading were uniformly low across all preschool cognitive measures. As found by others (Share et al. 1988; Shafrir and Siegel 1994), children with arithmetic plus reading disability were the most impaired group, both on preschool tasks and in school achievement. Their below average language performance suggests that, unlike the pure arithmetic disability group, their poor arithmetic may be attributable to verbal deficits common to both reading and arithmetic (Share et al. 1988).

The finding that the two groups of children with reading disability did not differ from controls in birth problems and illness suggests that adverse environmental factors in early life did not play a significant role in their learning problems. Recent genetic research suggests that the mathematical deficits of children who also have reading deficits are more heritable than are mathematical deficits in normal readers (Alarcón et al. 1997). Rourke (1993) pointed out that poor arithmetic, relative to reading, is characteristic of children with disabilities in which brain impairment is thought to be a principal feature. The adverse birth and early medical history of the children specifically impaired in arithmetic in the current study suggests that brain damage, probably predominantly right-sided (Rourke 1993), may play a role in many cases of arithmetic deficits.

Many of the gender differences evident when we averaged across scores of individual years (total sample) were not observed in the subgroups with persistent learning disability. Unlike girls of the total sample, girls with a learning disability showed as much preschool inattentiveness and as many behavior problems as boys. They had suffered as much illness, and did not differ from boys of the learning disability groups in preschool cognitive skills or in later reading or arithmetic scores. Contrary to findings for the total sample, girls with a learning disability were significantly lower than boys in verbal IQ and were lower than the boys within their groups. This study suggests that the preschool girl at risk for a learning disability, and especially for reading disability, is likely to have suffered more illness than other girls, to be inattentive and have behavior problems, and to be relatively low both in verbal IQ and on other preschool cognitive tasks.

Prediction of Mean School Achievement of the Total Sample. A mean achievement score for the eight grades was obtained for each child for each school achievement measure, and the contributions of birth, infant, and medical factors, as well as preschool measures to mean school achievement, were examined. The only significant correlation of either birth or infant adaptability problems with mean school achievement was the small, but significant, negative correlation of birth problems with arithmetic. That is, the larger the number of problems in the pre- and neonatal periods, the greater the likelihood of a later arithmetic impairment. Illness in the preschool years was significantly and negatively correlated with all school achievement measures, except listening comprehension. It is possible that children who suffered serious illnesses as preschoolers continued to have more illness in the school years, and that absence due to illness had an adverse effect on school learning without affecting oral language comprehension. As a history of illness was also significantly associated with inattentiveness and with lower preschool verbal IQ, the negative correlations with school achievement could be by means of these variables.

There are few studies predicting arithmetic or mathematics from preschool or kindergarten tasks. One exception is the study of Stevenson and Newman (1986), in which mathematics and reading at grades 5 and 10 were predicted by cognitive tasks given before kindergarten. A subset of the prekindergarten measures continued to be significant predictors of reading and arithmetic through grade 10. The same measures (WRAT Arithmetic, letter naming) predicted both reading and arithmetic. The prekindergarten WRAT Arithmetic was the best predictor of both reading and arithmetic at grade 10.

In the present study, all preschool subtotals and verbal IQ correlated significantly with all measures of mean school achievement. Preacademic skills, including letter naming, were the best predictor of both reading and arithmetic, and also of number concepts and spelling. Listening comprehension was better predicted by preschool language and verbal IQ. Although visual-motor skills correlated significantly with all school achievement measures, its highest correlation was with arithmetic. In a five-year follow up of children tested before kindergarten, the drawing of a person was among the best predictors of arithmetic for both boys and girls, and form copying also contributed for girls (Badian 1983). The visual-motor skills subtotal includes these two measures.

After preacademic skills entered into regression analyses, verbal IQ added a further significant proportion of variance to the prediction of both reading and arithmetic. Language was the only other variable that added variance to reading. The only variables accounting for additional variance in arithmetic were visual-motor skills and illness (in a negative direction). As found by Stevenson and Newman (1986), the preschool measures in the current study accounted for a larger proportion of the variance in reading than in arithmetic.

CONCLUSIONS

The present study is limited by the fact that birth and infancy data were retrospectively obtained at ages four to five and by the fact that individual testing of the total sample was carried out only before kindergarten entry. Nevertheless, the study confirms that, even as preschoolers, the small percentage of children at risk for a specific arithmetic disability differed in some respects from those who later developed impairments in reading or in both reading and arithmetic. Furthermore, this was found to be especially true of boys. The evidence suggests that birth problems or early serious illness may be factors in specific arithmetic impairment, but not in reading disability. A finding of interest was that a preschool high verbal, low nonverbal profile may be a precursor of a specific arithmetic disability. A number of gender differences was found for the total sample, but those preschool girls who developed learning disabilities tended to have similar profiles to at-risk boys. These girls were lower in preschool verbal IQ, and were atypical, behaviorally and cognitively, for their gender.

The findings of the study highlight how important it is for researchers to differentiate between groups of children who have a disability only in reading or arithmetic, and those who have a disability in both, in order to prevent distorted results. It is probable, also, that children with a specific arithmetic disability will differ from those with an arithmetic plus reading disability in the type of remediation needed to help overcome their arithmetic impairment.

Correspondence for this paper should be addressed to Nathlie A. Badian, 101 Monroe Road, Quincy, Massachusetts 02169.

References

Alarcón, M., DeFries, J. C., Light, J. G., and Pennington, B. F. 1997. A twin study of mathematics disability. *Journal of Learning Disabilities* 30:617–23.

Badian, N. A. 1983. Dyscalculia and nonverbal disorders of learning. In *Progress in Learning Disabilities*, vol. 5. H. R. Myklebust, ed. New York: Grune and Stratton.

Badian, N. A. 1990. Background factors and preschool test scores as predictors of reading: A nine-year longitudinal study. *Reading and Writing: An Interdisciplinary Journal* 2:307–26.

Barakat, M. K. 1951. A factorial study of mathematical abilities. *British Journal of Psychology*, Statistical Section 4:137–56.

Cone, T. E., Wilson, L. R., McDonald Bradley, C., and Reese, J. H. 1985. Characteristics of LD students in Iowa: An empirical investigation. *Learning Disability Quarterly* 8:211–20.

Cox, T. 1987. Slow starters versus long term backward readers. *British Journal of Educational Psychology* 57:73–86.

Davis, J. T., Parr, G., and Lan, W. 1997. Differences between learning disabled subtypes classified using the revised Woodcock-Johnson Psycho-Educational Battery. *Journal of Learning Disabilities* 30:346–52.

Finucci, J. M., and Childs, B. 1981. Are there really more dyslexic boys than girls? In *Sex Differences in Dyslexia*. A. Ansara, N. Geschwind, A. Galaburda, M. Albert, and N. Gartrell, eds. Towson, MD: Orton Dyslexia Society.

Gardner, E. F., Rudman, H. C., Karlsen, B., and Merwin, J. C. 1982. *Stanford Achievement Test*. New York: Psychological Corporation.

Ginsburg, H. P. 1997. Mathematics learning disabilities: A view from developmental psychology. *Journal of Learning Disabilities* 30:20–33.

Jastak, J. F., and Jastak, S. R. 1965. *Wide Range Achievement Test*. Wilmington, DE: Guidance Associates of Delaware.

Koppitz, E. M. 1968. *Psychological Evaluation of Children's Human Figure Drawings*. New York: Grune and Stratton.

Kosc, L. 1974. Developmental dyscalculia. *Journal of Learning Disabilities* 7: 164–77.

Liberman, I. Y., and Shankweiler, D. 1985. Phonology and the problems of learning to read and write. *Remedial and Special Education* 6:8–17.

Light, J. G., and DeFries, J. C. 1995. Comorbidity of reading and mathematics disabilities: Genetic and environmental etiologies. *Journal of Learning Disabilities* 28:96–106.

McGee, R., Williams, S., and Silva, P. A. 1988. Slow starters and long-term backward readers: A replication and extension. *British Journal of Educational Psychology* 58:330–37.

Olson, R., Wise, B., Conners, F., Rack, J., and Fulker, D. 1989. Specific deficits in component reading and language skills: Genetic and environmental influences. *Journal of Learning Disabilities* 22:339–48.

Olson, R. K., Wise, B., Johnson, M. C., and Ring, J. 1997. The etiology and remediation of phonologically based word recognition and spelling disabilities: Are phonological deficits the "hole" story? In *Foundations of Reading Acquisition and Dyslexia: Implications for Early Intervention*, B. Blachman, ed. Mahwah, NJ: Lawrence Erlbaum Associates.

Paulos, J. A. 1988. *Innumeracy: Mathematical Illiteracy and its Consequences*. New York: Hill and Wang.

Rivera, D. P. 1997. Mathematics education and students with learning disabilities: Introduction to the special series. *Journal of Learning Disabilities* 30:2–19, 68.

Rourke, B. P. 1993. Arithmetic disabilities, specific and otherwise: A neuropsychological perspective. *Journal of Learning Disabilities* 26:214–26.

Rourke, B. P., and Conway, J. A. 1997. Disabilities of arithmetic and mathematical reasoning; Perspectives from neurology and neuropsychology. *Journal of Learning Disabilities* 30:34–36.

Rourke, B. P., and Finlayson, M. A. J. 1978. Neuropsychological significance of variations in patterns of academic performance: Verbal and visual-spatial abilities. *Journal of Abnormal Child Psychology* 6:121–33.

Rourke, B. P., and Strang, J. 1978. Neuropsychological significance of variations in patterns of academic performance: Motor, psychomotor, and tactile-perceptual abilities. *Journal of Pediatric Psychology* 3:62–66.

Rutter, M. 1978. Prevalence and types of dyslexia. In *Dyslexia: An Appraisal of Current Knowledge*. A.L. Benton and D. Pearl, eds. New York: Oxford University Press.

Sattler, J. M. 1974. *Assessment of Children's Intelligence*. Philadelphia: W. B. Saunders.

Shafrir, U., and Siegel, L. S. 1994. Subtypes of learning disabilities in adolescents and adults. *Journal of Learning Disabilities* 27:123–34.

Share, D. L., Jorm, A. F., Maclean, R., and Matthews, R. 1984. Sources of individual differences in reading acquisition. *Journal of Educational Psychology* 76:1309–24.

Share, D. L., Moffitt, T. E., and Silva, P. A. 1988. Factors associated with arithmetic-and-reading disability and specific arithmetic disability. *Journal of Learning Disabilities* 21:313–20.

Shaywitz, S. E., Shaywitz, B. A., Fletcher, J. M., and Escobar, M. D. 1990. Prevalence of reading disability in boys and girls: Results of the Connecticut Longitudinal Study. *Journal of the American Medical Association* 264:998–1002.

Siegel, L. S. 1989. IQ is irrelevant to the definition of learning disabilities. *Journal of Learning Disabilities* 22:469–78, 486.

Siegel, L. S. 1992. An evaluation of the discrepancy definition of dyslexia. *Journal of Learning Disabilities* 25:618–29.

Stanovich, K. E. 1986. Matthew effects in reading: Some consequences of individual differences in the acquisition of literacy. *Reading Research Quarterly* 26: 360–407.

Stanovich, K. E. 1991. Discrepancy definitions of reading ability: Has intelligence lead us astray? *Reading Research Quarterly* 26:7–29.

Stevenson, H. W., and Newman, R. S. 1986. Long-term prediction of achievement and attitudes in mathematics and reading. *Child Development* 57:646–59.

Strang, J. D., and Rourke, B. P. 1983. Concept-formation/nonverbal reasoning abilities of children who exhibit specific academic problems with arithmetic. *Journal of Clinical Child Psychology* 12:33–39.

Wagner, R. K., and Torgesen, J. K. 1987. The nature of phonological processing and its causal role in the acquisition of reading skills. *Psychological Bulletin* 101:192–212.

Wechsler, D. 1963. *Wechsler Preschool and Primary Scale of Intelligence*. New York: Psychological Corporation.

Weinstein, M. C. 1980. Neuropsychological approach to math disability. *New York University Education Quarterly* 11:22–28.

Wright, S. F., Fields, H., and Newman, S. P. 1996. Dyslexia: Stability of definition over a five year period. *Journal of Research in Reading* 19:46–60.

Wrigley, J. 1958. The factorial nature of ability in elementary mathematics. *British Journal of Educational Psychology* 28:61–78.

Developmental Dyslexia:
Related to Specific or General Deficits?

Victor van Daal

Free University Amsterdam
The Netherlands
and

Aryan van der Leij

University of Amsterdam
The Netherlands

The present study was designed to examine the question of whether developmental dyslexia in 12-year-old students at the beginning of secondary education in the Netherlands is confined to problems in the domain of reading and spelling or also is related to difficulties in other areas. In particular, hypotheses derived from theories on phonological processing, rapid automatized naming, working memory, and automatization of skills were tested. To overcome the definition and selection problems of many previous studies, we included in our study all students in the first year of secondary special education in a Dutch school district. Participants were classified as either dyslexic, garden-variety, or hyperlexic poor readers, according to the degree of discrepancy between their word recognition and listening comprehension scores. In addition, groups of normal readers were formed, matching the poor readers in either reading age or chronological age. A large test battery was administered to each student, including phonological, naming, working memory, speed of processing, and motor tests. The findings

Annals of Dyslexia, Vol. 49, 1999
ISSN 0736-9387

indicate that dyslexia is associated with deficits in (1) phonological re-coding, word recognition (both in their native Dutch and in English as a second language), and spelling skills; and (2) naming speed for letters and digits. Dyslexia was not associated with deficits in other areas. The results suggest that developmental dyslexia, at the age of 12, might be (or might have become) a difficulty rather isolated from deficiencies in other cognitive and motor skills.

INTRODUCTION

The finding that children with developmental dyslexia perform poorly when reading nonwords has been replicated in many laboratories all over the world, and has been interpreted as a "phonological recoding deficit" (Rack, Snowling, and Olson 1992). When processing time is limited by flashing the non-words, the dyslexics are at even more of a disadvantage. This suggests that dyslexics may suffer from an "automatic decoding deficit" (Yap and Van der Leij 1993, 1994), which limits their ability to develop fluent and relatively effortless reading skills. However, it is still unclear whether such a deficiency is a symptom of a more general deficit. Although there is a general consensus that reading deficits include impairments in processing phonological aspects of language (Snowling 1987; Stanovich 1988; Stanovich and Siegel 1994), there is disagreement as to whether children with dyslexia suffer from more than phono-logical problems (e.g., Miles 1983). Recently, Bowers and Wolf (1993) have proposed a double deficit hypothesis, according to which the most severely affected dyslexic children have trouble with rapid automatized naming in addition to, but not separate from, their so-called phonological processing deficit (Wolf, Bowers, and Biddle in press). Alternatively, De Jong (1998) pro-poses that both phonological and naming speed deficits may be related to a lack of working memory capacity for the concurrent processing and storage of verbal information. Taking a more radical point of view, other authors have argued that children with dyslexia, in addition to many language- and memory-related problems, also may have a more general difficulty auto-matizing any skill whether phonological, visual, or motor (Nicolson and Fawcett 1990; Fawcett, Nicolson, and Dean 1996).

In this article, we review studies which illustrate the differ-ent points of view in the debate, draw attention to possible methodological flaws in relevant studies, and suggest an im-proved methodology for a study which is aimed at the examination of whether the problems in children with developmental dyslexia are indeed confined to reading and the phonological aspects of language, or whether they extend to deficits outside of these areas. The results of such a study will be presented and discussed.

THE PHONOLOGICAL PROCESSING DEFICIT

Stanovich and Siegel (1994) found the following evidence for the position that dyslexia is to be viewed as a specific deficit: (1) differences between dyslexics and both chronological and reading age-matched controls pertain to phonological skills, and (2) differences between dyslexics and other nondiscrepant poor readers (the so-called garden-variety poor readers) concern general language and memory skills, but not reading and phonological skills. It is for these reasons that their hypothesis is called the Phonological-Core Variable-Difference Model. In their metalinguistic study (Stanovich and Siegel 1994), data from several different studies were aggregated, resulting in a total of 401 good readers, 341 dyslexic readers (poor reading with normal IQ), and 167 poor readers with low IQ (garden-variety poor readers). Because the latter two groups showed similar phonological processing deficits, Stanovich and Siegel (1994) claimed that reading problems are independent from general intelligence.

RAPID NAMING

Denckla and Rudel (1976) and Spring and Capps (1974) were the first to demonstrate that severely disabled readers were slower to name arrays of common stimuli such as letters, digits, objects, and colors than were normal readers. Because this was originally regarded as a name retrieval problem (Ellis 1981) and because it was not clear whether naming problems do co-occur with, cause, or result from reading problems, naming difficulties were seen as part of the phonological processing deficit. However, given recent evidence to show that naming speed correlates only moderately with phonological skills (Wolf et al. in press; De Jong and Van der Leij in press), it has been suggested that deficits in rapid automatized naming constitute a second independent characteristic of reading-impaired children. Nevertheless, phonological and naming skills could share a common base. For the current research, it is important to note Wolf et al.'s (in press) hypothesis that, in the most severe cases of developmental dyslexia, phonological processing deficits go together with naming deficits.

WORKING MEMORY

The role of verbal memory in reading problems has been explored by many authors (for reviews see Elbro 1996 and Brady 1997). Recently, De Jong (1998) has suggested that reading disabled children suffer from a lack of working memory capacity for the concurrent processing and storage of verbal information. According to De Jong, however, the deficit is not restricted to the language domain, but is also manifest in certain numerical tasks.

With respect to phonological decoding, naming speed, and working memory, Ellis and Large (1987, 1988) have confirmed in a longitudinal study that normally intelligent children with a specific reading deficit differ from their better-reading peers on relatively few tasks (phonological segmentation, verbal memory, and rapid automatized naming), whereas children with generalized reading disability (poor reading with low IQ) differ in nearly all respects from their better-reading peers.

In sum, at least three hypotheses of a rather specific and reading-related nature have been supported with empirical evidence: a phonological processing deficit, a double deficit including difficulties with phonological processing and rapid naming, and a deficit in working memory capacity. In each case it has been argued that these deficits do not relate to general cognitive skills.

A PATTERN OF DIFFICULTIES?

Miles (1983, 1998) views dyslexia as a pattern of difficulties, a view based primarily on clinical observations that culminated in the development of a widely used dyslexia screening test, the Bangor Dyslexia Test (Miles 1982). The test items on the Bangor Dyslexia Test concern domains that are not exclusively phonological. For example, they assess left-right confusions over body parts, subtraction tables, knowledge of the sequence of the months both forward and backward, and digit span. The items also include familial incidence of reading and spelling problems, the occurrence of b-d confusions in materials written by the participant, and a memory task that is clearly phonological. That task involves repeating polysyllabic words such as "statistical," and can be considered a nonword repetition task since most of the stimulus words are unrecognizable to low-level readers. Although some empirical support has been found for the utility of these test items in distinguishing between children with dyslexia and children without dyslexia (Miles 1983; Miles and Haslum 1986), a theoretical framework which explains why these test items are indicators of dyslexia has not been developed yet.

DYSLEXIC AUTOMATIZATION DEFICIT (DAD) AND CONSCIOUS COMPENSATION (CC)

In an attempt to provide a theoretical framework for a more general deficit, Nicolson and Fawcett (1990) have proposed that children with dyslexia fail to automatize any skill fully. Their Dyslexic Automatization Deficit (DAD) hypothesis predicts that dyslexics will be unable to acquire fluency in either reading skills or in various skills outside reading and spelling, including phonological, speed, memory, and motor skills. Nicolson and Fawcett claim that ". . . there is no support . . . for any of the theories that attempt to tie dyslexia to one specific modality or type of process" (1994, p. 228). In most of their empirical studies (e.g., Nicholson and Fawcett 1999; Nicolson, Fawcett, and Dean 1996), Nicolson and his colleagues have compared dyslexic readers with normal readers on a series of motor balance tasks. The dyslexic children's performance was at the level of chronological age-matched controls in a simple baseline condition, but tended to deteriorate with increasing complexity of task conditions. For example, differences in speed appeared in a selective choice RT task ("push the button when the tone is low; don't push when it is high"), but not in a simple reaction time (RT) task ("push the button when a tone is heard"). Furthermore, performance on a balance task—a skill which should be fully automatized by the age of 11 years—deteriorated when it was combined with an attention-consuming task such as counting backward from 100 by 3s. To explain the difference in performance in the simple versus complex conditions, Nicolson and Fawcett (1990) supplemented their DAD hypothesis with the Conscious Compensation (CC) hypothesis, stating that dyslexics can mask their automatization deficit in many instances—when not constrained by time or required to divide their attention to perform complex tasks—by committing a considerable part of their attentional resources to the task under study.

Fawcett, Nicolson, and Dean (1996) have further speculated that the phonological problems in dyslexia may have a similar cause as deficits traditionally assumed to reflect cerebellar impairment such as balance and time estimation. They suggest that mild cerebellar impairment may limit articulatory control leading to difficulty in building up phonological representations, and also cause problems with most complex motor tasks.

Challenging as the DAD/CC hypotheses may be, attempts to replicate the findings of Nicolson and Fawcett (1990, 1994) have not been entirely successful. For example,Yap and Van der Leij (1994) reported partial support for the automatization deficit, finding deficits in only one of two dual task conditions presented. However, Wimmer, Mayringer, and Landerl (1998), and Stringer and Stanovich (1998) were unable to find any supporting evidence. Therefore, although a general automatization deficit hypothesis is attractive to many clinical workers who are faced with dyslexic persons who present problems outside the domain of reading and spelling, the validity of the DAD/CC hypothesis is still to be assessed.

ON THE METHODOLOGY IN DYSLEXIA RESEARCH

As the studies reviewed are inconclusive concerning the generality of deficits associated with developmental dyslexia, we turn to two methodological concerns with dyslexia research. The first issue deals with the definition of dyslexia, and the second with comorbidity.

A definition of dyslexia must be precise but say nothing about the causes of the disorder because they are yet to be established (Tønnessen 1997). In this respect, the work of Aaron (1991), Siegel (1988, 1989, 1992), and Stanovich (1991) is especially important because it shows that, for example, IQ and reading disability are independent factors which must be separately defined. Thus, it seems worthwhile to start with a rather limited operational definition of dyslexia that refers only to the most obvious and highly quantifiable symptoms (Tønnessen 1997).

Difficulty with the recognition of single words (Lyon 1995), resistant to proper treatment, in combination with normal listening comprehension (Aaron 1991), seem to be good candidates for the components of an ideal operational definition. It is generally agreed that difficulty with word recognition is the main component. Also, in order to be certain that the reading problems are truly resistant to treatment, deficits resulting from poor educational opportunities must be excluded. Finally, studies on the relation of reading and IQ suggest that the IQ criterion should be replaced by listening comprehension, or, to put it in a broader sense, verbal competence. To support this decision, it may be argued that verbal competence is a product of learning actively stimulated by one's environment and is, therefore, more comparable to reading than spatial ability or other aspects of general intelligence. Moreover, verbal competence and reading are both skills in the verbal domain, which makes the discrepancies between them an intriguing issue to be examined. Why is learning the written form of the language so difficult for some students who are able to learn the spoken language? To study this question, the comparison to students who do not show such a discrepancy (chronological and reading age-matched controls) is relevant. We should also include students with the opposite reading profile, hyperlexia, characterized by strong word recognition skill with much weaker listening comprehension. Whatever deficiencies are related to dyslexia should not be detectable in students with hyperlexia. Furthermore, to be able to test the hypothesis that dyslexia (or specific reading disability) is not related to general intelligence (and thus, presumably, unrelated to listening comprehension), it is worthwhile to include a group of garden-variety poor readers who perform poorly at both word recognition and listening comprehension.

Obviously, the operational definition suggested here is quite different from the approach proposed by Miles (1994) who seeks to reconcile within one taxonomy: anatomical findings (that is, structural anomalies in the brain of dyslexic people); impairments in the visual system of persons with dyslexia; genetic aspects of dyslexia; problems in auditory processing; impaired phonological processing; clinically supported pattern of difficulties mentioned earlier. That pattern also gets support from the "that's our Johnnie" effect, by which parents tend not to restrict their reports of difficulties or typical behaviors to only those relevant to reading and spelling. In contrast to the proposed limited operational definition of dyslexia, the co-occurrence of all these phenomena has not yet been established.

In order to establish reliably whether problems in reading and spelling are linked to problems in other domains, we must define the unique characteristics of persons with developmental dyslexia. This is, in essence, a question of comorbidity that can only be answered in a large, randomly selected sample (e.g., Caron and Rutter 1991). Unfortunately, many studies seem to suffer from small sample size because costs are high or from selection bias, perhaps because clinic samples are more easily accessible to researchers. For example, it has been suggested by Wimmer, Mayringer, and Landerl (1998) that the effects found by Nicolson and Fawcett (1990) may be attributed to preselection which has resulted in a high incidence of both dyslexia and attentional disorders among participants. In order to prevent selection bias, we decided to test all students meeting our operational criteria for dyslexia from an entire school district, and to compare them to other relevant groups from that same district.

HYPOTHESES

We reasoned that if developmental dyslexia is related to deficits in phonological processing, naming, working memory, and/or automatization of skills, students with dyslexia would score lower on tasks that require these skills than normal students of the same chronological age (CA controls), and at or below the level of younger students matched for reading age (RA controls).

In addition, by comparing dyslexics to hyperlexics and to garden-variety poor readers, two more hypotheses can be tested. First, if any of the aforementioned deficits is related to poor word recognition only, and not to listening comprehension, it should not affect hyperlexics but should affect both dyslexic and garden-variety poor readers. Second, if the hypothesis of a variable difference outside the domain of reading is correct, dyslexics should outperform both garden-variety poor readers and hyperlexics on tasks that tap general learning abilities.

METHOD

GENERAL DESIGN

In the Dutch school system, children enter secondary schools at age twelve. Classes are tracked according to ability and career goals. Most students receive either low or middle vocational training, or are prepared for tertiary education at various levels. In addition to these main tracks, special schools exist for students with learning disabilities. At secondary level, children whose IQs are within the normal range are routed to schools designed to cope specifically with learning disabilities. Still another type of school exists for children with mild retardation.

We chose to conduct our study at the secondary level in a school district that is representative of an average district in the Netherlands. In particular, only a few nonnative speakers took part. This number would have been much larger had we worked in a large city. In order to keep costs as low as possible, the present study is not longitudinal, but instead focuses on 12-year olds because at that age, reading problems have stabilized (Smart, Sanson, and Prior 1996) and there is little likelihood of misdiagnosis (either false positives or negatives). All 12-year olds who attended the same secondary school for primary learning-disabled children took part in the study so as to represent wide variations on any measure. In fact, we expected our sample to include many dyslexics, nondyslexics, and garden-variety poor readers, all with comparable school careers in special education. We predicted that the dyslexic participants would all have received some form of treatment, but would still need a special school to help compensate for their dyslexia. Our study also included all 12-year olds who attended a secondary school in the same district for children with mild retardation in an effort to find even more garden-variety poor readers and possibly hyperlexics (children who proficiently decode and recognize words, but have trouble understanding what they read). Two CA control groups containing whole classes of 12-year olds were formed: one from a school for low vocational training, and one from a school for middle vocational training. An RA control group was formed by selecting ten fourth graders who read at the same level as the poorest readers in special education, but were two years younger. In addition to normal readers, we expected that classes of 12-year olds from low and middle vocational training would also include a few dyslexics, hyperlexics, and nondiscrepant poor readers.

In addition to the tasks that were used to classify participants (word recognition and listening comprehension), we used a wide range of tasks to test our hypotheses. Reading-related tasks included nonword reading, spelling, and word recognition in English as a second language. Phonological processing tasks involved sound blending, sound analysis, and nonword repetition. Language-related timed tasks included rapid naming and articulation speed. In addition, we presented tasks assessing working memory, speed of processing, and motor skill in both baseline and dual-task conditions. Verbal and nonverbal intelligence tests served as covariates.

The present study was set up to examine as many representative 12-year-old children as possible on a wide range of tests. The purpose of this format was to help us discover characteristics unique to dyslexic students, in comparison to chronological and reading age controls, and to garden-variety and hyperlexic readers.

PARTICIPANTS

All children studied were from the Breda school district in the southern Netherlands. All 73 students from the first classes of a school for learning disabled children were included, along with all 15 children in the first class of a school for children with mild retardation (see Van der Leij 1987 for a detailed description of the special school system in the Netherlands). To avoid selection bias in the CA control group, we included two entire classes from regular schools: 21 children from the first year of a school for low vocational training and 23 from the first year of a school for middle vocational training. Nearly all of these children were 12 years old, although a few were a year older. Finally, ten children in primary education (grade 4) were selected as RA controls for the dyslexic participants. Thus, the total number of participants in our study was 140. In the school for primary learning disabled children, one boy was under psychiatric treatment and one girl suffered from loss of hearing. Both were excluded from the subsequent analyses, reducing the number of evaluable participants to 138.

Among the CA control samples, small subgroups with dyslexic and hyperlexic profiles were found. The first subgroup showed far better listening comprehension than reading skill, although their reading skill still fell within normal limits. The second group showed far better reading than listening skill although, again, the deficient skill was within age-appropriate levels. Despite the fact that both subgroups had very interesting features, it was decided to exclude their results from the analyses in the present research in order to obtain a CA control group which was as homogeneous as possible. This homogeneity was expected to increase the power of the analyses. In Appendix 1, the distribution of the different types of readers over the groups is provided. Thus, our analyses include 118 (138–20) participants.

PROCEDURES

All participants were given all tests described below, either in classes or individually, but always double-blind. Classifications into different types of readers were carried out afterward when all data had been collected. Only the word recognition test of the participants from the school for primary learning disabilities was scored first, in order to select reading-age-matched controls. Due to children's absences, we do not have data for all participants on some tests.

TESTS

Altogether, some 40 different tests and subtests were administered, covering the following domains:

1. Word recognition and listening comprehension (used for classification of the participants).
2. Reading-related measures such as nonword reading, spelling, and word recognition in English as a second language.
3. Tests for the measurement of phonological skills, including sound blending, sound analysis, and nonword repetition.
4. Language-related timed tasks such as rapid naming and articulation speed.
5. Tasks for working memory (Digit Span and the Star Counting Test).
6. Tasks for general speed of processing and motor skill in both baseline and dual-task conditions.
7. Verbal and nonverbal intelligence tests as control measures for general learning ability.
8. Arithmetic and reading comprehension as other academic skills.

Tests for the Classification of Participants. Word recognition was measured by means of the Eén-Minuut Test (One-Minute Test), developed by Brus and Voeten (1973). In this test, the participant is required to read real words aloud as quickly and as accurately as possible. The words (nouns, verbs, and the like) are printed on a card with 116 words arranged in four columns in order of increasing difficulty. The raw score is the number of words correctly read within one minute. Recently, this test has been standardized for the Dutch school population by Van den Bos et al. (1994). Parallel test and test-retest reliabilities were over .80 as reported by Brus and Voeten (1973) and more recently by Van den Bos et al. (1994).

Listening comprehension was assessed by administering the experimental form of the Listening subtest of the BELL 1996 (Van den Bos 1996). For this subtest, the participant selects the one picture out of a group of four that best fits with a spoken sentence. To perform well, the participant should know word meanings and understand syntactic and semantic relations. The test has 34 items of increasing difficulty and has recently been standardized in a large-scale survey (n = 1700) involving first-year students in secondary education (Van Daal and Van der Leij in preparation). Two parallel forms were used, the A and the B forms, which (in the sample of the current study) had homogeneity reliabilities (Cronbach's α) of .63 and .69, respectively.

All participants were classified as either a garden-variety poor reader, a dyslexic reader, a hyperlexic reader, or a normal reader on the basis of the standard scores ($M = 10$; $SD = 3$) obtained on the word recognition test and the listening comprehension test. A dyslexic reader was defined as scoring 7 or less on the reading test and over 7 on the listening comprehension test, with a discrepancy of at least 3 points between the two measures. All participants scoring just over 7 on reading, but having a listening comprehension score of at least 3 points more were also considered dyslexic. In the whole sample of 138, only six such participants could be found. Participants with a listening comprehension score of less than 7 and a reading score at least 3 points higher were treated as hyperlexic readers. Here we had only two participants who scored just over 7 on the listening comprehension test, but had a far better reading score. Finally, the group of garden-variety poor readers included those participants who scored below 7 on both the reading and the listening comprehension tests. Here, no participants with a large discrepancy between reading skill and listening comprehension were encountered.

Reading-related Tests. The first test used to measure reading- and language-related skills was the Klepel (Van den Bos et al. 1994). This test was constructed by changing vowels or consonants in words of the Eén-Minuut Test under the restriction that the pronunciation rules of Dutch were not violated. The score is the number of nonwords correctly read within two minutes. Van den Bos et al. (1994) report reliabilities over .90 for this test.

All participants were also given a standardized spelling test consisting of 135 words of increasing difficulty. The score on this test is the number of correctly spelled words.

As the students in the first year of secondary education also receive formal instruction in the reading and writing of English, an English word recognition test was administered. This test, the English version of the One-Minute Test, consists of words of increasing difficulty which occurred in all commonly used teaching methods in the Netherlands (Van Daal, in preparation). The participant's task is to read aloud the words as quickly and as accurately as he can. The score is the number of words read correctly within one minute. Cronbach's α for this test is .90.

Measures Tapping Phonological Skills. The following three tests were administered with the help of an Apple Macintosh Plus computer on which a program written in AuthorWare was run. In the Auditory Analysis task, the computer presented the spoken form of a nonword (from the parallel version of the aforementioned Klepel) in digitized speech. All speech used was uttered at a rate of one syllable per second by a professional speech trainer, recorded in a studio on DAT tape, and digitized on the computer's hard disk at a sampling rate of 44 kHz. It was the participant's task to say the smallest sounds of the word, as quickly as possible, and in correct order. The experimenters were trained to press the space bar as soon as the participant started speaking so that the latencies of the responses were recorded by the computer. Accuracy in all of these computer-administered tasks was immediately assessed by the experimenter who literally transcribed each error into the system. When the response was scored, the next item was presented. Thus, both the accuracy and the latencies of the responses could be analyzed. The KR-20 reliability of the Auditory Analysis task—which consisted of 20 items—was .87.

For the Sound Blending task, the isolated phonemes of nonwords were presented auditorily by the computer and it was the participant's task to say the whole word as quickly as possible. The KR-20 reliability for this test (20 items) was .69.

A nonword repetition test also was administered with the help of the computer. Here participants were again instructed to respond as quickly as they could after the computer had said the nonword. Subsequent items increased in number of syllables, from one, KES, to four, WAPELBROEGER. The KR-20 reliability for this test (20 items) was .55.

Language-related Timed Tasks. The rapid naming test comprised six subtests, each of which contained 50 items printed on a card. The participants were asked to name the items on each card as quickly as they could without hesitations or errors. Mean total naming times per card were computed for alphanumeric stimuli (digits [0-9], capital letters [A-Z], and a mix of digits and capital letters) and objects and colors (one card with five different familiar objects, and one card with five different colors). The sixth subtest consisted of a mix of letters, digits, and colors for which the total naming time was also recorded by the experimenter in an individual testing situation. Errors were not analyzed as they rarely occurred.

Articulation time was measured with an identical procedure in each of two trials. In the first trial, the participant was asked to repeat ZUS AAPJE BOTERVLOOT (sister monkey butterdish) five times, as quickly as possible and without errors. In the second trial, JAS AUTO KIPPENHOK (coat car chicken-hutch) was repeated. Word combinations were taken from a standard list used by speech trainers to assess speech problems in Dutch, and were pronounced by the experimenter at a rate of about one syllable per second. Articulation speed was timed only after the participant was able to repeat the target phrase once without errors. The number of trials to achieve accuracy was also recorded by the experimenter.

Working Memory. Digit Span (WISC-R) was administered in the classrooms. To avoid cheating (writing the numbers down then reversing them) only forward items were used. Three trials at each string length were used to increase the reliability of the test. The total number of items correctly recalled was scored.

The Star Counting test was originally developed by De Jong and Das-Smaal (1995) and has 22 items on which the participant is allowed to work for a total of 30 minutes. The score is number of items correctly solved. A single item of the Star Counting test consists of a 5 x 5 array of stars (*), plus signs (+), and minus signs (–). A value is given to start with, say 25, and instruction is provided on how many to add (2) and to subtract (3). Thus, if the first row of the array is +**–*, the result would be $25 + 2 + 2 = 29 – 3 = 26$. According to the memory model by Baddeley (1986), this task can be perceived as a task for dual processing because a slave system simply has to count, while an executive master system looks for whether addition or subtraction is required.

Measures of General Speed of Processing and of Motor Skill. As a baseline measure of Simple Reaction Time (RT), participants were asked to press the space bar as soon as possible after hearing a tone. A visual signal warned the participant that the next stimulus was about to come with a random latency of 0.5 second (sec) to 1.5 sec after the visual signal. Mean RTs were computed.

In the selective choice RT task, participants were asked to press the space bar as quickly as possible when a high tone was presented, but to refrain from pressing when a low tone was presented. For this task, RTs for hits and false alarms were recorded, as were numbers of hits, misses, correct rejections, and false alarms. A measure of d-prime (d') was also computed (McNicol 1972).

Two balance and motor tests were also presented, using a dual task paradigm. The Two Board Balance task (after Henderson and Sugden 1992) requires the child to balance with one foot in front of the other on a narrow board which is positioned like a seesaw on top of a second board. The experimenter can hear a click whenever a child loses balance, causing the two boards to collide. We measured how much time had passed before the participant caused the boards to click. There were two baseline conditions: one with the dominant foot in front of the other foot, the other with the dominant foot at the rear of the board. On two additional trials, participants were blindfolded, and on another two trials they counted backward from 30 by ones, while balancing. Each type of trial was done once with the dominant foot in front of the other foot, then repeated with the dominant foot at the rear of the board. Participants were allowed to practice for 10 seconds before each trial.

The other motor balance task was Walking Backwards (original version by Henderson and Sugden 1992). Participants were required to walk backward over a line, 3 cm wide, touching toe to heel at each step. We measured how many steps each child could make (with a maximum of 15) while properly touching toe to heel and without going off the line with more than half of the foot. The test was repeated with the added task of counting backward from 30 by 1s. Two test trials were run before scoring in order to verify that the instructions were understood.

It must be noted that the procedures for scoring the balance and motor tasks in this study were more objective than the methods used by Nicolson and Fawcett (1990) who measured the degrees of swaying and the waving of the arms, as recorded on video tapes.

Intelligence. For some of the participants, intelligence test scores had been used for school entrance decisions in special education, so were available for use in our study. Results from both a test for verbal intelligence, the OTIS (Dutch version by Maussen 1971), and one for nonverbal intelligence, the Raven's Progressive Matrices (Raven, Court, and Raven 1979) were gathered from the school files of all children who had been assessed on these measures within the last two years.

Other Academic Achievement Tests. Reading comprehension was measured by means of the Reading subtest of the BELL 1996 (Van den Bos 1996). To complete this task, participants first read a sentence, then turn over the page and select the picture that best corresponds to that sentence. The test consists of 34 items of increasing difficulty and its format largely parallels that of the listening comprehension test. Here again, both A and B forms were used, and had reliabilities (Cronbach's α) of .74 and .81, respectively.

Arithmetic speed was measured by means of the Tempo Test Rekenen (Speeded Test of Arithmetic, De Vos 1992) which consists of five subtests. For this measure, participants are instructed to solve as many simple calculations as they can using paper and pencil within one minute. The subtests are divided into measures of addition, subtraction, multiplication, division, and a mixture of all four operations.

RESULTS

Multiple regression analyses were carried out using a regression-based variable for decoding/listening comprehension as the dependent variable, and all tests entered as independent variables. Fifty-six percent of the total variance could be explained, $F (26, 79) = 3.94$, $p < .001$. Significant predictors included rapid naming of alphanumeric items and nonword reading. No other variable explained additional variance in the regression-based variable for decoding/listening comprehension. For the sake of simplicity, analyses of differences between discrete groups on individual measures are presented below in detail. Analyses of variance were conducted with Bonferroni tests to assess the significance of pairwise comparisons.

GROUP DIFFERENCES IN CLASSIFICATION VARIABLES

The means and standard deviations for both classification variables (listening comprehension and word recognition) are presented in Table I. Differences between groups were significant on word recognition. Garden-variety poor readers read fewer words per minute than any other group, and both dyslexics and RA controls read fewer words than either hyperlexics or CA controls.

Between-group differences were also found on the listening comprehension test. In this case, CA controls and dyslexics were better at listening comprehension than were the garden-variety poor readers, hyperlexics, or RA controls. Therefore, we can say that the classification of the participants was generally successful, although the garden-variety poor readers were less competent at word recognition than the dyslexic readers. Also, the listening comprehension test (which had been designed for 12-year olds) proved too hard for the younger, RA-matched controls.

GROUP DIFFERENCES ON READING-RELATED TESTS

As seen in table I, group differences were also found on all three reading-related tests. On nonword reading, garden-variety and

Table I. Mean scores (and *SD*s)
of reading groups on classification
and reading-related variables.

	Poor Readers			Control Groups		
	Garden-variety	Dys-lexic	Hyper-lexic	CA Match	RA Match	F-Value
n	13	41	16	34	10	
Classification Variables						
Word Recognition:						
Words read in one	42.7[a]	58.0[b]	81.0[c]	79.0[c]	68.5[b]	43.69***
minute	(15.8)	(9.3)	(10.3)	(10.7)	(7.1)	df (4,113)
Listening Comprehension:						
Number correct	16.5[a]	27.0[b]	17.8[a]	25.8[b]	18.4[a]	67.15***
(max = 34)	(2.8)	(2.8)	(3.4)	(2.8)	(2.4)	df (4,113)
Reading Related Tests						
Nonword reading:						
Words read within	27.6[a]	35.6[a]	74.8[b]	68.5[b]	64.0[b]	50.80***
2 minutes	(13.7)	(11.0)	(15.8)	(17.1)	(9.2)	df (4,113)
Words correctly	73.1[a]	106.3[b]	120.4[c]	122.1[c]	98.9[b]	34.80***
spelled	(26.3)	(13.8)	(9.7)	(8.0)	(10.1)	df (4,112)
Foreign language:						
English words	32.8[a]	32.6[a]	53.5[b]	55.6[b]	—	19.36***
read in one minute	(1.9)	(8.4)	(19.6)	(17.6)	—	df (4,88)

Note: Results of post-hoc comparisons indicated by superscripts; different superscripts in a given row indicate those comparisons that are significantly different. CA match = chronological age match; RA match = reading age match.

***$p < .001$

dyslexic poor readers decoded fewer nonwords than RA controls, CA controls, or hyperlexics.

On spelling, garden-variety poor readers spelled fewer words correctly than any other group, and both RA controls and dyslexics spelled fewer words correctly than hyperlexics or CA controls. On English word recognition, hyperlexics and CA controls successfully read more English words than dyslexics or garden-variety poor readers. Therefore, we can say that the classification of the subjects is supported by the results on the reading-related tasks.

PHONOLOGICAL SKILLS

In table II, statistics are presented for the phonological tasks of auditory analysis, auditory synthesis, and nonword repetition.

Although no significant differences were found on the latency measures, groups did differ in their accuracy on each measure. Garden-variety readers were less accurate than CA controls on both nonword repetition and auditory synthesis tasks, and less accurate than RA controls on auditory analysis. Interestingly, only on nonword repetition were the dyslexic readers more accurate than the garden-variety readers.

Thus, on the phonological processing tests, we failed to find the differences that would be predicted by the Phonological-Core Variable-Difference Model.

Table II   Mean accuracy and latency scores (and *SD*s) of reader groups on phonological processing tests.

| | Poor Readers | | | Control Groups | | |
	Garden-variety	Dys-lexic	Hyper-lexic	CA Match	RA Match	ANOVA F-Value
n	13	41	16	34	10	
Auditory Analysis						
Percentage correct	51[a]	62[a]	51[a]	61[b]	89[b]	2.99*
	(33)	(25)	(31)	(29)	(11)	df (4,97)
Latency (seconds)	.87	1.04	1.14	1.13	1.31	1.84, *ns*
	(.25)	(.34)	(.37)	(.45)	(.28)	df (4,97)
Auditory Synthesis						
Percentage correct	69[a]	86[b]	79[a]	86[b]	86[a]	3.30**
	(17)	(16)	(19)	(12)	(6)	df (4,97)
Latency (seconds)	.44	.36	.40	.34	.34	2.15[ns]
	(.12)	(.11)	(.10)	(.08)	(.15)	df (4,94)
Nonword Repetition						
Percentage correct	86[a]	96[b]	90[a]	96[c]	92[c]	4.36**
	(16)	(6)	(8)	(6)	(7)	df (4,97)
Latency (seconds)	.26	.25	.26	.23	.26	< 1, *ns*
	(.07)	(.07)	(.06)	(.07)	(.04)	df (4,97)

Note: *$p < .05$; **$p < .01$

Results of post-hoc comparisons indicated by superscripts; different superscripts in a given row indicate those comparisons that are significantly different. CA match = chronological age match; RA match = reading age match.

LANGUAGE-RELATED TIMED TASKS

Group performances on timed language tasks are presented in table III. On the rapid naming of alphanumeric items, significant group differences were found such that garden-variety poor readers were slower than all other groups except the RA controls, and dyslexics were slower than hyperlexics and CA controls. Although there was an overall group effect on the rapid naming of symbols and colors, no pairwise comparison reached significance.

On the first wordstring of the articulation test, RA controls needed more trials than the CA controls, hyperlexics, and dyslexics, but there were no differences on the second wordstring. Garden-variety poor readers were slower in articulating

Table III Mean scores (and *SD*s) of reader groups on language-related timed tasks.

| | Poor Readers | | | Control Groups | | |
	Garden-variety	Dys-lexic	Hyper-lexic	CA Match	RA Match	ANOVA F-Value
n	13	41	16	34	10	
Rapid Naming Measures						
Number of seconds to name letters/digits	32.4[a] (9.1)	27.8[b] (4.5)	21.8[c] (3.5)	23.2[c] (3.9)	26.0[a] (3.7)	13.04*** df (4,111)
Number of seconds to name objects/colors	46.4 (7.8)	42.0 (7.7)	38.4 (5.5)	39.4 (9.0)	44.5 (5.1)	3.07, *ns* df (4,112)
"Zus aapje botervloot"						
Trials to articulate	1.6[a] (.9)	1.4[b] (.7)	1.3[b] (.5)	1.2[b] (.5)	2.8[a] (3.3)	4.18** df (4,112)
Seconds to articulate five times	9.6[a] (3.3)	7.0[b] (2.3)	7.7[a] (2.6)	6.9[b] (1.5)	8.2[a] (2.3)	3.90*** df (4,112)
"Jas auto kippenhok"						
Trials to articulate	1.4 (.7)	1.2 (.5)	1.3 (.8)	1.0 (.2)	1.3 (.7)	1.40, *ns* df (4,112)
Seconds to articulate five times	8.4[a] (2.4)	6.3[b] (2.3)	6.9[a] (1.5)	6.2[b] (1.3)	8.1[a] (1.6)	4.70* df (4,112)

Note: $^*p < .05$; $^{**}p < .01$; $^{***}p < .001$

Results of post-hoc comparisons indicated by superscripts; different superscripts in a given row indicate those comparisons that are significantly different. CA match = chronological age match; RA match = reading age match.

than dyslexics and chronological age controls, both on the first and second wordstrings.

In general, our results agreed with what would be predicted by the naming deficit hypothesis. We should, however, cite three points of diversion from expected results:

1. Garden-variety readers were slower than dyslexics.
2. The naming deficit did not generalize to nonalphanumeric stimuli.
3. Naming deficits tended to go along with articulation problems.

WORKING MEMORY

As shown in Table IV, garden-variety poor readers remembered fewer digits than all other groups on the WISC Digit Span subtest. They also made fewer correct calculations on the Star Counting Test than any other group.

On working memory tests, therefore, garden-variety readers performed less well than the other groups.

Table IV   Mean scores (and *SDs*) of reader groups on memory measures.

| | Poor Readers | | | Control Groups | | |
	Garden-variety	Dys-lexic	Hyper-lexic	CA Match	RA Match	ANOVA F-Value
n	13	41	16	34	10	
Digit Span						
Number of items recalled	4.1[a]	4.8[b]	4.7[b]	5.0[b]	4.5[b]	3.16[*]
	(1.1)	(.7)	(1.1)	(.7)	(.5)	*df* (4,112)
Star Counting Test						
Number of items correct	6.2[a]	12.8[b]	13.6[b]	13.4[b]	13.6[b]	6.23[***]
	(6.3)	(4.1)	(4.5)	(4.8)	(4.5)	*df* (4,112)

Note: [*]$p < .05$; [***]$p < .001$

Results of post-hoc comparisons indicated by superscripts; different superscripts in a given row indicate those comparisons that are significantly differ-

TESTS FOR GENERAL SPEED OF PROCESSING AND MOTOR SKILL IN BASELINE AND DUAL-TASK CONDITIONS

On the simple reaction time task, CA controls were faster than RA controls (see table V). On the choice reaction task, however, no differences at all were found for d-prime or for latencies for hits. Only on latencies for false alarms were the reading age controls slower than the chronological age controls. The differences found can be explained easily by maturation effects.

As seen in table V, on none of the motor and balance tasks were differences between any two groups found. Therefore, no support for the DAD/CC hypothesis was found.

VERBAL AND NONVERBAL INTELLIGENCE

In table VI, scores for nonverbal and verbal intelligence are presented. As mentioned previously, these measures were available only for students attending the school for primary learning disabled. Among these children, hyperlexics scored lower on average than dyslexics on the Raven's test ($F[3,53] = 3.87$, $p = .014$), whereas the garden-variety poor readers performed less well than the dyslexics and CA controls on the OTIS ($F[3,54] = 4.79$, $p = .005$).

Thus, as in other language-related tasks, garden-variety poor readers performed less well on verbal intelligence and on nonverbal intelligence.

OTHER ACADEMIC ACHIEVEMENT TESTS

Scores on reading comprehension and speeded arithmetic are presented in table VI. Significant group differences were found on reading comprehension, with garden-variety poor readers scoring lower than hyperlexics, dyslexics, and CA controls. Reading-age controls scored lower than dyslexics and CA controls. On the speeded arithmetic test, the garden-variety poor readers were less competent than all other groups except the reading-age controls.

DOUBLE DEFICIT

As discussed earlier, a double deficit involving both nonword reading and letter naming speed may characterize a subgroup of dyslexics; such students should have the most severe reading impairments. However, it should be noted that the correlation between nonword reading and naming speed was rather high in the whole group ($r = .68$), probably because the nonword reading task involved speed as well. Interestingly, this correlation dropped to .35 when only dyslexics were taken into account.

Table V.　Mean scores (and SDs) on baseline and dual-task measures of general speed of processing and of motor skill.

	Poor Readers			Control Groups		ANOVA
	Garden-variety	Dys-lexic	Hyper-lexic	CA Match	RA Match	F-Value
Speed of Processing						
Simple RT (secs)	.80[a,b]	.76[a,b]	.86[a,b]	.68[b]	1.00[a]	3.75***
(baseline condition)	(.22)	(.22)	(.24)	(.20)	(.30)	$df(4,97)$
Choice reaction:						
d' (dual-task	1.43	1.34	2.01	1.57	1.47	1.66,ns
condition)	(1.02)	(.69)	(1.49)	(.68)	(.41)	$df(4,97)$
Choice reaction:	1.7	1.9	1.8	1.6	1.9	1.78ns
latency of hits (secs)	(.5)	(.5)	(.6)	(.4)	(.2)	$df(4,97)$
Choice reaction:						
false alarm	1.1[a,b]	1.2[a,b]	1.0[a,b]	.9[b]	1.6[a]	2.69*
latency (secs)	(.5)	(.6)	(.4)	(.3)	(.9)	$df(4,97)$
Two-Board Balance						
Secs in balance	2.8	4.8	5.8	3.9	4.1	ns
preferred foot in front	(1.6)	(5.2)	(6.0)	(3.0)	(3.6)	$df(4,97)$
Secs blindfolded	3.1	4.6	5.1	3.9	4.8	ns
preferred foot behind	(2.1)	(4.3)	(5.2)	(3.4)	(4.9)	$df(4,97)$
Secs blindfolded	1.3	1.8	2.1	1.7	1.8	ns
preferred foot in front	(.9)	(1.1)	(1.5)	(1.3)	(.9)	$df(4,97)$
Secs in balance	1.5	2.0	1.6	1.7	1.6	ns
preferred foot behind	(1.3)	(1.9)	(1.1)	(1.3)	(.5)	$df(4,97)$
Secs counting backward	1.0	3.5	4.9	3.2	2.9	ns
preferred foot in front	(1.3)	(3.6)	(4.9)	(2.9)	(2.6)	$df(4,97)$
Secs counting backward	1.4	4.7	3.2	3.1	3.4	ns
preferred foot behind	(2.2)	(5.2)	(2.8)	(2.6)	(4.0)	$df(4,97)$
Walking Backward						
Number of steps	8.2	9.4	7.2	10.2	12.3	ns
	(6.3)	(5.2)	(5.4)	(5.7)	(3.6)	$df(4,97)$
Number of steps						
while counting	5.7	8.6	6.8	8.4	9.5	ns
backward	(4.5)	(5.8)	(5.8)	(5.6)	(6.1)	$df(4,97)$

Note: *$p < .05$; ***$p < .001$

Results of post-hoc comparisons indicated by superscripts; different superscripts in a given row indicate those comparisons that are significantly different. CA match = chronological age match; RA match = reading age match.

Table VI. Mean scores (and *SD*s) on tests of intelligence and academic achievement tests. (Raven's and OTIS scores available only students from school for primary learning disabled).

	Poor Readers			Control Groups		
	Garden-variety	Dys-lexic	Hyper-lexic	CA Match	RA Match	ANOVA F-Value
Intelligence Measures	*n* = 5	*n* = 30[#]	*n* = 6	*n* = 17		
Raven's						
(nonverbal)	105.2[a,b]	113.7[b]	102.2[a]	109.8[a,b]		3.87*
IQ Points	(4.0)	(8.7)	(9.9)	(8.9)		*df* (3,53)
OTIS (verbal)	87.4[a]	100.5[b]	91.0[a,b]	101.6[b]		4.79**
IQ points	(6.7)	(8.7)	(8.6)	(10.9)		*df* (3,54)
Achievement Measures	*n* = 13	*n* = 41	*n* = 16	*n* = 34	*n* = 10	
Reading						
comprehension:	15.6[a]	24.5[c]	22.5[b,c]	26.0[c]	19.0[a,b]	18.50***
no. correct	(5.3)	(3.8)	(4.7)	(3.8)	(4.2)	*df* (4,112)
Speeded arithmetic:						
no. correct	74.4[a]	111.8[b]	115.6[b]	123.8[b]	96.3[a,b]	7.46***
in five mins	(35.5)	(25.3)	(33.7)	(28.8)	(18.2)	*df* (4,112)

[#]Note: In Dyslexic group, *n* = 29 for the OTIS measure.

Within this group, we found eight students who had neither deficit, nine who had both deficits (scoring 1 *SD* below the general mean on both variables), and 26 students with a single deficit. Those with only one deficit always had a decoding problem (scoring 1 *SD* below the general mean). In a secondary analysis, we compared the group with the double deficit to the group with the single nonword reading deficit. Differences were found only on naming speed measures themselves, including the naming of both alphanumeric stimuli, $F(1,22) = 31.12$, $p < .001$ and nonalphanumeric items, $F(1,22) = 10.36$, $p = .004$. No significant difference was found on any other variable.

DISCUSSION

The outcomes of the current study are straightforward. The dyslexic group differed from the CA-matched control group in two respects only: they had extreme difficulties with single-word measures including nonword reading and recognition of high-frequency words in a foreign language (English); and with spelling. Of course, these difficulties come as no surprise. The analyses revealed that dyslexic students were below RA level when reading nonwords and at RA level in word recognition (due to our matching procedure). Because the two tasks, Klepel for nonword reading and EMT for word recognition, are equivalent except for the semantic element, the hypothesis of a phonological recoding deficit (Rack, Snowling, and Olson 1992) is supported by our findings. Because dyslexic students also did poorly on recognizing foreign words which they had practiced, and because all three reading tasks involved speed, the results are consistent with the automatic decoding deficit hypothesis as well (Yap and Van der Leij 1993). According to this hypothesis, it is the automatization of reading skill that is deficient; therefore, the reading of overlearned or very familiar words remains slow, even when a high level of accuracy is attained. Moreover, reading performance will break down when task demands are increased by presenting, for example, less frequent words, nonwords, longer real words, or words with complex orthographic structures. Another way to increase the task demands is to emphasize speed of response (for more details, see Van der Leij and Van Daal 1999). In addition, because automatization of reading is deficient, no robust orthographic representations (Share 1996, 1998) are built up, a fact reflected in dyslexic students' performance in spelling.

The second and only significant finding outside the area of reading and spelling concerns a naming deficit. The fact that this deficit only appeared when letters and/or digits had to be named and not with symbol/color naming, favors the idea that an automatic decoding deficit (in the sense of an impaired retrieval speed for letter names) exists as well. Our data do not, however, support the position of a more general naming deficit. Much to our surprise, we were not able to find any other significant difference between dyslexic and normal readers, whether matched on CA or RA. The hypotheses of a general phonological processing deficit, of a general naming deficit, of a general deficit in working memory, and of a more general automatization deficit were all unsupported by our findings.

In contrast, garden-variety poor readers differed from dyslexic readers and the CA and RA control groups on a variety of tasks that assessed phonological skills (analysis, blending, nonword repetition), rapid naming (letters and digits), articulation speed, and working memory (Digit Span, Star Counting Test). The garden-variety poor readers seemed to match the cognitive profiles predicted by the aforementioned hypotheses better than the dyslexics. The only profile that the garden-variety poor readers did not match was that predicted by the general automatization deficit: they did not differ from other groups on the reaction tasks or on the motor tasks. Consistent with their weaker verbal intelligence, garden-variety poor readers scored lower on both reading comprehension and speeded arithmetic. However, it should be noted that the garden-variety group in the current study, with an average nonverbal IQ of 105 and verbal IQ of 87, were of low-average intelligence and could easily have been placed in the dyslexic group in other studies. If this is in fact the case, our findings strongly suggest that the hypothesized deficits may not appear in dyslexics across the intelligence continuum. This casts doubt not only on the validity of the various hypotheses regarding deficits outside the area of reading, but also on the independence of developmental dyslexia from general learning disabilities.

In line with our predictions, the hyperlexic readers were better than dyslexic readers at phonological recoding, English word recognition, spelling, and rapid naming (letters and digits), but scored lower on nonverbal intelligence. Differences in verbal intelligence and reading comprehension were in the expected direction, but were not significant.

Now we will discuss our findings with regard to the different hypotheses in more detail. Regarding the phonological processing deficit hypothesis, no differences between the dyslexics and CA control groups were found on three phonological processing tasks (synthesis, analysis, and nonword repetition), although nonword reading was certainly impaired in the dyslexics. It should be noted that the mean accuracy percentages on blending and analysis do not indicate a ceiling effect. It may be that at this age, a phonological processing deficit is no longer characteristic of dyslexics. A phonological processing deficit may be bound to a younger age, and, more important, a lower reading age (the mean score of the dyslexics on the classification variable EMT—58.0 words correctly read per minute—equalled a reading age at the end of grade 3). Support for this view may be found in a longitudinal study that showed that, in Dutch, phonological skills and word reading are correlated only in the first stages of reading development (De Jong and Van der Leij 1999). As we will discuss later, the emerging picture seems to be that young dyslexics who perform poorly on a variety of tasks may, over time, move into the normal range on some of these tasks. In fact, in 12-year olds, we found little support for the part of the Phonological-Core Variable-Difference Model that relates to pure phonological processing. Moreover, our findings did not reveal total independence of the phonological core from general intelligence because the garden-variety students performed less well than the dyslexic students on all phonological processing tasks (blending, analysis, and nonword repetition).

The naming deficit hypothesis as a more general deficit was also not supported by our findings because our dyslexics were not impaired on all naming tasks: the twelve-year-olds in this study were normally proficient at the naming of objects and colors. However, as suggested by other authors such as Wolf et al. (in press), a double deficit may be characteristic of a subgroup of dyslexics; that is, the most severely dyslexic subgroup may show all the predicted differences in comparison to a dyslexic subgroup that is less affected. In a secondary analysis, we were able to classify participants into two groups based on whether they had an additional naming deficit apart from their nonword reading deficit. The only difference in performance between these two groups concerned the rapid naming of symbols and colors. Therefore, we can conclude that the most severely affected group has a general naming problem. It may make sense to differentiate subtypes based on these two measures but this topic requires more thorough investigation, especially because we found a relation with articulation speed in the whole group.

We were not able to find support for the hypothesis of a general deficit in working memory. Our findings are more directly comparable with the work of our Dutch colleague and coworker De Jong (1998) than with studies from other countries. Whereas the dyslexic students in De Jong's study also were selected from special schools for primary learning disabled children, they were two to three years younger (10 instead of 12.5 years) than the participants in the current study, and their reading age (on the same word recognition test) was about one year lower (end grade 4 instead of end grade 5). Across these studies, a comparison of the results on the Star Counting Test suggests that the dyslexic students tend to catch up when they grow older, whereas the scores of the CA controls tend to level off with age. This phenomenon also has been noticed by Nicolson and Fawcett (1994) who compared dyslexic groups at the ages of 8, 13, and 17 years, and found "a heartening developmental trend" (p. 224). They mean by this that differences between CA-matched groups tended to decrease over time, on measures for memory, articulation, and processing speed. Of course, only a longitudinal study (which, to our knowledge, has never been done for children aged twelve and over), could provide an answer. Note, however, that Nicolson and Fawcett

(1994) also suggested that the developmental trend toward normal performance may not appear for all skills. In their research, even the 17 year olds with dyslexia still performed poorly on various tests of phonological skill, naming speed, and motor skills, with particular deficits evident in the one-foot-balance and blindfold-balance tasks. In their view, these deficits, when found at an older age, can be interpreted as a more general automatization deficit.

This portion of Nicolson and Fawcett's (1994) results was not confirmed by our findings. We found no differences on tests for speed of processing (simple/choice reaction), or on a motor task (in simple and dual conditions). Although the performance of the dyslexic students on the motor tasks (walking backward and two-board balance) decreased in the dual-task condition (counting backward), the same was true for all other groups as well. We suggest three possible reasons for the discrepancy in findings: differences in the selection of participants, task demands, and the classification of participants.

With respect to selection of the participants, most of the studies mentioned have been carried out in countries where English is the native language. It is known that English orthography is more difficult than Dutch because it has more irregular spelling-sound correspondences. As a consequence, it could well be that participants in our study were less severely reading impaired in an absolute sense. Nonetheless, our participants did meet the traditional criteria for dyslexia, with mean IQs of 113.7 (nonverbal) and 100.5 (verbal), and mean reading delay of about 3.5 years at the age of 12 to 13. In addition, they showed the reading profile that is predicted by the hypotheses of both a phonological recoding deficit (Rack, Snowling, and Olson 1992), and of an automatic decoding deficit (Yap and Van der Leij 1994), a strong discrepancy in word-nonword reading, and a low retrieval speed for overlearned orthographic stimuli like letters and (English) words. Moreover, our participants represented the most severe cases of an entire school district (with a population of about 60,000). To support our claim that our participants accurately represented the dyslexics in our country and that their dyslexia was the most severe we could find, it is important to note that the participants of our study and in the study of De Jong (1998) are very much alike. If you divide reading age according to years of instruction and practice in reading, both groups progressed at about half the normal rate of development.

With respect to the tasks we used in the current study, they were certainly neither too easy nor too difficult, as no ceiling or floor effects were found. Instead, there was wide variation in performance in all groups. The difficulty of the task demands could, however, still be decisive. Returning to the issue of comparisons of studies across orthographies, a study of Landerl, Wimmer, and Frith (1997) is relevant because the Dutch orthography resembles the German orthography more than it does the English. Landerl, Wimmer, and Frith (1997) compared 12-year old dyslexic students in Austria (German orthography) and the United Kingdom (English orthography) with CA- and RA-groups on equivalent tasks in their own language, and concluded that dyslexics from both countries suffered from the same phonological processing deficit. The task they used in that study—which required children to exchange the consonant onsets of two words (boat-fish becomes foat-bish)—was far more complex than the phonological blending, analysis, and nonword repetition tasks that we used. It is possible that dyslexic students in our sample may have been trained in the kind of tasks we presented because practicing the phonological route has become part of the curriculum in the special schools. One possible way to test the phonological processing deficit hypothesis at the age of 12 and over is through a task that taps analysis, blending, and phonological working memory all at once, as in the task of Landerl, Wimmer, and Frith (1997). Although our tasks may not have been demanding enough to reveal a phonological processing deficit, our other tasks seem to have been designed or selected properly. They indicated the expected effects of maturation (RA students showed slower speed in rapid naming, articulation, and simple and choice reaction), general learning abilities (garden-variety students performed more poorly at reading comprehension, working memory tasks, and arithmetic), and educational experience (RA students were at reading level at spelling, reading comprehension, and arithmetic). However, a direct comparison between findings across countries (and orthographies) may be possible only when the tasks used are exactly equivalent. Alternatively, if these cannot be constructed, the structures of covariances between tasks must be analyzed. Thus, the time has come to execute a large-scale international study on the characteristics of developmental dyslexia.

The validity of our classification, based on word recognition and listening comprehension, is supported by the findings that the dyslexic and garden-variety groups performed equally (at or below RA level) on the other reading tasks and spelling, but differed in scores on reading comprehension and verbal IQ (garden-variety below and dyslexics equal to CA level). The hyperlexic group performed slightly better than expected on tasks related to listening comprehension, but otherwise met expectations. That is, they matched the CA group in reading and spelling, and their reading comprehension skill and verbal intelligence was somewhat lower than CA level. To conclude, although the classification into dyslexic and garden-variety groups was confirmed by other findings, the hyperlexic classification was only partially confirmed. However, we suggest that it still may be worthwhile to differentiate hyperlexic readers from the other groups, in light of the fact that the verbal IQ (91) for the hyperlexic group nearly matched the garden-variety level (87) and was much lower than the dyslexic level (101). To support this idea further, it should be noted that the hyperlexic students performed at the expected CA level on all tasks that tap speed, working memory, and automatization.

Two issues remain to be discussed: (1) why did our findings not support most of the hypotheses that relate dyslexia to other variables of cognitive functioning and information processing? and (2) why do our findings differ from the general automatization deficit hypothesis? With regard to the hypotheses within the language domain (phonological processing, naming speed, working memory), we draw the tentative conclusion that, at this age, most differences with chronological peers tend to disappear by means of the combined mechanisms of levelling off in normal performance, and catching up in dyslexic performance. Of course, this hypothesis should be tested in a proper, longitudinal design. In such a study, the way to operationalize the phonological tasks should be reconsidered as well. A phonological processing deficit still may appear at this age when task demands require complex phonological processing, as evidenced by data from the students in the study of Landerl, Wimmer, and Frith (1997), who were only slightly younger.

Regarding the hypothesis of a more general automatization deficit, our interpretation is less straightforward. We failed to find any association between group membership (dyslexics/ CA/RA) and performance on general speed and motor tasks in either simple or dual conditions. Moreover, two recent studies also failed to replicate the results obtained by Nicolson and Fawcett (1994) and Fawcett, Nicolson, and Dean (1996). Wimmer, Mayringer, and Landerl (1998) report that all differences between dyslexics and control participants on various balance tasks disappeared when participants with ADHD were removed from their (Austrian) sample (see also Wimmer, Mayringer, and Raberger 1999). And Stringer and Stanovich

(1998) failed to replicate Nicolson and Fawcett's (1994) findings on a duration estimation task. Weak performance by dyslexics on this task is thought to be critical for the cerebellum hypothesis, which states that both the motor problems and the reading problems in dyslexics stem from improper functioning of the cerebellum. Stringer and Stanovich (1998) found that time duration accounted for no unique variance in reading performance once age and intelligence were controlled for. The only recent study that replicated part of the original findings of Nicolson and Fawcett (1990, 1994) was carried out in our own lab (Yap and Van der Leij 1994), and included a clinical sample of dyslexics. This means that, unless we go back to the files, we cannot rule out that some students may have suffered from ADHD as well. Thus, it could be that the relatively small groups of participants in the Nicolson and Fawcett studies were preselected in some way that influenced their results. In the present research, where we have tried to avoid such selection problems, we were not able to find support for the DAD/CC hypotheses. We concede that there is always the possibility that our motor tasks—walking backward and two-board balance, with and without counting backward and with and without being blindfolded—did not conform to the dual-task paradigm. Perhaps, for example, the single task of walking backward, meant to tap automatic processing, required too much attention because it is such an unusual motor activity. On the other hand, in our measures of speed of processing within the same paradigm, we did not find the expected interaction between group (dyslexics/CA/RA) and condition (simple/choice reaction) either, although the dyslexic, CA, and RA students performed equally well in the simple condition.

To conclude, the findings of our study confirm that dyslexia at the age of twelve to thirteen is related to problems in phonological recoding, in speed of word recognition, and in rapid naming of letters and digits. Thus, our results support the hypothesis of a very specific automatic decoding deficit (Yap and Van der Leij 1993; Van der Leij and Van Daal 1999). Furthermore, our findings suggest that, at least at this age, dyslexic students do not suffer significantly from more general deficits in the domains of phonological processing, naming speed, working memory, and automatization. In our sample, it was the performance of the garden-variety students, rather than that of the dyslexics, that seemed more in line with the predicted characteristics. This finding suggests that, in order for such deficits to be present at this age, pure dyslexia must be surrounded by a more general learning

APPENDIX 1 Distribution of different types of readers across schools. Percentage is based on total study sample.

	Poor Readers			Chronological Age Controls			Reading Age Controls	
	Garden-variety	Dyslexic	Hyperlexic	Normal Profile	Dyslexic Profile	Hyperlexic Profile	Age Controls	Total
Special Education: Retarded Children	8 5.8%	1 0.7%	5 3.6%	1 0.7%				15
Regular Education: Low Vocational Training		8 5.8%	4 2.9%	3 2.2%	1 .7%	5 3.6%		21
Regular Education: Middle Vocational Training		3 2.2%	3 2.2%	12 8.7%	3 2.2%	2 1.4%		23
Special Education: Primary Learning Disabled	5 3.6%	32 23.2%	6 4.3%	17 12.3%	8 5.8%	1 0.7%		69
Primary Education: Grade 4							10 7.2%	10
All Schools Included	13	44	18	33	12	8	10	138

disability such as specific language impairment or lower intelligence. These tantalizing conclusions should be regarded as tentative, and we eagerly await further investigation on this subject.

ACKNOWLEDGMENTS

We thank Wil Pas and Coby Beurkens for their help in constructing, revising, and administering the tests; and for organizing the whole process of data collection, the staffs and teachers of the participating schools for their generous collaboration; Fulco Stiva for the computer programming; and Marion van der Steen, Saskia Stroombergen, Barbara Wessels, Mostafa Habini, and Marga van Engelen for their assistance in the test administrations.

Address for correspondence: Victor van Daal, Free University, Department of Special Education, Van der Boechorststraat 1, 1081 BT Amsterdam, Netherlands, vhp.van.daal@psy.vu.nl; Aryan van der Leij, University of Amsterdam, Department of Education, Wibautstraat 4, 1091 GM Amsterdam, Netherlands, avdleij@educ.uva.nl.

References

Aaron, P. G. 1991. Can reading disabilities be diagnosed without using intelligence tests? *Journal of Learning Disabilities* 24:178–86.

Baddeley, A. D. 1986. *Working Memory*. Oxford, England: Clarendon Press.

Bowers, P. G., and Wolf, M. 1993. Theoretical links between naming speed, precise timing mechanisms and orthographic skill in dyslexia. *Reading and Writing: An Interdisciplinary Journal* 5:69–85.

Brus, B. Th., and Voeten, M. J. M. 1973. Eén-Minuut-Test [One-Minute Test]. Nijmegen (Netherlands): Berkhout.

Caron, C., and Rutter, M. 1991. Comorbidity in child psychopathology: Concepts, issues and research strategies. *Journal of Child Psychology and Psychiatry* 32:1063–80.

De Jong, P. F. 1998. Working memory deficits of reading disabled children. *Journal of Experimental Child Psychology* 70:75–96.

De Jong, P. F., and Das-Smaal, E. A. 1995. Attention and intelligence: The validity of the Star Counting Test. *Journal of Educational Psychology* 87:80–92.

De Jong, P. F., and Van der Leij, A. 1999. Phonological abilities and reading acquisition. *Journal of Educational Psychology* 91:450–76.

De Vos, T. 1992. *Tempo Test Rekenen [Speeded Arithmetic Test]*. Nijmegen (Netherlands): Berkhout.

Denckla, M., and Rudel, R. 1976. Rapid automatized naming (R.A.N.): Dyslexia differentiated from other disabilities. *Neuropsychologia* 14:471–78.

Elbro, C. 1996. Early linguistic abilities and reading development: A review and a hypothesis. *Reading and Writing: An Interdisciplinary Journal* 8:1–33.

Ellis, N. 1981. Visual and name coding in dyslexic children. *Psychological Research* 43:201–18.

Ellis, N., and Large, B. 1987. The development of reading: As you seek so shall you find. *British Journal of Psychology* 78:1–28.

Ellis, N., and Large, B. 1988. The early stages of reading: A longitudinal study. *Applied Cognitive Psychology* 2:47–76.

Fawcett, A. J., and Nicolson, R. I. 1994. Speed of processing, motor skill, automaticity and dyslexia. In *Dyslexia in Children. Multidisciplinary Perspectives*. A. J. Fawcett and R. I. Nicolson, eds. New York: Harvester Wheatsheaf.

Fawcett, A. J., Nicolson, R. I., and Dean, P. 1996. Impaired performance of children with dyslexia on a range of cerebellar tasks. *Annals of Dyslexia* 46:259–83.

Henderson, S. E., and Sugden, D. A. 1992. *Movement Assessment Battery for Children*. Kent, England: The Psychological Corporation Ltd.

Lyon, G. R. 1995. Toward a definition of dyslexia. *Annals of Dyslexia* 45:3–27.

Maussen, L. H. M. 1971. *OTIS Test*. Nijmegen (Netherlands): Berkhout.

McNicol, D. 1972. *A Primer of Signal Detection Theory*. London: George Allen & Unwin Ltd.

Miles, T. R. 1982. *The Bangor Dyslexia Test.*Wisbech, England: Learning Development Aids.

Miles, T. R. 1983. *Dyslexia: The Pattern of Difficulties*. St Albans, England: Granada Publishing Co.

Miles, T. R. 1994. A proposed taxonomy and some consequences. In *Dyslexia in Children. Multidisciplinary Perspectives*. A. J. Fawcett and R. I. Nicolson, eds. New York: Harvester Wheatsheaf.

Miles, T. R., Haslum, M. N., and Wheeler, T. J. 1998. Gender ratio in dyslexia. *Annals of Dyslexia* 48:27–55.

Miles, T. R., and Haslum, M. N. 1986. Dyslexia: Anomaly or normal variation? *Annals of Dyslexia* 36:103–17.

Nicolson, R. I., and Fawcett, A. J. 1990. Automaticity: A new framework for dyslexia research? *Cognition* 30:1–33.

Nicolson, R. I., and Fawcett, A. J. 1994. Comparison of deficit severity across skills: Towards a taxonomy for dyslexia. In *Dyslexia in Children. Multidisciplinary Perspectives*. A. J. Fawcett and R. I. Nicolson, eds. New York: Harvester Wheatsheaf.

Rack, J. P., Snowling, M. J., and Olson, R. K. 1992. The nonword reading deficit in developmental dyslexia: A review. *Reading Research Quarterly* 27:28–53.

Raven, J. C., Court, J. H., and Raven, J. 1979. *Manual for Raven's Progressive Matrices and Vocabulary Scales*. Section I General Overview. London: H.K. Lewis & Co.

Siegel, L. S. 1988. Evidence that IQ scores are irrelevant to the definition and analysis of reading disability. *Canadian Journal of Psychology* 42:202–15.

Siegel, L. S. 1989. I.Q. is irrelevant to the definition of learning disabilities. *Journal of Learning Disabilities* 22:469–78.

Siegel, L. S. 1992. Dyslexics vs. poor readers: Is there a difference? *Journal of Learning Disabilities* 25:618–29.

Smart, D., Sanson, A., and Prior, M. 1996. Connections between reading disability and behavior problems: Testing temporal and causal hypotheses. *Journal of Abnormal Child Psychology* 24:363–83.

Snowling, M. J. *Dyslexia: A Cognitive Developmental Perspective*. Oxford, England: Basil Blackwell Ltd.

Spring, C., and Capps, C. 1974. Encoding speed, rehearsal, and probed recall of dyslexic boys. *Journal of Educational Psychology* 66:780–86.

Stanovich, K. E. 1988. Explaining the differences between the dyslexic and the garden-variety poor reader: The phonological-core variable-difference model. *Journal of Learning Disabilities* 21:590–604.

Stanovich, K. E. 1991. Discrepancy definitions of reading disability: Has intelligence lead us astray? *Reading Research Quarterly* 26:7–29.

Stanovich, K. E., and Siegel, L. S. 1994. Phenotypic performance profile of children with reading disabilities: A regression-based test of the phonological-core variable-difference model. *Journal of Educational Psychology* 56:24–53.

Stringer, R., and Stanovich, K. E. 1998. On the possibility of cerebellar involvement in reading disability. Paper read at the 4th conference of the SSSR, April 1998, San Diego.

Tønnessen, F. E. 1997. How can we best define 'dyslexia'? *Dyslexia* 3:78–92.

Van Daal, V. H. P. In preparation. Learning to read in a foreign language.

Van Daal, V. H. P., and Van der Leij, A. In preparation. Large-scale screening and diagnosis of dyslexia in secondary education.

Van den Bos, K. P. 1996. *BELL96.* Groningen University (Netherlands): Department of Special Education.

Van den Bos, K. P., Lutje Spelberg, H. C., Scheepstra, A. J. M., and De Vries, J. 1994. *De Klepel. Vorm A en B.* Een test voor de leesvaardigheid van pseudowoorden. Verantwoording, handleiding, diagnostiek en behandeling [The Klepel. Form A and B. A test of reading pseudowords]. Nijmegen (Netherlands): Berkhout.

Van der Leij, A. 1987. Special education in the Netherlands. In *Encyclopedia of Special Education, Vol. 2.* C. R. Reynolds and L. Mann, eds. New York: Wiley & Sons.

Van der Leij, A., and Van Daal, V. H. P. 1999. Automaticity, automatization and dyslexia. In *Dyslexia: Advances in Theory and Practice.* I. Austad, I. Lundberg, and F. E. Tønnessen, eds. Dordrecht, Netherlands: Kluwer Academic Publishers.

Van der Leij, A., and Van Daal, V. H. P. In press. Automatization aspects of dyslexia: Speed limitation in word identification, sensitivity to increasing task demands, and orthographic compensation. *Journal of Learning Disabilities.*

Wimmer, H., Mayringer, H., and Landerl, K. 1998. Poor reading: A deficit in skill automatization or a phonological deficit? *Scientific Studies of Reading* 2:321–40.

Wimmer, H., Mayringer, H., and Raberger, Th. 1999. Reading and dual-task balancing: Evidence against the automatization deficit explanation of developmental dyslexia. *Journal of Learning Disabilities* 32:473–78.

Wolf, M., Bowers, P. G., and Biddle, K. in press. Naming-speed process, timing, and reading: A conceptual review. *Journal of Learning Disabilities.*

Yap, R. L., and Van der Leij, A. 1993. Word processing in dyslexics: An automatic decoding deficit? *Reading and Writing: An Interdisciplinary Journal* 5:261–79.

Yap, R. L., and Van der Leij, A. 1994. Word processing in dyslexics: An automatic decoding deficit? In *Dyslexia in Children. Multidisciplinary Perspectives.* A. J. Fawcett and R. I. Nicolson, eds. New York: Harvester Wheatsheaf.

Development of Dyslexic Subgroups: A One-Year Follow Up

Franklin R. Manis

Mark S. Seidenberg

Lynne Stallings

Marc Joanisse

Caroline Bailey

Laurie Freedman

Suzanne Curtin

University of Southern California
Los Angeles, California

Patricia Keating

University of California
Los Angeles, California

There is a consensus that dyslexia is on a continuum with normal reading skill and that dyslexics fall at the low end of the normal range in phonological skills. However, there is still substantial variability in phonological skill among dyslexic children. Recent studies have focused on the high end of the continuum of phonological skills in dyslexics, identifying a "surface" dyslexic, or "delayed" profile in which phonological skills are not out of line with other aspects of word recognition. The present study extended this work to a longitudinal context, and explored differences among subgroups of dyslexics on a battery of component reading skills. Third grade dyslexics (n = 72) were classified into two subgroups, phonological dyslexics and delayed dyslexics, based on comparisons to younger normal readers at the

Annals of Dyslexia, Vol. 49, 1999

same reading level (RL group). The children were tested at two points (in third and fourth grade). The results revealed that the classification of dyslexics produced reliable, stable, and valid groups. About 82 percent of the children remained in the same subgroup category when retested a year later. Phonological dyslexics were lower in phoneme awareness and expressive language. Delayed dyslexics tended to be slower at processing printed letters and words but not at rapid automatic naming of letters, and relied more heavily on phonological recoding in reading for meaning than did phonological dyslexics. A subset of the delayed dyslexics with the traditional "surface dyslexic" pattern (relatively high pseudoword and low exception word reading) was also identified. The surface subgroup resembled the RL group on most measures and was not very stable over one year. The results are discussed in light of current models of dyslexia and recent subgrouping schemes, including the Double-Deficit Hypothesis.

DEVELOPMENT OF DYSLEXIC SUBGROUPS: A ONE-YEAR FOLLOW-UP STUDY

While there is a developing consensus among researchers that dyslexia represents the lower end of a normal distribution of reading skills (e.g., Shaywitz, Escobar, Shaywitz, Fletcher, and Makuch 1992), there is considerable interest in the question of how reading disabled individuals differ among themselves. Differences may occur in underlying cognitive skills as well as in patterns of reading development. Numerous attempts to identify subgroups of dyslexia have been made over the past two decades. This work is important, both to an understanding of the causes of reading failure, and to its prognosis and treatment. Earlier subtyping efforts utilized multivariate statistical methods to sort profiles of performance on large batteries of neuropsychological and educational tasks. This work was disappointing as it failed to reach consensus on a small number of reliable subcategories of dyslexia, and it was not grounded in a theory of how various neuropsychological tasks were related to reading (Fletcher and Morris 1986; Hooper and Willis 1989; Lyon 1985; Satz and Morris 1981; Stanovich 1991). More recent studies have used classification systems that are consistent with current views of the cognitive bases of dyslexia (Castles and Coltheart, 1993; Manis, Seidenberg, Doi, McBride-Chang, and Peterson 1996; Morris, Stuebing, Fletcher, Shaywitz, S. E., Shankweiler, Katz, Francis, and Shaywitz, B. A. 1998; Wolf and Bowers in press). In the present paper, we apply a developmental, connectionist model of reading (Harm and Seidenberg 1999) to the issue of dyslexic subgroups. An important advantage of connectionist models is that the effects of hypothesized cognitive deficits on the reading system can be simulated, leading to interesting proposals about the nature of dyslexic reading deficits.

Three main approaches to dyslexic subgroups have been utilized in recent years. One approach relies on the phonological core hypothesis of dyslexia. According to this view, dyslexic children have poorly developed representations of words and their constituent sounds in memory. Evidence for the phonological core hypothesis is provided by repeated observations that dyslexic children have deficits on nonreading tasks involving the processing of phonological information including measures of phoneme awareness, verbal short-term memory, and rapid naming of symbols (Lyon 1995; Shankweiler, Crain, Katz, Fowler, Liberman, A. M., Brady, Thornton, Lundquist, Dreyer, Fletcher, Stuebing, Shaywitz, S.E., and Shaywitz, B. A. 1995; Stanovich 1988; Wagner and Torgesen 1987). Phonological deficits appear to have a strong genetic basis as well (Castles, Datta, Gayan, and Olson 1999; Olson, Wise, Conners, Rack, and Fulker 1989). These difficulties are thought to have widespread effects on learning to read words and may be manifested as deficits in orthographic knowledge of words at later stages of reading (Ehri 1992; Ehri and Saltmarsh 1996).

Morris et al. (1998) exemplified the phonological core framework in their cluster analytic study of poor reader subgroups. They identified seven subgroups of poor readers and two subgroups of good readers. Two poor reader subgroups were marked by a severe, global deficit across many, primarily language-based, tasks. Five subgroups had more specific deficits involving combinations of four variables: phonological awareness, verbal short-term memory, visual-spatial ability and rate of processing (including rapid automatic naming, or RAN tasks). Phonological deficits were found in four of the five specific subgroups, underlining the importance of phonological skills in reading disability. The fifth subgroup was a rate-deficient group that tended to have reading deficits on measures of reading rate but not accuracy.

In a second approach to subgrouping poor readers, Bowers and Wolf (Bowers and Wolf 1993; Wolf and Bowers in press) have argued that the rate of naming familiar symbols is a source of variation in reading ability that is partially independent of phonological skill. The hypothesis is supported by studies showing that naming speed accounts for reliable variance in reading that is not accounted for by IQ, verbal memory, and phonological awareness (e.g., Badian 1997; Bowers and Wolf 1993; Felton and Brown 1990; Manis, Seidenberg, and Doi 1999). The hypothesis is also supported by the identification of a rate-deficient subgroup in the Morris et al. (1998) cluster analytic study. Bowers and Wolf (Bowers 1995; Wolf and Bowers in press) showed that a deficit in phonological awareness and rapid naming was associated with more severe reading deficits than either deficit alone. Children with isolated rate deficits appeared to have difficulties with fluency and not accuracy of reading words (Bowers 1995; Morris et al. 1998).

Phonological deficits have also figured prominently in a third line of theoretically driven subtyping research that focuses on the processes by which words are recognized (Castles and Coltheart 1993; Castles et al. 1999; Manis et al. 1996; Murphy and Pollatsek 1994; Stanovich, Siegel, and Gottardo 1997). These studies distinguish between two main subgroups of disabled readers. Phonological dyslexics have poor phonological decoding skills (as on pseudoword reading tasks) relative to their word recognition skill (measured typically with an exception word reading task), whereas surface dyslexics show the opposite pattern (poor exception word reading relative to pseudoword pronunciation). In the dual-route model of reading used in some of these studies (q.v., Coltheart, Curtis, Atkins, and Haller 1993), phonological dyslexia is viewed as a deficit in sublexical aspects of reading, and surface dyslexia as a deficit in an independent reading mechanism operating at the lexical (whole word) level . Beginning with a series of case studies (e.g., Coltheart, Masterson, Byng, Prior, and Riddoch 1983; Temple and Marshall 1983) and continuing in several studies with large samples (e.g., Castles and Coltheart 1993; Manis et al. 1996; Stanovich et al. 1997), phonological and surface dyslexia have been shown to be valid and reliable classifications of dyslexic children. For example, phonological and surface dyslexics have been shown to differ in theoretically expected directions on tests of phoneme awareness, verbal short-term memory and orthographic knowledge, as well as in the pattern of their reading errors on words (Castles et al. 1999; Manis et al. 1996; Murphy and Pollatsek 1994; Stanovich et al. 1997).

Two interesting findings have emerged in recent studies of surface and phonological dyslexia. First, it is apparent that most dyslexics are "mixed"; that is, they have deficits in both exception word reading and nonsense word reading. Pure subgroups (children who are normal on one task and deficient on the other) are rare, and as it turns out, appear to have milder reading difficulties (Harm and Seidenberg 1999; Manis et al. 1996; Stanovich et al. 1997). A second finding is that only one of the subgroups appears to be developmentally distinctive. Surface dyslexics do not appear to differ from younger normal readers matched on overall word reading skill on a wide variety of measures, including nonword reading, phonological awareness, verbal short-term memory, orthographic skill and pattern of word mispronunciations (Manis et al. 1996; Stanovich et al. 1997). In contrast, phonological dyslexics are low on several tests of phonological skill, while scoring within or above the range of younger normal readers on orthographic and exception word tasks. Manis et al. (1996) hypothesized that surface dyslexics had delayed, but otherwise normal, word reading development, whereas phonological dyslexics deviated from the normal pattern. Longitudinal data are necessary to test this prediction. Stanovich et al. (1997) suggested that surface dyslexics might have mild phonological difficulties in combination with external environmental factors such as poor learning opportunities or low print exposure.

Castles and Coltheart (1993) interpreted the phonological and surface dyslexic profiles within the dual-route model of reading (e.g., Carr and Pollatsek 1985; Coltheart 1978; Coltheart, Curtis, Atkins, and Haller 1993). In this framework, phonological dyslexics have a deficit in a sublexical procedure that utilizes grapheme-phoneme conversion rules, and surface dyslexics are deficient in a lexical, or whole word recognition procedure by which a reader accesses a storehouse of information about whole word pronunciations.

An alternative to the dual-route model was presented by Harm and Seidenberg (1999). They proposed a comprehensive, developmental account of dyslexic subgroups using a connectionist model originally developed by Seidenberg and McClelland (1989; see also Plaut, McClelland, Seidenberg, and Patterson 1996). In this type of model, the reader gradually forms and strengthens associations between three types of units—orthographic units (which can be instantiated at the single-letter or multi-letter levels), phonological units, and semantic units—within a connectionist network that includes intervening layers of "hidden" units. The orthographic and phonological part of the model has been implemented as a computer simulation which first learns phonology, then is exposed to learning trials with a corpus of 3,123 printed monosyllabic words (Harm and Seidenberg 1999). The model learns to read both regular and exception words, and also acquires the ability to make generalizations to unfamiliar words and pseudowords.

Harm and Seidenberg (1999) and Manis et al. (1996) argued that connectionist models account for two phenomena that the dual-route model does not. First, most dyslexics have deficits on both pseudowords and real words, and differ primarily in the degree of such deficits rather than in some absolute sense; indeed many dyslexics have a "mixed" profile. The connectionist model produces a mixed pattern if the phonological units are damaged, simulating problems with the quality of phonological representations in memory. A slight amount of damage affects primarily pseudoword reading, but greater damage has effects on both pseudowords and exception words (Harm and Seidenberg 1999). The dual-route model accounts for pure cases (who have one deficit but not the other) but not for mixed cases. Secondly, the dual-route model, with its emphasis on grapheme-phoneme conversion, does not take the strong evidence for phonological deficits on nonreading tasks into account, whereas connectionist simulations have the ability to examine explicitly the effects of poor phonological representations on reading.

Harm and Seidenberg also simulated the effects of a variety of deficits in nonphonological processes within the model. What is interesting about these simulation studies is that several deficits tended to produce the delayed but normal pattern characteristic of surface dyslexia. Thus, deficits in the amount of hidden unit resources, deficits in overall learning rate, visual-orthographic deficits, and lowered print exposure all had the same effect, producing a general retardation in the development of orthographic to phonological associations that made the model look like models in the early phases of learning. During early phases, the models generally have learned regular words but have not mastered many of the exception words, much like the surface dyslexic pattern.

The Harm and Seidenberg model leads to an interesting set of predictions about the kinds of reading deficits that should be seen. Dyslexic children should fall into two broad categories: those with phonological deficits and those with delayed but normal reading acquisition. Surface dyslexics may be identifiable but would be a subset of individuals in the general delay category. The delayed group most likely has a heterogeneous set of causes and might be broken down further into subgroups associated with these causes. However, it is difficult to make inferences about causes from concurrent data on test batteries, so caution must be exercised.

How do the two subtyping frameworks reviewed earlier intersect with the connectionist model? Children with deficits in phonological awareness and verbal short-term memory identified by Morris et al. (1998) should tend to fall into the phonological dyslexic category, whereas children with deficits in other types of skills (e.g., visual-spatial ability or low overall cognitive ability) should tend to fall either in the delayed category or the normal reader category. Deficits in processing rate (or in RAN performance) might be found in both the phonological and delayed subgroups, as many children with phonological deficits may have double deficits, and some children with general delays might have mild phonological deficits in combination with slow RAN times. Slow symbol naming may be related to exception word learning, as both tasks involve accessing arbitrary item-specific information from the point of view of the connectionist model (see Manis et al. 1999 for a more extended discussion of RAN within a connectionist model). However, exception word reading deficits in the absence of serious phonological difficulties would tend to place an individual in the delayed dyslexic category. Children with RAN-only deficits might be deficient in reading fluency rather than accuracy, and, therefore, not be identified as poor readers using accuracy-based reading tests (Morris et al. 1998; Wolf and Bowers in press).

In sum, the recent literature on dyslexic subgroups seems to converge on two points: (1) phonological deficits are prominent among dyslexic children and appear to be the most valid classification variables; and (2) there are dyslexic children who do not appear to have core phonological deficits. The latter subgroup seems to fit a developmentally normal but delayed pattern. However, the nature of the cognitive deficit in this group is not clear.

The present study was designed to extend the recent work on dyslexic subgroups by assessing a younger sample of dyslexics that could be followed longitudinally. Dyslexics were divided into two subgroups based on comparisons to younger normal readers matched on word recognition skill (referred to hereafter as the reading level, or RL, comparison group): a phonological subgroup (deficient on phonological awareness or pseudoword reading); and a delayed subgroup (equally delayed in word recognition but not deficient on either of the phonological tasks).

Defining dyslexic subgroups based on a RL comparison group is a straightforward application of Harm and Seidenberg's (1999) simulation studies, as well as previous studies in which dyslexics emerged as either phonologically impaired or delayed in reading. Subgroups defined in this way will not necessarily resemble pure phonological and surface dyslexics; some of the phonological cases defined here would be pure phonological cases, and some of the delayed cases would be expected to have a surface dyslexic profile. Phonological dyslexics in the current scheme have the lowest phonological skill in the sample, and according to the Harm and Seidenberg model, would be expected to have both nonword and exception word reading difficulties, as well as deficits in orthographic knowledge. Delayed dyslexics do not have serious phonological deficits but read at about the same grade level. Therefore, they can be expected to be comparable in exception word and orthographic skills to the phonological group. An important question will be whether the delayed subgroup has anything that distinguishes it from a normalbut delayed pattern. Measures of expressive language, rapid automatic naming, speed of processing printed letters and words, orthographic skill, and phonological coding in reading were administered as a means of further describing the profile of cognitive strengths and weaknesses in the phonological and delayed subgroups. The longitudinal nature of the design allowed us to investigate the stability of the subgroups over a one-year period and to begin to examine directly the deficit versus delay distinction.

METHOD

SUBJECTS

A total of 162 subjects were selected for this study from two cohorts totalling 230 children who were participating in a longitudinal study. Subjects who were not utilized in the present analyses generally had Wechsler Vocabulary scores that were too low, or Woodcock Word Identification scores that did not fit the range proscribed for a particular group. Data from assessments conducted in Fall 1996, 1997, and 1998 are reported in this paper. Normally achieving readers in grades 1, 2, and 3, and dyslexics in grade 3 were nominated by teachers at the outset of the study. After obtaining consent, screening criteria were applied. Children were not included in the study if they were rated by school staff as having limited English proficiency (these ratings were based on interviews with the child by a speech-language therapist). Other exclusionary criteria were severe cognitive or neurological impairments, severe hearing loss, or visual impairments, based on school records.

The dyslexic group consisted of 72 third-grade children with a mean age of 8 years, 6 months (range 7 years, 11 months to 9 years, 4 months). The group was more diverse than a typical dyslexic sample as it included some children with below average expressive language skills. The criteria for inclusion in the group was a scaled score on the WISC-III Vocabulary test (Wechsler 1992) of 7 or higher, and a score at or below the 26th percentile on the Woodcock Reading Mastery Test - Word Identification (Woodcock 1987).

A group of 44 same-age normal readers in the third grade (the CA group) was obtained as well. All were reading at or above the 40th percentile on the Woodcock Word Identification test and had a Vocabulary scaled score of 7 or higher. The mean age was 8;5 (range 7;11 to 9;3).

A total of 46 younger normal readers (the RL groups) were tested in January to March of the same academic years as the dyslexics and the CA group. There were two RL groups, one for comparison to the dyslexics in year 1 of the study, and one for comparison in year 2. The year 1 RL group consisted of 27 first and 6 second graders who had a very similar mean and range of Woodcock Word Identification scores as the dyslexic group. The mean age was 6;9 (range: 6;1 to 7;10). The RL group for year 2 consisted of 18 second graders from the year 1 RL group (who were first graders in year 1) and an additional group of 12 first graders. The mean age of this group was 7;3 (range: 6;1 to 7;11).

The initial identifying information for the subject groups in year 1 (mean and range for Woodcock Word Identification grade equivalent and percentile and WISC-III Vocabulary scores) is shown in table I. The normally achieving reader groups were higher in Vocabulary than the dyslexic group, a fact considered in the analyses described below.

Table I. Mean word identification and vocabulary scores at time 1 (standard deviations in parentheses).

| Subject Groups | Woodcock Word Identification | | WISC-III Vocabulary |
	Grade Equivalent	Percentile	Scaled Score
Dyslexics (n = 72)	2.21 (0.36)	11.69 (7.85)	9.29 (1.80)
Reading Level (RL)			
Comparison Group (n = 33)	2.17 (0.39)	83.55 (13.92)	12.91 (2.82)
Chronological Age (CA)			
Comparison Group (n = 44)	4.07 (0.60)	70.02 (15.81)	10.54 (264)

PROCEDURES

Subjects were run individually over five 30-minute test sessions in 1996 (cohort 1) or 1997 (cohort 2) , and four 30-minute test sessions in 1997 or 1998. All testing was conducted at the schools during normal school hours.

Woodcock Reading Mastery Test - Word Identification. Form G was administered to children as a measure of sight word vocabulary in both years of the study. The items on the test are a representative sample of English words. About 25 percent of the words fit the general criteria for exception words utilized in the present study (for example, the pronunciation violates one or more common spelling-sound correspondences, or represents an orthographically "strange" combination of letters).

Pseudoword Reading. A list of 70 pseudowords was created for the study. The items ranged from simple CVC patterns (*nug*) to patterns with two or more letter clusters (*chome, scridge*). Some two-syllable items were included as well (*stining, namsion*). The items were ordered in difficulty based on pilot data. Children read the items aloud. Testing was discontinued when children made ten consecutive mistakes. The internal consistency reliability (Cronbach's alpha) was 0.96 for year 1. The task was administered in year 2 with a slight reordering of items.

Exception Word Reading. A list of 70 exception words also was created. The items were ordered in difficulty from easiest to hardest based on frequency and grade norms (Adams and Huggins 1986; Carroll, Davies, and Richman 1971) (e.g., *have, people, island, yacht, silhouette*). The task was discontinued when children made six consecutive mistakes. Internal consistency reliability for this task was high (Cronbach's alpha = 0.96).

Phoneme deletion. A task of the type devised by Bruce (1964) was administered in two parts. In part one, subjects repeated a familiar word that was spoken on a tape. The speaker on the tape asked the subject to repeat the word but with a specified part missing such as "snow" without the /s/ and "act" without the /k/. A single phoneme or a blend of two phonemes was deleted from the beginning, middle, or end of the word. There were 25 items, and testing was discontinued if the child made five mistakes in a row. Cronbach's alpha was 0.88. In part two, the items were all pseudowords such as "kimp" without the /m/. There were 15 items, and testing was discontinued if the child made five mistakes in a row. Cronbach's alpha for the pseudowords was 0.84. Scores were combined across the two tasks for the present analyses.

Wechsler Intelligence Scale for Children-III Vocabulary.
The Vocabulary subtest of the WISC-III (Wechsler 1992) was administered. The task required children to define a series of words as best they could.

Clinical Evaluation of Language Fundamentals (CELF) Recalling Sentences.   The Recalling Sentences subtest of the CELF (Semel, Wiig, and Secord 1995) was administered in year 2. Children listened to tape recorded sentences and repeated them back. Sentences gradually increased in length and grammatical complexity as well as word length and difficulty.

Three tasks were presented on laptop computers (Letter Matching, Orthographic Choice, and Semantic Categorization). For each task, the child viewed one or two letter strings or words on the screen and pushed a button to indicate the response. Responses were timed and latency was calculated for correct trials only.

Letter Matching.   This task required children to decide if a string of five letters contained two letters that were the same or not and press a button (gtaVA = "yes"; pNhB = "no"). On some "same" trials, the matching letters were both in the same case (e.g., HntKt) and on others they were alternating case (e.g., gtaVA); therefore, the task required children to process letters to the point of recognition rather than making comparisons strictly on the basis of low-level physical features. Cronbach's alpha for the accuracy scores was .86. The procedure was based on a similar task employed by Bigsby (1988).

Orthographic Choice.   This task required children to view two strings of letters displayed side by side on the screen and decide which item represented a correctly spelled word. They pressed a button to indicate which side of the screen had the correctly spelled item. Half of the items contained at least one exception word (*sponge, spunge*) and half contained two regular words (*sheap, sheep*). All of the foil items were identical phonologically to the correct exemplar items and hence the child could not rely on phonological recoding of the items to recognize the answer. This task taps the ability to recognize specific spellings of words. There were 48 items in all. Six practice trials were given. Cronbach's alpha for the accuracy scores was equal to 0.75, somewhat lower than the other tasks. The task was adapted from a similar measure used by Olson et al. (1989).

Semantic Categorization.   For this task, children saw a printed category displayed on the screen (e.g., a fruit, a part of your body). The category was read aloud by the experimenter. It then disappeared from the screen and was replaced a second later by a word. The children decided if the item was a member of the category or not and pressed a button. There are four types of items that could be presented: actual exemplars (*pear*), alternative exemplars (*peach*), homonym foils (*pair*), and visual foils (*peer*). Only the last three types of items were shown. Subjects had to respond "yes" to alternative exemplars and "no" to foils. The task measures the extent to which subjects rely on phonological recoding when reading words for meaning. Children who are unable to reject homonym foils display evidence of relying on phonological recoding (accepting *pair* because it sounds exactly like *pear*). The visual foils were designed to share as many letters with the actual word (*pear*) as did the homonym foils to control for guessing based on visual similarity. There were sixteen categories and 40 items in all displayed (16 alternative exemplars, and 12 each of homonym foils and visual foils). There were 6 practice trials. Cronbach's alpha for the accuracy data was 0.58. The task was adapted from a similar measure developed by Van Orden for adults (Van Orden 1987) and by Sprenger-Charolles, Siegel, and Bechannec (1998) for children. The stimuli are listed in the Appendix.

Rapid Automatic Naming - Letters.   Children named letters in an array as rapidly as they could and overall time was recorded. In year 1, the version of the RAN used by Torgesen et al. (1997) was presented. There were 36 letters arranged in four rows of 9. Only six unique letters were used (a, c, k, n, s, t), and these letters were ordered randomly and repeated in blocks of six. Two trials of 36 letters were presented. Test/retest reliability was 0.76. In year 2, the original Denckla and Rudel (1976) stimuli were used. There were five unique letters (a, d, s, o, and p) arranged in five rows of ten with random ordering within each block of five. Two trials of 50 letters were presented. Test/retest reliability was 0.78. Speeds in items per second were calculated to permit comparisons across years.

Title Recognition Test.   Children were shown 45 book titles on a sheet and listened as the experimenter read them aloud one at a time. The child then rendered a judgement as to whether the book was a "real" book. They were encouraged to say "I don't know" if a book title was unfamiliar. There were 15 phony book titles. Children were warned that "some titles were not real books" and told not to guess. The total score on the task was the proportion of correct book titles chosen by the child minus the proportion of incorrect titles chosen by the child. This score corrects for guessing in the manner devised by Cunningham and Stanovich (1990). The task was designed to measure the general amount of print exposure for each child. The reliability for hits was .82 (Cronbach's alpha).

RESULTS

Analyses centered on three questions. First, how stable were the classifications of the dyslexics? Second, what cognitive deficits were associated with each subgroup pattern, particularly the delayed pattern? And third, how did the subgroup classification overlap with other leading subtyping schemes such as the phonological/surface dyslexia and double-deficit schemes?

Subgroup Definitions and Stability. Dyslexics were divided into subgroups in the first year of the study, based on the performance of the younger normal readers. For the Pseudoword Reading and Phoneme Deletion tasks, z-scores were created, based on the means and standard deviations for the RL group. Dyslexics were assigned to the phonological dyslexic subgroup ($n = 32$) if their score on either the Phoneme Deletion or Pseudoword Reading task fell at or below –0.9. Dyslexics were assigned to the delayed dyslexic subgroup ($n = 40$) if their score on both Phoneme Deletion and Pseudoword Reading was at or above –0.9. Since the younger normals were equated to the dyslexics on word recognition skill, this procedure results in one subgroup whose phonological skills are considerably lower than expected based on word recognition, and another whose phonological skills are on a par with their word recognition.

The distributions of Phoneme Deletion and Pseudoword Reading scores for year 1 are shown in figures 1 and 2 as a function of Woodcock Word Identification skill for the dyslexic subgroups, the RL group ($n = 37$), and the CA group ($n = 52$). Some data points overlap and are not shown in the graph. The graphs serve to make two important points that are basic to the present study. First, the relation between Word Identification and the phonological measures is strongly linear, consistent with the phonological core hypothesis. Second, there was considerable variability in phonological skill among the dyslexics, with some scoring as high as the CA-matched group. It is this variability that motivates an examination of subgroups of dyslexics. The distributions for the RL group and for the phonological group do not overlap completely, consistent with the definition of the subgroup, whereas the distributions for the delayed and RL group overlap very closely. Means on all tasks given in the first year are shown in table II.

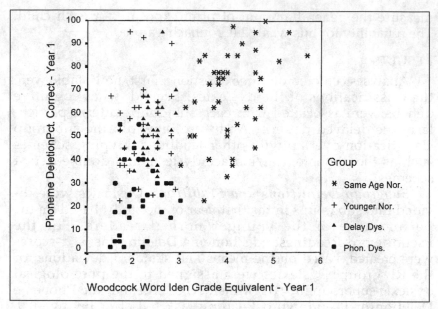

Figure 1.   *Scatterplot of phoneme deletion scores as a function of*
               Woodcock Word Identification grade equivalent scores in
               Year 1.

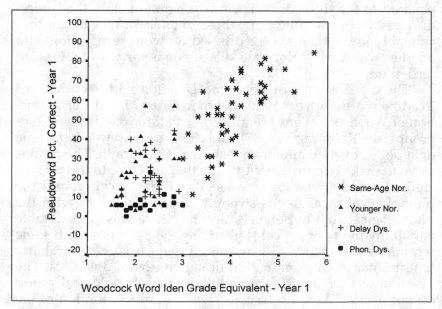

Figure 2.   *Scatterplot of pseudoword reading scores as a function of*
               Woodcock Word Identification grade equivalent scores in
               Year 1.

Table II. Means, standard deviations and group differences for the test variables in year 1.

| | Subject Groups | | | |
| | Dyslexic Subgroups | | Comparison Groups | |
Variables	Phonological (*n* = 32)	Delayed (*n* = 40)	RL Group (*n* = 33)	CA Group (*n* = 44)
Pseudoword Reading (%)	8.6 (6.8)	23.9 (11.0)	23.3 (14.6)	53.1 (17.8)
Phoneme Deletion (%)	23.4 (14.5)	50.8 (12.4)	52.5 (18.6)	67.2 (20.3)
Excep. Word Reading (%)	28.7 (12.4)	32.7 (9.2)	31.3 (12.5)	64.0 (10.4)
Orthographic Choice (%)	66.2 (10.3)	64.6 (9.5)	61.9 (13.2)	77.2 (8.0)
Letter Match (%)	83.6 (9.5)	86.7 (9.5)	82.8 (14.7)	82.6 (11.8)
Letter Match RT (in ms)	2434 (544)	2601 (696)	3055 (702)	2360 (671)
RAN-Letters (items/sec)	1.55 (0.29)	1.59 (0.27)	1.45 (0.24)	1.77 (0.32)

To determine whether the groups were distinct in year 1, a MANOVA was conducted on all of the measures from year 1, comparing phonological and delayed dyslexics and the RL group. The CA group was not included in this analysis as it was clearly superior to the other groups on the defining measures and the critical comparisons involved the groups matched on reading level. The groups differed significantly, $F(16, 170) = 8.32$, $p < .001$ (Pillai's trace, and at the .001 level on Wilks' Lambda and Hotelling's trace). Univariate ANOVAs revealed group differences on Letter Matching RT, Pseudowords, Phoneme Deletion, and Vocabulary scaled score. Post hoc tests (Tukey's test) indicated that the phonological subgroup performed more poorly than both the delayed subgroup and the RL group on Pseudoword Reading (p's < .001) and Phoneme Deletion (p's < .001). The phonological subgroup was lower on both measures. In addition, the phonological and delayed subgroups were lower than the RL group on Wechsler Vocabulary ($p < .05$), suggesting that the group differences on the reading tasks might be mediated by poor oral language ability. However, when Vocabulary was entered as a covariate in the MANOVA, this did not reduce the level of significance of group differences on the other measures. The three groups did not differ from each other on the exception, orthographic choice, and Woodcock tasks, indicating that their level of word-specific orthographic knowledge was comparable. These analyses established that the groups had clear operational definitions in year 1.

Since the Tukey test is conservative, it is possible that it might fail to detect differences that would be of interest. Therefore, t-tests also were conducted for each pairwise group difference among the dyslexics and RL group. The only additional group differences that were found were that both dyslexic subgroups were faster than the RL group on Letter Matching ($p < .01$) and the delayed group was faster than the RL group on RAN-Letters ($p < .05$).

The children's scores one year later on the same tasks, relative to the RL group for year 2 ($n = 57$), were used to classify them again. Of the 26 phonological dyslexics who returned for the second year of the study, 21 were in the same subgroup, which represents 80.8 percent stability. Similarly, of the 32 delayed dyslexics who returned, 27 were in the same subgroup for a stability of 84.4 percent. There were five cases in each group who switched subgroups over the one-year period. Most of these were children whose scores fell near the borderline for the subgroup division.

Correlations among the measures in year 2.   Correlations among the measures given in year 2 are shown in table III for the dyslexic sample. It is important to point out that the current sample of dyslexics is highly selected and has a restricted range on many variables (particularly those relating to word recognition and phonological decoding) which may affect the correlations. Of particular interest was the pattern of relationships among the timed measures. Letter Match RT correlated with Orthographic choice RT, but neither of them correlated with RAN-Letters. Surprisingly, RAN-Letters did not correlate with Orthographic Choice accuracy, although it did with Woodcock Word Identification and Exception Word Reading. The phonological tasks (Phoneme Deletion and Pseudoword Reading) were correlated with each other, and Pseudoword Reading also correlated with word-level tasks such as Woodcock Word Identification, Exception Word Reading, and Semantic Categorization (alternative exemplars). These data indicate that phonological recoding is a very important part of reading words aloud, and silently for meaning among the dyslexic sample. Phoneme Deletion also correlated with Title Recognition. This surprising finding suggests that children with better phoneme awareness have higher print exposure. Title Recognition was

Table III. Correlations between the variables in year 2 (vocabulary is year 1) for dyslexics (n = 72). values over 0.27 are significant at p < .05.

Year 2 Variable	1	2	3	4	5	6	7	8	9	10	11	12	13	14
1. Woodcock Word Iden. Grade Equivalent														
2. Vocab. SS (yr 1)	0.17													
3. CELF Rec. Sent.	0.07	0.33												
4. Pseudoword Reading	0.52	0.14	0.13											
5. Phoneme Deletion	0.27	0.25	0.22	0.38										
6. Excep. Word Reading	0.81	0.10	0.02	0.37	0.01									
7. Ortho. Choice %	0.45	-0.35	-0.17	0.27	-0.10	0.47								
8. Ortho. Choice RT	-0.18	-0.05	-0.19	0.23	0.08	-0.26	-0.09							
9. Letter Match %	-0.12	-0.06	-0.17	0.03	0.10	0.00	0.11	0.24						
10. Letter Match RT	-0.06	-0.03	-0.04	0.25	-0.02	-0.14	0.00	0.40	-0.07					
11. RAN (items/sec.)	0.35	0.15	-0.02	0.11	0.11	0.35	0.05	-0.08	0.08	-0.19				
12. Title Recognition	0.27	0.22	-0.05	0.08	0.29	0.14	0.02	0.03	0.25	-0.26	-0.14			
13. Sem. Cat.-Alt. Ex.	0.56	-0.02	0.16	0.37	-0.03	0.62	0.50	0.04	0.14	0.14	0.11	-0.04		
14. Sem. Cat.-Hom. Foil	0.10	-0.05	-0.15	-0.20	-0.07	0.16	0.08	-0.10	0.03	-0.19	0.00	0.24	0.05	

not correlated with measures of word reading and orthographic skill, as has been the case in past studies with unselected samples of children (e.g., Cunningham and Stanovich 1990). CELF Recalling Sentences correlated with Vocabulary, but not with the phonological tasks, suggesting that it tapped into more general verbal skills rather than specific phonological skills.

Comparisons of the groups in year two.   Analyses of the year 2 data were conducted on the groups as classified in year 1 (including the newly consituted RL group). The CA group had a 100 percent return rate, but five children had fallen below the 40th percentile on the Woodcock and were excluded from analyses.

The first question concerned whether the subgroups' test profiles were similar in years 1 and 2. Mean scores in year 2 on all of the tasks carried over from year 1 are listed in table IV.

Table IV.   Means, standard deviations and group differences for the test variables in year 2.

| | Subject Groups | | | |
| | Dyslexic Subgroups | | Comparison Groups | |
Variables	Phonological (*n* = 26)	Delayed (*n* = 32)	RL Group (*n* = 30)	CA Group (*n* = 39)
Pseudoword Reading (%)	22.3 (13.9)	35.4 (13.3)	39.7 (16.9)	63.4 (17.6)
Phoneme Deletion (%)	33.6 (14.9)	52.5 (13.6)	56.2 (19.2)	71.0 (17.7)
CELF Recalling Sent. SS	7.9 (3.2)	9.8 (2.8)	13.3 (8.9)	11.1 (4.8)
Excep. Word Reading (%)	50.8 (12.0)	49.2 (13.3)	45.4 (13.8)	74.4 (9.5)
Orthographic Choice (%)	72.2 (10.7)	71.9 (8.3)	72.0 (8.9)	82.1 (8.2)
Orthographic Choice RT	2045 (600)	2683 (1573)	2916 (1777)	1927 (472)
Letter Match (%)	85.9 (12.9)	88.2 (11.3)	92.0 (6.0)	91.3 (9.6)
Letter Match RT (in ms)	2139 (540)	2491 (622)	2680 (825)	2208 (629)
RAN-Letters (items/sec)	1.79 (0.29)	1.69 (0.27)	1.56 (0.22)	1.97 (0.30)
Title Recognition Score	.16 (.21)	.26 (.17)	.14 (.15)	.31 (.13)

Additional variables present in the second year were Orthographic Choice Latency, CELF Recalling Sentences scaled score, and Title Recognition Test corrected score. An initial MANOVA conducted on all of the variables is shown in table IV (the CA group was once again excluded from this analysis). There was a significant overall effect of group, $F(32, 86) = 3.189$, $p < .001$. Univariate ANOVAs were significant for CELF Recalling Sentences, Pseudoword Reading, Phoneme Deletion, and Letter Matching RT. Using Tukey post-hoc tests, phonological dyslexics differed from the RL group on the two phonological tasks and CELF Recalling Sentences (p values all less than .002), as well as from the delayed group (p values all less than .05). Thus, in addition to showing stability on the defining measures, phonological dyslexics performed poorly on an additional measure tapping linguistic processes. The fact that CELF Recalling Sentences correlated with Vocabulary but not Phoneme Awareness suggests that it taps into more general expressive language skills. Delayed dyslexics closely resembled the RL group on both phonological tasks, as well as the two measures of word-specific orthographic knowledge (Orthographic Choice and Exception words). The only other difference significant by Tukey post hoc test was that phonological dyslexics were faster than the RL group on the Letter Matching task ($p < .05$).

Planned contrasts using the t-test revealed several additional significant differences. Delayed dyslexics scored lower than the RL group on CELF Recalling Sentences ($p < .05$). Phonological dyslexics were faster on Letter Matching compared to both delayed dyslexics ($p < .05$) and the RL group ($p < .01$), and phonological dyslexics were marginally faster than delayed dyslexics on Orthographic Choice ($p < .06$) and marginally lower on the Title Recognition Test than the delayed dyslexics ($p < .07$). Delayed dyslexics scored higher than the RL group on the Title Recognition Test ($p < .05$). Phonological and delayed dyslexics did not differ on the RAN-Letters task.

The results indicate that the only salient area of difference favoring phonological dyslexics over delayed dyslexics is in the area of rate of processing, but this difference did not extend to the RAN task, limiting the generality of the deficit. There was no evidence that delayed dyslexics had a slower learning rate, based on the fact that they were not falling behind the phonological dyslexics on any of the reading or decoding tasks (e.g., Pseudoword and Exception Word Reading, Woodcock Word Identification, and Orthographic Choice), and indeed made as good or better progress than the phonological group on these tasks (see tables II and IV). In addition, delayed dyslexics did not differ from the RL group on any of these tasks.

Delayed dyslexics by definition had relatively good phonological skills, although they were still below the level of the CA group. It is of interest, therefore, to explore the extent to which they relied on phonology in reading for meaning. Previous studies have shown that reliance on phonology among normal readers increases with reading experience and with increases in decoding skills (e.g., Doctor and Coltheart 1980; Sprenger-Charolles et al. 1998). Delayed dyslexics may show appropriate levels of reliance on phonology for their reading level in keeping with their delayed profile. Alternatively, they may show enhanced reliance on phonological recoding, possibly implicating this as a compensatory mechanism. Reliance on a phonological recoding strategy in reading for meaning was assessed by means of the semantic categorization task. Readers who rely strongly on phonological codes in processing words for meaning are expected to find it difficult to reject a homonym for a word that fits the category prompted (e.g., flower–ROWS) (Sprenger-Charolles et al. 1998; Van Orden 1987).

Results for semantic categorization are shown in table V for all four groups. It is notable that all three groups had considerable difficulty rejecting the homonym foils in comparison to their performance on both the visual foils and the alternative exemplars. The visual foils provide a control for the possibility that dyslexics select homonyms because of a general tendency to process printed words only partially. An ANOVA comparing the phonological, delayed, and RL groups on all three conditions of the semantic decision task revealed significant main effects of group and condition as well as an interaction between group and condition, $F(4, 158) = 3.89$, $p < .01$. Planned contrasts

Table V.   Mean percent correct in each condition of semantic categorization (standard deviations in parentheses).

| | Subject Groups | | | |
| | Dyslexic Subgroups | | Comparison Groups | |
Variables	Phonological	Delayed	RL Group	CA Group
Alternative Exemplars	82.8 (12.3)	86.5 (11.5)	86.8 (8.9)	92.8 (7.4)
Visual Foils	75.7 (19.3)	81.6 (17.5)	87.1 (13.2)	93.8 (8.2)
Homonym Foils	51.8 (14.9)	43.9 (15.1)	54.2 (20.1)	59.5 (18.2)

by *t*-test indicated that the phonological dyslexics had a lower score than the RL group on the visual foils ($p < .025$) and the delayed dyslexics had a lower score than the RL group on the homonym foils, ($p < .05$). Delayed dyslexics showed a trend toward lower scores on the homonym foils than the phonological dyslexics ($p < .06$). The results indicate that phonological dyslexics make more guesses based on visual approximations than the RL group, but that delayed dyslexics showed a stronger tendency to rely on phonological codes when reading for meaning.

Overlap between the current subtyping scheme and other subtyping schemes. The analyses up to this point indicate that, aside from a greater reliance on phonological coding in reading for meaning (see Discussion for further comments), the delayed dyslexics are very similar to the RL group in both years of the study. However, a question that arises is whether there are salient subgroups *within* the general category of delayed dyslexics that have more distinctive cognitive profiles. Two subtyping schemes are relevant to the measures utilized in this study: the phonological/surface distinction and the double-delay scheme. Both schemes are explored below.

Earlier in the paper, it was pointed out that surface dyslexics, who have poor Exception Word Reading and relatively good phonological skills, would fall, by definition, into the delayed subgroup. We identified nine surface dyslexics in year 1 who met the criteria for the delayed subgroup, and in addition, showed an Exception Word Reading *z*-score below zero and a discrepancy of at least .5 standard deviations between Exception Word and Pseudoword Reading. Mean scores on the variables for both years are shown in tables VI and VII.

Six of the eight subjects returning in year 2 were classified as delayed and two were classified as phonological dyslexics. Only two of the surface dyslexics were reclassified as surface dyslexics in year 2. Therefore, this subgroup is very unstable. It is apparent from tables VI and VII that despite their low scores on Exception Word Reading and relatively high scores on Pseudoword Reading in year 1, the surface dyslexics were largely indistinguishable from the RL group in year 2. *T*-tests comparing surface dyslexics in year 2 with phonological dyslexics revealed differences in Pseudoword Reading and Phoneme Deletion favoring the surface dyslexics (p values less than .025) , but no differences in Exception Word Reading, Letter Matching, Orthographic Choice, RAN-letters, and Semantic Categorization. Surface dyslexics were lower than

Table VI.   Means, standard deviations and group differences, including surface dyslexics, for the test variables in year 1.

	Subject Groups			
	Dyslexic Subgroups		Comparison Groups	
Variables	Phonological (n = 32)	Surface (n = 9)	RL Group (n = 33)	CA Group (n = 44)
Pseudoword Reading (%)	8.6 (6.8)	29.5 (8.7)	23.3 (14.6)	53.1 (17.8)
Phoneme Deletion (%)	23.4 (14.5)	42.8 (5.2)	52.5 (18.6)	67.2 (20.3)
Excep. Word Reading (%)	28.7 (12.4)	21.4 (3.8)	31.3 (12.5)	64.0 (10.4)
Orthographic Choice (%)	66.2 (10.3)	59.4 (12.4)	61.9 (13.2)	53.1 (17.8)
Letter Match (%)	83.6 (9.5)	85.4 (8.8)	82.8 (14.7)	82.6 (11.8)
Letter Match RT (in ms)	2434 (544)	2700 (552)	3055 (702)	2360 (671)
RAN-Letters (items/sec)	1.55 (0.29)	1.59 (0.23)	1.45 (0.24)	1.77 (0.32)

the RL group on the homonym foil trials of the Semantic Categorization task ($p < .05$), but did not differ reliably from the RL group on any of the other measures. The most parsimonious interpretation of the data is that the surface group resembles the delayed dyslexic category.

The correspondence between the present subtyping scheme and the double-deficit scheme was explored by classifying subjects into four groups in year 1: (1) low phoneme deletion; (2) slow RAN time; (3) a double deficit; or (4) a deficit on neither task. A cutoff of one standard deviation below the CA group's mean was utilized. Table VIII reveals that most of the phonological dyslexic subgroup fell into either the phonological deficit or double-deficit group. In contrast, delayed subjects either fell into the slow RAN group or the no deficit group, with the majority falling in the no deficit group. By way of comparison, most of the CA subjects were in the no deficit group, although 7 were in the slow RAN group. These data indicate that roughly half of the slow RAN subjects were normal readers on an accuracy measure (the Woodcock Word Identification test), a result which parallels Morris et al.'s (1998) findings.

Table VII. Means, standard deviations and group differences, including surface dyslexics, for the test variables in year 2.

| | Subject Groups | | | |
| | Dyslexic Subgroups | | Comparison Groups | |
Variables	Phonological (n = 26)	Surface (n = 9)	RL Group (n = 30)	CA Group (n = 39)
Pseudoword Reading (%)	22.3 (13.9)	35.0 (15.5)	39.7 (16.9)	63.4 (17.6)
Phoneme Deletion (%)	33.6 (14.9)	55.0 (21.6)	56.2 (19.2)	71.0 (17.7)
CELF Recalling Sent. SS	7.9 (3.2)	10.8 (1.8)	13.3 (8.9)	11.1 (4.8)
Excep. Word Reading (%)	50.8 (12.0)	42.1 (15.4)	45.4 (13.8)	74.4 (9.5)
Orthographic Choice (%)	72.2 (10.7)	68.0 (9.4)	72.0 (8.9)	82.1 (8.2)
Orthographic Choice RT	2045 (600)	2175 (864)	2916 (1777)	1927 (472)
Letter Match (%)	85.9 (12.9)	85.9 (8.7)	92.0 (6.0)	91.3 (9.6)
Letter Match RT (in ms)	2139 (540)	2231 (362)	2680 (825)	2208 (629)
RAN-Letters (items/sec)	1.79 (0.29)	1.71 (.32)	1.56 (0.22)	1.97 (0.30)
Title Recognition Score	.16 (.21)	.21 (.14)	.14 (.15)	.31 (.13)

Table VIII. Correspondence between the phonological and delayed classification and the double deficit classification in year 1.

| | Double Deficit Classification | | | |
Phonological/Delayed Groups	Low Phoneme Awareness	Slow RAN	Double Deficit	No Deficit
Phonological Dyslexics	15	2	10	5
Delayed Dyslexics	0	8	1	31
CA Group	3	7	0	34

DISCUSSION

Previous empirical studies, and the results of connectionist simulations of developmental dyslexia (Harm and Seidenberg 1999), suggest that dyslexic children are heterogeneous but that they might be parsimoniously placed into two general categories: phonological dyslexia, and delayed dyslexia. The goal of the present study was to present a rationale for this subgrouping scheme and to report initial data from an ongoing longitudinal investigation. The study yielded results that shed light on three empirical issues: (1) the stability of the subgroups; (2) the nature of correlated reading and language deficits in the subgroups; and (3) the developmental trend over one year.

To summarize, phonological and delayed dyslexics both showed better than 80 percent stability over one year. They were distinguishable from each other, as well as from younger normal readers, on several tasks. Phonological dyslexics continued to be poor one year later on the classification tasks, and on an additional expressive language task, CELF Recalling Sentences. Delayed dyslexics showed evidence of slow processing of letter-level and orthographic information. Their latencies were comparable to the RL group, who were one and a half years younger on average. Delayed dyslexics also showed evidence of relying more strongly on phonological codes in the Semantic Categorization task. Despite these differences, the overall profile across the test battery resembled that of the RL group, supporting the designation of this subgroup as delayed but normal. The amount of progress on Woodcock Word Identification over one year was roughly comparable for the two subgroups, indicating that delayed dyslexics were not simply learning to read at a slower rate than the phonological dyslexics. If anything, phonological dyslexics made slightly less progress in overall word reading over the year.

The findings on stability are the first to be reported for these particular subgroups of reading difficulty. Longitudinal data reported by Torgesen et al. (1997) are consistent with the present data as they indicated that phonological deficits (e.g., phonological awareness and pseudoword reading) were quite stable in a large sample of dyslexics, although the children in that study were selected for low phonological decoding ability. Studies by Snowling, Goulandris, and Defty (1996) and Manis, Custodio, and Szeszulski (1993) found that phonological difficulties tended to persist and even to become more distinct from word reading skill over a two-year period in unclassified samples of dyslexic children.

A central issue concerns whether the classification scheme presented here provides a clearer understanding of the variability among dyslexic children than other potential subtyping schemes. It is important to remember that any dyslexic classification scheme makes arbitrary distinctions in what is largely a continuous distribution of scores (Castles et al. 1999). Subgrouping is a tool to understand the variability among dyslexics, not an end in itself, and subtyping schemes can change as theories of the cognitive deficits underlying dyslexia evolve. The present scheme was derived from an explicit computational model of developmental dyslexia that produces profiles in simulation studies that resemble the present two subgroups.

We explicitly compared our classification scheme to two of the current approaches, the phonological/surface distinction (e.g., Castles and Coltheart 1993; Manis et al. 1996; Stanovich et al. 1997) and the double-deficit framework (Bowes and Wolf 1993; Wolf and Bowers in press). Surface dyslexics were unstable over the one year of the study, and were found to be a subset of the delayed subgroup who did not show any characteristics that would distinguish them from the larger group. Thus, while it is possible that surface dyslexia has unique distinguishing features, this was not apparent from the tasks given in the present study. The children were also crossclassified as having single or double deficits using Bowers and Wolf's double-deficit framework. The two frameworks overlapped to some extent as many phonological dyslexics were placed in either the double-deficit or single phonological-deficit category. The delayed dyslexics were mostly classified as having no deficit in the Bowers-Wolf scheme, but a few of them had single deficits in naming speed. Half of the children in the slow naming speed group were normal readers. The two approaches thus appear to be applicable to somewhat different populations of poor readers, although there is significant overlap.

This brings us to the most puzzling issue in the study. How do we characterize the delayed dyslexic subgroup? Recall that in the connectionist model, this group may be a hodgepodge of different deficits, ranging from cognitive deficits (visual-orthographic deficits) to experiential problems (low print exposure), but no one profile may dominate enough to produce a distinctive pattern of test performance. It is possible that such a state of affairs existed in the present sample, but this will require in-depth analysis of individual cases. What can be said about the delayed subgroup at present is that they were slow on two visual-orthographic tasks relative to phonological dyslexics, and that they relied to an unusual extent on phonological recoding in the semantic categorization task. While further testing of delayed dyslexics is necessary to determine whether these patterns are indeed robust, some preliminary hypotheses about the cognitive profile we observed can be evaluated.

First, are delayed dyslexics actually phonological dyslexics who have been partially or largely remediated? They fit the overall profile reported in past studies for remediated phonological dyslexics (e.g., Olson, Wise, Johnson, and Ring 1996; Torgesen, Wagner, and Rashotte 1997): relatively good phonological awareness and decoding in the context of continued slow and inaccurate word recognition. However, the intervention histories we obtained from the children's teachers indicate that if anything, the phonological dyslexics received more remediation. Sixteen of the 32 phonological dyslexics received such intervention during the third grade as did 13 of the 40 delayed dyslexics. The intervention most commonly involved 50 minutes, four days a week of small group, phonics-oriented instruction, although some children received less. Therefore, the data do not support the hypothesis that the delayed group was a remediated form of the phonological group.

Second, delayed dyslexics might represent a group of children with mild phonological deficits and low print exposure as proposed by Stanovich et al. (1997) for their sample of surface dyslexics. Delayed dyslexics in our sample clearly did not have low print exposure as measured by the Title Recognition Test, but this test may be somewhat unreliable (Castles et al. in press). Delayed dyslexics did appear to have mild phonological deficits as they were low relative to the CA group but not the RL group. However, delayed dyslexics had about the same degree of impairment as phonological dyslexics on various word reading tasks such as the Woodcock Word Identification, Exception Word Reading, and Orthographic Choice. Therefore, mild phonological deficits *alone* are not sufficient to explain the delayed group's deficit. In addition, because reading and phonological skill are most likely reciprocally related, phonological deficits could be a by-product of slow progress in overall reading.

A third possibility is that delayed dyslexics have inefficient word decoding and recognition as indicated by their slow performance on some tasks, and by the observation that they have learned to rely more strongly on phonological recoding (e.g., in the semantic categorization task). The possibility that at least some delayed dyslexics have not developed rapid and automatic word recognition skills is being explored in the third year of the study.

Finally, it is possible that delayed dyslexics represent a group of poor readers who lag behind good readers (for any of a number of reasons, such as poor preparation for schooling), but who will eventually catch up. Although there was no evidence of catch-up in the present study, the one-year period of study does not provide enough of a time span to really test this hypothesis.

CONCLUSION

There is a great deal of interest in the nature and sources of variability within the dyslexic population. The present study utilized a connectionist model of word reading (Harm and Seidenberg 1999) to explore the variability question. We defined two subgroups of dyslexics on the basis of accuracy-based measures of reading. Phonological dyslexics had deficits in nonword reading and phoneme awareness, in relation to an RL group equated on word recognition, whereas delayed dyslexics had phonological skills on a par with the RL group. The subgroups were found to be moderately stable (82 percent) and to be distinct on a number of theoretically interesting measures. The subgroups showed a different profile of deficits on measures of oral language, orthographic skill, and reliance on phonology in reading for meaning. Phonological dyslexics had isolated deficits in phonology and expressive language, whereas delayed dyslexics resembled the RL group across all reading tasks. The delayed group was not synonymous with general cognitive delays or general deficits in rate of processing. Instead, the data suggest that this subgroup of dyslexics has difficulties with the development of orthographic skills, including the acquisition of rapid, automatic word recognition, and possibly differences in word recognition strategies. The data validate the phonological/delayed distinction proposed by Harm and Seidenberg (1999), and highlight the need to explore the nature and source of the difficulty in delayed dyslexics.

APPENDIX

Semantic Categorization Stimuli

Prompt	Actual Exemplar	Alternative Exemplar	Visual Foil	Homonym Foil
forest animal?	deer	bear	dare	dear
flower?	rose	tulip	rise	rows
part of boat?	sail	mast	soil	sale
number?	four	nine	fur	for
part of face?	nose	eye	note	knows
eyes can do?	stare	blink	store	stair
very hot thing?	sun	fire	sum	son
part of dog?	tail	paw	tile	tale
color?	blue	yellow	blow	blew
holds water?	pail	glass	peel	pale
type of fruit?	pear	peach	peer	pair
Halloween costume?	witch	monster	watch	which

ACKNOWLEDGMENTS

We are grateful to the Long Beach Unified School District, and to the many teachers, principals, and students who participated in the study. We would also like to thank the following people for their help in collecting, scoring, and analyzing data: A. Giraco, S. Kohanbashiri, K. Lindsey, B. Shuford, M. Ichikawa, M. Harm, P. Fang, R. Russell, A. Styskal, K. Willits, Y. LaFontaine, B. Pedersen, J. A. Martino, J. Heley, P. Bolandian, M. Guardiani, L. Cunningham, M. Munoz, C. Kelly, L. Woomer, and L. Gonnerman. Thanks are also extended to A. Fowler and three anonymous reviewers for their comments on an earlier version of the paper. This research was supported by a grant to the first author from the National Institute of Health (HD 29891). The article is based on a paper presented at the 49th Annual Conference of the International Dyslexia Association®, San Francisco, California, November, 1998.

Address for correspondence: Frank Manis, Psychology Department, University of Southern California, Los Angeles, California 90089-1061. E-mail: manis@rcf.usc.edu.

References

Adams, M. J., and Huggins, A. W. F. 1985. The growth of children's sight word vocabulary: A quick test with educational and theoretical implications. *Reading Research Quarterly* 20:262–81.

Badian, N. A. 1997. Dyslexia and the double deficit hypothesis. *Annals of Dyslexia* 47:69–87.

Bowers, P. G. 1995. Tracing symbol naming speed's unique contribution to reading disabilities over time. *Reading and Writing: An Interdisciplinary Journal* 7:189–216.

Bowers, P. G., and Wolf, M. (1993). Theoretical links among naming speed, precise timing mechanisms, and orthographic skill in dyslexia. *Reading and Writing: An Interdisciplinary Journal* 5:69–85.

Carr, T. H., and Pollatsek, A. 1985. Recognizing printed words: A look at current models. In *Reading Research: Advances in Theory and Practice*, Vol V, D. Besner, T. G. Waller, and G. E. MacKinnon, eds. Orlando, FL: Academic Press.

Carroll, Davies, and Richman. 1971. *Word Frequency Book*. American Heritage

Castles, A., and Coltheart, M. 1993. Varieties of developmental dyslexia. *Cognition* 47:149–80.

Castles, A., Datta, H., Gayan, J., and Olson, R. K. 1999. Varieties of developmental reading disorder: Genetic and environmental influences. *Journal of Experimental Child Psychology* 72:73–94.

Coltheart, M. 1978. Lexical access in simple reading tasks. In *Strategies of Information Processing*, G. Underwood, ed. London: Academic Press.

Coltheart, M., Curtis, B., Atkins, P., and Haller, M. 1993. Models of reading aloud: Dual-route and parallel-distributed processing approaches. *Psychological Review* 100:589–608.

Coltheart, M., Masterson, J., Byng, S., Prior, M., and Riddoch, J. 1983. Surface dyslexia. *Quarterly Journal of Experimental Psychology: Learning Memory and Cognition* 18:718–29.

Denckla, M., and Rudel, R. G. 1976. Rapid "automatized" naming (RAN): Dyslexia differentiated from other learning disabilities. *Neuropsychologia* 14:471–79.

Ehri, L. C. 1992. Reconceptualizing the development of sight word reading and its relationship to recoding. In *Reading Acquisition*, P. B. Gough, L. C. Ehri, and R. Treiman, eds. Hillsdale, NJ: Lawrence Erlbaum Associates.

Fletcher, J. M., and Morris, R. 1986. Classification of disabled learners: Beyond exclusionary definitions. In *Handbook of Cognitive, Social and Neuropsychological Apects of Learning Disabilities*, Vol. I, S. Ceci, ed. Hillsdale, NJ: Lawrence Erlbaum Associates.

Harm, M. W., and Seidenberg, M. S. 1999. Phonology, reading and dyslexia: Insights from connectionist models. *Psychological Review*.

Hooper, S. R., and Willis, W. G. 1989. *Learning Disability Subtyping: Neuropsychological Foundations, Conceptual Models and Issues in Clinical Differentiation*. New York: Springer-Verlag.

Lyon, G. R. 1985. Educational validation of learning disability subtypes. In *Neuropsychology of Learning Disabilities: Essentials of Subtype Analysis*, B. R. Rourke, ed. New York: Guilford Press.

Lyon, G. R. (1995). Toward a definition of dyslexia. *Annals of Dyslexia* 45:3–27. *Journal of Experimental Child Psychology* 66:211–35.

Manis, F. R., Seidenberg, M. S., Doi, L. M., McBride-Chang, C., and Peterson, A. 1996. *Cognition* 58:157–95.

Manis, F. R., Custodio, R., and Szeszulski, P. A. 1993. Development of phonological and orthographic skill: A 2-year longitudinal study of dyslexic children. *Journal of Experimental Child Psychology* 56:64–86.

Manis, F. R., Seidenberg, M. S., and Doi, L. M. 1999. See Dick RAN: Rapid naming and the longitudinal prediction of reading subskills in first and second graders. *Scientific Studies of Reading* 3:129–57.

Morris, R. D., Stuebing, K. K., Fletcher, J. M., Shaywitz, S. E., Lyon, G. R., Shankweiler, D. P., Katz, L., Francis, D., and Shaywitz, B. A. 1998. Subtypes of reading disability: Variability around a phonological core. *Journal of Educational Psychology* 90:347–73.

Murphy, L., and Pollatsek, A. 1994. Developmental dyslexia: Heterogeneity without discrete subgroups. *Annals of Dyslexia* 44:120–46.

Olson, R. K., Wise, B., Connors, F., Rack, J., and Fulker, D. 1989. Specific deficits in component reading and language skills: Genetic and environmental influences. *Journal of Learning Disabilities* 22:339–48.

Olson, R. K., Wise, B., Ring, J., and Johnson, M. 1997. Computer-based remedial training in phoneme awareness and phonological decoding: Effects on the post-training development of word recognition. *Scientific Studies of Reading* 1:235–53.

Plaut, D., McClelland, J. L., Seidenberg, M. S., and Patterson, K. 1996. Understanding normal and impaired word reading: Computational principles in quasi-regular domains. *Psychological Review* 103:56–115.

Satz, P., and Morris, R. 1981. Learning disability subtypes: A review. In *Neuropsychological and Cognitive Processes in Reading*, F. J. Pirozzolo and M.C. Wittrock, eds. New York: Academic Press.

Seidenberg, M. S., and McClelland, J. L. 1989. A distributed, developmental model of word recognition and naming. *Psychological Review* 96:523–68.

Semel, E., Wiig, E., and Secord, W. 1995. *Clinical Evaluation of Language Fundamentals*, 3rd ed. San Antonio, TX: Psychological Corporation.

Shankweiler, D., Crain, S., Katz, L., Fowler, A. E., Liberman, A. E., Brady, S. A., Thornton, R., Lundquist, E., Dreyer, L., Fletcher, J. M., Stuebing, K. K., Shaywitz, S. E., and Shaywitz, B. A. 1995. Cognitive profiles of reading disabled children: Comparison of language skills in phonology, morphology and syntax. *Psychological Science* 6:149–56.

Snowling, M. J., Goulandris, N., and Defty, N. 1996. A longitudinal study of reading development in dyslexic children. *Journal of Educational Psychology* 88:653–69.

Stanovich, K. E. 1988. Explaining differences between the dyslexic and the garden-variety poor reader: The phonological-core variable-difference model. *Journal of Learning Disabilities* 21:590–612.

Stanovich, K. E. 1991. Discrepancy definitions of reading disability: Has intelligence led us astray? *Reading Research Quarterly* 26:1–29.

Stanovich, K. E., Siegel, L. S., and Gottardo, A. 1997. Converging evidence for phonological and surface subtypes of reading disability. *Journal of Educational Psychology* 89:114–28.

Temple, C. M., and Marshall, J. C. 1983. A case study of developmental phonological dyslexia. *Bristish Journal of Psychology* 74:517–33.

Torgesen, J. K., Wagner, R. K., Rashotte, C. A., Burgess, S., and Hecht, S. 1997. Contributions of phonological awareness and rapid automatic naming ability to the growth of word-reading skills in second- to fifth-grade children. *Scientific Studies of Reading* 1:161–85.

Van Orden, G. C. 1987. A ROWS is a ROSE: Spelling, sound, and reading. *Memory and Cognition* 15:181–98.

Wagner, R. K., and Torgesen, J. K. 1987. The nature of phonological processing and its causal role in the acquisition of reading skills. *Psychological Bulletin* 101:192–212.

Wechsler, D. A. 1992. *Wechsler Intelligence Scale for Children-III*. San Antonio, TX: Psychological Corporation.

Wolf, M., and Bowers, P. G. in press. The double-deficit hypothesis for the developmental dyslexias. *Journal of Educational Psychology*.

Woodcock, R. W. 1989. *Woodcock Reading Mastery Tests-Revised*. Circle Pines, MN: American Guidance Service.

PART III
Phonology and Spelling

These three papers on the intersection between phonology and spelling among schoolchildren suggest that this is a topic that merits our attention.

In chapter 6, Diane Sawyer, Sally Wade and Jwa Kim analyze a large corpus of spelling errors among 100 schoolchildren (aged 7 to 15 years) diagnosed with dyslexia. The resulting database is important in (mostly) confirming patterns of difficulty among poor readers that can only be inferred from studies of typically developing readers currently available. Among other findings, the study confirms that phonetically confusable letters dominate the errors among both consonants and vowels, with vowels causing the greatest difficulty; this is also true among nondyslexic readers. At the same time, reversals of p, b,and d account for a sizable 7.41 percent of the errors among this dyslexic group (on this, it would be worthwhile to have comparable data on a nondyslexic sample). Although Sawyer et al. report a strong associaton between reading and spelling, as in typical students, this dyslexic sample appears to be unlike poor readerswith regard to sequence of develoment. Previous research on normal readers suggests that phonetic skill in spelling precedes phonetic skill in reading, but in this dyslexic sample there is no consistent advantage for reading or spelling. The paper not only succeeds in convincing us that spelling errors are a useful window on phonology, but will motivate others to make explicit comparisons of the spelling erorrs of children with and without dyslexia.

The second spelling-and-phonology paper, by Yolanda Post and colleagues, converges nicely with he paper by Sawyer et al., asking explicitly about the relationship between reading skill and the identification and spelling of vowels. That paper is important in presenting identification and spelling data on second to fourth graders who span the entire range of reading skill from poor to excellent. Consistent with the results from Sawer et al., Post also finds short front vowels to be particularly problematic, and suggests that phonetic confusability conbributes greatly to the difficulty of the poorest readers.

For chapter 8, C. K. Leong has collected data on a large number of experimental measures in an attempt to define the most important predictors of spelling accuracy among children in grades 4 to 6. His results suggest that rapid and automatic processing of phonological/orthographic information (deciding whether *bloe* or *blog* sounds like a real English word) accounts for 50% of the variation in spelling, with verbal memory accounting for an additional 18%. In this group word specific knowledge added some, but not much additional variation in spelling and even there it was more the ability to recognize that *juice moose* rhymed than that *have cave* did not. These results confirm prior research in demonstrating that acquiring the regularities of spelling is what is critical—not only for reading but for spelling and that discriminating the "outlaws" plays a much more modest role than one might expect.

Spelling Errors as a Window on Variations in Phonological Deficits Among Students with Dyslexia

Diane J. Sawyer, Ph.D.

Middle Tennessee State University
Murfreesboro, Tennessee

Sally Wade, Ph.D.

State University of New York, Geneseo
Geneseo, New York

Jwa K. Kim, Ph.D.

Middle Tennessee State University
Murfreesboro, Tennessee

Characteristics of spelling development and spelling error patterns were examined in 100 schoolchildren (aged 7 to 15 years) previously identified as dyslexic with specific phonological weaknesses. Within a severely restricted range, spelling development generally followed a normal course despite wide individual variation. The group was divided using two different spelling criteria: (1) global spelling stage, and (2) a split based on the number of spelling confusions involving phonetically similar consonants. Comparisons using either criterion led to the conclusion that better spellers are also better readers and are more skilled in phoneme manipulation. Regression analyses suggested that measures of phonemic segmenting and manipulation make

Annals of Dyslexia, Vol. 49, 1999
Copyright© 1999 by The International Dyslexia Association®
ISSN 0736-9387

independent contributions to the acquisition of word reading. Phoneme segmenting explained significant variance only when students were subdivided according to errors in coding confusable consonants. Implications for instruction are considered.

INTRODUCTION

Dyslexia is a condition characterized by extreme difficulty in acquiring reading and spelling. It is presumed to stem from a core deficit that limits the ability to process phonological information. This deficit is observable when tasks requiring phoneme segmentation and manipulation are presented (Lyon 1995). To date, a strong relationship has been established between phonological abilities and reading and spelling (Lundberg, Frost, and Peterson 1988; Rhol and Tunmer 1988; Stuart and Masterson 1992; Treiman 1991; Wagner and Torgesen 1987; Wimmer, Mayringer, and Lander 1998). In the search to understand dyslexia, spelling error patterns have been viewed as a rich source of information about the phonological abilities of students with dyslexia (Bruck 1993; Lenox and Siegel 1998; Moats 1994, 1995; Varnhagen, Varnhagen, and Das 1992). Spelling provides a direct link to students' representation of spoken phonemes in written form and might provide a window on the nature of phonological abilities and deficits that specifically affect students with dyslexia.

At this time, little is known about the pattern of spelling growth among children with phonological dyslexia. Frith (1985) hypothesized that among normally developing readers, spelling acquisition precedes reading acquisition until repeated exposure to irregularly spelled words helps to build the memory for spelling patterns. This pattern of early spelling and reading acquisition was documented in studies of normally developing students (Durkin 1966; Chomsky 1970). However, one might reasonably question the direction of this relationship among students with phonological dyslexia. Spelling is often the most impaired skill in their literacy package. It would be reasonable to assume that the reading phase and spelling stage status of such students might be more closely aligned, reflecting more parallel or simultaneous development in each domain. We were interested in examining the pattern of reading and spelling development and in exploring possible reasons for the depressed development in spelling among students with dyslexia. Specifically, this study examined spelling performance among phonological dyslexics to:

1. Infer the relationship between spelling and reading development.
2. Discern types of errors commonly made.
3. Evaluate relationships among word reading, selected phonological abilities, and spelling behavior across a range of ages and opportunities for instruction (years in school).

METHOD

PARTICIPANTS

One hundred students were drawn from the population of students diagnosed in the Tennessee Center for the Study and Treatment of Dyslexia. The profile of dyslexia applied for purposes of identification in the center may be summarized as follows:

1. Listening Comprehension and IQ are average or above, with spelling and word reading scores at least 15 standard score points lower than listening comprehension and IQ. In addition, phonological analysis and sequencing abilities (segmenting phonemes and manipulating sounds in spoken words) are well below age level expectations.
2. Spelling and word attack (nonsense words) scores are typically at least one-half standard deviation lower than scores associated with reading real words in isolation, some of which may have been learned as whole units.

Prior to assessment in the center, all participants had been labeled in their schools as having a learning disability in reading and/or written language that could not be attributed to intelligence, experience, speech/language, hearing, or vision difficulties. They ranged in age from 7 years 3 months to 15 years 3 months with grade placement ranging from first to eighth. There were 71 males and 29 females. Seventy-nine percent of the sample clustered in the age group 8 to 11 years; 80 percent clustered in grades 2 to 5. This distribution is representative of the population of students identified as dyslexic in the center over a three-year period. Individual full scale IQs ranged from 85 ($n = 1$) to 135 ($n = 1$) with a mean of 100.3 and a standard deviation (SD) of 9.83.

DATA COLLECTION

Raw scores obtained on the day of center diagnosis were recorded for the following tests and subtests:

Weschler Individual Achievement Test (WIAT; Psychological Corporation 1992). On the Basic Reading Subtest, student reads a list of common words. On the Spelling Subtest, student spells a list of common words from dictation.

Developmental Spelling Analysis (DSA; Ganske 1993). Student spells words dictated until passing criteria are not met. Entry list determined by performance on a screen. Each of four lists taps a different level of pattern complexity (for example, c-v-c, c-c-v-c, c-v-c-c, on Letter Name list; c-v-ce, c-v-v-c, c-v-c-c-c, on Within Word list).

Decoding Skills Test (DST; Western Psychological Services 1985)—Subtest II Monosyllable Words (Real). Student reads lists of words grouped by levels of decoding complexity (c-v-c, c-c-v-c, c-v-c-e, c-v-v-c, and so on).

Lindamood Test of Auditory Conceptualization (LAC; Riverside Publishing 1979)—Part III. Student must show the addition, deletion, or transposition of sounds in a nonsense syllable spoken by the examiner. Colored blocks are used.

Test of Awareness of Language Segments (TALS; PRO-ED 1987)—Part C—Words-to-Sounds. Student hears a one-syllable real word which represents the individual sounds using colored blocks.

Woodcock Reading Mastery Test-Revised (WRMT-R; American Guidance Service 1987)—Word Analysis Subtest. Student reads a list of nonsense syllables.

On the day of diagnosis, the center staff also estimated the developmental phase of reading acquisition for each student following criteria outlined in figure 1. Our reading phase checklist is based on the work of Frith (1985; 1986) and Ehri (1994). Within this phase sequence, nonreaders or very beginning readers are judged to be at the logographic phase. A somewhat more skilled reader would be judged to be at the early alphabetic phase and so on. Interrater reliability for assigning students to phases of development using this checklist has consistently reached .90–.95 among several center staff over four years.

LOGOGRAPHIC PHASE
- can segment spoken sentences into words
- can segment spoken words into syllables (*ba-na-na*)
- understands *concept of word* and word boundaries in print
- identifies most alphabet letters by name
- can write most alphabet letters
- can recognize some familiar words
- can recognize rhyming words

NOVICE ALPHABETIC PHASE
- can identify initial sound in spoken words
- can identify final sound in spoken words
- can say the sound associated with most consonants
- can segment spoken words of two or three phonemes (*s-o, t-a-p*)
- can read and spell most initial and final consonants in one-syllable words
- can produce rhyming words

TRANSITION
- can segment spoken words of four or more phonemes (*d-e-s-k, b-l-a-s-t*)
- can manipulate phonemes in words of 3 phonemes
- can distinguish among short vowel sounds in spoken words
- can read and spell consonant blends correctly
- codes a vowel sound in every c-v-c words

MATURE ALPHABETIC PHASE
- can read pseudowords which are of comparable difficulty to real words read (c-v-c; c-c-v-c; c-v-c-c)
- can delete one phoneme from a blend in spoken words
- can distinguish between the short and long vowel sound in spoken words
- can read and spell preconsonant nasals correctly (la*m*p, po*n*d)

TRANSITION
- gaining automaticity of word recognition
- has mastered reading and spelling short vowels in one-syllable words
- has mastered reading and spelling long vowel-silent *e* pattern in one-syllable words
- reads simple two-syllable, closed syllable words

RELATIONAL ORTHOGRAPHIC PHASE
- has mastered reading and spelling high frequency long vowel patterns in one-syllable words
- has mastered reading and spelling *r*-controlled vowel patterns in one-syllable words
- has mastered reading and spelling most common vowel digraphs in one-syllable words
- spells most homophones correctly
- gaining automaticity in reading passages
- spells plurals and inflectional endings correctly (e.g., *s, es, ing*, all pronunciations of ed)

HIERARCHICAL ORTHOGRAPHIC PHASE
- understanding syllable patterns
- learning prefixes, suffixes, and root words
- learning about stressed and unstressed syllable
- learning the conventions of combining syllables
- continuing to gain fluency in reading and writing

Figure 1.   Developmental Reading Phases (after Frith 1985, 1986 and Ehri 1994)

ANALYSIS OF SPELLING ERRORS

Performance on the Developmental Spelling Analysis was examined. Individuals' spelling levels were evaluated and classified according to qualitative stages proposed by Bear, Invernizzi, Templeton, and Johnston (1996). Individual spelling performance was classified into nine stages, based on the dominant pattern observed. Notations on table I show the performance criteria applied in assigning spelling stages and reading phases. A score of 22 out of 25 items correct was considered to be mastery level on any given spelling list. If a score in this range was attained on the initial list administered, the next, more difficult, list provided in the DSA was also administered. Sixty-one students were given only the Letter Name list (one-syllable, short vowel words), 32 students were administered both the Letter Name list and the Within Word list, and 7 students were administered only the Within Word list (with long vowel patterns and complex consonant clusters such as in *steep*, *smoke*, *might*, *bridge*, and *patch*). No student was administered a more advanced list.

Spelling errors were further analyzed according to the system of categories developed by Moats (1995) to describe phonologically inaccurate spellings. This analysis yielded a quantitative description of error types. Two categories of errors, consonant substitutions and vowel substitutions, were further analyzed according to characteristics of speech production. Vowel substitution errors in spelling were also compared to those word reading errors—Decoding Skills Test—which involved an incorrect vowel (Richardson and Dibenedetto 1985).

RESULTS AND DISCUSSION

RELATIONS BETWEEN READING ACQUISITION AND SPELLING ACQUISITION

Table I shows that reading development is extremely restricted but spelling development spans a somewhat broader range. Analysis of word reading accuracy on the DST showed that only three students confidently read words containing short vowels and words containing the final-*e* pattern. None had begun to gain control over tasks associated with the orthographic phase in reading as delineated on the developmental checklist. In the orthographic phase, students begin to evidence ability to adjust expectations regarding letter/sound correspondences. At this

Table I. Classification of participants in terms of Reading Phases (presented in columns) and spelling stages (presented in rows).

Spelling Stages	Reading Phases*					Orthographic	
	Logographic (whole words)	Novice (initial /; (final c)	Alphabetic		Transition (short Vs; c-v-ce)	Relational (r-control v; c-v-c)	Hierarchical (syllable patterns)
			Transition (blends some vowels)	Mature (nasals pseudowords)			
Pre-Literate (marks on page)							
Semi-Phonemic (random letters)		1					
Early Phonemic (initial/final con) (+ 0-4 Letter Name List)	2	10	8	2			
Late Phonemic (vowels in all attempts) (+ 5-12 Letter Name List)	2	12	9	2			
Early Letter Name (blends, pre-con nasals) (+ 12-21 Letter Name List)		7	20	2			
Late Letter Name (All short vowels; 22 + Letter Name List)		1	2	3	2		
Transition (long vowels; + 5-12 Within Word List)		2	4	7			
Morphemic (long vowels; + 12-21 Within Word List)			1	1	1		
Syllabic (22+ Within Word List)				1			
Totals	4	33	44	16	3		

*Note. Characteristics of each reading phase are specified in figure 1.

phase, students can recognize that some spelling patterns, such as vowel teams and vowel-plus-*r*, require a shift in decoding strategy from one-letter/one-sound to recognition that specific pairings of letters, within the context of a word, yield a particular and different sound than does each letter independently. The DST is uniquely designed to tap student recognition of shifts in letter/sound associations as cued by different spelling patterns. Spelling development detailed in table I shows that 25 students confidently spelled short vowels (late letter name stage and beyond) and four were well established in spelling words containing long vowel patterns (morphemic and syllabic stages). Forty-six students were struggling to represent every sound in one-syllable words (semi-phonemic stage through late phonemic stage) while simultaneously struggling to decode consonant elements (novice through transitional alphabetic phase). Forty-five students appear to have generally more advanced skills in spelling than in reading. Twenty-one appear to have had more advanced skills in reading words than spelling words. One-third of all subjects (34) demonstrated essentially parallel development in reading and spelling, the pattern we originally hypothesized. Among phonological dyslexics in this sample, the pattern of association between levels of reading and spelling acquisition appears to be generally inconsistent with the pattern of decoding competence shadowing spelling competence found among normally developing readers (Durkin 1966; Chomsky 1970). Table I also reveals wide individual variations in the developmental progress of reading and spelling abilities within this sample, despite the fact that only high frequency letter-to-sound patterns are considered.

PHONOLOGICAL CHARACTERISTICS OF SPELLING ERRORS

Spelling is the act of encoding speech with letters. To examine the association between spoken units and coding responses, errors exhibited by students in this sample were analyzed. Every word attempted on any spelling list of the Developmental Spelling Analysis (excluding the Screen) was considered.

One hundred students attempted a total of 2863 words appropriate to their developmental status in spelling. Of these, 2025 words (70.7 percent) contained spelling errors. Each error was classified using the categories posed by Moats (1995) for phonologically inaccurate spellings. Each error is classified in only one category. The categories for which errors were noted, and the number of errors noted for each type, are presented in table II. An additional category, Reversals, is also included.

Table II. Phonological coding errors by type, number, and
percent of total errors (2025).

	n	%
[a]Nasals (add/delete/substitute—*m* or *n*)	104	5.14
[b]Substitutes nasal for liquid	4	.04
[c]Liquids (add/delete/substitute—*l* or *r*)	88	4.35
[d]Omitted consonant (excludes *m, n, l, r*)	63	3.11
[e]Substitutes consonants	334	16.49
[f]Adds consonant	62	3.06
[g]Adds final *e*	222	10.96
[h]Substitutes vowel	805	39.75
[i]Omits vowel	45	2.22
[j]Omits final *e*	64	3.16
[k]Incorrect sequence	41	2.02
[l]Substitutes word	35	1.73
[m]Reversal	15	7.41

[a]Nasals = add, delete, or replace *m* or *n* (*stemp* for *steep*; *bop* for *bump*);
[b]Substitution of a nasal for a liquid (*nap* for *lap*); [c]Add, delete, or substitute
l or *r* (*sed* for *slid*); [d]Errors of consonant omission (*sep* for *ship*; *tip* for *trip*);
[e]Substitution of one consonant with another (*jem* for *drum*; *fid* for *fit*);
[f]Adding a consonant (*whent* for *went*; *wripe* for *ripe*); [g]Adding final *e* (*fede* for
fed); [h]Substitution of one vowel with another (*desh* for *dish*); [i]Omission of a
vowel (*cost* for *coast*; *ft* for *fit*); [j]Omission of final *e* (*cap* for *cape*);
[k]Inappropriate sequence of letters (*hlep* for *help*); [l]Substitution of one word for
another (*it* for *chop*); [m]Reversing the form of a letter (*b* for *d* or *p*).

The category containing the greatest proportion of errors
was vowel substitutions (805 errors or 39.75 percent). Collectively, consonant coding errors of substitution or omission
constituted the second largest category and accounted for 32
percent of all errors. Although correctly coding the vowel was
extremely difficult for these students, appropriate coding of the
consonants was only somewhat less problematic. One nonphonological error category also was examined. One hundred
fifty errors (7.4 percent of all coding errors) were associated
with letter reversals (for example, *b/d* and *p/q*). Although these
errors were most evident among students aged 7 to 10 years, 28
percent of all reversal errors were noted among students aged
11 years to 14 years. Phonological coding errors were dominant,

but it is clear that many students with dyslexia also struggle with issues of positional orientation of letters throughout their elementary school years.

DISCERNING PHONOLOGICAL MISPERCEPTIONS

To ascertain the extent to which spelling errors might be associated with misperceptions of spoken sounds, all consonant substitutions not involving liquids or nasals were classified as either (1) possibly related to faulty sound classification (such as confusing *s* and *sh*, *t* and *th*, *j* for *dr*); or (2) as not likely to be associated with distinguishing between sounds (as in *kat* for *cat*; *rat* for *hat*; *qwite* for *quite*, *cut* for *cute*). Many (139) consonant substitutions appeared related to possible misperceptions of similar sounds, making up 41.6 percent of all errors in that category. The consonant errors which involved phonetically confusable letters were then classified according to the voicing and place of articulation of each error and its target (see Moats 1995, p. 5).

The greatest number of these consonant substitution errors (106/139) involved substituting one voiceless consonant letter (e.g., *t*, *s*, *sh*, *c*, *f*) with another. Of these replacements, 86 (81 percent) involved consonants that are articulated in the same or in an immediately adjacent location. For example, the consonants represented by the *t* in *top* and *th* in *with* are articulated immediately adjacent to each other at the front of the mouth: for *t*, air is stopped by the tongue; for *th*, air slips around the tongue. Other letter substitution errors involving same or immediately adjacent places of articulation include *s* for *sh*, *f* for *th*, *c* or *k* for *ch*, *t* for *th*, or *sh* for *ch*, *j* for *ch*. Substitution errors may result if distinctions between the consonant phonemes are not well established, if motor patterns involved in production are not explicitly attended to, and/or if children are imprecise in their execution (i.e., "slushy speech").

Analysis of all 139 possible consonant perception errors in terms of oral production suggests that 93.5 percent involve letters used to code either voiceless consonant sounds in contiguous locations (*s*/*sh*) or voicing contrasts when the place of articulation is identical (*p*/*b*). Coding voiceless consonants that are articulated in immediately adjacent positions appears to be most problematic.

A similar analysis was completed for all 805 vowel substitution errors noted. Substitutions that accounted for 1 percent or more of all the vowel substitutions noted were *e* for / ĭ/ (16.9 percent), *o* for /ŭ/ (9 percent), *i* for /ĕ/ (4 percent), *a* for /ĕ/ (2.9 percent), and *a* for /ŏ/ (1.4 percent). In the judgment of these researchers, it is reasonable to conclude that perhaps only the most frequently occurring substitutions (*e* for / ĭ/; *o* for /ŭ/; perhaps *i* for /ĕ/) may be considered systematic replacements among the students in this study. When the most common substitutions (*e* for / ĭ/, *o* for /ŭ/) are considered in light of place of articulation, they can be interpreted as reflecting confusions rooted in imprecise jaw position while producing or reproducing the vowel sound in the target word (see figure I, page 9 in Moats 1995 for an illustrative chart). Both errors involve a slight dropping of the jaw while retaining similar laxness of tongue. This close proximity for articulation of elements in each pair might explain the prominence of these replacement errors.

The production of different vowel sounds involves very fine coordination of jaw height with tongue tension. Among many students in this study, the associations established between letters that code short vowel sounds and the precise articulation coordinates for each sound may not be reliable. As for consonants, this lack of reliability could be the result of failure to distinguish between sounds articulated in adjacent positions, or the result of imprecise articulation of sounds emanating from adjacent locations. Further investigation is suggested.

READING WORDS CONTAINING "I" AND "U"

To examine the likelihood that similar vowel errors occur in misspellings and misreadings of the same student, we counted and compared all errors noted for spelling /ŭ/ and / ĭ/ on the Letter Name list of the DSA and in reading real monosyllable words on the DST.

On the DSA, 62 students made substitution errors involving *e* for / ĭ/ and 53 made errors substituting *o* for /ŭ/. Among these students, 45.8 percent of the time, *e* was used to code / ĭ/. Similarly, *o* was used to code /ŭ/ 35.1 percent of the time. On the DST (which has two words for each vowel sound), these same students misread one-syllable words containing *i* 14.5 percent of the time and misread words containing *u* 28.3 percent of the time. In reading (unlike spelling) vowels are decoded within the context of other letters that may provide semantic or experiential cues to pronunciation, such as familiar word bodies (the written analogy to spoken rimes). For example, *i* in *hit* could be processed as / ĭt / + /h/ = *hit*. Spelling requires perception of the spoken word, segmentation of its phonemic elements, and translation of each phoneme into a graphemic representation. Accurate spelling of vowel sounds requires much greater reliance on the auditory discrimination of fine differences. These differences might explain the inconsistent pattern of reading/spelling errors associated with the short vowel sound of /ĭ/. However, this does not appear to explain the fairly consistent pattern of difficulty noted for coding the short sound of /ŭ/ in both reading and spelling one-syllable words. Rather, unique issues attendant on auditory discrimination of this phoneme, perhaps also affecting its articulation, must be considered in trying to explain the pattern observed among this sample of students. Further, at the beginning levels of reading and spelling, there are markedly fewer rimes containing /u/ spelled with *u* in comparison to rimes containing /ĕ/, /ĭ/, or /ŏ/ and spelled with those letters. Whereas /ŭ/ is spelled with /u/ in *cup, sun,* and *but,* its spelling in such words as *come, does, love,* and *mother* may be a source of confusion for immature and/or poor spellers. Experience with high-frequency words, in and of itself, must be considered a possible source of decoding and encoding difficulties observed among these students at the beginning stages of reading and spelling. In short, the issue of vowel coding confusions among students in this sample may be explained only partly by possible misperceptions of confusable phonemes.

CHARACTERISTICS OF SUBJECTS WHO DO AND DO NOT MAKE SPELLING ERRORS INVOLVING CONFUSABLE CONSONANT SOUNDS

Twenty-nine students made three or more spelling errors that might be associated with consonant misperceptions. Among the remaining 71 students, 42 made one or two such errors and 29 made none. Since one or two such errors could be due to chance or to attention lapses, children who made 0 to 2 errors were collapsed into a single group to be compared with those who made 3 to 9 such errors.

As evident in table III, students with ≥ 3 consonant coding confusion errors on the DSA performed significantly lower on a variety of measures when compared to students making two or fewer such errors. Differences were significant for test performance on all but sound segmenting (TALS-C). Removing the 29 students who exhibited no errors suggestive of misperceptions in coding consonants had little impact on the overall pattern. Although data are not presented here, differences on these measures were evident when students who made 0 errors were

Table III. Means and standard deviations (SDs) on study measures in dyslexic students grouped by a number of consonant confusion errors in spelling.

Measure	0–2 Errors ($n = 71$)		3–9 Errors ($n = 29$)		F-test
	M	SD	M	SD	df (1,98)
TALS-C	13.07	3.1	12	3.1	2.28
LAC-3	6.3	2.2	5.1	2.4	6.28**
Decoding Skills Test	21.7	11.4	14	11	9.14**
DSA	19.2	10.4	11.9	7.9	11.58**
Word Attack on WRMT-R	13.4	5.6	6.9	5.8	24.61***
WIAT Spelling	18.9	4.9	14.8	5.5	13.69**
WIAT Basic Reading	22.3	6.4	17.5	7.3	10.74**

*p < .01, **p < .001, ***p<.0001

Abbreviations: TALS-C = Test of Awareness of Language Segments-Part C; LAC = Lindamood Test of Auditory Conceptualizaton-Part 3; DSA = Developmental Spelling Analysis; WRMT-R = Woodock Reading Mastery Test-Revised; WIAT = Wcchsler Individual Achievement Test.

compared to those who made 1 to 2 errors. Because students with > 2 consonant coding confusions ranged in age from 7 years, 7 months to 15 years, 3 months, maturation and school experience do not appear to be plausible explanations of the high number of consonant coding confusions.

THE RELATIONSHIP AMONG VARIABLES ASSOCIATED WITH ACHIEVEMENT IN READING AND SPELLING

Correlational analyses were conducted to infer the degree of linear relationship among the variables of interest. These correlations are presented in table IV. Moderate but highly significant correlations were obtained for all achievement variables with the LAC-3 (phoneme sequencing). The TALS-C (phoneme segmenting) bore a modest but significant correlation with performance on only DSA (spelling regular words) and Word Attack (reading nonsense words). Performance on the TALS-C was essentially independent of performance on the LAC-3 ($r = .025$). These two measures of phonological awareness appear to have different implications for reading and spelling achievement

Table IV. Table of correlations.

	TALS-C	LAC-3	DSA	DST	BRd	WSp	WAt
	(n = 100)	(n = 100)	(n = 100)	(n = 100)	(n = 100)	(n = 100)	(n = 100)
IQ	−.025	−.132	−.015	.070	−.185	−.106	−.063
TALS-C		.025	.224*	.159	−.069	.052	.300*
LAC-3			.410***	.421***	.373***	.401***	.423***
DSA				.704***	.662***	.787***	.692***
DST					.690***	.657***	.712***
BRd						.749***	.590***
Wsp							.629***

*p < .05, **p < .001, ***p < .0001

IQ = WISC-R; TALS-C = Test of Awareness of Language Segments-Part C; LAC-3 = Lindamood Test of Auditory Conceptualization - Part 3; DSA = Developmental Spelling Analysis; DST = Decoding Skills Reading Monosyllable (real) words; BRd = Basic Reading Subtest of Weschler Individual Achievement Test; WSp = Spelling subtest of Weschler Individual Achievement Test; WAt = Word Attack subtest of Woodcock Reading Mastery Test-Revised

within this sample of students with a documented deficit in phonological abilities.

PREDICTING READING PERFORMANCE

We next went on to examine the power of selected variables to predict reading on the norm-referenced measure. We were interested to see if the prediction model would yield significantly different results when focus was shifted from the assumption of homogeneity among this sample of students with phonological dyslexia to the assumption of qualitative differences associated with the two criteria used to split the group into two. The means and standard deviations noted for subsets of the group established by clustering students according to these different criteria are presented in table V.

No differences in age, grade, or IQ are apparent across the subgroups. However, significantly better achievement on several measures is apparent among students classified as better spellers, however that classification is made (DSA stages 5 to 9; consonant confusion errors 0 to 2).

Hierarchical regression analyses were conducted to assess the relative contributions on measures arranged along a developmental continuum. Selection of the predictor variables and their

Table V. Means and standard deviations for subgroups derived from analysis of spelling performance along two dimensions: Developmental stages of spelling knowledge and consonant coding errors suggestive of perceptual confusion.

	Spelling Stages		Coding Confusions	
	1-4 (n = 46)	5-9 (n = 54)	3-9[a] (n = 29)	0-2 (n = 71)
Age	10.3	10.5	9.9	10.6
	(2.0)	(1.7)	(1.8)	(1.8)
Grade	3.8	4.2	3.6	4.2
	(1.9)	(1.5)	(1.8)	(1.6)
IQ	99.1	101.4	100.4	100.3
	(9.6)	(10.0)	(11.3)	(9.3)
Reading Phase	2.4	3.2**	2.5	2.9*
	(0.69)	(0.83)	(0.74)	(0.88)
TALS-C	12.2	13.2	12.00	13.1
	(3.2)	(3.0)	(3.1)	(3.1)
LAC-3	5.2	6.6*	5.1	6.3*
	(2.4)	(2.1)	(2.4)	(2.2)
WIAT Rdg	17.7	23.6**	17.5	22.6*
	(5.9)	(6.8)	(7.3)	(6.4)
WIAT Spel	14.3	20.7**	14.8	18.9**
	(3.8)	(4.8)	(5.5)	(4.9)
DST	12.5	25.2**	14.0	21.7*
	(8.7)	(10.9)	(11.0)	(11.4)
DSA	9.3	23.4**	11.9	19.2*
	(4.7)	(9.1)	(7.9)	(10.4)
WAT	8.0	14.3**	7.0	13.4**
	(5.3)	(5.7)	(5.8)	(5.6)
Con Err	2.8	1.1**	4.2	.87**
	(2.1)	(1.2)	(1.5)	(.83)

*$p < .05$; **$p < .0001$

Note. [a]22 students in this group were represented in the spelling 1–4 group.

order of inclusion in the model was based on Frith's phase theory of reading acquisition as well as previous research. For example, although both skills are related to spelling, the ability to segment words into phonemes is generally recognized as an earlier developing ability than is the ability to manipulate phonemes; therefore, segmentation is entered earlier than manipulation. As discussed earlier, previous research has shown that the ability to spell words precedes the ability to read words in typically developing students. Finally, the ability to read and spell words that conform to the one-letter/one-sound pattern, with the exception of consonant digraphs, generally precedes the ability to read and spell words with more complex letter-to-sound patterns such as *plate, lean, leave, believe, weigh, sigh*, and the like (see Bear et al. (1996) for a detailed discussion of the developmental sequence of spelling patterns for encoding and decoding).

Our goal was to examine the power of criterion-referenced measures of elements of Frith's theoretical framework to predict word reading as measured by the WIAT Basic Reading subtest. We hypothesized that the earlier developing phonological skills would account for a greater amount of the variance explained by the model when applied to a subgroup of comparatively poorer spellers, whether relative status was based on spelling stage or consonant coding confusions.

At the outset, we observed an unusual pattern in how TALS-C correlated with reading across subsets of the sample. Scatter plot analysis led to the decision to delete two extreme outlyers (TALS-C scores < 4 but WIAT reading scores > 20). Subsequent regression analyses involving the two different characterizations of spelling abilities within the sample were based on a total N of 98. These results are presented in table VI.

The full model, including TALS-C, LAC-3, DSA, and DST, accounted for the greatest amount of variance in word reading on the WIAT when applied to the two subgroups of qualitatively poorer spellers (65 percent and 77 percent). Substantially less variance was accounted for when applied to the two subgroups of qualitatively better spellers (48 percent and 50 percent). Although all children in this sample qualified as phonological dyslexics, the predictive power of the variables in this model is apparently attenuated in the presence of more accurate coding of confusable consonants as well as in the presence of generally more consistent ability to spell increasingly complex letter-to-sound patterns.

Performance on the DSA accounted for the greatest amount of the total variance in word reading within the total group and within the two clusters of comparatively better spellers. In contrast, among the poorer spellers, decoding words with essentially invariant letter-to-sound correspondences (c-v-c, c-v-ce) on the DST made a substantial contribution (28 percent to 31 percent) to the variance in WIAT reading over and above the

Table VI. Predicting WIAT Basic Reading Scores from four predictor variables in 100 dyslexic students classified according to various spelling criteria. (Regression weights are presented in brackets, semi-partial r^2 in parenthesis.)

Classification	Intercept	Predictor Variables				Variance Accounted for
		TALS-C	LAC-3	DSA	DST	
Total Group (N = 100)	17.34	[-.533] (0.007)	[.136] (.14)	[.259] (.35)	[.268] (.10)	59%
DSA stage 1–4 (n = 44)	12.05	[-.140] (.000)	[-.199] (.11)	[.213] (.26)	[.494] (.28)	65%
DSA stage 5–9 (n = 54)	10.61	[-.70] (-0.056)	[.133] (.05)	[.325] (.31)	[.189] (.07)	48%
Coding confusions >2 (n = 27)	17.15	[.474] (.07)	[-2.05] (.17)	[-.218] (.23)	[.697] (.31)	77%
Coding confusions 0–2 (n = 71)	19.56	[-.545] (.005)	[.054] (.06)	[.299] (.37)	[.187] (.07)	50%

Abbreviations: TALS-C = Test of Awareness of Language Segments-Part C; LAC = Lindamood Testof Auditory Conceptualization-Part 3; DSA = Developmental Spelling Analysis; WRMT-R = Woodcock Reading Mastery Test-Revised; WIAT = Wechsler Individual Achievement Test.

variance accounted for by DSA. This statistical finding supports the importance of the reading development > spelling development, a pattern that was documented among 21 students in the full sample (refer to table I).

Although it consistently loaded into the model first, a substantial contribution by TALS-C was noted only when students were divided according to errors in coding confusable consonants (errors > 2 = 7 percent; 0-2 = 5.6 percent). It is important to note that TALS-C evidenced strong levels of internal consistency (Chronbach Alphas .80–.93) and test-retest reliability (Pearson r's .80–.87), across several age/grade samples in studies associated with its development. When achievement on the WIAT was considered in light of possible phoneme misperceptions, the earlier developing phonological ability explained a significant amount of variance in reading words that typically did not reflect the one-letter/one-sound pattern. In contrast, the contribution of the later developing skill of phoneme manipulation (LAC-3) was strong and fairly stable when the total group (14 percent) and the two characterizations of poorer spellers are considered (11 percent and 17 percent). However, its contribution, when the model is applied to the two different characterizations of better spellers, is substantially diminished but still significant (5 percent and 6 percent). The underlying competencies tapped by these two measures of phonemic awareness appear to support word reading on the WIAT with different degrees of intensity when subgroups of the total sample are considered.

TESTING THE INDEPENDENCE OF THE INDEPENDENT VARIABLES IN THE REGRESSION MODEL

Fairly large differences noted in the contribution of the variables in the regression equations led to the decision to test the independence of each variable from all others in the equation for each subgroup obtained using the two different classifications of spelling status. Tolerance indexes were obtained for each regression analysis computed. Tolerance, an index of independence of each predictor variable from all other predictor variables, can be computed by first developing a regression line to predict each selected predictor variable using all other predictor variables. Then $1-R^2$ of the regression line, the tolerance index, is calculated. A high tolerance index for a given predictor variable denotes a greater degree of independence from all other predictor variables. The resulting estimates of independence are reported in table VII.

The tolerance index clearly shows that TALS-C segmenting performance retains a high degree of independence from all other independent variables in all prediction equations. The amount of variance explained for WIAT word reading by performance on this task is a function of its unique demands rather than its order of entry into the regression model. In contrast, the degree of independence noted for phoneme manipulation (LAC-3) in the model applied to the subgroup representing consonant coding confusions > 2 is substantially reduced when compared to its tolerance index within other subgroups. The tolerance index suggests that among those exhibiting apparently systematic consonant coding confusions, phoneme segmenting is a useful index of the source of their difficulties in acquiring literacy.

A strong interplay of abilities tapped by measures of phoneme manipulation, reading words, and spelling words is suggested in this study. These tasks all tap phonological recoding. The increased degree of independence apparent among these variables when the two subsets of relatively better spellers are considered suggest that the role of phonological recoding, per sé, is reduced among those who are gaining control over the spelling process through the amalgamation of word-specific knowledge. The inferences drawn from the contrasting patterns of independence and interdependence among the predictor variables that we see in table VII are consistent with the theoretical perspective offered by Gough and Wren (1998). They suggest that knowledge of letter/sound correspondences provides the foundation for word reading, that word-specific knowledge builds on this foundation to establish the superstructure of decoding, and that phonemic awareness is the cornerstone of this whole process. The tolerance indexes associated with estimates of these abilities among better and poorer spellers in this study appear to reflect precisely these interactions in the course of development.

Table VII. Index of independence of each variable from all others within each classification category (tolerance).

Classification	TALS-C	LAC-3	DSA	DST
Total Group	.95	.81	.49	.49
Spelling Stages 1–4	.97	.75	.58	.51
Spelling Stages 5–9	.95	.91	.69	.72
Coding Confusions >2	.96	.70	.31	.27
Coding Confusions 0–2	.90	.89	.57	.61

CONCLUSIONS

Students in this study exhibited a pattern of development in the acquisition of knowledge about spelling that is consistent with the pattern of normal development. However, the expected pattern of reading acquisition shadowing spelling development was apparent for only 45 percent of the sample. Individual variation in development of reading and spelling within this sample was greater than expected.

Degrees of delayed development within a normal pattern of spelling acquisition among these 100 students suggest individual variation in the impact of phonological deficits on spelling. Twenty-nine percent of the total group evidenced a pattern of consonant coding errors that may be linked to poor phoneme differentiation and/or production. It is reasonable to conclude that differences in knowledge about spelling as well as differences in the ability to code confusable sounds may be important intragroup variables to consider in future research aimed at more fully specifying the phonological core deficit among students with dyslexia. A recent longitudinal study reported by Snowling, Goulandris, and Defty (1998) lends support to this call for attention to intragroup variation in developing a better understanding of dyslexia.

IMPLICATIONS

Results of this study suggest the need to differentiate among characteristics that might be transient (developmental) and those which might be reflecting a true disorder. Eleven of the 29 students revealing apparently systematic consonant coding errors (>2) ranged in age from 10 to 15. Among these students, phonological recoding difficulties are probably not developmental. The same approach to instructional intervention for all 29 students would probably yield better outcomes for many of the younger children whose difficulties may well be the consequence of a developmental lag. Among the 11 older students, however, intervention that specifically targets the formation of sounds for articulation, in association with letter-sound pairings, might be crucial for their future success in decoding and spelling.

Similarly, the inference of a growing foundation of automatic letter/sound associations among the 54 students at spelling stages 5 to 9 also suggests the need to differentiate among currently available instructional programs for students with dyslexia. Some programs specifically developed to instruct severely disabled readers are highly repetitive, begin all students at the same point, and focus on the one-letter/one-sound pattern over an extended period of time. A more complex pattern, typically c-v-ce, is not introduced until the previous pattern is mastered. Such programs are, perhaps, most appropriate for students whose limited skills place them at the early through late phonemic stages (see table 1), as well as for those who are so severely impaired that generalizations about letter/sound correspondences are exceptionally difficult to establish; for example, the child who can decode "mit" and "ten," but not "mitten." However, students who have already established a good foundation at the late letter name stage might benefit more from a program which offers greater opportunities to acquire word-specific knowledge that can generalize to a broader spectrum of vocabulary. Programs that promote learning more complex phonograms through inductive or deductive reasoning, as in the use of word sorts, may be more efficient in promoting growth in both decoding and encoding among students at these stages of development.

The patterns of association observed in this study tend to suggest that the diagnosis of dyslexia does not, in itself, provide sufficient information to specifically guide intervention for the diverse group who bear this label. Defining differences among students with dyslexia, within research samples, might serve to further our understanding of this complex disability and might help to explain the fact that different studies of the contribution of phonological variables among poor readers can yield discrepant results. Perhaps the question of identifying subtypes of dyslexia, which has received considerable attention recently, is less important at this stage in our understanding of dyslexia than is the question of subsets of students with phonological dyslexia, and how differences among them might inform both identification and intervention.

ACKNOWLEDGMENTS

The authors wish to express their gratitude to Cynthia Minnis, Donna Ritenour, and Caresa Young for their invaluable contributions during the data gathering phase of this study.

Address for correspondence: Diane J. Sawyer, Tennessee Center for the Study and Treatment of Dyslexia, 610 W. College, Suite 120, Murfreesboro, Tennessee 37130.

References

Bear, D. R., Invernizzi, M., Templeton, S., and Johnston, F. 1996. *Words Their Way*. Columbus, OH: Prentice-Hall Publishers, Inc.

Bruck, M. 1993. Component spelling skills of college students with childhood diagnosis of dyslexia. *Learning Disabilities Quarterly* 16:171–84.

Chomsky, C. 1970. Write first, read later. *Childhood Education* 47:296–99.

Durkin, D. 1966. *Children Who Read Early*. New York: Teacher's College Press.

Ehri, L. 1994. Development of the ability to read words: Update. In *Theoretical Models and Processes of Reading*, 4th ed., R. Ruddell, M. Ruddell, and H. Singer, eds. Newark, DE: International Reading Association.

Frith, U. 1985. Beneath the surface of developmental dyslexia. In *Surface Dyslexia*, K. Patterson, M. Coltheart, and J. Marshall, eds. London: Lawrence Erlbaum Associates, Inc. Publishers.

Ganske, K. 1993. *Developmental Spelling Analysis*. Barboursville, VA: Author.

Gough, P. B., and Wren, S. 1998. Decomposition of decoding. In *Reading and Spelling Development and Disorders*, C. Hulme and R. M. Joshi, eds. Mahwah, NJ: Lawrence Erlbaum Associates, Inc. Publishers.

Lennox, C., and Siegel, L. S. 1998. Phonological and orthographic processes in good and poor spellers. In *Reading and Spelling: Development and Disorders*, C. Hulme and R. M. Joshi, eds. Mahwah, NJ: Lawrence Erlbaum Associates, Inc., Publishers.

Lindamood, C. H., and Lindamood, P. C. 1979. *Lindamood Auditory Conceptualization Test*. Chicago: Riverside Publishing.

Lundberg, I., Frost, J., and Petersen, O. P. 1988. Effects of an extensive program for stimulating phonological awareness in preschool children. *Reading Research Quarterly* 23:263–84.

Lyon, G. R. 1995. Toward a definition of dyslexia. *Annals of Dyslexia* 45:3–27.

Moats, L. 1995. *Spelling Development Disability and Instruction*. Baltimore: York Press.

Moats, L. 1994. Assessment of spelling in learning disabilities research. In *Frames of Reference for the Assessment of Learning Disabilities: New Views on Measurement Issues*, G. R. Lyon, ed. Baltimore, MD: Paul H Brookes Publishing Co.

Psychological Corporation. 1992. *Wechsler Individual Achievement Test*. San Antonio, TX: Harcourt Brace and Co.

Richardson, E., and Dibenedetto, B. 1985. *Decoding Skills Test*. Los Angeles: Western Psychological Services.

Rohl, M., and Tunmer, W. E. 1988. Phonemic segmentation skill and spelling acquisition. *Applied Psycholinguistics* 9:335–50.

Sawyer, D. J. 1987. *Test of Awareness of Language Segments*. Austin, TX: PRO-ED.

Snowling, M., Goulandris, N., and Defty N. 1998. Development and variation in developmental dyslexia. In *Reading and Spelling Development and Disorders*, C. Hulme and R. M. Joshi, eds. Mahwah, NJ: Lawrence Erlbaum Associates, Inc. Publishers.

Stuart, M., and Masterson, J. 1992. Patterns of reading and spelling in 10 year old children related to prereading phonological abilities. *Academic Press* 54:168–87.

Treiman, R. 1991. Phonological awareness and its roles in learning to read and spell. In *Phonological Awareness in Reading: The Evolution of Current Perspectives*, B. Fox and D. J. Sawyer, eds. New York: Springer-Verlag.

Varnhagen, C., Varnhagen, S., and Das, J. P. 1992. Analysis of cognitive processes and spelling errors of average ability and reading disabled children. *Reading Psychology: An International Quarterly* 13:217–39.

Wagner, R., and Torgesen, J. 1987. The nature of phonological processing and its causal role in the acquisition of reading skills. *Psychological Bulletin* 101:192–212.

Wimmer, H., Magringer, H., and Lander, K. 1998. Poor reading: A deficit in skill automatization or a phonological deficit? *Scientific Studies of Reading* 2(4):321–40.

Woodcock, R. W. 1987. *Woodcock Reading Mastery Tests* (rev. ed.). Circle Pines, MN: American Guidance Service.

Identification of Vowel Speech Sounds by Skilled and Less Skilled Readers and the Relation with Vowel Spelling

Yolanda V. Post

Neuhaus Education Center
Bellaire, Texas

Paul R. Swank

University of Houston
Houston, Texas

Merrill Hiscock

University of Houston
Houston, Texas

Anne E. Fowler

Haskins Laboratories
New Haven, Connecticut

Reading and spelling errors of vowels are reported in many studies (Bryson and Werker 1989; Fowler, Liberman, and Shankweiler 1977; Fowler, Shankweiler, and Liberman 1979; Goswami 1993; Landerl, Wimmer, and Frith 1997; Shankweiler and Liberman 1972). The present study tested the hypothesis that spelling errors involving vowels

Annals of Dyslexia, Vol. 49, 1999
ISSN 0736-9387

are linked to difficulties in vowel perception. Second to fourth graders (total n = 155) *were divided into five groups according to reading skill and were tested on a variety of measures involving vowel identification, vowel discrimination, and vowel spelling. Despite little difficulty on the vowel discrimination tasks, participants made many errors on the vowel identification measures. Vowel identification errors were linearly associated with reading skill with least skilled readers having significantly more difficulty with stressed "short" vowels as in* dip *than with stressed "long" vowels as in* deep, *presented in identical contexts. Vowel identification errors were also associated with vowel spelling errors. It is hypothesized that errors in vowel spelling may relate to weak access to the phoneme at the oral language level and may indicate a lack of constancy in the representation of vowels by less skilled readers. Weaknesses in vowel perception can be detected with a simple vowel identification test in which phonological similarity of test items is used as linguistic manipulation, and where phonemes must be identified based on presentation of a single test item in a forced choice format.*

INTRODUCTION

Reading and spelling are dependent on phonological processing of speech sounds and syllables. The obligatory nature of phonological processing in reading has been demonstrated for alphabetic orthographies (Berent and Perfetti 1995; Van Orden, Pennington, and Stone 1990), for orthographies that use partially overlapping alphabets (Lukatela and Turvey 1998), and for logographic writing systems (Perfetti and Zhang 1995; Tan, Hoosain, and Siok 1996) (see Coltheart 1978 for a different view). However, the phonological processing necessary for reading and spelling appears not to be as immediate or precise in persons who manifest reading and spelling disabilities (e.g., Rubin and Liberman 1983). Such persons show deficits in phonemic awareness (Bradley and Bryant 1978; Lundberg, Olofsson, and Wall 1980; Morais 1987) and in underlyng perceptual abilities (Brady 1997; Fowler 1991; McBride-Chang 1995) such as discrimination of speech sounds (Godfrey, Syrdal-Lasky, Millay, and Knox 1981; Kraus et al. 1996; Reed 1989). They also have difficulties with pronunciation (Apthorp 1995; Lieberman et al. 1985), and show slow access to the lexicon (Bowers and Wolf 1993). If the underlying linguistic ability to discriminate speech sounds is directly linked to reading and spelling acquisition, it is important to determine which linguistic segments are perceived less accurately by children with reading and spelling problems, in what context a segment is less well perceived, and what the consequences are for the spelling of these segments.

READING AND SPELLING ACCURACY OF VOWELS

Many reading and spelling studies have noted that readers have difficulties with vowels (Bryson and Werker 1989; Fowler, Liberman, and Shankweiler 1977; Fowler, Shankweiler, and Liberman 1979; Goswami 1993; Landerl, Wimmer, and Frith 1997; Shankweiler and Liberman 1972). In the study by Shankweiler and Liberman (1972) vowel reading errors were twice as frequent as initial and final consonant reading errors combined, whereas almost no vowel errors were made in oral speech repetition. Vowels were equally difficult to read in initial, medial, and final position in one-syllable words (Fowler, Liberman, and Shankweiler 1977), independent of word or nonword status (Fowler, Shankweiler, and Liberman 1979). In a reading study by Ehri, Wilce, and Taylor (1987), children had difficulty with the categorization of the short vowel in CVC[1] words, especially when the following consonant was the velar stop consonant /g/ or /k/.

The fact that readers in English show more difficulties with the reading and spelling of vowels than consonants could be an artifact of the consistency with which the vowel is spelled in English (Berndt, D'Autrechy, and Reggia 1994). German is considered to be a language possessing the same word roots as English but with a more consistent orthography. In a study in which German words, English words, and pseudowords were equated, English children made many vowel errors and misread real words for pseudowords, whereas the German children did not make such errors (Frith, Wimmer, and Landerl 1998).

Although variations in orthographic regularity affect how fast children become aware of the phonological idiosyncrasies in their language (Wolf et al. 1994; Zinna, Liberman, and Shankweiler 1986), vowel reading and spelling errors also occur in some orthographically consistent languages such as Finnish. Finnish persons with a reading impairment show a particular difficulty in mapping letters onto (phonetically) short and long vowels (Lyytinen et al. 1995) in consistently spelled words.

---

[1]Here and elsewhere, CVC refers to Consonant-Vowel-Consonant; CV for Consonant-Vowel, etc.

Hence, difficulties with reading English vowels may reflect more than the fact that there are many possible spelling mappings for any given vowel phoneme.

Why is it so difficult for less skilled readers of English to remember the accurate spelling of vowels? Writing in an alphabetic orthography does not merely transcribe speech sounds. It reveals the underlying speech structure and forces the writer into conscious awareness of the relation between speech sounds and written symbols. As expressed by Olson (1996), "to learn to read any script is, at base, to find or detect aspects of one's own implicit linguistic structure that can map onto or be represented by elements of that script" (p. 93). In addition, Olson (1996) stresses that "such awareness is not just implicit linguistic knowledge brought to consciousness but rather a matter of sorting sounds into the categories provided by the script" (p. 95). If, as this view suggests, learning to read in an alphabetic writing system requires the discovery of language structure, the errors in reading or spelling vowels may imply a more fundamental underlying oral language deficit with respect to vowels.

THE PERCEPTION OF VOWELS

Deficits in perceiving vowels have only been observed in persons with reading deficits when natural speech is altered in some way (Apthorp 1995; Brady, Shankweiler, and Mann 1983; Bryson and Werker 1989; Lieberman et al. 1985). For example, in the Lieberman et al. (1985) study, adult dyslexics had so much difficulty when asked to repeat synthesized vowels varying only in formant frequency that they were retested, with the same results. Despite such reports, there has been little follow-up research on the perception of vowels among persons with reading deficits.

In order to assign a speech sound to a phoneme, the relational properties of speech segments must be taken into account because phonemes are realized differently, depending on position in the word (Jakobson and Halle 1968) and on surrounding phonemes (Denes and Pinson 1963). To cite just one example, English vowels are lengthened dramatically before voiced stop consonants. According to Chen (1970), in CVC words, vowel duration of the /ă/[2] before the voiceless /p/, /t/, /k/, and /ŋk/ is 155, 170, 158, and 165 ms, respectively, whereas before

---

[2]We remind readers that the so-called long and short vowels of modern English differ less in length than they do in laxity, vowel height, and presence or absence of diphthongs. Because no single phonetic feature reliably distinguishes the two groups of vowels (e.g., the /ă/ is arguably both long and

the voiced /b/, /d/, /g/, and /ŋg/ the vowel lasts twice as long, at 300, 308, 357, and 288 ms, respectively. The voiced stop consonant extends its influence through the nasal to the preceding vowel. For example, the short vowel /ĕ/ located before the /d/ in *send* lasts 147 ms, but before the unvoiced /t/ in *sent* lasts only 123 ms. It should be noted that the voiced stop consonant does not assert this influence when it belongs to the following syllable. The vowel /ă/ in *ample* and *amble* were of the same duration, 148 and 147 ms, respectively, according to Chen's measurements.

Thus, the extent to which vowel duration varies in English is highly dependent on the immediate context in which the vowel is uttered. Vowel length variation contributes to the discrimination between voiced and voiceless consonants. The longer the closure time for voiceless consonants, the shorter the vowel length, and vice versa, perhaps to "assure a relatively even flow of syllables" (Chen 1970, p. 145). Vowels also differ in sound quality depending on consonantal context. For instance, vowel formants adapt to the formants of preceding and following consonants (Denes and Pinson 1963; Olive, Greenwood, and Coleman 1993).

If vowels vary in segment duration and sound quality depending on linguistic context, the establishment of a speech sound concept that entails such allophonic variation becomes very important. There is considerable evidence that the speaker/listener is biologically equipped to extract and use such speech sounds at an implicit level; indeed our speech processes are equipped with the flexibility and adaptability not only to abstract across the different realizations of a speech sound within a speaker but also to do so across speakers and dialects (Nygaard and Pisoni 1998). This feat is accomplished in the act of listening without conscious awareness of the phonemic units (Liberman, Cooper, Shankweiler, and Studdert-Kennedy 1967), and is referred to by such terms as "perceptual invariance" (Kent 1997) or "perceptual constancy" (Lively and Pisoni 1997). In contrast, the explicit awareness of these same

---

tense unlike other short vowels), and because readers are more likely to be familiar with the orthographic terms long and short, we have elected to use the conventional diacritic markers used in dictionaries. Listed here are the vowel phonemes (presented in slashes) and a keyword for each: /ĭ/ as in *bit*; /ē/ as in *beat*; /ĕ/ as in *bet*; /ā/ as in *bait*; /ŭ/ as in *but*; /ū/ as in the first syllable of *beauty*; /ŏ/ as in *pot*; /ō/ as in *boat*; and /ă/ as in *bat*. The associated phonetic representations are presented in brackets in table I.

phonemes involves the cognitive ability to abstract, classify, and manipulate segments of spoken language (Liberman 1973, 1978). This ability is referred to as "phoneme identity" (Byrne and Fielding-Barnsley 1990; Murray 1998). The ability to partition an utterance into its component phonemes (Diehl 1986; Scott and Cutler 1984) depends on achievement of perceptual constancy and is referred to as phoneme segmentation in reading research (Høien et al. 1995; Lundberg, Frost, and Petersen 1988).

A letter can be considered a conceptual model that unites the different realizations of a speech sound under a single, visual label (Olson 1996). Indeed, there is some evidence that in skilled readers this conceptual model of speech (orthography) comes to dominate the phonetic perception of a word such that a literate person "hears" words through their representation in writing. They no longer notice, for instance, separate speech segments when the orthography ignores segmentation such as the /ks/ in ox (Moats 1994). In persons with a reading deficit, less coactivation between linguistic and orthographic representation is observed (Landerl, Frith, and Wimmer 1996), perhaps because they have never established secure phoneme identity. In order to use the orthographic component as a model for speech representation, perception of a speech sound may gradually changes with growth in literacy, allowing for greater reading and spelling efficiency (Ehri and Saltmarsh 1995, but see Wimmer, Mayringer, and Landerl 1998). Establishing a consistent, abstracted identity for a vowel, irrespective of consonantal context, would facilitate the cognitive ability of linking a speech segment with the correct spelling of such a segment.

HYPOTHESIS AND DESIGN

The present study tested the hypothesis that spelling errors involving vowels are linked to vowel perception deficits, following up on a prior study suggesting an association between vowel perception and reading skill. In that study (Post, Foorman, and Hiscock 1997), less skilled readers in second and third grade had more difficulties than highly skilled readers in perceiving two high vowels. The groups did not differ, however, in their production of words containing these same vowels, nor did they differ in their perception of the initial stop consonants /d/ and /t/.

Four experimental tasks were developed for the present study, both to clarify the vowel perception deficit observed in the Post et al. study, and to link this deficit with vowel spelling. A vowel discrimination task (task 1) established whether comparing short and long high vowels, in two items presented in sequence, induced perception errors in less skilled readers. Vowel identification of four different short versus long vowel pairs (task 2) probed whether short/long vowel contrasts necessarily induce less skilled readers to make errors when each task item is presented singly in a forced choice format. A third task required identification of two short vowels to determine whether, apart from the short versus long contrast, other vowel contrasts present difficulties for less skilled readers. The three tasks give converging information about speech perception processes because the consonantal context surrounding the vowel in these three tasks was kept the same. In contrast with the Post et al. (1997) study, the tasks contain one- as well as two-syllable words. Finally, a spelling task that required insertion of a vowel letter into phonologically similar words (task 4) was administered to check for accuracy of spelling of the same vowels tested in the vowel identification tasks. Standardized measures of verbal memory and receptive vocabulary were used to describe the sample of students. Furthermore, the relation between vowel identification and performance on a standardized test of phonemic awareness was examined.

METHODS

EXPERIMENTAL MEASURES

Task 1: Discrimination of the Vowels /ĭ/ and /ē/. Vowel discrimination was tested with pseudowords with a CVC or CVCV word structure. Stimuli for this task included 16 one- and 16 two-syllable words with /d/ or /t/ as initial consonant, and /b/ or /p/ as middle or end consonant (see the first column of table 1). The two-syllable words differed from the one-syllable words by adding the word ending "–y" (/ē/). Addition of the "–y" shifts the syllable boundary from a position directly after the final consonant to the position immediately after the vowel.* A few slots in the CVC(V) word structure matrix were already occupied by existing dictionary words.

On each trial of the vowel discrimination task, the participants listened to two stimuli that differed only in vowel quality

---

*Contrasting views about the syllable boundary are described in Akmajian, Demers, Farmer, and Harnish (1991), Treiman and Danis (1988), and Dollaghan and Biber (1993).

(the short high vowel /ĭ/ as in *dip* or the long high vowel /ē/ as in *deep*) and were asked to decide whether they were the same or different (an AX paradigm). Half of the 32 word pairs were identical and half were not. Participants listened first to the one-syllable word pairs, then, after a short break, to the two-syllable word pairs. An equal number of words in first position of the different condition contained a long vowel or a short vowel. Participants were asked to point to two identical blocks when they thought the words were the same and to two different blocks when they were different. The blocks in the different condition had contrasting colors (red and green instead of two green blocks) with pictures glued on top (rabbit and turtle instead of two rabbits). For half the participants, the different blocks were placed on the right and the identical blocks on the left. For the other half, the position of the blocks was reversed. Two word pairs were given as examples, one pair being different and the other the same. Then the children were asked to demonstrate their understanding of the task on three more trials with feedback. The vowel discrimination task had a coefficient-α reliability of .82.

   Task 2: Identification Tasks Involving Four Vowel Contrasts.   Vowel identification consisted of four separate tasks in which the following vowels were contrasted: /ĭ/–/ē/ as in *dip* — *deep*; /ĕ/–/ā/ as in *Deb* — *tape*; /ŭ/–/ū/ as in *tub* — *tube*; and /ŏ/–/ō/ as in *top* — *dope*. Each vowel identification task contained 16 items: half of the items contained a short vowel; the other half a long vowel. The word structures in which the short or long vowels were embedded were the same as in the discrimination task (see table I). The items were not presented in pairs as in task 1 but rather one at a time. Participants were asked to indicate whether they had heard the short vowel by pointing to one block, or the long vowel by pointing to two blocks. For half of the participants, the two blocks were placed on the right and the one block on the left; the position was reversed for the other half. At the beginning of each 16-item task, five demonstration trials were given. The coefficient-α reliability ranged from .80 for the /ĭ/–/ē/ task to .88 for the /ĕ/–/ā/ task, with reliability values of .82 for the /ŭ/–/ū/ task and .81 for the /ŏ/–/ō/ task. Across the four sets of contrasts (64 items), the reliability was .92.

   Task 3: Identification of the Vowels /ĕ/ Versus /ă/.   In this identification task, the participants were asked to make a forced choice between /ĕ/ and /ă/. Instead of blocks, male and female Barbie dolls (Ken and Pam) were used to indicate the vowels /ĕ/

Table I. List of items for vowel discrimination and identification.				
SHORT VOWELS				
Stressed syllable /ĭ/=[ɪ]	/ĕ/=[ɛ]	/ŭ/=[ʌ]	/ŏ/=[ɑ]	/ă/=[æ]
d__b (y) dĭb(y)	dĕb(y)	dŭb(y)	dŏb(y)	dăb(y)
d__p (y) dĭp(y)	dĕp(y)	dŭp(y)	dŏp(y)	dăp(y)
t__b (y) tĭb(y)	tĕb(y)	tŭb(y)	tŏb(y)	tăb(y)
t__b (y) tĭp(y)	tĕp(y)	tŭp(y)	tŏp(y)	tăp(y)
LONG VOWELS				
Stressed syllable /ē/=[iy]	/a/=[ey]	/u/=[juw]	/ō/=[ow]	
d__b (y) dēb(y)	dāb(y)	dūb(y)	dōb(y)	
d__p (y) dēp(y)	dāp(y)	dūp(y)	dōp(y)	
t__b (y) tēb(y)	tāb(y)	tūb(y)	tōb(y)	
t__b (y) tēp(y)	tāp(y)	tūp(y)	tōp(y)	

Note: Dictionary notation is used to indicate the so-called short and long vowels; brackets indicate the phonetic realization of a phoneme. Despite the label, length does not reliably distinguish the two sets. For example, the phoneme /ă/ (or [æ]) can be as long in duration as the long vowels. For the set of items used, the long vowels were phonetically realized with a glide.

and /ă/. The participants were asked to point to Pam when they heard the vowel /ă/ as in *Pam* or *Pammy*, and to point to Ken when they heard the /ĕ/ as in *Ken* or *Kenny*. The words *Debby*, *dab*, and *tap* were used as three more feedback trials. Apart from the change in procedure, the administration of the test followed the same format as the short/long vowel identification tasks, including use of the same CVC(y) word structure. The 16 items are shown in the upper half of the second and fifth columns of table I. This task had a coefficient-α reliability of .86.

Task 4: Vowel Spelling. The words in the spelling test consisted of a family of Latin loan words ending in *-tion*. Each word in the spelling test lacked the vowel letter in the stressed syllable located immediately before the word ending *-tion* (see table II). The students were asked to fill in the missing letter after the word was dictated to them two times. Their choice of letter was not limited to two as was the case in the vowel identification tasks (forced choice tasks).

The words ending in *-tion* have highly consistent vowel spellings. The prefinal syllable of the test words comprised the short vowels /ĭ/, /ĕ/, /ŭ/, or /ă/, consistently spelled with the

TABLE II.   Vowel Spelling Test (Vowel letter insertion).

SHORT VOWELS	/ĭ/ =[ɪ]	/ĕ/=[ɛ]	/ŭ/=[ʌ]	/ă/ =[æ]
	friction	section	suction	caption
	eviction	invention	eruption	faction
LONG VOWELS	/ē/ =[iy]	/ā/=[ey]	/ū/=[juw]	
	secretion	elation	evolution	
	completion	ovation	resolution	

Note: Participants are required to insert the appropriate vowel (underlined here) in the syllable before -*tion*. This is an open-ended task.

Slashes denote the underlying phoneme; brackets denote the phonetic realization of the phoneme. In contrast to the short vowels, the long vowels are phonetically realized with a glide in English.

letters *i, e, u,* or *a,* respectively, followed by a consonant (*friction, section, suction, caption*), or the long vowels /ē/, /ā/, /ū/, consistently spelled with the letters *e, a, u* (*secretion, elation, evolution*). Because the number of words containing an /ŏ/ or /ō/ in prefinal position (*concoction, lotion*) is limited, they were not included.

The 14 items of the vowel spelling task had a coefficient-α reliability of .70. Separately, the reliability was .55 for the four words containing /ĭ/ and /ē/, .50 for the /ĕ/ and /ā/ words, .56 for the /ŭ/ and /ū/ words, and .36 for words with /ă/ and /ĕ/.

The experimental words for the first three tasks were pronounced on tape by a female speech-language pathologist speaking standard northeastern American English (see table I)[3]. The short vowels were pronounced on tape as monophthongs and the long vowels as diphthongs. Vowels in American dialects differ in degree of diphthongization (Olive et al. 1993; Treiman and Cassar 1997). The dictation words in task 4 (see table II) were pronounced by the intervention teacher when she administered the test in each classroom. She spoke the same northeastern dialect as the speech-language pathologist.

STANDARDIZED MEASURES

Test of Phonological Awareness (TOPA) (Torgesen and Bryant 1994). The TOPA was administered for comparison with the vowel identification task. The early elementary version

---

[3]Because this study was conducted in eastern Texas, the Northeastern dialect in which stimuli were presented differed from that of all of the children who were black, white, Hispanic, and Asian.

of the TOPA requires recognition of shared final consonants in illustrated one-syllable words. The TOPA has a coefficient-α of .89 for 8-year-old children.

Digit Span subtest of the WISC-lll (Wechsler 1991). This digit span measure tests short-term verbal memory. The split-half correlation for 8-year-old children is .84.

Peabody Picture Vocabulary Test, third edition (PPVT-III) (Dunn and Dunn 1997). The PPVT-III tests receptive vocabulary and has a coefficient-α of .95 for 8-year-old children.

Woodcock-Johnson Psycho-Educational Test Battery (WJ-R) (Woodcock and Johnson 1989). The Basic Reading Cluster includes the Word Attack and Letter-Word Identification subtests of the WJ-R. Percentile scores for each participant use age as the basis for comparing norms. These percentile scores were then used to group participants in terms of reading skill. The Basic Reading Cluster reliability for 9 year olds is .96.

PROCEDURE

The Woodcock-Johnson, the vowel discrimination and identification tasks, the TOPA, the PPVT-III, and the WISC-III Digit span were part of two testing sessions for an intervention study, and were interspersed between other tests. In the first session, the tests were administered in the following order: vowel discrimination, TOPA, digit span, and the Woodcock-Johnson. The order of testing in the second session two weeks later was vowel identification of the first three short/long contrasts, PPVT, and the final two vowel identification contrasts (/ŏ/–/ō/ and /ĕ/–/ă/). The tests were administered individually in two 45-minute sessions in a quiet room provided by the schools. The spelling test of vowel-letter insertion was administered in each classroom.

Vowel discrimination, identification of short versus long and short versus short vowels, and vowel spelling will be described as four separate tasks. Although the 14 items in the spelling test were not administered in vowel pairs, they were analyzed in short/long or short/short pairs to make the task comparable to the vowel identification task.

PARTICIPANTS

A total of 164 second, third, and fourth graders attending two public schools in eastern Texas were given the Word Attack and Letter-Word Identification subtests of the WJ-R (Woodcock and Johnson 1989). Seven children were excluded from the study because they scored two or more standard deviations below the mean on the Peabody Picture Vocabulary Test - III (Dunn and Dunn 1997) or on the Digit subtest of the WISC-III (Wechsler 1991). Two additional children were dropped because they were not available for both testing sessions. The remaining 155 participants were native speakers of English and had no history of speech or hearing deficits, or of emotional problems. In terms of SES, the participants were homogeneously lower middle class; all children lived in the same area. The sample consisted of black (77 percent), white (16 percent), Hispanic (6 percent), and Asian (1 percent) children. Overall, slightly more females (81) than males (74) were available for testing. In second grade, the ratio was equal (29 female, 29 male); in third grade, girls were outnumbered by boys (22 female, 30 male), and in fourth grade, girls predominated (30 female, 15 male).

The participants were divided into five groups based on their percentile score on WJ-R Basic Reading Cluster. Group 1 (the least skilled readers) scored at or below the 25th percentile, group 2 scored between the 25th and 51st percentile, group 3 between the 50th and the 76th percentile, group 4 between the 75th and 91st percentile, and group 5 above the 90th percentile. Although a cutoff at the 25th percentile designates poor readers in most studies (Siegel and Heaven 1986; Bowers 1995), a division into five groups was chosen because of preliminary data (Post 1997, manuscript) that suggested even intermediate readers lack fully accurate vowel perception. In correspondence with recent evidence that reading skill is distributed normally independent of intelligence (Foorman et al. 1996; Stanovich and Siegel 1994), the reading level of the children is described in terms of reading skill only, rather than in terms of discrepancy-based criteria.

The reading percentile range, reading group, gender, and grade of the remaining 155 children are described in table III. With the exception of Asian children (only 2), each race was represented in each reading group. The number of participants in each reader group ranged from 22 to 45.

Within each grade sampled, the very skilled readers (group 5) were the youngest and the least skilled (group 1) the oldest. Because these patterns are consistent across groups and age-adjusted scaled reading scores were used, age in months is collapsed over grade. As shown in table III, the less skilled the readers, the older they were; the more errors they made on the TOPA, and the lower their PPVT and WISC-III scores.

Multivariate analyses of variance (repeated measures) were chosen to analyze the data. A more appropriate analysis would

TABLE III. Descriptive Measures (mean and SD) for five groups of readers drawn from grade 2 through 4 .

Group	Basic Cluster Percentile Range	n	Gender F	Gender M	Age in Months	PPVT SS	TOPA Errors	WISC-III Digits	WJ BASIC Cluster SS
1	(<26th percentile)	(29)	13	16	111.4	84.6	7.8	7.1	83.5
					(10.8)	(10.9)	(4.7)	(2.2)	(5.5)
2	(26–50 percentile)	(45)	28	17	108.0	89.7	6.8	8.1	94.5
					(9.8)	(11.1)	(4.1)	(2.2)	(3.3)
3	(51–75 percentile)	(35)	18	17	105.1	91.4	4.4	9.3	104.3
					(11.0)	(13.5)	(3.3)	(2.6)	(2.8)
4	(76–90 percentile)	(24)	11	13	106.7	100.1	3.4	10.9	114.5
					(10.9)	(10.3)	(3.0)	(3.3)	(2.6)
5	(>90th percentile)	(22)	11	11	99.0	104.9	1.4	11.8	132.2
					(10.0)	(11.7)	(1.7)	(2.6)	(7.2)

Note. F=Female; M=Male; SS = Standard Scores; PPVT = Peabody Picture Vocabulary Test - III (Dunn and Dunn 1997); TOPA = Test of Phonological Awareness (Torgesen and Bryant 1994); BR = Basic Reading Cluster (Woodcock and Johnson 1989): Group 1 least skilled and group 5 very skilled readers; WISC = Wechsler Intelligence Scale for Children-third edition (Wechsler 1991).

be categorical data modeling but there were insufficient data for such an analysis with the number of conditions present. An alpha level of .05 was used for all statistical tests. With each statistical test, the probability of obtaining a particular value of the computed statistic was reported (Dixon 1998). In all analyses, reader (R) referring to five groups, was the between-group variable. When the omnibus test of main effects and interactions with the factor Reader was significant, the data were further analyzed with subsequent linear (L), quadratic (Q), cubic (C), and quartic (QR) polynomial contrasts. Multivariate analyses (Wilk's lambda) were reported because of violation of the assumption of sphericity.

RESULTS AND DISCUSSION

TASK 1: VOWEL DISCRIMINATION

In task 1, discrimination of the short and long high vowels /ĭ/ as in *dip* and /ē/ as in *deep* was assessed in one- and two-syllable words. The question posed was whether less skilled readers could detect if vowel pairs were the same or different.

Few errors were made on the 32 pairs of items, but the least skilled readers made the most errors. Whereas group 1 made 2.6 errors on average, the other four groups made less than 1 error (.9, .8, .5, and .4 for groups 2 to 5). A two-way ANOVA was performed with reader group as the between-subjects variable and with repeated measures on same–different pairs. Neither the main effect of condition (same versus different) nor the interaction between condition and reader group were significant. The main effect of reader group was significant, $F(4, 150) = 4.2$, $p = .003$, particularly the linear contrast indicating a linear trend with poorer readers making more errors, $F(1, 150) = 11.3$, $p = .001$. Because the differences among reader groups were constant across same and different words, the responses were collapsed over this variable. When the variables of syllable, initial, and middle/final consonant and interactions with reader group were considered separately, no interactions with reader group were found.

The vowel errors declined linearly with increases in reading ability; however, even the least skilled readers (group 1) made few errors. Thus, the same-different task was easy, even for the least skilled readers. Apparently, less skilled readers can hear the contrast between the vowels /ĭ/ and /ē/ when two pseudowords containing these vowels are presented in direct sequence, even when the 32 items in the task are highly similar phonologically. Perhaps they only get confused when they have to consult the stored representation of a vowel, as in the vowel identification task involving the high vowels / ĭ/ and /ē/ (Post et al. 1997).

To explore this possibility, we tried to replicate the vowel identification task of Post et al. (1997), including the same 16 items used in task 1, but expanding our focus to other short/long vowel contrasts as well. We anticipated that less skilled readers would have difficulty with all short/long vowel contrasts presented singly in a forced choice format. We also hypothesized that vowel identification skills would be linearly related to reading skill (Foorman et al. 1996; Stanovich and Siegel 1994).

TASK 2: VOWEL IDENTIFICATION OF SHORT AND LONG VOWELS

Apart from the / ĭ/ versus /ē/ contrast (*dip* versus *deep*), task 2 examines identification of three other contrasts: /ĕ/ versus /ā/ (*Debby* — *tape*), /ŭ/ versus /ū/ (*dub* — *tube*), and /ŏ/ versus /ō/ (*top* — *dope*). Before the results of the vowel identification tasks are examined, possible confounds on task performance were ruled out. These included age of the participants and lexical status of the stimuli. Links between perception and awareness will be explored by comparing vowel identification accuracy with performance on the elementary version of the TOPA (Torgesen and Bryant 1994).

Vowel Identification Errors Over Grade. Given evidence that the predictive power of phonemic awareness tests declines with reading age (Schatschneider, Francis, Foorman, and Fletcher in press), could vowel identification errors decline in higher grades or is it a stable characteristic? Although the mean (*SD*) of vowel errors in second grade was 15.2 (12.8), in third grade 16.7 (13.4), and in fourth grade 13.3 (10.2), an ANOVA of reader-group by grade indicated that neither grade nor the interaction between reader-group and grade was significant. Therefore, vowel identification seems to be a stable characteristic over these ages. Age differences will be ignored and the vowel identification data will be collapsed over grade.

Lexical Status of Items in the Vowel Identification Tasks. A second possible confound concerns lexical status of the items in the tasks. When phonological similarity between experimental words is used by exhausting the possibilities of a specific word structure (CVC and CVC/y/), a few slots are usually occupied by existing dictionary words. Such words, shown in Table III, are *dub*, *dip(py)*, *Deb(by)*, *tip(py)*, *tub(by)*, *top*, *tape*, *taupe* (pronounced /tōp/), *Toby*, *dope*, *dopey*, *tube*, *dupe*, *deep*, and *teepee*.

When the errors on words and comparable pseudowords were summed separately, and their sums were compared with repeated measures on words and pseudowords, their means were comparable: $F(1, 150) = .003$, $p = .96$. In view of the significant interaction between the five groups of readers and the factor word/pseudoword ($F[4, 150] = 2.9$, $p = .02$), the least skilled readers (group 1) showed processing deficits with pseudowords. Because there was no difference of lexical status, subsequent analyses ignored the distinction between words and pseudowords in the vowel identification tasks.

Vowel Identification of the Short and Long Vowel. In the first analysis, the four vowel pairs (P) were compared in terms of their status as short or long vowels (V). In particular, the question was, "If the less skilled readers do worse on vowel identification in general, would the difference be the same for short and long vowels?" It was expected that the differences would be linear across groups. Several alternative approaches have been suggested for this type of problem (Allerup and Elbro 1998). We used the repeated measures approach because there was no constraint on the data to be better in one condition than the other; that is, we were not concerned with gains. Also, the better readers typically made few errors in either condition, which would have led to substantial missing data in methods which look at odds ratios or ratios relative to potential gain. In three subsequent analyses, the factors of Syllable (S: one or two-syllable), Initial Consonant (#C: /d/ or /t/), or Middle/Final Consonant (C#: /b/ or /p/) were added.

Step 1: Vowel Identification Three-way ANOVA (Reader x Pair x Vowel). Histograms for the four separate short/long vowel pairs are shown in figure 1. In a three-way ANOVA, the three main factors of reader ($F[4, 150] = 16.2$, $p = .001$), pair ($F[1, 150] = 11.5$, $p = .001$), and vowel ($F[1, 150] = 25.4$, $p = .001$) were significant. Interactions of reader with the other two factors were not significant except for the interaction of reader x vowel ($F[4, 150] = 4.6$, $p = .002$). The interaction of vowel and the linear contrast on reader was significant ($F[1, 150] = 10.3$, $p = .002$), as was the interaction of vowel and the quadratic contrast ($F[1, 150] = 6.3$, $p = .01$). This signifies that the differences between the short and long vowel were not constant across the groups of readers. The curvature of the short and long graphs is dissimilar: the contrast is more linear for the short vowel than for the long vowel. In Figure 2, the linear decline of errors for the five groups of readers is shown for the short and long vowel errors collapsed over the four vowel pairs. More errors were made on the short vowel than on the long vowel by the two least skilled groups, with the errors for the short and long vowel converging for groups 3, 4, and 5.

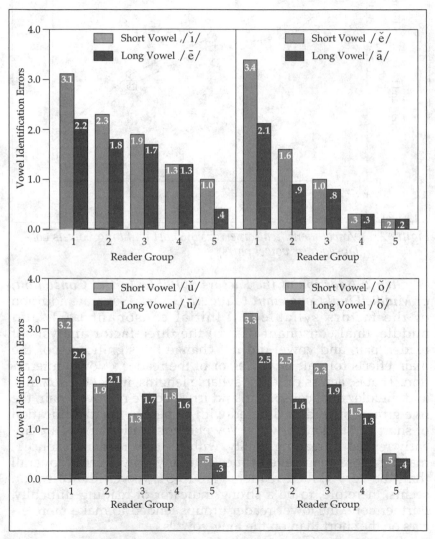

Figure 1.   Histograms of identification errors for 4 pairs of short and long vowels.

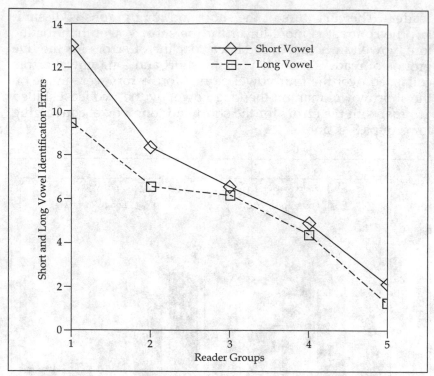

Figure 2.   *Vowel identification errors of short and long vowels collapsed over vowel pairs.*

**Step 2: Addition of the Factors Syllable, Initial Consonant,
or Middle/Final Consonant to the ANOVAs.**   Separate addition
of the factors syllable (S), initial consonant (#C), and
middle/final consonant (C#) to the three-factor analysis of
reader, pair, and vowel did not change the significance of the
main effects for pair or vowel, or of the reader x vowel interaction. That is, across different syllable lengths, initial consonants,
and middle/final consonant, and irrespective of vowel pair, the
five groups of readers differed with respect to the identification
of short versus long vowels. Vowel identification errors are linearly related to reading ability, with the low readers (group 1)
making more than seven times as many vowel errors overall
than the very skilled readers (group 5). Vowel identification
seems, therefore, to be a strong indicator of reading difficulty.
Furthermore, the lower reader groups tended to make more errors on the short than on the long vowels.

Discussion.   Given the preponderance of errors in identifying short vowels in two-syllable words, we speculated that

some participants might have associated the number of blocks with the number of syllables instead of with short and long vowels. However, such a strategy should also lead to many errors in representing the long vowel in one-syllable words. Few such errors were made. Furthermore, the short vowel was difficult for the low readers (group 1) in all four vowel pairs, whereas groups 3 to 5 did not show this bias.

The answers in the first vowel identification task could also have been influenced by the presence of the unstressed word ending "-y" (pronounced /ē/ in two-syllable words). Perhaps the word ending facilitated the recognition of the long high vowel /ē/ in the first syllable of two-syllable words and limited the recognition of the short vowel / ĭ/ in two-syllable words. Although this was exactly the result we observed, the same pattern was also evident for the three other vowel pairs. Vowel pair and reader group did not interact, and histograms for three of the four pairs (except the pair /ĕ/-/ā/) are remarkably similar.

Another possibility is that vowel identification is difficult for less skilled readers because they cannot remember the association between vowel type and number of blocks. If so, perhaps this task (and not vowel discrimination) accurately reflects the difficulty less skilled readers have in associating a representation of a linguistic segment with an abstract symbol, the very task required in mastering phoneme-grapheme associations.

We next compared children's ability to discriminate vowels (assessed in task 1) with their ability to identify the same high vowels (required in task 2). As shown in Figure 3, only the vowel identification task gave rise to errors, such that there were large differences in variance across tasks. Nevertheless, an ANOVA was performed, which showed significant effects of reader group ($F[4,150] = 8.6$, $p = .001$); type of task ($F[1,150] = 117.5$, $p = .001$); and a significant interaction between reader group and type of task ($F[4,150] = 3.2$, $p = .01$). The interaction of type of task and the linear contrast on reader was also significant ($F[1, 150] = 12.5$, $p = .001$). This means that the differences between identification and discrimination errors were constant across the groups. Thus, type of task is important in establishing perceptual impairment for vowels in less skilled readers.

TASK 3: VOWEL IDENTIFICATION OF /ĕ/ AND /ă/

After having established that the short/long contrast in identification is difficult for less skilled readers, we next considered the contrast between two short vowels in an identification task. Stark and Heinz (1996) observed that children with language

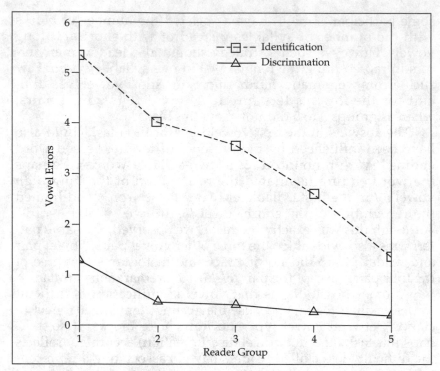

Figure 3. Vowel discrimination and identification errors for high front vowels /ĭ/ and /ē/.

problems show deficits discriminating the /ĕ/ and /ă/. Although the /ă/ is longer in duration than the /ĕ/ in natural speech (Peterson and Lehiste 1980) and the two vowels also differ in sound quality, it was assumed that the contrast between the two short vowels would be hard to explain to children. Therefore, dolls instead of blocks were introduced as objects of sound association. In task 3, the two short vowels /ĕ/ and /ă/, as in *Debby* and *dab*, are contrasted. We expected that short vowels in the same consonantal context would be equally difficult to identify.

Findings. In a two-way ANOVA of reader group and vowel with repeated measures on the two short vowels, reader group ($F[4, 150] = 9.4$, $p = .001$) and the interaction between reader and vowel ($F[4, 150] = 2.9$, $p = .02$) were significant, but there was no main effect of vowel. Thus, the overall means on /ĕ/ and /ă/ were the same: $M = 1.0$, $SD = 1.6$ versus $M = 1.0$, $SD = 1.5$. The linear contrast of the interaction of vowel x reader was significant ($F[1,150] = 4.9$, $p = .03$). This signifies that the /ĕ/ was more difficult than the /ă/ for the less skilled readers (groups 1 and 2), whereas the more skilled readers (group 3 through 5) made more errors on the /ă/. Errors for both types of vowels declined from group 1 to group 5 (see third and fourth column in table IV).

When the factors of syllable, initial consonant, and middle/final consonant were added separately, the interaction of reader x vowel remained significant, as did the linear contrast for this interaction. However, no other interactions with reader were significant except syllable x reader ($F[1, 150] = 2.9$, $p = .02$). Fewer errors were made on the /ă/ in one-syllable items ($M = .4$, $SD = .8$) than on the /ă/ in two-syllable items ($M = .6$, $SD = .9$), whereas the errors in one- and two-syllable items remained the same for the /ĕ/ ($M = .5$, $SD = 1.0$ and $M = .5$, $SD = .9$, respectively).

Less skilled readers made errors in the short vowel task, even with the changed procedure. Thus, vowel identification errors are not restricted to the short/long vowel contrast. As hypothesized, the number of overall errors made on the /ĕ/ and /ă/ was comparable.

Discussion. The presence of fewer errors on the /ĕ/ in the short/short vowel contrast (task 3) than in the short/long contrast (/ĕ/ versus /ā/ in task 2) can have four explanations. First, it may be that the forced choice between two short vowels is easier than between a short and a long vowel. Second, the results may be attributed to the change in task instructions. Dolls with well-known names (*Ken* and *Pam*) were used instead of blocks. The task with the dolls might have been more appealing to the children than the tasks with the blocks. Third, the names *Ken* and *Pam*, ending in the nasal /m/ or /n/, may have served to heighten the distinction between /ĕ/and /ă/. Finally, the enhanced accuracy may stem from the fact that each target vowel was associated with a well-known name containing that vowel, instead of with an arbitrary symbol (the block).

Table IV.   Vowel identification errors (mean and *SD*) for /ĕ/–/ā/ and /ĕ/–/ă/ comparisons.

Reader Group	/ĕ/=[ɛ]	/ā/=[ey]	/ĕ/=[ɛ]	/ă/=[æ]
1	3.4 (2.3)	2.1 (2.0)	2.3 (2.0)	2.1 (1.9)
2	1.6 (2.0)	0.9 (1.5)	1.2 (1.8)	0.8 (1.4)
3	1.0 (1.6)	0.8 (1.5)	0.4 (1.0)	0.8 (1.3)
4	0.3 (0.8)	0.2 (0.7)	0.4 (1.4)	0.8 (1.5)
5	0.1 (0.5)	0.2 (0.7)	0.1 (0.3)	0.3 (0.6)
M (SD)	1.4 (2.0)	0.9 (1.6)	1.0 (1.6)	1.0 (1.5)

Some insights may be gained from looking at how well reading disabled adults (n = 36) perceived these same short vowels when the same (paper and pencil) format was used across all five vowel identification tasks described thus far. These adult literacy students made an equal number of errors on the /ĕ/ as on the /ă/ in the short/short-vowel task (/ĕ/: M = 2.6 SD = 1.9 and /ă/: M = 2.6 SD = 1.6). This number was also equivalent to the number of errors in identifying /ĕ/ (M = 2.7 SD = 1.8) when it was presented in comparison to the long vowel /ā/. In adults, number of errors on a specific vowel remained constant independent of the type of vowel contrast in the task. Further research is necessary to establish whether vowel identification errors are affected by the type of vowel contrast in the vowel pair.

In the demonstration examples, with the adults as well as with the children, the names *Pam* and *Ken* were used. Therefore, the use of dolls with well-known names instead of blocks must have simplified the task for the children. Instead of forcing an association between a vowel sound and a symbol (one or two blocks), a more direct comparison between the vowel sound in the first names *Ken* or *Pam* and the vowel in the presented experimental word could be made. In this respect, the /ĕ/–/ă/ identification task is more comparable to task 1 (vowel discrimination) in which two words presented in sequence were compared. The /ĕ/–/ă/ identification task with high frequency lexical exemplars is also similar to phoneme identity tasks used in research by Byrne and Fielding-Barnsley (1990, 1991) and Murray (1998) and in asssessment tools such as the TOPA (Torgesen and Bryant 1994) or the *Batty*, *Betty*, and *Bitty* task (Ehri et al. 1987).

From tasks 1 through 3, we can conclude that the vowel identification test possesses unique characteristics. Our results indicate that less skilled readers do make vowel perception errors and that these errors can be induced through single presentation of phonologically similar words from which listeners must extract the appropriate vowel and pair it with an arbitrary symbol (block). Could vowel-spelling errors be induced when phonologically-related words are presented for spelling dictation?

TASK 4: VOWEL SPELLING

In task 4, vowel spelling in the *-tion* words is examined. The words are orthographically consistent and form a phonological neighborhood in that they are phonetically similar to one another (Luce and Pisoni 1998). The spelling of this group of words had not been studied systematically in the participating schools and the words functioned, therefore, as pseudowords. Note that the classroom spelling test was administered to only 145 children because of the absence of 10 of the children at the time of administration of the spelling test. These 10 children were distributed evenly over the five groups and three grades.

Short Versus Long Vowels. The spelling errors for the short and long vowels declined linearly with the largest number of errors observed in the low skilled readers (group 1) and the least number by the very skilled (group 5). A three-way ANOVA was performed with five groups of readers (R) as the between-subjects variable and with repeated measures on the three vowel pairs (P) and on short versus long vowel (V). The main effect of reader group was significant ($F[4,140] = 17.3, p = .001$) as was the linear contrast among the five groups of readers ($F[1, 140] = 65.3, p = .001$). That is, errors declined with increasing reading skill. The main effect of vowel type was significant ($F[1,140] = 7.5, p = .007$) but not the interaction between vowel type and reader group ($F[4, 140] = .6, p = .63$). In other words, all reader groups made more errors on short rather than on the long vowels. The interaction between pair and vowel was significant ($F[2,139] = 15.7, p = .001$) but not the interaction of pair x vowel x reader. In pairwise comparisons, the vowel pair / ĭ/ –/ē/ as well as the pair /ĕ/–/ā/ differed significantly from /ŭ/–/ū/. This means that all readers made more spelling errors on the short vowels / ĭ/ and /ĕ/ than on the long vowels /ē/ and /ā/, whereas they made the same number of errors on short /ŭ/ versus long /ū/. It should be noted that in the first two pairs, the spelling for short and long vowels changes from *i* to *e* and from *e* to *a*. In the third pair, the spelling is *u* for both members of the vowel pair (see figure 4).

Two Short Vowels. Whereas almost no errors were made on the /ă/ spelled with the letter *a*, many errors were made on the /ĕ/ spelled with the letter *e*. In an ANOVA with repeated measures on vowel, Reader group was significant ($F[1, 150] = 10.4, p = .001$) as was the linear contrast ($F[1,] = 34.7, p = .001$). The main effect of vowel ($F[1, 140] = 101.5, p = .001$), the interaction of vowel x reader ($F[4, 140] = 5.4, p = .001$), and the vowel by linear contrast was also significant ($F[1, 140) = 16.2, p = .001$). Thus, spelling errors on both short vowels declined over the five groups, but with a much steeper decline for the /ĕ/ than for the /ă/ (see figure 5).

Discussion. The short/long vowel contrasts showed the expected linear decline in spelling errors from low readers to

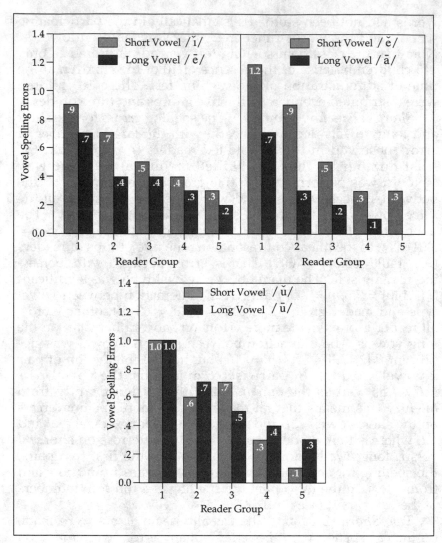

Figure 4.   *Histogram of short/long vowel spelling errors.*

very skilled readers. Furthermore, more errors were made on the short /ĭ/ and /ĕ/ than on the long /ē/ and /ā/. However, on the /ŭ/ and /ū/, the number of errors was comparable. Almost no errors were made on the short vowel /ă/, spelled as *a*. In Ehri et al. (1987) it was noticed that the short /ĕ/ and /ĭ/ are often confused in spelling. Apparently, it is easier to spell the speech sound /ă/ with the letter *a*.

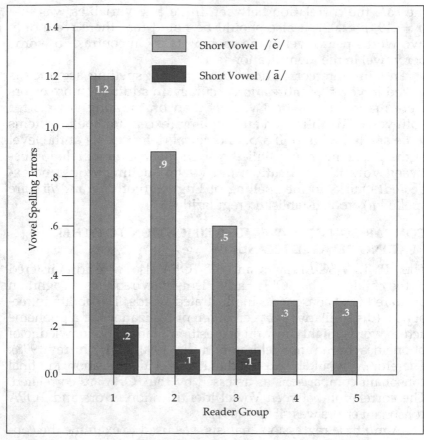

Figure 5.   Histogram of short vowel comparison spelling errors.

THE RELATION BETWEEN VOWEL
IDENTIFICATION AND SPELLING

Categorization of spelling errors as errors against a specific phoneme instead of errors against an orthographic convention makes it possible to show the relation between vowel identification and vowel spelling. The correlation between vowel identification and vowel spelling for the short vowels (.52) was higher than that for the long vowels (.24). Separately, vowel spelling was significantly correlated with vowel identification ($p = .01$) for all vowels except /ŭ/ ($r = .15, p = .07$) and /ū/ ($r = .03, p = .20$). The correlations were .34 for the / ĭ/ , .31 for the /ē/, .41 for the /ĕ/, .35 for the /ā/, .19 for the / ă/ , and .29 for the /ĕ/ in the short-vowel contrast. Because few vowel-identification ($M = .99, SD = 1.5$) or vowel-insertion errors ($M = .39 \ SD = 1.3$) were made on the /ă/, the correlation between these two variables was low ($r = .19$, $p = .02$). It also should be noted that there were only two words per vowel in the spelling tasks in contrast to words per vowel in the identification task.

In sum, intercorrelations indicate that spelling accuracy is linked to vowel identification accuracy. In addition, more errors were made on the short vowels than on the long vowels for both vowel identification and spelling (except for spelling items to be spelled with u). If a phonological deficit exists at the level of the phoneme in less skilled readers, such a direct relation between vowel identification and vowel spelling would be expected. Quirks in the spelling of English (both /ŭ/ and /ū/ are spelled u) erode established regularities.

COMPARISON OF VOWEL IDENTIFICATION TO OTHER READING-RELATED MEASURES

The PPVT, WISC-III digits, and the TOPA also were administered to the children. The TOPA-Early Elementary requires recognition of shared final consonants in illustrated words. The ability to recognize (dis)similarity between different realizations of a phoneme across words might draw on acquisition of identity knowledge of phonemes (Byrne and Fielding-Barnsley 1990, 1991; Murray 1998). Therefore, it would be expected that vowel identification and final consonant comparisons as assessed by the TOPA are correlated. The correlation between Vowel Identification errors and TOPA consonant errors was .45 ($p = .001$).

A multiple regression analysis was used to examine the contribution of vowel identification to the reading score controlling for the PPVT, digit memory, and the TOPA. When all four variables were entered into the model, they predicted 49.9 percent of the variance in reading scores ($F[4, 150] = 37.4$; $p < .01$). Examination of the regression parameters indicated that each variable predicted significant variance over and above the other variables in the model (all t with 150 df, all $p < .01$): −4.0 for vowel identification; −2.8 for TOPA; 3.9 for digit memory; and 3.6 for the PPVT. To examine the degree of unique contribution of each predictor over and above the others, squared part correlations were computed. These indices represent the variance in the dependent variable predicted by the independent variable after partialing out the variance of the other independent variables from the predictor in question. These indices (.054 for vowel identification, .026 for TOPA, .050 for memory, and .042 for the PPVT) indicate that while there is considerable overlap in the predictors, the vowel discrimination task contributed at least as much, if not more, unique variance to the prediction of reading as any other predictor.

GENERAL DISCUSSION

In four tasks, discrimination, identification, and spelling of vowels were examined. Second, third, and fourth graders, divided into five groups according to reading skill, were tested with forced-choice vowel identification tasks of four short/long vowel contrasts (as in *Debby* and *tape*) and with a task contrasting the two short vowels /ĕ/ and /ă/ (as in *Deb* and *dab*). The short / ĭ/ (*dip*) versus long /ē/ (*deep*) contrast was also tested with a vowel discrimination task. Linguistic manipulation (Papagno and Vallar 1992) consisted of the exhaustion of a CVC and CVC(*y*) word formation. Some of the items belonged, therefore, necessarily to the category word. Because of the phonological similarity among the items, the coefficient-α reliability of the four short/long vowel identification tasks was high (.92). Vowel identification errors were linearly related with reading skill with the two least skilled reader groups making more errors on the short vowel than the long vowel, and the three more skilled reader groups making an equal number of errors on both type of vowels. Although fewer errors were made on the short vowel /ĕ/ in the short vowel contrast (/ĕ/–/ă/ as in *Debby* and *dab*) than in the short/long contrast (/ĕ/–/ā/ as in *Debby* and *tape*), this difference could be attributed to a change in task explanation. The results of the vowel discrimination and identification tasks point to a less stable core representation of the vowel in less skilled readers. Intercorrelations showed that spelling accuracy is linked to vowel identification accuracy.

If a phonological deficit exists at the level of the phoneme in less skilled readers, such a direct relation between vowel identification and vowel spelling would be expected. The results from this study show that vowels should not be neglected in the teaching of spelling or in preparatory speech awareness activities. Although errors in reading and spelling vowels was noticed in many studies (Bryson and Werker, 1989; Fowler, Liberman, and Shankweiler 1977; Fowler, Shankweiler, and Liberman 1979; Goswami, 1993; Landerl, Wimmer, and Frith 1997; Shankweiler and Liberman 1972; Steffler, Varnhagen, Treiman, and Friesen 1998), these errors have not been linked directly to less stable vowel representation in less skilled readers.

COMPARISON OF THE RESULTS WITH
OTHER VOWEL STUDIES

In a replication of the reading study by Fowler, Shankweiler, and Liberman (1979), Bryson and Werker (1989) noted that both skilled and less-skilled readers had no difficulty in detecting same versus different vowel pairs in a vowel discrimination task. Reed (1989) also found no vowel deficits when two short vowels were presented in sequence in her vowel discrimination task. In that study, children were trained to respond to the two short vowels /ĕ/ and /ă/ which were presented in sequence with an interstimulus interval (ISI) of 400 ms. Each vowel had a duration of 250 ms. Participants were first trained to associate a response key with each one of the two vowels, and were then asked to indicate the temporal order in which the two vowels were presented by pressing the two keys in the same order. There were four possible sequences of stimuli.

The reason that both reading disabled and typically reading children performed well on the vowel discrimination tasks used by Bryson and Werker (1989) or in the study by Reed (1989) could pertain to the successive presentation of two vowels. This type of presentation was comparable to the same/different presentation in task 1 (vowel discrimination of the short and long high vowel /ĭ/–/ē/) in the research presented here, a task on which the less skilled readers also made few errors. Therefore, it appears that task presentation of two stimuli in sequence is not demanding enough to trigger vowel errors in less skilled readers without further manipulation.

PHONEMIC AWARENESS TASKS VERSUS
PHONEMIC IDENTITY

Phonemic awareness tasks such as rhyming, blending, and segmentation predict reading quite accurately. However, most tasks provide a global test of the presence or absence of phonemic awareness (Torgesen and Bryant 1994; Yopp 1995), but specific speech sound sensitivity is not tested. If a reading deficit is due to the failure to establish phonological immediacy in reading or spelling, a deficit at the level of the specific phoneme should also be expected. If a phonological representation is required for the purpose of holding a word in working memory (Baddeley, Eldridge, and Lewis 1981; Kleiman 1975) and this representation is incomplete or underspecified (Frost 1998) regarding vowel length, efficient use cannot be made of orthographic cues such as the silent letter *e* to indicate a preceding long vowel (for example, *lame*). Therefore, phonemic awareness could better be defined as a set of specific linguistic subskills the presence of which stimulates the immediate presence of phonological representation in reading and spelling, rather than as a global unified concept. The ability to recognize quickly and consistently the different realizations (allophones) of a single phoneme in spoken word context (Byrne 1998; Murray 1998) is one important component in the development of literacy. The tasks that probe for this type of awareness are easier to administer and less frustrating for less skilled readers to complete than are phonemic awareness tasks that focus on segmentation and deletion. Phoneme identity tasks could also be used to develop alphabetic insight when directly linked with letter identification (Byrne and Fielding-Barnsley 1990).

For less skilled readers, phoneme identity might never be secure enough to establish phonological immediacy in reading and spelling. It is possible, therefore, that they will not establish the knowledge of orthographic patterns that may alter their phonological representation for greater reading efficiency (Moskowitz 1973; Ehri and Wilce 1980). Earlier reading studies established that less skilled readers are insensitive to contextual regularities in English orthography (Bryson and Werker 1989; Fowler et al. 1979). The vowel identification test highlights insensitivity toward contextual regularities in English phonology as exhibited in allophony.

TEACHING STRATEGY AND THE FORCED CHOICE TASK

Because successful readers link spelling patterns to invariant phonetic categories extracted from the speech signal, instruction could direct the learner's attention to perceptual constancy through the use of minimal word pairs (Byrne 1998; Lively and Pisoni 1997). In this way, the attention of beginning readers could be directed to the systematic impact of surrounding segments on the phonetic quality of the vowel and of the vowel on the adjacent consonants. Reading and spelling methods that introduce new letters in strict sequence always practice their newly introduced letters in neighborhoods of phonologically similar words that are orthographically transparent (Cox 1984). The forced-choice task could simplify the introduction to a new group of similar words even more. Instead of asking a reading disabled student to read a whole row of similarly spelled words, one could start by showing the student one word and asking whether that word (*man*) is the word *man* or *men*. A yes/no question could force the student to acknowledge that the contrasting vowels are also spelled differently. A subsequent contrast between *man* and *mam* could show that the two vowels belong to one phoneme and are spelled with the same letter, although their articulation is slightly different. In beginning literacy instruction, systematic vowel nuances within the phoneme are usually glossed over. Now that we begin to understand the phonological intricacies of our speech and the difficult transition from speech to literacy code, perception research suggests that apart from phonemic awareness activities, reading and spelling instruction should include very systematic development of speech sound identity in direct relation to spelling. Reading is the effective adaptation of basic language skills (Cox 1988).

ACKNOWLEDGMENTS

This research was instigated and supported by Neuhaus Education Center in Houston, Texas. Part of the results were presented at the Conferences of the Society for the Scientific Studies of Reading (San Diego, April 1998; Montreal, April 24 1999). Permission for testing in a school district in eastern Texas was gratefully accepted. We thank all the children who participated in the study. The help in data collection of Cheryl K. Wiederhold and, specifically, Martha Laplante was appreciated. The tape preparation by the T. L. C. Speech Laboratory in Galveston, headed by Monica McHenry, Ph.D., is herewith acknowledged. This paper results from Yolanda Post's doctoral dissertation at the University of Houston where Professor Barbara R. Foorman guided her first steps in the field of reading research.

Address correspondence to: Yolanda Post, Neuhaus Education Center, 4433 Bissonnet, Bellaire, TX 77401-3233. E-mail: ypost@neuhaus.org.

References

Akmajian, A., Demers, R., Farmer, A., and Harnish, R. 1991. *Linguistics*. Cambridge, MA: MIT Press.

Allerup, P., and Elbro, C. 1998. Comparing differences in accuracy across conditions or individuals: An argument for the use of log odds. *The Quarterly Journal of Experimental Psychology* 51A (2):409–24.

Apthorp, H. S. 1995. Phonetic coding and reading in college students with and without learning disabilities. *Journal of Learning Disabilities* 28 (6):342–52.

Baddeley, A. D., and Lewis, V. J. 1981. Inner active processes in reading: The inner voice, the inner ear and the inner eye. In *Interactive Processes in Reading*, A. M. Lesgold and C. A. Perfetti, eds. Hillsdale, NJ: Lawrence Erlbaum Associates.

Berent, I., and Perfetti, C. A. 1995. A rose is a REEZ: the two-cycles model of phonology assembly in reading English. *Psychological Review* 102(1):146–84.

Berndt, R. S., D'Autrechy, C. L., and Reggia, J. A. 1994. Functional pronunciation units in English words. *Journal of Experimental Psychology: Learning, Memory, and Cognition* 20(4):977–91.

Bowers, P. G. 1995. Tracing symbol naming speed's unique contributions to reading disabilities over time. *Reading and Writing: An Interdisciplinary Journal* 7:189–216.

Bowers, P. G., and Wolf, M. 1993. Theoretical links among naming speed, precise timing mechanisms and orthographic skill in dyslexia. *Reading and Writing: An Interdisciplinary Journal* 5:69–85.

Bradley, L., and Bryant, P. E. 1978. Difficulties in auditory organisation as a possible cause of reading backwardness. *Nature*, 271:746–47.

Brady, S. A. 1997. Ability to encode phonological representations: An underlying difficulty of poor readers. In *Foundations of Reading Acquisition and Dyslexia: Implications for Early Interventions*, B. Blachman, ed. Mahwa, NJ: Lawrence Erlbaum Associates.

Brady, S., Shankweiler, D., and Mann, V. A. 1983. Speech perception and memory coding in relation to reading ability. *Journal of Experimental Child Psychology* 35:345–67.

Bryson, S. E., and Werker, J. F. 1989. Toward understanding the problem in severely disabled readers Part 1: Vowel errors. *Applied Psycholinguistics* 10:1–12.

Byrne, B. 1998. *The Foundation of Literacy. The Child's Acquisition of the Alhabetic Principle.* Hove, UK: Psychology Press, Ltd.

Byrne, B., and Fielding-Barnsley, R. 1990. Acquiring the alphabetic principle: A case for teaching recognition of phoneme identity. *Journal of Educational Psychology* 82 (4):805–12.

Byrne, B., and Fielding-Barnsley, R. 1991. Evaluation of a program to teach phonemic awareness to young children. *Journal of Educational Psychology* 83 (4):451–55.

Chen, M. 1970. Vowel length variation as a function of the voicing of the consonant environment. *Phonetica* 22:129–59.

Coltheart, M. 1978. Lexical access in simple reading tasks. In *Strategies of Information Processing*, Underwood, ed. New York: Academic Press.

Cox, A. R. 1984. Structures and Techniques. *Multisensory Teaching of Basic Language Skills.* Cambridge, MA: Educators Publishing Service, Inc.

Delattre, P. 1962. Some factors of vowel duration and their cross-linguistic validity. *Journal of the Acoustical Society of America* 34:1141–43.

Denes, P. B., and Pinson, E. N. 1963. *The Speech Chain. The Physics and Biology of Spoken Language.* Baltimore, MD: Waverly Press, Inc.

Diehl, R. L., Buchwald McCusker, S., and Chapman, L. S. 1981. Perceiving vowels in isolation and in consonantal context. *Journal of the Acoustical Society of America* 69(1):239–48.

Dixon, P. 1998. Why scientists value p values. *Psychonomic Bulletin of Review* 5(3):390–96.

Dollaghan, C., Biber, M., and Campbell, T. 1993. Constituent syllable effects in a nonsense-word repetition task. Research note. *Journal of Speech and Hearing Research* 36:1051–54.

Dunn, L., and Dunn, L. 1997. *Peabody Picture Vocabulary Test-III.* Circle Pines, MN: American Guidance Service.

Ehri, L. C., and Saltmarsh, J. 1995. Beginning readers outperform older disabled readers in learning to read words by sight. *Reading and Writing* 7:295–326.

Ehri, L. C., and Wilce, L. S. 1987. Does learning to spell help beginners learn to read words? *Reading Research Quarterly* 22:47–65.

Ehri, L. C., Wilce, L. S., and Taylor, B. B. 1987. Children's categorization of short vowels in words and the influence of spellings. *Merrill-Palmer Quarterly* 33:393–421.

Foorman, B. R., Francis, D. J., Fletcher, J. M., and Lynn, A. 1996. Relation of phonological and orthographic processing to early reading: Comparing two approaches to regression-based, reading-level-match designs. *Journal of Educational Psychology* 88(4):639–52.

Fowler, A. E. 1991. How early phonological development might set the stage for phoneme awareness. In *Phonological Processes in Literacy. A Tribute to Isabelle Y. Liberman*, S. A. Brady and D. P. Shankweiler, eds.. Hillsdale, NJ: Lawrence Erlbaum Associates.

Fowler, C. A., Liberman, I. Y., and Shankweiler, D. 1977. On interpreting the error pattern of the beginning reader. *Language and Speech* 20:162–73.

Fowler, C. A., Shankweiler, D., and Liberman, I. Y. 1979. Apprehending spelling patterns for vowels: A developmental study. *Language and Speech* 22:243–52.

Frith, U., Wimmer, H., and Landerl, K. 1998. Differences in phonological recoding in German- and English-speaking children. *Scientific Studies of Reading* 2(1):31–54.

Frost, R. 1998. Towards a strong phonological theory of visual word recognition: True issues and false trails. *Psychological Bulletin* 123(1):71–99.

Godfrey, J. J., Syrdal-Lasky, A. K., Millay, K. K., and Knox, C. M. 1981. Performance of dyslexic children on speech perception tests. *Journal of Experimental Child Psychology* 32:401–24.

Goswami, U. 1993. Toward an interactive analogy model of reading development: Decoding vowel graphemes in beginning reading. *Journal of Experimental Child Psychology* 56:443–75.

Henry, M. K. 1988. Beyond phonics: Integrated reading and spelling instruction based on word origin and structure. *Annals of Dyslexia* 38:258–75.

Henry, M. K. 1989. Children's word structure knowledge: Implications for decoding and spelling instruction. *Reading and Writing: An Interdisciplinary Journal* 2:135–52.

Høien, T., Lundberg, I., Stanovich, K. E., and Bjaalid, I.-K. 1995. Components of phonological awareness. *Reading and Writing: An Interdisciplinary Journal* 7:171–83.

Jakobson, R., and Halle, M. 1968. Phonology in relation to phonetics. In *Manual of Phonetics*, B. Malmberg, ed. Amsterdam: North-Holland Pub. Comp.

Kent, R. D. 1997. *The Speech Sciences*. San Diego: Singular Pub. Group.

Kleiman, G. M. 1975. Speech recoding in reading. *Journal of Verbal Learning and Verbal Behavior* 14:323–39.

Kraus, N., McGee, T. J., Carrell, T. D., Zecker, S. G., Nicol, T. G., and Koch, D. B. 1996. Auditory neurophysiologic responses and discrimination deficits in children with learning problems. *Science* 273:971–73.

Landerl, K., Wimmer, H., and Frith, U. 1997. The impact of orthographic consistency on dyslexia: A German-English comparison. *Cognition* 63:315–34.

Liberman, I. Y. 1973. Segmentation of the spoken word and reading acquisition. *Bulletin of the Orton Society* 23:65–77.

Lieberman, P., Meskill, R. H., Chatillon, M., and Schupack, H. 1985. Phonetic speech perception deficits in dyslexia. *Journal of Speech and Hearing Research* 28:480–86.

Lively, S. E., and Pisoni, D. B. 1997. On prototypes and phonetic categories: A critical assessment of the perceptual magnet effect in speech perception. *Journal of Experimental Psychology: Human Perception and Performance* 23(6):1665–79.

Luce, P. A., and Pisoni, D. B. 1998. Recognizing spoken words: The neighborhood activation model. *Ear and Hearing* 19(1):1–36.

Lukatela, G., and Turvey, M. T. 1998. Reading in two alphabets. *American Psychologist* Sept:1057–72.

Lundberg, I., Frost, J., and Peterson, O. 1988. Effects of an extensive program for stimulating phonological awareness in preschool children. *Reading Research Quarterly* 23:263–84.

Lundberg, I., Olofsson, A., and Wall, S. 1980. Reading and spelling skills in the first school years, predicted from phonemic awareness skills in kindergarten. *Scandinavian Journal of Psychology* 21:159–73.

Lyytinen, H., Leinonen, S., Nikula, M., Aro, M., and Leiwo, M. 1995. In search of the core features of dyslexia: Observations concerning dyslexia in the highly orthographically regular Finnish language. In *The Varieties of Orthographic Knowledge ll; Relations to Phonology, Reading, and Writing,* V. W. Berninger, ed. Dordrecht, The Netherlands: Kluwer Academic Pub.

McBride-Chang, C. 1995. Phonological processing, speech perception, and reading disability: An integrative review. *Educational Psychologist* 30(3):109–21.

Moats, L. C. 1994. The missing foundation in teacher education: Knowledge of the structure of spoken and written language. *Annals of Dyslexia* 44:81–102.

Morais, J. 1987. Phonetic awareness and reading acquisition. *Psychological Research* 49:147–52.

Moskowitz, B. 1973. On the status of the vowel shift in English. In *Cognitive Development and the Acquisition of Language,* T. Moore, ed. New York: Academic Press.

Murray, B. A. 1998. Gaining alphabetic insight: Is phoneme manipulation skill or identity knowledge causal? *Journal of Educational Psychology* 90 (3):461–75.

Olive, J. P., Greenwood, A., and Coleman, J. 1993. *Acoustics of American English Speech. A Dynamic Approach.* New York: Springer-Verlag.

Olson, D. R. 1996. Towards a psychology of literacy: On the relations between speech and writing. *Cognition* 60:83–104.

Papagno, C., and Vallar, G. 1992. Phonological short-term memory and the learning of novel words: The effect of phonological similarity and item length. *Quarterly Journal of Experimental Psychology* 44A:47–67.

Perfetti, C. A., and Zhang, S. 1995. Very early phonological activation in Chinese reading. *Journal of Experimental Psychology: Learning, Memory, and Cognition* 21(1):24–33.

Peterson, G. E., and Lehiste, I. 1960. Duration of syllable nuclei in English. *Journal of the Acoustical Society of America* 32:693–703.

Post, Y. V. 1997. Perception of high vowels in readers with intermediate reading skills. Unpublished manuscript.

Post, Y. V., Foorman, B. R., and Hiscock, M. 1997. Speech perception and speech production as indicators of reading difficulty. *Annals of Dyslexia* 47:3–27.

Reed, M. A. 1989. Speech perception and the discrimination of brief auditory cues in reading disabled children. *Journal of Experimental Child Psychology* 48:270–92.

Rubin, H., and Liberman, I. Y. 1983. Exploring the oral and written language errors made by language disabled children. *Annals of Dyslexia* 33:111–20.

Schatschneider, C., Francis, D. J., Foorman, B. R., and Fletcher, J. M. in press. The dimensionality of phonological awareness: An application of item response theory. *Journal of Educational Psychology.*

Scott, D. R., and Cutler, A. 1984. Segmental phonology and the perception of syntactic structure. *Journal of Verbal Learning and Verbal Behavior* 23:450–66.

Shankweiler, D., and Liberman, I. Y. 1972. Misreading: A search for causes. In *Language by Ear and by Eye: The Relationships between Speech and Reading,* J. F. Kavanagh and I. G. Mattingly, eds. Cambridge, MA: M.I.T Press.

Siegel, L. S., and Heaven, R. K. 1986. Categorization of learning disabilities. In *Handbook of Cognitive, Social, and Neurological Aspects of Learning Disabilities,* Vol.1, S. Ceci, ed. Hillsdale, NJ: Lawrence Erlbaum Associates.

Stanovich, K. E., and Siegel, L. S. 1994. Phenotypic performance profile of children with reading abilities: A regression-based test of the phonological-core variable-difference model. *Journal of Educational Psychology* 86(1):24–53.

Stark, R. E., and Heinz, J. M. 1996. Vowel perception in children with and without language impairment. *Journal of Speech and Hearing Research* 39:860–69.

Steffler, D. J., Varnhagen, C. K., Treiman, R., and Friesen, C. K. 1998. There's more to children's spelling than the errors they make: Strategic and automatic processes for one-syllable words. *Journal of Educational Psychology* 90(3):492–505.

Tan, L. H., Hoosain, R., and Siok, W. W. T. 1995. Activation of phonological codes before access to character meaning in written Chinese. *Journal of Experimental Psychology: Learning, Memory, and Cognition* 22(4):865–82.

Torgesen, J. K., and Bryant, B. R. 1994. *Test of Phonological Awareness.* Austin, TX: PRO-ED.

Treiman, R., and Cassar, M. 1997. Can children and adults focus on sound as opposed to spelling in a phoneme counting task? *Developmental Psychology* 33(5):771–80.

Treiman, R., and Danis, C. 1988. Short-term memory errors for spoken syllables are affected by the linguistic structure of the syllables. *Journal of Experimental Psychology: Learning, Memory, and Cognition* 14(1):145–52.

Van Orden, G. C., Pennington, B. F., and Stone, G. O. 1990. Word identification in reading and the promise of subsymbolic psycholinguistics. *Psychological Review* 97(4):488–522.

Wechsler, D. 1991. *Wisc-III. Wechsler Intelligence Scale for Children-third edition.* San Antonio: Harcourt Brace & Company.

Wilkinson, I. A. G. 1998. Dealing with diversity: Achievement gaps in reading literacy among New Zealand students. *Reading Research Quarterly* 33(2):144–67.

Wimmer, H., Mayringer, H., and Landerl, K. 1998. Poor reading: A deficit in skill-automatization or a phonological deficit? *Scientific Studies of Reading* 2(4):321–40.

Wolf, M., Pfeil, C., Lotz, R., and Biddle, K. 1994. Towards a more universal understanding of the developmental dyslexias: The contribution of orthographic factors. In *The Varieties of Orthographic Knowledge I: Theoretical and Developmental Issues,* V. W. Berninger, ed. Dordrecht: Kluwer Academic Publishers.

Woodcock, R. W., and Johnson, M. B. 1989. *Woodcock-Johnson Psycho-Educational Battery-Revised.* Allen, TX: DLM.

Yopp, H. K. 1995. A test for assessing phonemic awareness in young children. *The Reading Teacher* 49(1):20–29.

Zinna, D. R., Liberman, I. Y., and Shankweiler, D. 1986. Children's sensitivity to factors influencing vowel reading. *Reading Research Quarterly* 21 (4):465–80.

Phonological Coding and Children's Spelling

Che Kan Leong

College of Education, University of Saskatchewan,
Saskatoon, Saskatchewan, Canada

The goal of this study was to predict children's spelling from their performance on pseudohomophone choice and rhyme matching tasks. A total of 222 nine- to twelve-year-old children in grades 4, 5, and 6 participated. The children were given, individually, a computerized pseudohomophone choice task with 30 item pairs in two conditions, and a computerized rhyme matching task with 68 word pairs in four conditions. Accuracy and speed of processing were assessed. Three memory tasks, a Spoonerism task, a general ability test, and a written spelling test were also administered. Analyses of variance and multiple regression analyses showed that both accurate and rapid choice of pseudohomophones sounding like real words and rhyme matching contributed substantially to variations in spelling. Orthographic knowledge played a role in spelling as shown by the contribution of word pairs that rhymed but were orthographically dissimilar. Phonological coding as tested by pseudohomophone choice was also important.

INTRODUCTION

In learning to read and spell English, children need to appreciate the alphabetic principle. They need to learn that printed symbols represent systematic phonemes and other sublexical segments such as onsets and rimes. Readers need to map

Annals of Dyslexia, Vol. 49, 1999

accurately and rapidly the correspondences between graphemes and speech sound segments; and spellers, the connection between phonemes and sublexical segments to graphemes (Goswami and Bryant 1990).

Graphemes are defined as minimal lexical contrastive units in writing. They are analogous, but not entirely parallel, to phonemes, which are the minimal contrastive segments in speech (Henderson 1985; Venezky 1970). Graphemes and phonemes bear a probabilistic relationship in that graphemes can assume different forms in different orthographic environments, in the same way that phonemes can have different phonetic renderings in varying phonological environments. An example of allophonic variation is the phoneme category of /p/, which varies from the voiced to the unvoiced allophone according to varying speech sound environments (e.g., spit versus pit). Similarly, the front vowel /æ/ varies dramatically in "sat" versus "sand". To illustrate the case of graphemic variation, the phoneme /k/ can be represented as <c> in cap, as <k> in king, or as <ch> in chord.

In spelling, children need to be aware that graphemes can assume different canonical forms in different orthographic environments (e.g., spelling /sh/ as a palatalized <t> as in nation). As defined by Ehri (1980), the orthographic form that children need to be aware of is, ". . . a sequence of letters bearing systematic relationships to phonological properties of the word" (p. 313). Thus, orthographic or spelling patterns and phonological forms of lexical items are closely intertwined.

The present study used two computerized tasks designed to examine the contribution to children's spelling of each of: (1) phonological translation of pseudohomophone item pairs sounding like real English words (e.g., kard, brane); and (2) rhyme matching of word pairs (e.g., cold-bold, moose-juice). To decide if a pseudohomophone (e.g., kard) sounds like a real English word, children probably process the base phonological form (/ka:d/ as in card). It is hypothesized that this processing skill may relate to their reading and spelling abilities (Pring and Snowling 1986).

One-syllable word pairs rhyme because they share the same *rime*, which includes the vowel and any consonants that come after it (e.g., /it/ in beat and /ist/ in feast). Children's facility with rhyme is attributed to their ability both to process rimes and to segment onsets (the prevocalic consonants or consonant clusters such as b in beat) (Bryant, MacLean, Bradley, and Crossland 1990; Kirtley, Bryant, MacLean, and Bradley 1989).

METHOD

PARTICIPANTS

The sample comprised 78 fourth graders (36 boys and 42 girls), 65 fifth graders (34 boys and 31 girls), and 79 sixth graders (44 boys and 35 girls) for a total of 222 participants, all from two "average" schools in a midwestern Canadian city. Those children with intellectual, sensory, and physical disabilities were not included in the analyses. The mean ages in months and standard deviations for the three grades were, respectively: 114.09 (4.63), 125.92 (3.70), and 138.39 (3.95). On the Matrix E subtest of the British Ability Scales (BAS) (Elliott, Murray, and Pearson 1978) given as an index of general ability, the mean scaled scores were: grade 4—103.89 (*SD* 16.52); grade 5—103.86 (*SD* 15.93); and grade 6—113.47 (*SD* 13.66). A one-way ANOVA showed a significant effect of grade on BAS, F (2,219) = 9.90, p = .001. Pairwise comparisons indicate that grade 6 scores were higher than those of grades 4 and 5. Spellings scores on the Wide Range Achievement Test-Revised (WRAT-R) (Jastak and Wilkinson 1984) did not differ as a function of grade, $F(2,219)$ = .90, p = .408. Mean scaled scores were: grade 4—105.00 (*SD* 15.13); grade 5—102.75 (*SD* 13.39); and grade 6—105.77 (*SD* 12.69).

PROCEDURE

All 222 students were tested individually in a quiet room on two computerized tests of pseudohomophone choice and rhyme matching. The accuracy and automaticity with which these students processed the pseudohomophones and rhyming word pairs provided an index of the students' sensitivity to the English spelling-to-sound mapping and might explain their spelling performance. Automaticity was measured from reaction time scores in milliseconds.

Each of the computerized tasks took about 15 minutes per child. In addition, paper-and-pencil tasks were given either individually or to small groups of students. To determine whether a memory component might also play a role in spelling, three of these tasks tapped short-term and working memory. In addition to the tasks tapping memory, a Spoonerism task was included to test children's ability to segment words and to apply a novel phonological rule.

TASKS

Pseudohomophone Choice.   The pseudohomophone choice task offers a simple and effective way to examine children's access to phonological information inherent in words or pseudowords. Participants must decide if a letter string sounds like a real word on the basis of both orthographic and phonologic information. The computerized task consisted of 30 pairs of pseudohomophone items, displayed in lower case (see Appendix 1). The item pairs were presented in random order. Both members of the pair appeared simultaneously, one to the left and the other to the right, of the central fixation point on the computer screen. Participants were asked to select (accurately and rapidly) the one letter string that *sounded* like a real English word. There were 15 item pairs of four letters in length, 12 item pairs with five letters, and 3 item pairs with three or six letters. Members of each item pair were matched for orthographic patterns and onsets of initial consonants or consonant clusters (e.g., *bloe*, blog).

There were two conditions defined in terms of printed word frequency (using norms from Carroll, Davies, and Richman 1971). For the 15 higher frequency item pairs, the mean frequency of the base words was 871; for the 15 lower frequency item pairs, the mean frequency of the base words was 252. An example of a higher frequency item pair is *leeve*-meave (leave has a frequency of 964); an example of a lower frequency item pair is *shurt*-shart (shirt has a frequency of 222). The full set of the 30 item pairs is shown in Appendix 1. The general idea is that selecting the target pseudohomophone necessarily involves accessing the base word in lexical memory (e.g., *bloe* from blow and *reech* from reach). There is some evidence that latencies in making pseudohomophonic choice may be unrelated to the frequencies of the base words, as discussed in subsequent sections.

Rhyme Decision.   The computerized rhyme task comprised 68 word pairs (see Appendix 2) matched for word length (either four- or five-letter real English words), and required accurate and rapid rhyme decision. The four rhyme conditions were: (1) Rhyme-Orthographic (R-O) where word pairs both rhymed and looked alike (orthographic similarity) such as *cold-told*; (2) Rhyme-only (R) where word pairs rhymed but were orthographically dissimilar, such as *moose-juice*; (3) Word-Orthographic (W-O) where word pairs were orthographically similar but did not rhyme, such as *some-home*; and (4) Words (W) as control items, where word pairs neither looked alike, nor rhymed, such as *shirt-witch*.

Taking into account the printed frequencies of both members of the item pair, the mean printed frequencies according to Carroll et al. (1971) were 570.46 for the R-O condition, 759.58 for the R condition, and 2856.17 for the W-O condition. We did not measure word frequency in the control condition (W). As in the pseudohomophone choice task, word pairs were presented in random order, and each item of the pair appeared randomly to the left or right of the central fixation point on the computer screen.

The general idea of rhyme matching or decision for word pairs shown on the computer screen is that subjects will need to inspect the orthographic patterns and make use of the rime units in order to make an accurate and rapid decision. It is expected that rhyme decision reaction times will be markedly slowed where there is a conflict between phonologic and orthographic patterns (in the R and W-O conditions), and that rhyme matching efficiency should predict spelling proficiency.

Working Memory Task. In this task, students in small groups were asked to listen to randomly arranged sets of two, three, four, or five unrelated declarative sentences spoken at an even pace by a female experimenter with training in language and linguistics. After the oral presentation of each doublet, triplet, quartet, or quintet set of sentences, the students were asked to write down the answer to one comprehension question (related to any but the final sentence of the set), and to record in order the very last word of each of the sentences in that set. This Working Memory task has been shown by both the present author and others to be predictive of reading, but is not much used with spelling (Swanson 1992).

Short-Term Memory Task. In this task, children were asked to listen to 12 sets of phonemically confusable monosyllabic words (e.g., man, mad, mat, pan) spoken by the same female experimenter. Children were asked to repeat the items in each set in the correct serial order. This task was based on the work of Baddeley (1986) and has been shown to be effective in studying spelling (Leong 1997).

Sentence Repetition Task. This task was based on sentence elicitation inventories and was modified by Leong, Cheng, Lundberg, Olofsson, and Mulcahy (1989) in studies relating cognitive processing to academic achievement. There were 24 ten-word sentences varying in grammatical complexity. Each child listened to each sentence spoken by the same experimenter and was asked to repeat each of the 10-word sentence in the correct serial order.

Spoonerism. Individual children were asked to listen to 12 sets of two word pairs or two item pairs, and to report them orally in such a way that their first sounds were exchanged or reversed. For example, sun-shine would become shun-sine and thin-stair would be uttered as stin-thair. Similar Spoonerism tasks were used by Gillon and Dodd (1994) in studying 8- to 10-year-old poor readers, and by Perin (1983) in studying spelling (see Appendix 3 for stimuli).

RESULTS

Before the main statistical analyses, all the reaction time (RT) data in milliseconds (ms) were scrutinized for outliers. The Winsorizing technique was applied to replace those responses *more than* two standard deviations above the mean by RTs *at* two standard deviations above the mean (Barnett and Lewis 1984). All the RT scores related to correct items for both computerized tasks. Scatterplots of mean accuracy scores against mean reaction times for the 222 participants show no speed and accuracy trade-off. Although summary data on both accuracy and latency are presented, results of most statistical analyses are presented only for the more sensitive latency data. Also, for each of the variables shown in table 1 except for the Working Memory task, separate 3 (grade) x 2 (gender) ANOVAs showed no gender difference. Therefore, all the main analyses dealt with groups by grade and spelling ability, collapsing across gender.

The first question related to the overall patterns on the computerized and paper-and-pencil tasks. Did they sample what they purported to sample? If the processing of the two levels of the pseudohomophone task and the three levels (excluding the control words) of the rhyme decision task depend on perceiving the orthographic pattern and the inherent rime part as the basis of accurate and rapid lexical decision, then the five subtasks should cluster together. Similarly, the three memory tasks should also form a cluster. The other variables should either factor with these components or form a different component.

This first question was addressed using a principal components analysis. Table 1 shows the correlation matrix of the five RT subtasks and the paper-and-pencil tasks together with chronological age (in months). Table 2 shows the principal component analysis followed by varimax rotation. There were three components using Cattell's (1966) criterion of the scree test for factors or components with eigenvalues greater than unity.

The first component had very high loadings on the latency of the five computerized phonological subtasks. As the tasks in this component focused on accurate and rapid pseudohomophonic choice and on making rhyme decision, the component appears to tap rapid processing of related phonological and orthographic information. The second component, with high loadings on the three memory tasks, might be termed a memory component. The third component—showing high loadings of Spoonerism, age, and the WRAT-R spelling test—might be termed "sensitivity to phonological rules." It should, however, be noted that written spelling loaded almost equally on the three components. Together, these components accounted for 80 percent of the total variation in spelling. The principal component analysis suggests that, by and large, the main computerized tasks and the paper-and-pencil tasks sampled the components as hypothesized.

The next question revolved around the differential effect of the pseudohomophonic choice task and the rhyme-matching task on spelling performance and development.

PSEUDOHOMOPHONE CHOICE

Data for pseudohomophone choice are shown in table III. The results of a 3 (grade) x 2 (condition) repeated measures ANOVA on latency showed significant main effects for grade, $F(2, 219) = 6.23$, MSE = 2.96, $p = .002$, and for condition, $F(1,219) = 6.35$, MSE = .194, $p = .012$. Pairwise contrasts showed that the grade differences were between grades 4 and 6 only, and that the difference between conditions resulted from faster RTs on the lower frequency item pairs.

Scaled scores from the WRAT-R spelling task were used to divide the children in each grade into subgroups of low (L), medium (M), and high (H) spellers with cutoff scores of 91 (the lowest 27 percent of each grade) for the low groups and 117 (the top 13 percent of each grade) for the high groups. The numbers of L, M, and H spellers for grades 4, 5, and 6 were, respectively: 13, 50, and 15; 14, 42, and 9; and 9, 56, and 14. The 3 (grade) x 3 (spelling) x 2 (condition) ANCOVA with the last factor repeated and Working Memory as the covariate showed significant main effects of spelling group, $F(2, 212) = 21.45$, MSE = 2.42, $p = .000$, and of condition, $F(1, 213) = 5.38$, MSE = .197, $p = .021$, with fastest RTs in the low frequency condition. The Working Memory task was used for possible adjustment because among the three memory tasks, this task showed both a gender difference and an overall grade difference. The accuracy and latency results are shown in figures 1 and 2, respectively.

How is children's spelling associated with accurate and rapid processing of real English rhyming word pairs? In

Table I. Intercorrelations, means (*M*), and standard deviations (*SD*) of variables for grades 4, 5 and 6 students (*n* = 222).

Variables	1	2	3	4	5	6	7	8	9	10	11	12	M	SD
1. Chronological Age (Months)	—												126.20	11.039
2. BAS Matrix	.266	—											107.29	15.990
3. WRAT-R Spelling	.030	.379	—										104.62	13.785
4. Short-Term Memory	.128	.304	.322	—									65.032	11.737
5. Working Memory	.181	.163	.258	.391	—								23.473	5.765
6. Spoonerism	-.024	.255	.405	.253	.200	—							27.514	10.353
7. Sentence Repetition	.210	.366	.397	.550	.437	.289	—						149.50	9.375
8. Pseudo-homophone Choice (HF) RT	-.260	-.282	-.496	-.244	-.160	-.205	-.179	—					3197	1285
9. Pseudo-homophone Choice (LF) RT	-.273	-.273	-.502	-.211	-.211	-.223	-.213	.883	—				3093	1282
10. Rhyme-Orthographic RT	-.369	-.319	-.440	-.237	-.194	-.158	-.308	.735	.716	—			2168	746
11. Rhyme Only RT	-.359	-.284	-.469	-.222	-.214	-.164	-.298	.744	.714	.900	—		2284	776
12. Word-Orthographic RT	-.316	-.227	-.345	-.230	-.147	-.079	-.207	.555	.535	.773	.696	—	2784	977

Note. Latency (RT) in milliseconds.

Table II. Varimax rotated components for 12 variables (sorted) by principal component analysis for students in grades 4, 5, and 6 ($n = 222$).

Variables	I	II	III	h^2
Rhyme-Orthographic RT	.909			.871
Rhyme Only RT	.897			.842
Pseudohomophone Choice (HF) RT	.880			.815
Pseudohomophone Choice (LF) RT	.858			.784
Word-Orthographic RT	.780			.652
Sentence Repetition		.819		.693
Short-Term Memory		.752		.590
Working Memory		.689		.480
BAS Matrix	-.268	.514		.349
Spoonerism		.345	.679	.593
Chronological Age	-.373	.361	-.619	.653
WRAT-R Spelling	-.476	.366	.568	.684
Eigenvalues	5.033	1.823	1.149	
Percentage Total Variance	50.34	18.22	11.49	
Percentage Common Variance	62.88	22.76	14.36	

Note. Only loadings >.250 reported.

Table III. Mean latency (in milliseconds) and accuracy (in percentages) of pseudohomophone choice in three grades on two conditions: Higher Frequency (HF) and Lower Frequency (LF) of the base words of the pseudohomophones.

Grade	Higher Frequency (HF)		Lower Frequency (LF)	
	RT	% Correct	RT	% Correct
4	3476	78.6	3362	82.6
($n = 78$)	(1988)	(17.3)	(2036)	(8.7)
5	3163	82.4	3047	81.9
($n = 65$)	(1727)	(14.6)	(1617)	9.7
6	2835	83.1	2700	85.6
($n = 79$)	(1514)	(14.9)	(1448)	(14.9)

particular, is the association stronger when the experimental conditions increase in complexity from item pairs that are congruent in phonology to those which are in conflict? These questions were addressed with the rhyme decision task.

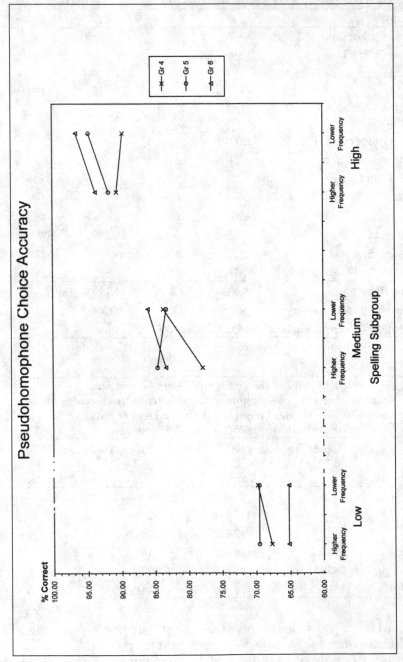

Figure 1.   Mean accuracy of pseudohomophone choice by spelling subgroup, grade, and printed frequency of base words of pseudohomophones.

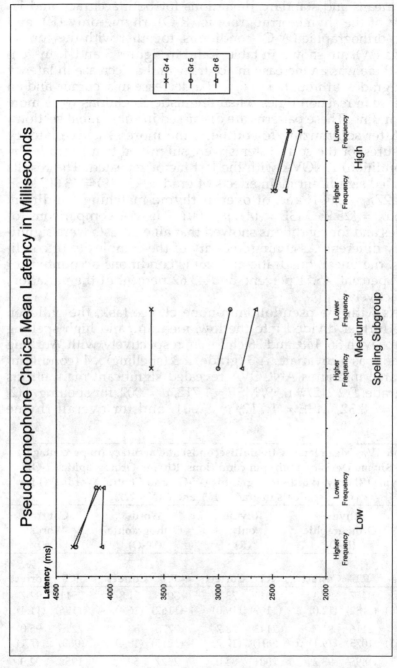

Figure 2. Mean latency (in ms) of pseudohomophone choice by spelling subgroup, grade, and printed frequency of base words of pseudohomophones.

RHYME DECISION

The means and standard deviations for both accuracy and latency of the rhyme-orthographic (R-O), rhyme-only (R), and word-orthographic (W-O) conditions, together with the control words (W), are shown in table 4 and in figures 3 and 4. In general, there was an increase in accuracy and a decrease in latency from grades 4 through 5 to 6, and a decrease in accuracy and an increase in reaction times when linguistic conditions were more demanding. These patterns are discussed in subsequent sections.

After scrutinizing for outliers, the more sensitive latency measures for the correct items were submitted to a 3 (grade) by 4 (condition) ANOVA with the last factor repeated. The results revealed significant main effects of grade: $F(2,219) = 13.39$, MSE $= 2.027$, $p < .001$, and of overall rhyme matching condition: $F(3,657) = 125.23$, MSE $= .141$, $p < .001$. Pairwise comparisons for grades and for conditions showed that all contrasts were significantly different. Assuming linearity of the complexity of conditions, the linear, quadratic and cubic conditions accounted for 10.67 percent, 45.71 percent, and 43.62 percent of the variation, respectively.

As with the pseudohomophone choice task, the children were further divided into the low, medium, and high spelling groups with 36, 148, and 38 children, respectively, with Working Memory as a covariate. A 3 (grade) x 3 (spelling) x 4 (condition) repeated measures ANCOVA revealed significant main effects for grade: $F(2,212) = 6.59$, MSE $= 1.712$, $p = .002$, for spelling: $F(2, 212) = 18.32$, MSE $= 1.712$, $p < .001$, and for overall rhyme

Table IV. Mean latency (in milliseconds) and accuracy (in percentages) of Rhyme Decision with four conditions: Rhyme-Orthographic (R-O), Rhyme (R) only, Word-Orthographic (W-O), and Control Words (W) for students in grades 4, 5, and 6 ($N = 222$).

Grade	Rhyme-Orthographic (R-O)		Rhyme only (R)		Word-Orthographic (W-O)		Control Words (W)	
	RT	% Correct	RT	% Correct	RT	% Correct	RT	% Correct
4	2477	87.4	2549	73.8	3026	51.8	2511	92.7
($n = 78$)	(1182)	(12.0)	(1169)	(19.0)	(1162)	(16.4)	(1196)	(11.4)
5	2116	91.7	2143	78.7	2778	53.0	2215	95.0
($n = 65$)	(1075)	(9.1)	(901)	(17.2)	(1215)	(16.4)	(963)	(7.1)
6	1898	93.2	2001	84.0	2527	59.3	1958	92.9
($n = 79$)	(872)	(4.9)	(853)	(13.7)	(1021)	(15.7)	(808)	(12.0)

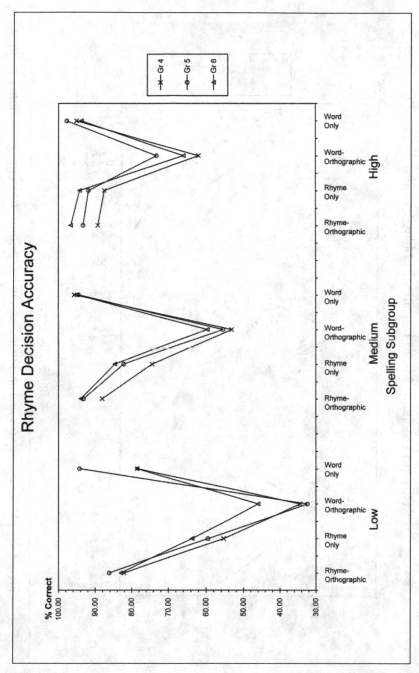

Figure 3.   Mean accuracy of rhyme decision by spelling subgroup, grade, and condition.

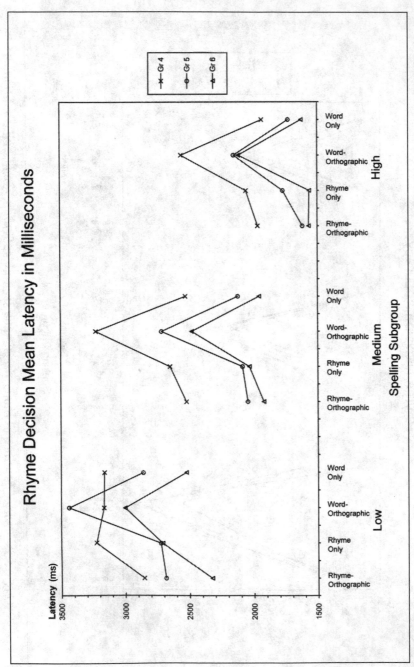

Figure 4.   *Mean latency (in ms) of rhyme decision by spelling subgroup, grade, and condition.*

matching condition: $F(3, 639) = 70.88$, MSE $= .139$, $p < .001$. The linguistic conditions showed significant linear, quadratic, and cubic trends which contributed 13.94 percent, 48.90 percent, and 37.16 percent, respectively, to the variation. These results are shown in figure 4, which highlights the interaction between spelling performance and condition.

MULTIPLE REGRESSION ANALYSES

To further investigate the contribution of pseudohomophone choice and rhyme decision to WRAT-R spelling, separate stepwise multiple regression analyses were carried out for each grade. The predictor variables were the latency measures of the different linguistic conditions of the pseudohomophone choice and rhyme decision tasks, the scores of the 3 memory tasks and Spoonerism, and the scaled general ability index from Matrix E. The criterion variable was WRAT-R spelling.

For grade 4, pseudohomophone choice (higher frequency set) contributed 27 percent (multiple $R = .520$) of the variation to spelling. This was followed by sentence repetition (12 percent) and spoonerism (4 percent), making a conjoint contribution of 44 percent. For grade 5, pseudohomophone choice (lower frequency set) explained most of the variation with a multiple R of .553, accounting for 31 percent of the variation. This was followed by: spoonerism (16 percent), sentence repetition (7 percent), and Matrix E (3 percent). The conjoint contribution of these four tasks was 56 percent of the variation. For grade 6 pseudohomophone choice (lower frequency set) with a multiple R of .519 accounted for 27 percent of the variation, followed by sentence repetition (9 percent), rhyme decision (R condition) (3 percent), and spoonerism (4 percent). The total conjoint contribution was 42 percent.

For all three grades, the pseudohomophone choice task, with its two subsets, contributed 27 percent to 31 percent to spelling with further variation explained by the memory component, the rhyme-only condition of rhyme decision task, and sensitivity to novel phonological rules (Spoonerism).

The above pattern of individual contributions to spelling changed somewhat when the accuracy scores for pseudohomophone choice and rhyme decision tasks were used in lieu of the latency measures. For grades 4 and 5, the rhyme decision rhyme-only (R) condition contributed 35 percent of the variation with a multiple R of .595 for grade 4; and 38 percent of the variation with a multiple R of .619 for grade 5. For grade 4, short-term memory contributed a further 7 percent, making a total contribution of 42 percent together with rhyme decision rhyme-only (R) condition. For grade 5, Matrix E contributed 9 percent, Spoonerism 4 percent, and rhyme decision word-only (W-O) condition another 3 percent, making a total conjoint contribution of 54 percent of the variation to spelling. For grade 6, it was the pseudohomophone choice (lower frequency set) that was the most predictive of spelling with a multiple R of .649, explaining 42 percent of the variation. This was followed by the rhyme-only condition (9 percent), rhyme-orthographic condition (5 percent), sentence repetition (4 percent) and pseudohomophone choice (higher frequency set) (3 percent). These five tasks accounted for a conjoint contribution of 62 percent of the variation.

It would appear that the analyses using the coarser-grained accuracy scores highlight the contribution of the different conditions of the pseudohomophone choice and rhyme decision tasks, and complement the multiple regression analyses using fine-grained reaction time measures in examining differential contributions.

DISCUSSION

Results of a principal components analysis on a number of phonology-related measures yielded three major components. The first component (loading on pseudohomophone choice tasks) appeared to tap rapid processing of phonological and orthographic information, the second heavily loaded on memory measures, and the third seemed to involve sensitivity to phonological rules. Together, the three components explained an impressive 80 percent of the total variation in spelling. Considered individually, the pseudohomophone-choice component accounted for 50 percent of the total variation (63 percent of the common variance); the memory component accounted for 18 percent of the total variation (23 percent of the common variance); and the sensitivity-to-phonological-rule component accounted for 12 percent of the total variation (14 percent of the common variation). These findings suggest that accurate and rapid perception of, and response to, the rime part in pseudowords, and the ability to make rhyme decisions (also based on rime), contribute substantially to spelling performance in children between 9 and 12 years of age.

Although latency data alone from the pseudohomophone choice task accounted for considerable varation in spelling performance, both the memory component and the Spoonerism task made additional contributions. Accuracy, too, was related to spelling. For grades 4 and 5, it was the accuracy in rhyme-only (R) condition with orthographically dissimilar word pairs (e.g., *moose-juice*) that explained some 35 percent to 38 percent of the variation; for grade 6 it was the pseudohomophone choice task (lower frequency set of base words) that was most predictive (42 percent of the variation), followed by the rhyme-only condition of the Rhyme Decision task. The analyses for the low, medium, and high spelling groups for the pseudohomophone choice and rhyme-matching tasks (figures 1, 2, 3, and 4) all further confirm the principal component analysis results.

It should be noted that in terms of the component loadings, the WRAT-R spelling loaded moderately highly (from .48 to .57) on the components tapping rapid processing of phonology and orthography and sensitivity to phonological rules; it loaded .37 on the memory component. These loadings can be explained in terms of the two main strategies in children's spelling: a rule-based strategy and a lexical strategy (Ehri 1986; Kreiner 1992; Kreiner and Gough 1990). The rule strategy refers to the mapping of phonemes onto graphemes to represent them and are probabilistic in nature. The lexical strategy emphasizes orthographic knowledge and word-specific memory, and is especially important for exception words.

Current psycholinguistic studies suggest that rule-based and lexical strategies for spelling are continuous and are interrelated (Treiman 1993). Both probabilistic rules and word-specific lexical strategies are necessary for spelling; and neither approach by itself seems sufficient to explain spelling proficiency and spelling difficulties (Kreiner 1992; Kreiner and Gough 1990; Stage and Wagner 1992). In a study using paper-and-pencil tasks of spelling regular, exception, and pseudowords with many or few orthographic/phonologic "friends", Leong (1997) found some evidence for these interrelated approaches with 150 nine- to twelve-year-old children. This pattern also seems to apply here, although it was not the intent of the present project to examine rule-based and lexical processing strategies in particular.

PSEUDOHOMOPHONE CHOICE

From the multiple regression analyses of the latency data for each grade separately, the pseudohomophone choice task consistently explained between 27 percent to 31 percent of the variation of WRAT-R spelling. While it was the higher frequency base words (e.g., *world* from *world*) that was important for the fourth graders, it was the lower frequency base words (e.g., hoap from hope) that were predictive for fifth and sixth graders. It seems reasonable to suggest that correct and rapid responses to pseudohomophonic item pairs require readers and spellers to draw on their lexical knowledge, perform checks both on the phonology derived from the rime part of the base forms, and on spelling or orthographic patterns, and then make their choice (Davelaar, Coltheart, Besner, and Jonasson 1978).

There is also evidence that in decision tasks pseudohomophones take longer reaction times compared with corresponding control nonwords (e.g., warld in the item pair werld-warld). Further, the usual finding of quicker and more accurate responses to high or higher frequency base words of pseudohomophones may not quite apply, as shown by McCann and Besner (1987) in asking adult students to name aloud pseudohomophones and nonpseudohomophones. This interpretation that access to the base words of pseudohomophones may be governed by lexical frequency finds some evidence in the present study as shown in table 3 and figures 1 and 2. It has been further shown by Laxon, Masterson, Pool, and Keating (1992) in a series of naming experiments that it is the number of orthographic neighbors (N) that might affect accuracy and latency of naming pseudohomophones.

WHEN PHONOLOGY AND ORTHOGRAPHY COLLIDE

While multiple regression analyses of the latency data consistently pointed to the potency of the phonological decision involving pseudohomophones, the accuracy data showed that the Rhyme (R) only condition of the rhyme decision task was most predictive of grades 4 and 5 spelling (35 percent and 38 percent of the variation) and some 9 percent of the variation following pseudohomophone choice of lower frequency pseudohomophones for grade 6. This set of findings raises two questions: One concerns the convergence of latency and accuracy data, and the other the reason for the potency of the rhyming condition where the phonology and orthography of the word pairs collide or conflict (e.g., have-cave).

On the first question, it is possible that latency and accuracy do not necessarily reflect the same cognitive processes (Santee and Egeth 1982). It may well be that both reaction times and accuracy measures are important parameters, and that an entire speed-accuracy trade-off (SAT) function may provide even greater insight into information dynamics (Pachella 1974). In general, percentages of correct items serve as surrogates of the kind and amount of learning; and latency measures deal with real time and are much less susceptible to changes brought on by rescaling. Since reading and spelling are real time events, latency should be the variable of greater interest. For the two computerized tasks of main interest here (pseudohomophone choice and rhyme decision), latency likely reflects better the aggregate of the processes of retrieving the rime part of the base words for the pseudohomophonic items and of the rhyming or nonrhyming word pairs, verifying the spelling or orthographic patterns and making a decision.

Regarding the second question, the orthographically similar but nonrhyming word pairs or the word-orthographic (W-O) condition (e.g., some-home) proved to be the most cognitively and linguistically demanding. It was, however, the Rhyme (R) only condition where word pairs were orthographically dissimilar but rhymed (e.g., tool-rule) that discriminated the different spelling groups. The early studies of Meyer, Schvaneveldt, and Ruddy (1974), Seidenberg and Tanenhaus (1979), and Polich, McCarthy, Wang, and Donchin (1983) all point to the increase in reaction times in rhyme matching when there is a conflict between orthographic and phonologic cues.

It appears that experimental participants access both phonologic and orthographic information in rhyme decision and attempt to draw on the rime part on both dimensions to make the decision. This explanation applies even more to spelling than to reading because spellers need to apply details of the writing system to the phonological structure of the spoken language (Perfetti, Rieben, and Fayol 1997). This refers to applying word-specific knowledge from reading and using analogy to spell words (Ehri 1997; Ehri and Wilce 1980; Goswami 1986). The phonological base of rapid and accurate rime detection in pseudohomophonic items and rhyme decision, buttressed by an orthographic framework, also reflects the current view of a strong connection between reading and spelling (see Brown and Ellis 1994, and Perfetti 1997 for details).

From the instructional perspective, multiple sources of information—phonologic, orthographic, and morphological—need to be used for both spelling and reading (Perfetti 1997). Students need to be instructed explicitly and systematically in the principles of the alphabetic language system (Ehri 1997; Seymour 1992) so as to make the strong connections between sublexical, phonemic, and orthographic segments that are necessary to enhance spelling and reading. Sustained instruction with a great deal of practice is necessary, especially for children with dyslexia. Take as an example the spelling of the word "listening". The phoneme /s/ assumes the grapheme <st>. Teachers can help their students by providing similar examples, preferably in context, such as "fasten" [seat belts], "moisten" [the envelope], "hasten" [one's departure], and the like. Another example is the spelling of the word "thigh", where the grapheme <gh> lengthens the preceding short phoneme /i/ to create <igh>. The analogous examples are "high" and "sigh". Thus, spelling is the most accurate where the underlying morphophonemic structure corresponds more closely to the phonetic realizations of the word. The more connections that students see between or amongst the phonologic (speech sound), the orthographic (spelling pattern), and semantic (meaning) aspects of words, the more precise will be their spelling.

APPENDIX 1

PSEUDOHOMOPHONE CHOICE TASK

Instruction: *On the computer screen, a pair of nonwords or letter strings will appear side by side. Decide quickly and accurately which of the pair, when pronounced, sounds like a real English word. When this item sounding like a real English word appears to the left of the central point, you press the key on the left like this [demonstrate]. When this item sounding like a real English word appears on the right, you press the key on the right like this [demonstrate]. Do not say these nonwords; just choose the ones sounding like real English words and make quick and accurate choices.*

Examples:

bloe blog   traif **trane**   **fearce** fairce   **kake** dake

	Base words of Higher Frequency (HF)		Base words of Lower Frequency (LF)	
(1)	lait	lote	ait	afe
(2)	tirn	turt	baik	bape
(3)	bote	boaf	kard	carn
(4)	bair	beal	hoap	hote
(5)	caim	pame	fite	fipe
(6)	gaim	gome	fead	feem
(7)	veech	veash	seet	seaf
(8)	thrue	threp	saif	saip
(9)	ferst	filst	joak	jope
(10)	leeve	meave	hawl	harl
(11)	floar	ploar	craul	crail
(12)	thurd	thord	derty	dorty
(13)	werld	warld	flote	floap
(14)	broun	broan	shurt	shart
(15)	strate	strale	tracter	trastor

APPENDIX 2

RHYME DECISION TASK

Instruction: *On the computer screen, two words will appear side by side. Decide quickly and accurately if these two words rhyme. Press the YES key [demonstrate] if the pair rhymes; and the NO key if they do not rhyme [demonstrate]. Do not say the words; just decide quickly and accurately if they rhyme or not.*

Examples:

clot	blot	news	lose	done	hone	jazz	fill
grove	drove	stole	droll	rough	dough	grant	roast

Rhyme-Orthographic (R-O)		Rhyme only (R)		Word-Orthographic (W-O)		Control Words (W)	
clot	blot	news	lose	done	hone	jazz	fill
last	past	make	ache	said	paid	swim	east
tilt	wilt	tool	rule	home	some	door	sing
mark	dark	dial	mile	have	cave	half	talk
born	worn	wear	rare	dull	pull	from	gift
soft	loft	comb	foam	ward	card	turn	form
mink	pink	stole	droll	mink	pint	grant	roast
rung	sung	blare	stair	foul	soul	chain	think
cold	told	stare	flair	wand	hand	chair	start
made	fade	stain	crane	wasp	rasp	bless	stair
grove	drove	moose	juice	rough	dough	plate	steam
brush	crush	tough	stuff	could	mould	sheet	three
yield	field	great	state	couch	touch	learn	clear
porch	torch	fruit	shoot	freak	break	shirt	witch
poise	noise	spoon	prune	clove	glove	store	whole
crank	drank	phone	known	beard	heard	clear	group
pitch	ditch	reign	train	cough	rough	stack	brain

APPENDIX 3

SPOONERISM TASK

Instruction: *"I am going to say 2 words or 2 items. I will say them twice. When I have finished, please say the 2 words or 2 items in such a way that their first sounds are exchanged or reversed. In other words, the first sound of the first word becomes the first sound of the second word, and the first sound of the second word becomes the first sound of the first word. Let's try some examples. Please say the new words or items very clearly."*

Examples:

sun	shine	⟶	shun	sine
funny	joke	⟶	junny	foke
drink	shake	⟶	shink	drake
thin	stair	⟶	stin	thair

(1)	bram	blue	⟶	blam	brue
(2)	this	chap	⟶	chis	thap
(3)	sharp	chain	⟶	charp	shain
(4)	spurt	sheep	⟶	shurt	speep
(5)	shallow	thought	⟶	thallow	shought
(6)	smellow	thing	⟶	thellow	sming
(7)	brain	thrill	⟶	thrain	brill
(8)	attempt	unkempt	⟶	untempt	atkempt
(9)	inane	obtain	⟶	obane	intain
(10)	acclaim	inflame	⟶	inclaim	acflame
(11)	skunk	promp	⟶	prunk	skomp
(12)	crucial	pretend	⟶	prucial	cretend

ACKNOWLEDGMENTS

I gratefully acknowledge the assistance of the Social Sciences and Humanities Research Council of Canada through SSHRC Research Grant No. 410-96-0186. The cooperation of the teachers, parents, and students of St. Angela School and St. George School in Saskatoon are greatly appreciated. I thank W. K. Lai for the microcomputer programming and assistance in data analyses, and Rachele Akerman and Joslynn Surcon for conducting the studies in the schools and for working with the students. I also thank the editor and the two anonymous reviewers for their very insightful comments. Part of this work was presented at the 49th annual conference of the International Dyslexia Association® in San Francisco, U.S.A. in November, 1998.

Address correspondence to: CheKan Leong, Department of Educational Psychology and Special Education, College of Education, University of Saskatchewan, 28 Campus Drive, Saskatoon, Saskatchewan, Canada, S7N 0X1. Telephone: (306) 966-5257; Fax: (306) 966-8719/ (306) 966-7719; E-mail: leong@sask.usask.ca.

References

Baddeley, A. D. 1986. *Working Memory*. New York: Oxford University Press.

Barnett, V., and Lewis, T. 1984. *Outliers in Statistical Data*, 2nd ed. New York: John Wiley.

Brown, G. D. A., and Ellis, N. C. (Eds.). 1994. *Handbook of Spelling: Theory, Process and Intervention*. Chichester: John Wiley.

Bryant, P. E., MacLean, M., Bradley, L. L., and Crossland, J. 1990. Rhyme and alliteration, phoneme detection, and learning to read. *Developmental Psychology* 26:429–38.

Carroll, J. B., Davies, P., and Richman, B. 1971. *The American Heritage Word Frequency Book*. Boston: Houghton-Mifflin.

Cattell, R. B. 1966. The scree test for the number of factors. *Multivariate Behavioral Research* 1:245–76.

Davelaar, E., Coltheart, M., Besner, D., and Jonasson, J. T. 1978. Phonological recoding and lexical access. *Memory and Cognition* 6:391–402.

Ehri, L. C. 1980. The development of orthographic images. In *Cognitive Processes in Spelling*, U. Frith, ed. London: Academic Press.

Ehri, L. C. 1986. Sources of difficulty in learning to spell and read. In *Advances in Developmental and Behavioral Pediatrics: A Research Manual*, M. Wolraich and D. K. Routh, eds. Greenwich, CT: JAI Press.

Ehri, L. C. 1997. Learning to read and learning to spell are one and the same, almost. In *Learning to Spell: Research, Theory, and Practice Across Languages*, C. A. Perfetti, L. Rieben, and M. Fayol, eds. Mahwah, NJ: Lawrence Erlbaum Associates.

Ehri, L. C., and Wilce, L. 1980. The influence of orthography on readers' conceptualization of the phonemic structure of words. *Applied Psycholinguistics* 1:371–85.

Elliott, C. D., Murray, D. J., and Pearson, L. S. 1978. *British Ability Scales: Manual 3; Directions for Administration and Scoring/Manual 4: Tables of Abilities and Norms.* Windsor, Berks: National Foundation for Educational Research.

Gillon, G., and Dodd, B. J. 1994. A prospective study of the relationship between phonological, semantic and syntactic skills and specific reading disability. *Reading and Writing: An Interdisciplinary Journal* 6:321–45.

Goswami, U. C. 1986. Children' use of analogy in learning to read: A developmental study. *Journal of Experimental Child Psychology* 42:73–83.

Goswami, U. C., and Bryant, P. E. 1990. *Phonological Skills and Learning to Read.* Hillsdale, NJ: Lawrence Erlbaum Associates.

Henderson, L. 1985. On the use of the term "grapheme". *Language and Cognitive Processes* 1:135–48.

Jastak, S., and Wilkinson, G. S. 1984. *The Wide Range Achievement Test-Revised: Administration Manual.* Wilmington, DE: Jastak Associates.

Kirtley, C., Bryant, P., MacLean, M., and Bradley, L. 1989. Rhyme, rime, and the onset of reading. *Journal of Experimental Child Psychology* 48:224–45.

Kreiner, D. S. 1992. Reaction time measures of spelling: Testing a two-strategy model of skilled reading. *Journal of Experimental Psychology: Learning, Memory, and Cognition* 18:763–76.

Kreiner, D. S., and Gough, P. B. 1990. Two ideas about spelling: Rules and word-specific memory. *Journal of Memory and Language* 29:103–18.

Laxon, V., Masterson, J., Pool, M., and Keating, C. 1992. Nonword naming: Further exploration of the pseudohomophone effect in terms of orthographic neighborhood size, graphemic changes, spelling-sound consistency, and reader accuracy. *Journal of Experimental Psychology: Learning, Memory, and Cognition* 18:730–48.

Leong, C. K. 1997. Strategies used by 9- to 12-year-old children in written spelling. In *Reading and Spelling: Development and Disorders*, C. Hulme and R. M. Joshi, eds. Mahwah, NJ: Lawrence Erlbaum Associates.

Leong, C. K., Cheng, H. C., Lundberg, I., Olofsson, Å., and Mulcahy, R. 1989. Structural equation modelling of cognitive processing, language awareness, and achievement. *International Journal of Experimental Research in Education* 26:15–46.

McCann, R. S., and Besner, D. 1987. Reading pseudohomophones: Implications for models of pronunciation assembly and the locus of word frequency effects in naming. *Journal of Experimental Psychology: Human Perception and Performance* 13:14–24.

Meyer, D. E., Schvaneveldt, R. W., and Ruddy, M. 1974. Functions of graphemic and phonemic codes in visual word recognition. *Memory and Cognition* 2:309–21.

Pachella, R. G. 1974. The interpretation of reaction time in information-processing research. In *Human Information Processing: Tutorials in Performance and Cognition*, B. H. Kantowitz, ed. New York: John Wiley.

Perfetti, C. A. 1997. The psycholinguistics of spelling and reading. In *Learning to Spell: Research, Theory, and Practice*, C. A. Perfetti, L. Rieben, and M. Fayol, eds. Mahwah, NJ: Lawrence Erlbaum Associates.

Perfetti, C. A., Rieben, L., and Fayol, M. (Eds.). 1997. *Learning to Spell: Research, Theory, and Practice.* Mahwah, NJ: Lawrence Erlbaum Associates.

Perin, D. 1983. Phonemic segmentation and spelling. *British Journal of Psychology* 74:129–44.

Polich, J., McCarthy, G., Wang, W. S., and Donchin, E. 1983. When words collide: Orthographic and phonological interference during word processing. *Biological Psychology* 16:155–80.

Pring, L., and Snowling, M. 1986. Developmental changes in word recognition: An information-processing account. *Quarterly Journal of Experimental Psychology* 38A:395–418.

Santee, J. L., and Egeth, H. E. 1982. Do reaction time and accuracy measure the same aspects of letter recognition? *Journal of Experimental Psychology: Human Perception and Performance* 8:489–501.

Seidenberg, M. S., and Tanenhaus, M. K. 1979. Orthographic effects on rhyme monitoring. *Journal of Experimental Psychology: Human Learning and Memory* 5:546–54.

Seymour, P. H. K. 1992. Cognitive theories of spelling and implications for education. In *Psychology, Spelling and Education*, C. M. Sterling and C. Robson, eds. Clevedon, UK: Multilingual Matters.

Stage, S. C., and Wagner, R. K. 1992. Development of young children's phonological and orthographic knowledge as revealed by their spellings. *Developmental Psychology* 28:287–96.

Swanson, H. L. 1992. Generality and modifiability of working memory among skilled and less skilled readers. *Journal of Educational Psychology* 84:473–88.

Treiman, R. 1993. *Beginning to Spell: A Study of First-Grade Children*. New York: Oxford University Press.

Venezky, R. L. 1970. *The Structure of English*. The Hague: Mouton.

PART IV
Strategies for Remediation

The papers in this section explore multiple strategies for remediation of reading difficulties. The literature reviews are current, the techniques sophisticated, and the respect for empirical evidence outweighs (as it must) adherence to a particular philosophy of instruction.

In chapter 9, Sylvia Abbott and Virginia Berninger present a detailed curriculum for students in grades 4 to 7, contrasting two different ways to provide explicit instruction in the English orthography. For half the students the code-emphasis component focused exclusively on the phoneme-grapheme correspondences, the other half were also given explicit instruction to syllable types and morphological structure. The results are encouraging in finding that both groups made discernible gains in word recognition and reading comprehension over the four-month period; as did virtually every child in the study (individual data are provided). There was no evidence that instruction in syllables and morphemes had an obvious advantage. Readers will find this paper useful on a number of ways: for the explicit details in lesson plans which are tied to readily available commercial programs and for the result that the only limiting factor was RSN—and that limited not mastery of the code, but speed of word recognition. As the title suggests, the study indicates that 7th graders are not too old to benefit from instruction.

In chapter 10, Marshall Raskind and Eleanor Higgins provide some surprising and encouraging evidence that speech recognition technology designed to help persons compensate for reading limitations may in fact enhance reading and spelling as well—gains in word recognition, spelling, and reading comprehension were small but reliable after only one semester using this technology an hour a week. This carefully conducted study will be read with keen interest by all who struggle with how to support students who must continue in grade-level curriculum and yet also continue to learn to read. Combined with prior evidence that text readers help the poor reader, school systems, families and clinicians will be expanding their repertoire on aids to older students.

If you talk to any group of experienced reading instructors, you will find that their number one concern is how to enhance reading fluency. For even very effective code-emphasis interventions have not yielded sizable gains in reading fluency. In Chapter 11, Marianne Meyer and Rebecca Felton bring us up to date on what research finds regarding the efficacy of means to improve reading fluency, with particular emphasis on the "repeated readings" approach. This paper will be especially useful to reading instructors, as it is structured in a question answer format.

The final paper, chapter 12 by Joanne Martila Pierson offers an unusual—and very readable—combination of explicit code instruction and concern for the child's continued interest. What I like about this paper is the explicit documentation of what the child does and does not learn over the period covered and the honest reflections on what motivational efforts can and cannot do in promoting reading success. My suspicion will be that many clinicians will find their own attempts to "capture" a student's interest mirrored in this paper and will be encouraged to be creative in their efforts to spur interest, while at the same time keeping their eye on the mastery of the system.

It's Never Too Late to Remediate:
Teaching Word Recognition to Students with Reading Disabilities in Grades 4–7[1]

Sylvia P. Abbott and Virginia W. Berninger

University of Washington

Twenty children in fourth through seventh grade participated in 16 one-hour individual tutorials over a four-month period. Half of the children received structural analysis and alphabet principle training; half received only alphabetic principle training; all received training in orthographic and phonological skills, practice in oral reading of connected text, and monitoring strategies for comprehension. Results showed that the children improved reliably in reading and related measures. Treatment condition did not predict rate of growth. Only rapid automatic naming of letters predicted response to intervention and only on rate of real word reading. Results of this study indicate that upper elementary and middle school students who have not yet mastered accuracy and automaticity of word recognition should be given explicit instruction in word recognition, especially in the alphabetic principle. The benefits of structural analysis training were evident only in trends for individual students on hierarchical linear modeling (HLM) growth analyses.

[1]This dissertation research by the first author, and supervised by the second, was supported by Grant No. HD-33812 and Grant No. HD-25858-09 from the National Institute of Child Health and Human Development.

Annals of Dyslexia, Vol. 49, 1999
ISSN 0736-9387

INTRODUCTION

In her 1983 study, Chall made an important distinction between learning to read and reading to learn. The learning-to-read stage of instruction typically occurs during the primary grades, whereas the reading-to-learn stage typically begins during the intermediate grades. The timing of this developmental shift in focus of instruction may work well for many children who master basic word skills such as accurate and fluent word recognition in the primary grades. However, this developmental timing does not effectively accommodate those children who are still learning to read when the instructional shift occurs. For those children who continue to need explicit instruction in word recognition skills, the curriculum shifts its focus (from learning to read to reading to learn) too early. Such children are still in the learning-to-read stage, but can continue to make progress only if given explicit instruction at their level of development. A common scenario for these delayed readers is that not only is word recognition not explicitly taught in the intermediate grades but also the readability of the materials used is well beyond their instructional level. Little research has addressed this developmental mismatch between children's reading levels and the focus of curriculum. This developmental mismatch is especially problematic for students with dyslexia.

A growing body of research shows that early intervention (i.e., intervention before third grade) enhances the probability that students with reading disabilities will develop adequate reading skills (Lyon 1995). It does not follow, however, that early intervention alone is sufficient to meet the needs of all students with reading problems. Although many students benefit from the boost of early intervention (Abbott, Reed, Abbott, and Berninger 1997; Torgesen, Wagner, and Rashotte 1997; Vellutino, Scanlon, Sipay, Small, Pratt, Chen, and Denckla 1996), others will continue to need instructional support, sometimes for the remainder of their school years.

The research on early intervention has shed light on the beginning skills necessary for learning-to-read. Four skills need to be taught and learned at the beginning of the learning-to-read stage (Berninger 1998b). Children must acquire:

1. Orthographic knowledge in the form of naming letters, recognizing letters in words, and writing letters.
2. Phonological awareness in terms of segmenting spoken words into phonemes.

3. A knowledge of the alphabetic principle so that they can integrate letter and phoneme knowledge.
4. The ability to apply the alphabetic principle in decoding unfamiliar words and in recognizing familiar words.

However, additional skills must be acquired in order for children to deal with longer words and progress from the beginning to the advanced phase of learning to read. Adams and Henry (1997) discussed two skills needed to move beginning readers along the developmental continuum of word recognition: the six syllable patterns in written English; and morpheme patterns from the Anglo-Saxon, Romance (Latin and French), and Greek layers of the English language.

The working hypothesis of the research described in this article is that some students in the intermediate grades will need explicit instruction in beginning and/or advanced word recognition skills to become proficient readers. The research was designed to answer three questions:

1. Is instructional intervention effective in raising reading achievement in older, underachieving readers?
2. Is an instructional protocol that incorporates a beginning and an advanced skills component for word recognition more effective in raising reading achievement than one that incorporates only a beginning skills component?
3. Do individual differences in older, underachieving learners affect their response to instruction for word recognition?

EFFICACY OF REMEDIATION IN THE OLDER, UNDERACHIEVING READER

Prior research studies provided evidence for the hypothesis that instructional intervention directed toward learning to read may be effective for children with reading disabilities, even at a grade level when curriculum normally focuses on reading to learn.

In one study, Lovett and Steinbach (1997) tested the hypothesis that phonological deficits in reading can be remediated across the elementary grades. Their sample, which was significantly impaired in single-word reading (third to fourth percentile on average), spanned three grade groups: second/third, fourth, and fifth/sixth. They compared a treatment aimed at phonological decoding and a treatment aimed at word identification strategies; both treatments were significantly more effective than a control treatment aimed at classroom survival skills. Consistent with their hypothesis, the 35-hour treatment program, delivered to groups of two or three children, worked equally well at all grade levels. The older students were just as responsive as the younger students. Following treatment, the participants had made statistically significant improvements but still scored well below age-level norms on the Word Identification or Word Attack subtests of the Woodcock Reading Mastery Test-Revised (Woodcock 1987).

In a second study, Alexander, Anderson, Heilman, Voeller, and Torgesen (1991) evaluated the effectiveness of the *Auditory Discrimination in Depth Program* (ADD) in remediating the phonological decoding of ten students with severe dyslexia whose average age was 10.8 years. All but one had a discrepancy of at least 1.5 *SD* between their full scale IQ and a standardized measure of single-word reading. Children received, on average, 64 hours of individual training that used sensory feedback from the eye, ear, and mouth in identifying, classifying, and labeling consonant and vowel sounds. After children developed metalinguistic awareness of the motor characteristics of speech sounds, they learned to associate the sounds with corresponding alphabet letters. Following training, their average standard scores increased from 75.1 to 87.6 on the Word Identification subtest and from 77.2 to 98.4 on the Word Attack subtest of the 1973 version of Woodcock Reading Mastery Test.

Our study differed in four ways from these two studies:

1. Our inclusion criteria were less stringent. We hope that our sample may be more representative of the range of severity typically served in resource rooms. All participants had unexpectedly low achievement for their intelligence levels but were not necessarily at the very bottom of the reading distribution.
2. Our intervention was of shorter duration—about half that of Lovett and Steinbach (1997) and about a quarter that of Alexander et al (1991).
3. The instructional protocol was designed to aim the teaching in each session to all levels of language—subword, word, and text—to create a functional reading system (Berninger et al. 1997; Berninger 1998a; Berninger 1998b).

4. HLM analysis of growth curves (Bryk, Raudenbush, and Congdon 1996) was used to evaluate response to intervention for each individual and each treatment group.

RELATIVE EFFECTIVENESS OF BEGINNING SKILLS ONLY VERSUS COMBINED BEGINNING AND ADVANCED SKILLS

Considerable research evidence exists that training in orthographic knowledge, phonological awareness, alphabetic principle, phonological decoding, and word-specific reading is effective when a curriculum focuses on learning to read (e.g., Adams 1990; Ehri 1992; Gough, Juel, and Griffith 1992). The same kind of training may be effective in later years if these skills have not already been mastered. However when taught later, these skills may be learned more effectively if coupled with training in the advanced skills of syllable types and morpheme patterns. A word longer than one syllable is difficult to decode without analyzing the internal structure of the word. This skill of analyzing internal word structure—referred to as structural analysis—draws on syllable and morpheme knowledge in decomposing a word into its parts to derive its pronunciation and meaning.

In structural analysis approaches, students are taught not only to count the number of syllables in a word but also that each syllable contains a vowel sound. They also are taught that in polysyllabic words, one syllable is given primary stress, and that in English, the stressed syllable is often the first one in the word. Additionally, students are taught to distinguish among the six vowel-based syllable types in English: closed, open, silent *e*, vowel team, *r*-controlled, and *-le* (Moats 1995). Students also learn that words of Anglo-Saxon origin have characteristic vowel (V) and consonant (C) patterns—for example, VCCV, VCV, VCCCV, and CVVC—that can be used to segment long, unfamiliar words into syllables and then be decoded using spelling-phoneme knowledge. Balmuth (1982) showed that students have more difficulty recognizing written syllables than hearing syllables in spoken words. Segmentation of the written word does not always correspond in a one-to-one fashion with segmentation of the spoken word. For example, the written word *bunny* would be divided between the repeating *n*'s, but phonologically there is only one /n/ phoneme in the spoken word. Students also learn that accent patterns influence syllable patterns. Although the letter-sound correspondences in words derived from Romance languages are usually simple, the stress patterns are not. The schwa, or unstressed vowel sound, is common (e.g. excellent). Letter-sound correspondence alone cannot be used to determine the appropriate spelling of the schwa which is a reduced vowel; its spelling must be learned for specific word contexts.

Structural analysis approaches also introduce morphemic analysis; that is, analyzing words into their morphemes or meaning units. These units are either free or bound morphemes. Free morphemes can stand as whole words and cannot be divided without losing their meaning. Bound morphemes (for example, -s, -es, -ed, -er, -est) cannot stand alone but can be combined with a free morpheme such as clean, to modify its meaning. Most English words are of Anglo-Saxon, Romance, or Greek origin, each with distinct morpheme patterns. Anglo-Saxon morphemes consist of compound words, prefixes, and suffixes. Romance morphemes consist of roots (vis, tract, ped), prefixes, and suffixes. Greek morphemes consist of two equally important parts (tele + scope, auto + graph).

Unfortunately, this structural analysis approach is not taught in many classrooms in either the upper primary grades or intermediate grades. Henry (1988) assessed third through fifth grade students' ability to identify patterns within written words and found that they had limited knowledge of word structure. They had difficulty dividing words into syllables, and few used syllable division as a strategy for analyzing long, unfamiliar words. Henry also found that neither normally developing nor reading disabled students were able to identify or understand common morpheme patterns in words. One reason that many children are not taught morpheme patterns is that educators think students should master all letter-sound correspondences before learning to analyze the structure of polysyllabic words. Likewise, Just and Carpenter (1987) and O'Rourke (1974) reported that many grade school and high school students never master common prefixes and suffixes (bound morphemes), probably because they are not taught their meanings explicitly and do not infer the meanings on their own.

Research evidence supports the value of teaching structural analysis of words. Henry (1988) compared typical third, fourth, and fifth graders who received basal reader and spelling instruction to those who received decoding and word structure training based on word origin. Those who received both decoding and structural analysis improved more in reading and spelling performance than those who received only a basal approach. Henry, Calfee, and Avelar-LaSalle (1989) taught five specially designed units combining decoding and structural analysis. As a group, students improved from 15 percent to 50 percent correct on prefixes and from 18 percent to 55 percent correct on syllables. Based on her research, Henry (1990) published *Words*, a curriculum designed to make students aware of how different word patterns (letter-sound correspondence, syllable, and morpheme) are related to word origin. Readers are taught to look first for familiar morphemes in unfamiliar words, then for syllable divisions, and finally for letter-sound correspondences.

Based on the research of Henry and her colleagues, we tested the hypothesis that children would improve at word recognition more rapidly if given training in both the *beginning phase* (orthographic knowledge, phonological awareness, alphabet principle, decoding, and word specific practice) and the *advanced phase* (syllable types and morpheme patterns based on word origins) of word recognition, rather than training in the beginning phase only. We used portions of Henry's (1990) curriculum for the advanced phase and tested the hypothesis not only for treatment groups but also for individuals in treatment groups.

INDIVIDUAL DIFFERENCES IN UPPER ELEMENTARY LEARNERS

Rate of growth in response to instruction may be related to individual differences in students and not just to curriculum or instruction. Prior research has identified individual difference variables that predict slopes of growth curves in early intervention for reading problems. Such predictions include orthographic coding, phonological awareness, rapid automatized naming skills, and verbal IQ (Berninger, Abbott, Zook, Ogier, Lemos, and Brooksher 1999). We wondered whether these same individual difference variables would predict response to intervention in the upper elementary grades.

METHOD

PARTICIPANTS

Twenty students (13 males and 7 females) enrolled in fourth ($n = 4$), fifth ($n = 4$), sixth ($n = 10$), or seventh grade ($n = 2$) were identified as low achieving in reading as a result of testing at the University of Washington Learning Disabilities

Center in Winter 1997. These children's families were participating in a family genetics study; therefore, results may generalize to students whose families have multigenerational histories of learning disabilities. All students were underachieving in reading (more than a standard deviation between their score on WRMT-R Word Identification or Word Attack subtests and their prorated WISC-III Verbal IQ) and most were more than a standard deviation below the mean on those reading measures. Their average prorated Verbal IQ on the WISC-III (Wechsler 1991), which has a mean of 100 and a standard deviation of 15, was 102.55 (SD = 12.82). Their average Word Attack subtest score on the WRMT-R, which has a mean of 100 and a standard deviation of 15, was 83.90 (SD = 13.12) and their mean Word Identification subtest score on the WRMT-R, which also has a mean of 100 and a standard deviation of 15, was 81.25 (SD = 14.24) at the beginning of the study. The mean chronological age was 11.54 years (SD = 0.98 years) and ranged from 9.58 years to 13.16 years.

Background information was obtained for each participant from a questionnaire completed by the parents of all 20 participants. Parents answered questions about their educational level, ethnicity, family history of reading problems, child's educational history including current and past special services, and the amount of time the child reads outside of school. Ethnic background of the students was 90 percent European-American (7 girls and 11 boys) and 10 percent Asian-American (2 boys). Mothers' level of education, which is one index of socioeconomic status, included 25 percent high school, 50 percent community college or vocational technical, 15 percent college, and 10 percent some graduate study. Three children (15 percent) were left handed. Of the 20 children, 90 percent received resource room services prior to this study (35 percent had received services from first grade) and 70 percent continued to receive special services (from 20 to 60 minutes a day) during the study. None of the remaining 10 percent received special services for the first time during the study. Despite these special services, all students had struggled throughout their schooling with reading. Prior to the study, only one child reported no reading outside of school hours. The remaining 19 children reported reading outside of school from as little as 20 minutes a day (n = 1) to as much as two hours per day (n = 4); those that read for a longer time did not necessarily read more, as they may have read more slowly.

OVERVIEW OF INSTRUCTIONAL INTERVENTIONS

The students were assigned, on the basis of a random numbers table, to one of two treatment conditions. Table I summarizes both the variable and constant components of the two conditions. The two conditions differed in whether the students were given structural analysis training. The structural analysis group received 15 minutes of Henry's (1990) *Words* program that included explicit instruction in syllable types and morpheme patterns according to word origin. The study skills (control) group received 15 minutes of study skills training. The conditions also differed in how words were practiced during the phonological decoding and oral reading components of each lesson. In the phonological decoding component, children in the structural analysis group were encouraged to apply their knowledge of syllable structure and morpheme patterns. Similarly, when students made errors during text-level oral reading, tutors pointed out how syllable and morpheme information could be used to figure out correct pronunciations. In contrast, no mention of syllable structure or morpheme patterns was made to children in the study skills group during the phonological decoding or oral reading components. Children in both conditions received training in the components for beginning word recognition: phonological and orthographic awareness, alphabetic principle, phonological decoding, and oral reading of specific words. Children in these treatment conditions did not differ in mean age, grade, or mother's level of education.

Each student participated in one-hour individual tutorial sessions weekly for 16 weeks. These sessions began in March 1997, and were completed by the end of June 1997. Standard scripted lessons were designed based on the previously established, necessary components for developing a functional reading system (Berninger et al. 1997; Berninger 1998b). Lessons were designed for fast-paced tutor-student interaction and a high rate of student response. Elements of direct instruction (tutor modeling and student repeating response) were included, along with prescribed procedures for correcting children's errors. Each of the components is discussed in greater detail below.

Phonological and Orthographic Skills. Words taken from the vocabulary list at the beginning of each story in the *Decoding Strategies Student Book* (Engelmann, Meyer, Johnson, and Carmine 1988) were used for the phonological and orthographic activities at the beginning of each session. That is, phonological

Table I. Constant and varying[a] components in two instructional groups.

Language Level	Time (mins)	Structural Analysis Group (SA)	Study Skills Group (SS)
Subword	6	Phonological/ Orthographic Skills	Phonological/ Orthographic Skills
Subword	5	Alphabet Principle Training	Alphabet Principle Training
Word	10	*Phonological Decoding*[b]	*Phonological Decoding*[c]
Word(SA)/ Text (SS)	15	*Structural Analysis*	*Study Skills*
Text	24	Oral reading with *error correction,* comprehension monitoring, rereading for fluency	Oral reading with *error correction,* comprehension monitoring, rereading for fluency

[a]Varying components are bolded and italicized.

[b]Highlighting syllable/morpheme structure as well as alphabet principle

[c]Highlighting only alphabet principle

and orthographic skills were yoked to the vocabulary that children would read later in the session. For the *phonological training* component, the goal was to develop awareness of phonemes in the vocabulary words when spoken aloud. Tutors told the student to say a word (e.g., *turn*), then to say the target word without a designated phoneme (e.g., /t/). If the student responded correctly, the next word was presented. If the student answered incorrectly, the tutor demonstrated how to segment the sounds using colored disks to represent each sound segment. If the student could segment the word using the disks to represent the sounds, the next word was presented. If not, one more teaching and testing trial was presented, followed by the next word. For the *orthographic training* component, the goal was to develop awareness of each letter in the written version of the vocabulary word. Words from the story were printed on the board. The tutor swept her finger from left to right under the word and directed the student to look at the word. The tutor then covered the word and asked the student to spell the word. If the student did not spell the word correctly, the tutor pointed out the missed letters, then repeated the procedure before presenting the next word.

Alphabetic Principle Training. The goal of this component was to use skills acquired from orthographic and phonological training when learning specific spelling-sound correspondences. During this component, 109 of the most frequent spelling-sound correspondences of written English were explicitly taught using *Talking Letters* (Berninger 1998b) and a connectionist, nonrule-based approach. The spelling-sound correspondences were organized into "orders" based on the degree of predictability (see Appendix). These orders, derived from Venezky's (1995) theory, have been used in four of our prior studies. Orders 0-a and 0-b cluster as easy predictability, orders 1–4 cluster as moderate predictability, and orders 5, 6, and 7 cluster as low predictability (Berninger et al. in press). For each correspondence, the tutor would point to and name a letter or group of letters, then name a picture that contained the target phoneme associated with that 1- or 2-letter spelling unit, and finally produce the sound that went with the spelling unit. Next, as in direct instruction, the student repeated pointing to and naming the letter(s), naming the pictured word, and producing the phoneme (for example, *a*, *apple*, /a/).

Phonological Decoding. The goal of this component was to apply the alphabet principle to real words that would appear later in the reading selection. The Structural Analysis Group spent 10 minutes applying phonics and structural analysis to decoding vocabulary words. For each word, the student was asked to divide the word into syllables, sound out the spelling-sound correspondences within syllables, then blend the syllables to make a whole word (*boat/ing*, then *b-oa-t-i-ng*, then *boating*). If a student needed help, the tutor was to model use of the structural analysis strategies being taught.

In contrast, the Study Skills Group used synthetic phonics strategies to sound out the same words. They were asked to sound out each grapheme (/b/ /ō/ /t/ /ĭ/ /ng/) and blend the resulting phonemes to synthesize a whole word. If the student was unable to segment and blend a word, the tutor modeled the phoneme synthesis procedure but did not model analyzing the word into its syllables or morphemes.

Structural Analysis. Using *Words* (Henry 1990) tutors instructed students in layers of language based on word origin (Anglo-Saxon, Romance, and Greek). Syllable patterns, morpheme patterns, and strategies for decoding, reading, and spelling long words were covered. Students were taught to check for affixes and roots, then divide the word into syllables, and finally, if needed, to use letter-sound correspondence. When the *Words* lesson introduced spelling activities, children first repeated the word, then listened for syllables, and then identified common affixes and roots. They were encouraged to use letter-sound correspondences only after attempting the morpheme and syllable strategies.

Study Skills. The students in this condition used a commercially available study skills workbook (Drumm 1996). Lessons spanning grade levels 2 through 8 were used. The tutor worked with the students on such skills as outlining, writing paragraphs, note-taking, and using an index. Tutors invited students to relate their current classroom assignments to the lessons taught in the tutorial.

Oral Reading of Connected Text for Meaning. The final 24 minutes of the tutorial were spent orally reading and rereading stories taken from *Corrective Reading Skill Applications* (Englemann et al. 1988). Stories from student books B1, B2, and C were chosen, progressing from texts with tightly controlled syntax and vocabulary to less controlled texts that were more representative of texts typically encountered in classrooms. Procedures in the teacher's manual for this program were not followed. Our procedures for this research included comprehension monitoring but not explicit instruction in comprehension. As children read, corrections were made as needed, according to treatment condition. That is, those students in the Structural Analysis Group were told to divide the word into syllables, sound out the syllables, and then pronounce the word using the strategies taught. Students in the Study Skills Group were taught to use the letter-sound correspondences from Talking Letters to sound out difficult words. If a student in either group was still unable to read the word, the tutor spelled the word and then supplied the name of the word to form a connection at the whole word level.

TUTORS AND FIDELITY OF TREATMENT IMPLEMENTATION

Tutors included school psychologists and graduate students in school psychology or teacher education, and were trained by the first author prior to beginning tutoring. Once tutoring began, tutors audiotaped each tutoring session. Audiotapes were reviewed by the first author who discussed with tutors any deviations in standard implementation of procedures. Deviations were rare after the first two sessions. Tutors also met regularly to solve potential problems related to motivation or behavior.

LESSON PLANS

Part I of the Appendix contains the spelling-sound correspondences taught in the alphabet principle component, organized by order of difficulty (see Abbott et al. 1997 for a discussion of the theoretical rationale for orders and difficulty). Part II of the Appendix refers the reader to the actual page numbers from

Henry's *Words Program*, Drumm's *Social Skills Program*, and Englemann et al.'s *SRA Decoding Program* for each lesson.

OVERVIEW OF ASSESSMENT MEASURES

A time schedule for the administration of tests is presented in table II. The pretest battery included the following:

1. A prorated verbal IQ test based on the WISC-III (Wechsler, 1991) Information, Similarities, Vocabulary and Comprehension subtests.
2. Measures of orthographic knowledge including the University of Washington Letter Cluster Orthographic Coding Test (Berninger, Yates, and Lester 1991); the Colorado Perceptual Speed Test (DeFries 1985); and the Orthographic Choice Task (adapted from a computer-based test developed by Olson, Kliegl, Davidson, and Foltz 1985).
3. Measures of phonological processing include syllable deletion and phoneme deletion on the Modified Rosner Test of Auditory Analysis Skills (Berninger, Thalberg, DeBruyn, and Smith 1987). We also presented prepublication versions of phonological segmentation and nonword memory measures from Wagner and Torgesen's (1999) Comprehensive Assessment of Phonological Skills.
4. A reading comprehension measure (Woodcock 1987).
5. Qualitative Reading Inventory (QRI), an informal reading inventory for connected text that yields instructional level in grades (Leslie and Caldwell 1990) and of taught words.
6. A measure of rapid automatized naming (RAN) for letters (Wolf, Bally, and Morris 1986).
7. Measures of accuracy including the Word Identification and Word Attack subtests of the Woodcock Reading Mastery Test-Revised (1987) and prepublication speed of reading single real words or pseudowords (Wagner and Torgesen 1999).
8. Measures of spelling from the Wechsler Individual Achievement Test (WIAT, Psychological Corporation 1992) and Wide Range Achievement Test-Third Edition (WRAT-3, Wilkinson 1993).

At midtest, after 8 lessons, the single-word reading and spelling measures were repeated because they were thought to

Table II.   Time schedule for administration of tests.

	Pretest	Midtest	Posttest
WISC III:	X		
Information, Similarities, Vocabulary, and Comprehension subtests			
Letter Cluster Coding	X		X
Colorado Perceptual Speed Test	X		X
Orthographic Choice Task	X		X
Syllable and Phoneme Deletion	X		X
Phonological Segmentation	X		X
Nonword Memory Test	X		X
Qualitative Reading Inventory	X		X
Rapid Automatized Naming (RAN) of Letters	X		
Woodcock Johnson-Revised:			
Word Identification	X	X	X
Word Attack	X	X	X
Passage Comprehension	X		X
Real Word and Non-word Reading Efficiency Subtests	X	X	X
Wechsler Individual Achievement Test Spelling Subtest	X	X	X
Wide Range Achievement Test- 3rd Edition Spelling	X	X	X
Taught Words	X		X

be the most sensitive to the effects of structural analysis training. The Woodcock, WIAT, and WRAT-3 measures were age-corrected standard scores. The RAN measure was a time score in seconds. The QRI was a criterion-referenced grade level. All the other measures were accuracy scores.

At posttest, after 16 lessons, a battery was administered that included measures of phonological and orthographic skills, accuracy and speed of single-word reading, spelling, text reading, and comprehension. Table III reports the means and standard deviations for each measure administered at two time points, and for the one measure (RAN) other than verbal IQ that was

Table III. Means and standard deviations (SD) for each treatment group on outcomes measured only once or twice.

	Structural Analysis		Study Skills	
	Pretest Mean (SD)	Posttest Mean (SD)	Pretest Mean (SD)	Posttest Mean (SD)
Orthographic Letter Cluster	85.90 (8.41)	89.40 (7.89)	84.70 (5.68)	91.20 (3.16)
Colorado Perceptual Test	37.64 (9.98)	40.22 (12.04)	28.76 (9.32)	33.03 (12.21)
Orthographic Choice	79.23 (16.10)	81.54 (11.85)	76.92 (4.56)	75.16 (9.33)
Phoneme Segmentation	21.50 (4.97)	25.10 (5.71)	20.60 (3.10)	25.50 (2.46)
Syllable Segmentation	6.20 (2.20)	7.40 (2.01)	5.60 (2.37)	6.80 (1.40)
Wagner-Torgesen Segmentation	12.30 (4.06)	18.40 (4.77)	8.80 (2.62)	17.80 (4.24)
Wagner-Torgesen Memory	16.60 (3.66)	18.20 (3.85)	17.10 (3.35)	20.00 (0.39)
WRMT-R Passage Comprehension	87.40 (24.16)	95.90 (20.64)	80.60 (17.32)	88.70 (15.76)
QRI (instructional level for text reading)	3.80 (1.98)	4.80 (2.04)	2.78 (1.77)	3.33 (1.82)
RAN Letters	25.8 (5.1)		32.4 (7.8)	

given only once. Table IV reports the means and standard deviations for each measure administered at three time points.

RESULTS

ANALYSES

To answer the three research questions, a repeated measures ANOVA was used to examine effects over time for measures obtained at pretest and posttest (see table III), and HLM (Bryk et al. 1996) growth curve modeling (Bryk and Raudenbush 1987) was used to examine effects over time for measures that were obtained at pretest, midtest, and posttest (see table IV). (Three time points are needed for growth curve analysis.) There were no statistically significant differences between groups at pretest on any measure in Tables III or IV or in the amount of reading students did outside of school. We use Bryk and Raudenbush's HLM growth curve modeling rather than growth curves based on ordinary least squares regression for several reasons. First, HLM growth curve modeling handles missing data well. Second, HLM growth curve modeling has been shown to have smaller standard errors in cross-validation and, therefore, better reliability in estimating slopes of individual growth curves. Third, the regression is fitted with information from the individual's score and from all the members in the group. Finally, the multilevel feature allows us to compare treatments at the group level and to assess each student's growth in response to intervention at the individual level. Therefore, in this study, we analyzed response to treatment for both groups and individuals (see Abbott and Berninger 1995; Berninger and Abbott 1994).

Table IV. Means and standard deviations (SD) for each treatment group on outcomes measured at three timepoints.

	Structural Analysis			Study Skills		
	Pretest Mean (SD)	Midtest Mean (SD)	Posttest Mean (SD)	Pretest Mean (SD)	Midtest Mean (SD)	Posttest Mean (SD)
Word Identification	85.40 (16.29)	86.10 (20.11)	90.30 (15.85)	77.10 (11.15)	78.80 (7.82)	82.30 (9.50)
Word Attack	84.10 (16.80)	83.30 (14.68)	89.40 (12.18)	83.70 (9.02)	84.50 (11.68)	87.30 (9.46)
Taught Words	25.60 (10.72)	28.10 (9.89)	31.00 (8.59)	19.22 (8.50)	23.89 (8.33)	25.00 (8.94)
WIAT Spelling	82.40 (12.17)	87.20 (11.44)	86.80 (11.44)	80.00 (9.21)	82.44 (11.16)	83.78 (13.90)
WRAT-3 Spelling	86.40 (13.73)	87.70 (11.20)	89.60 (12.22)	81.22 (10.10)	80.89 (8.98)	81.33 (8.80)
Real Word Reading Efficiency	50.40 (14.27)	52.70 (13.93)	53.30 (13.90)	42.89 (5.90)	45.11 (7.20)	45.89 (8.22)
Nonword Reading Efficiency	22.89 (8.61)	23.44 (10.81)	24.56 (9.57)	16.57 (7.21)	18.72 (7.57)	17.71 (8.10)

EFFICACY OF REMEDIATION IN THE OLDER, UNDERACHIEVING READER

As shown in table V, there was a significant trials effect (improvement over 16 lessons) for each measure except orthographic choice that was measured at two time points. As shown in table VI, slopes were significant, indicating reliable improvement, on all measures at three time points, except nonword reading efficiency. Thus, with the exception of orthographic choice and nonword reading efficiency, children improved reliably on all reading, spelling, and related skills the intervention was designed to improve. For the standardized measures, these gains were in age-corrected standard scores which represent relative gains compared to age-peers.

Table V. Analysis-of-Variance results for outcomes measured at pretest and posttest.

	Treatment			Trials		Treatment x Trials		
	MS	F	MSE_a	MS	F	MS	F	MSE_b
Orthographic Letter Cluster	0.90	0.01	74.25	250.00	18.71***	22.50	1.68	13.36
Colorado Perceptual Test	644.97	2.81	229.78	117.01	11.08**	7.17	0.68	10.57
Orthographic Choice	188.57	0.81	232.18	0.75	0.03	41.39	1.92	21.58
Phoneme Segmentation	0.63	0.02	32.76	180.63	48.78***	4.23	1.14	3.70
Syllable Segmentation	3.60	0.67	5.36	14.40	5.02*	.00	.00	2.87
Wagner Segmentation	42.03	2.11	19.90	570.03	47.19***	21.03	1.74	12.08
Wagner Memory	13.23	0.77	17.18	50.63	15.28***	4.23	1.28	3.31
Passage Comprehension	490.00	0.67	733.67	688.90	15.24***	0.40	0.01	45.21
QRI (instructional level for text)	14.67	2.10	6.98	5.73	17.36***	0.47	1.42	0.33

* $p < .05$ ** $p < .01$ *** $p < .001$

MSE_a is used to test the treatment effect for significance.

MSE_b is used to test the trials and treatment x trials interaction for significance.

Table VI.	Intercepts and slopes of overall growth curves in total sample.			
	Intercept	t	Slope	t
Word Identification	59.77	23.59**	2.75	5.15***
Word Attack	21.68	12.10***	1.62	2.96**
Taught Words	23.35	10.60***	2.66	6.15***
WIAT Spelling	24.68	23.95***	1.48	4.05***
WRAT-3 Spelling	26.45	33.94***	0.61	3.68**
Real Word Reading Efficiency	47.29	18.88***	1.54	3.23**
Nonword Reading Efficiency	18.94	8.72***	0.92	1.93

** $p < .01$ *** $p < .001$

TREATMENT EFFECTS

Group Analyses. As shown in table V, neither the treatment effect nor treatment x trials effect was ever significant for measures obtained at two time points. As shown in table VII, treatment never reliably predicted the slope for measures obtained at three time points. The lack of a treatment effect is not due to preexisting differences between treatment groups as the intercepts in table VIII were not significantly different.

Individual Analyses. For measures with three data points, we were able to examine individual growth curves within each treatment. For measures with two data points, we examined change from pretest to posttest for individual subjects. In table IX, a check indicates that an individual child was a treatment responder (growth curve significantly different from chance or posttest higher than pretest) on a learning outcome measure. As evident on that table, there was a trend toward greater individual treatment response within the

Table VII.	Is treatment predictive of intercept and slope?			
	Intercept	t	Slope	t
Word Identification	−5.83	−1.16	0.20	0.19
Word Attack	−0.38	−0.10	−0.35	−0.32
Taught Words	−4.38	−0.99	−0.08	−0.08
WIAT Spelling	−0.45	−0.21	−0.45	−0.61
WRAT-3 Spelling	−1.28	−0.81	−0.48	−1.44
Real Word Reading Efficiency	−6.79	−1.39	0.18	0.18
Nonword Reading Efficiency	−3.40	−0.78	0.20	0.21

Table VIII.   Intercepts and slopes of growth curves in structural analysis and study skills treatments.

	Structural Analysis		Study Skills	
	Intercept	Slope	Intercept	Slope
Word Identification	62.68	2.65	56.85	2.85
Word Attack	21.87	1.80	21.48	1.45
Taught Words	25.53	2.70	21.16	2.63
WIAT Spelling	24.90	1.70	24.45	1.25
WRAT-3 Spelling	27.08	0.85	25.81	0.38
Real Word Reading Efficiency	50.68	1.45	43.89	1.63
Nonword Reading Efficiency	20.64	0.82	17.24	1.02

structural analysis group than within the study skills group on five of the seven measures for which three data points were available. This trend could be seen on all measures except WIAT (on which equal individual improvement was seen in the two groups) and nonword efficiency (on which the study skills group showed more improvement). For the two measures with only two data points, the structural analysis group included more treatment responders. When only the word-level measures—which were hypothesized to be more sensitive to structural analysis training—were considered (all but QRI which assesses text reading), a sign test showed significantly more positive outcomes at the individual level for the structural analysis group than for the study skills group ($p < .035$, one tailed).

To compare the amount of growth across treatment groups, we transformed the change in mean slope for the treatment responders in each group to grade equivalents based on published norms for the two reading measures. On average, the treatment responders in the structural analysis group advanced 8 months in word identification skill levels and the treatment responders in the study skills group advanced 7 months. On Word Attack, the treatment responders in the structural analysis group advanced an average of 11 months and the treatment responders in the study skills group advanced 5 months. Although the groups were nearly equivalent in the amount of gain in real word reading, the treatment responders in the structural analysis group gained more than those in the study skills group in pseudoword reading.

Table IX.   Improvement on measures for individual participants.

	Word ID	Word Attack	Taught Words	WIAT	WRAT	Word Effic.	Nonword Effic.	QRI level	Ortho choice
Structural Analysis Group									
1	√	√			√	√	√		√
2	√	√	√	√			√	√	√
3	√	√		√	√	√		√	
4	√	√	√	√					
6		√	√		√	√		√	
7	√	√		√	√	√		√	
12	√		√	√	√	√	√	√	√
15	√	√	√	√	√	√	√	√	√
17			√	√	√	√	√	√	
20	√			√	√	√			
Total Improved	8	7	5	7	9	8	5	7	4
Study Skills Group									
5				√	√	√	√	√	√
8		√		√		√	√		√
9	√			√		√	√		
10	√	√		√	√	√			
11	√	√	√	√	√			√	√
13	√	√				√	√		
14	√	√		√				√	
16	√		√				√	√	
18	√	√	√	√	√	√	√		
19				√		√		√	
Total Improved	7	6	3	7	5	6	7	5	3

[a]For the first seven measures, a check (√) means the growth curve was significantly different from chance. For the last two measures, it means that the posttest score was higher than the pretest score.

That treatment is received at all may be more important than which specific kind of treatment is received. As we have reported before in treatment studies based on a systems approach aimed at multiple components of a functional system (Abbott et al. 1997; Hart, Berninger, and Abbott 1997), all children participating responded to treatment on some learning outcome measures, regardless of which treatment group they were in.

INDIVIDUAL DIFFERENCES
IN UPPER ELEMENTARY LEARNERS

The multilevel features of HLM were used to examine whether the pre-intervention levels of individual difference measures were related to the intercept and slope of individual growth curves. Of the preintervention measures considered (phonological coding, orthographic coding, phonological nonword memory, instructional level on the QRI, prorated WISC-III VIQ, and RAN letters), only two predicted parameters of the growth curves. As shown in table X, prorated Verbal IQ predicted the intercept, or level of skill development prior to intervention, but not slope, or response to intervention. As shown in table XI, RAN letters predicted the intercept for taught words and nonword reading efficiency and the slope for real word efficiency.

DISCUSSION

Older, underachieving readers in the upper elementary and middle school grades benefit from instructional intervention in reading. Children improved about 5 standard score points (1/3 standard deviation) on standardized measures of single word reading after just sixteen 1-hour individual tutorials. These children started out at a low reading level, but not as low as that of the children in Lovett and Steinbach's (1997) study. They ended up at a higher level than the participants in that study but failed to reach the performance level achieved by participants in the Alexander et al. (1991) study, which provided about four times

Table X. Does Verbal IQ predict growth curve intercept and slope?				
	Intercept	t	Slope	t
Word Identification	0.70	5.43***	−0.08	−1.90
Word Attack	0.40	3.57**	−0.05	−1.15
Taught Words	0.51	3.83***	−0.04	−1.26
WIAT Spelling	0.19	2.74*	0.02	0.84
WRAT-3 Spelling	0.17	3.35**	−0.00	−0.18
Real Word Reading Efficiency	0.62	4.34***	0.02	0.50
Nonword Reading Efficiency	0.43	2.90**	0.03	0.73

*$p < .05$ **$p < .01$ ***$p < .001$

Table XI.   Does rapid automatized naming for letters predict growth curve intercept and slope?

	Intercept	t	Slope	t
Word Identification	−0.85	−2.77	0.08	1.04
Word Attack	−0.45	−1.88	0.03	0.34
Taught Words	−0.74	−2.76*	0.03	0.46
WIAT Spelling	−0.15	−1.06	−0.05	−0.95
WRAT-3 Spelling	−0.16	−1.55	−0.02	−0.83
Real Word Reading Efficiency	−0.58	−1.71	−0.16	−2.45*
Nonword Reading Efficiency	−0.76	−2.93**	0.03	0.46

$* p < .05$ $** p < .01$

as much instructional intervention. Clearly, severity of reading disability, as well as intensity and duration of treatment, affect learning outcome for remedial instruction.

At least four factors may help to explain the lack of treatment-specific effects for structural analysis training in the group analyses. First, due to small sample size (10 in each treatment group), we may have lacked sufficient power to detect treatment effects. The enormous within-group variation, reflected in the standard deviations, rendered the group effect statistically nonsignificant. Future research might investigate the effect of structural analysis training in larger samples or more homogenous samples.

Second, although the treatments were equally effective at the group level, the trends noted in the individual HLM growth curve analyses suggest that the group difference might have been apparent if the intervention had continued for a longer time (e.g., 64 instead of 16 sessions). The lessons designed by Henry are intended as 30–45 minute group lessons that extend over the school year. In our study students enjoyed one-on-one instruction and frequent opportunities for active participation but spent only 15 minutes a day on structural analysis. Clearly, further research with increased intensity and duration of intervention is needed for this hypothesis to be explained.

Third, the study skills treatment, which was linked to what children did at school, might have helped them to better organize themselves at school and thus benefit more from their regular program, even if it did not teach word recognition explicitly. Students in the upper elementary and middle school grades may benefit from explicit instruction in self-regulation and executive functions as well as in word recognition.

Finally, many of these students had not yet mastered beginning word recognition skills (phonological awareness and orthographic knowledge, knowledge of spelling-phoneme correspondence in the alphabet principle, and application of the alphabet principle to phonological decoding). In many cases, they may not have received systematic, explicit instruction in these skills during the primary grades due to the prevailing whole-language philosophy. Because training in beginning skills was not withheld from any participant, both on ethical and theoretical grounds (advanced skills build on beginning skills), results may indicate that all underachieving readers in the intermediate grades may benefit, to some degree, from the focused instruction on beginning skills. Again, a tutorial of longer duration may have revealed more robust evidence of the benefit from structural analysis in addition to alphabet principle, the cornerstone of beginning skills. Alphabet principle is a powerful component of word recognition; orthographic and phonological awareness support its acquisition and phonological decoding supports its application. However, the trend toward more individual treatment responding for word learning in the Structural Analysis Group, which would not have been found without the multilevel features of HLM growth curve analysis, suggests that children can benefit from structural analysis training before they master the alphabet principle. For this reason, instruction that focuses on all the beginning skills of learning to read (including alphabet principle and phoneme segmentation) and on structural analysis (including syllable structure and morpheme patterns) is recommended for older, underachieving readers, even if the benefits of combined alphabet principle and structural analysis training are not immediately apparent.

That RAN for letters was the only individual difference variable that predicted the slopes of the growth curve for any measure (real word efficiency) lends credence to the claim that the instruction these students were getting at school was not matched to their instructional needs. Earlier in the students' development, other individual difference variables may have exerted constraints on their reading acquisition, causing them to get off to a slower start. In another study with second graders, individual differences in RAN, phonological awareness, and orthographic processing predicted slopes of growth curves in response to intervention (Berninger et al. 1999). As students get older and gain reading skill, many of these individual difference variables may cease to be such major obstacles to learning. At this stage, instructional variables may be more important and continuing, explicit instruction in word recognition may be critical to students' success.

Even though Verbal IQ may set some limits for reading achievement level (pretreatment intercept), in this study it did not significantly influence rate of response (slope) to short-term intervention. Explicit instruction benefited all the children on multiple outcomes (see table IX). Results show that with systematic, short-term intervention, upper elementary and middle school students can keep moving up the reading continuum. Only longer term interventions, integrated with the children's regular and special programs at school, will show just how far up the reading continuum these students, who still require explicit instruction in word recognition, may advance.

APPENDIX

Part I. Alphabet principle training organized by order of predictability.				
Order 0-a		**Order 0-b**		**Order 1**
a (apple)	m (mountain)	c (cat)	bl (blocks)	pl (plant)
b (balloon)	n (numbers)	c (circle)	br (bread)	pr (presidents)
d (dog)	p (pumpkin)	g (girl)	cl (clock)	qu (question)
e (exit)	r (rocks)	g (giraffe)	cr (crayon)	sm (smoke)
f (fish)	t (ten)	s (sun)	dr (drum)	sn (snow)
h (hamburger)	u (umbrella)	s (eyes)	fl (flag)	sp (spoon)
i (insect)	v (valentine)	y (yoyo)	fr (frog)	st (stamp)
j (jet)	w (window)	y (fly)	gl (glasses)	sw (swan)
k (kite)	z (zebra)	o (dog)	gr (grapes)	tr (triangle)
l (letters)		o (octopus)	sc (scarf)	tw (twelve)
			sk (skeleton)	x (box)
			sl (sleep)	ck (truck)
Order 2		**Order 3**	**Order 4**	**Order 5**
a.e (ace)	sh (shoes)	oi (oil)	oa (boat)	el (elephant)
i.e (ice)	au (auto)	wh (wheel)	ow (window)	il (pill)
o.e (rose)	aw (claw)	oo (books)	ai (bandaid)	il (child)
o (volcano)	ch (chair)	oo (moon)	ay (play)	all, al (ball)

(continues)

Part I. (*continued*)

Order 2	Order 3	Order 4	Order 5
u (music)	ng (sing)	th (three)	ull (bull)
y (baby)	ow (owl)	th (feather)	ul (ruler)
	ou (house)	ph (phone)	ol (sold)
	oy (boy)		

Order 6	Order 7	Order 8 (schwa)	Order 9 (open syllable)
ar (dictionary)	ight (light)	a (bal*a*nce)	a (apron)
ar (star)	gh (eight)	e (elev*e*n)	e (equal)
er (letter)	gh (laugh)	o (mother)	i (dinosaur)
ir (girl)	dge (bridge)		
or (horse)	tch (watch)		
ur (church)	wr (wrench)		
kn (knife)			
mb (comb)			

Part II. Pages from published programs used in each lesson.

Lesson	Henry's Word Program	Drumm's Study Skills Program	Englemann's SRA Decoding Program
1	15-17	17-20	22-23, 28-29
2	18-19	21-26	63-64, 67-68
3	20-22	75-79	73-74, 75-76
4	23-24	80-85	95-96, 97-98
5	25-27	86-89	1-2, 3-4
6	28-30	90, 92-94	9-10, 11-12
7	31-32	38-42	83-84, 85-87
8	33-35	43-45	88-89, 90-91
9	36-38	61-65	17-18, 19-20
10	39-41	66-68	21-22, 23-24
11	42-44	95-99	33-34, 35-36
12	45-46	100-104	37-38, 39-40
13	47-48	90-92	110-111, 112-113
14	49-51	93-95	120-121, 131-132
15	52-55	96-100	145-146, 147-148
16	56-60	101-105	149-150, 153-154

Address correspondence to: Sylvia P. Abbott at Mukilteo Elementary, 2600 Mukilteo Drive, Mukilteo, WA 98275; or to Virginia W. Berninger at 322 Miller, Box 353600, University of Washington, Seattle, WA 98195-3600, E-mail <vwb@u.washington.edu>.

References

Abbott, R. D., and Berninger, V. W. 1995. Structural equation modeling and hierarchical linear modeling: Tools for identifying orthographic processes in reading and writing development. In *The Varieties of Orthographic Knowledge II: Theoretical and Developmental Issues,* V. Berninger, ed. Dordrect, The Netherlands: Kluwer Academic Publishers.

Abbott, S., Reed, E., Abbott, R. D., and Berninger, V. W. 1997. Year-long, balanced reading/writing tutorial: A design experiment used for dynamic assessment. *Learning Disabilities Quarterly* 20:249–63.

Adams, M. 1990. *Beginning to Read: Thinking and Learning About Print.* Cambridge, MA: MIT Press.

Adams, M., and Henry, M. 1997. Myths and realities about words and literacy. *School Psychology Review* 26:425–36.

Alexander, A., Andersen, H., Heilman, P., Voeller, K., and Torgesen, J. 1991. Phonological awareness training and remediation of analytic decoding deficits in a group of severe dyslexics. *Annals of the Orton Society* 41:193–206.

Balmuth, M. 1982. *The Roots of Phonics.* New York, NY: Teachers College Press.

Berninger, V. W. 1998a. Specific reading and writing disabilities in young children: Assessment, prevention, and intervention. In *Learning About Learning Disabilities,* 2nd ed., B. Wong, ed. NY: Academic Press.

Berninger, V. W. 1998b. *Process Assessment of the Learner: Guides for Intervention.* San Antonio, TX: The Psychological Corporation.

Berninger, V. W., and Abbott, R. D. (1994). "Redefining learning disabilities: Moving beyond aptitude-achievement discrepancies to failure to respond to validated treatment protocols." In *Frames of Reference for the Assessment of Learning Disabilities: New Views on Measurement Issues,* G. R. Lyon, ed. Baltimore, MD: Paul H. Brookes Publishing Co.

Berninger, V. W., Abbott, S., Greep, K., Reed, E., Sylvester, L., Hooven, C., Clinton, A., Taylor, J., and Abbott, R. D. 1997. Directed reading and writing activities: Aiming instruction to working brain systems. In *Prevention and Intervention Issues across the Life Span,* S. M. C. Dollinger and L. F. DiLalla, eds. Hillsdale, NJ: Lawrence Erlbaum Associates.

Berninger, V. W., Thalberg, S., DeBruyn, I., and Smith, I. 1987. Preventing reading disabilities by assessing and remediating phonemic skills. *School Psychology Review* 16:554–65.

Berninger, V. W., Yates, C., and Lester, K. 1991. Multiple orthographic codes in reading and writing acquisition. *Reading and Writing: An Interdisciplinary Journal* 3:115–49.

Berninger, V., Abbott, R., Zook, D., Ogier, S., Lemos, Z., and Brooksher, R. 1999. Teaching the alphabet principle within a connectionist framework. *Journal of Learning Disabilities.*

Berninger, V., Vaughan, K., Abbott, R., Abbott, S., Brooks, A., Abbott, S., Reed, E., Rogan, L., and Graham, S. in press. Early intervention for spelling problems:

Teaching spelling units of varying sizes within a multiple connections framework. *Journal of Educational Psychology.*

Bryk, A., and Raudenbush, S. 1987. Application of hierarchical linear models to assessing change. *Psychological Bulletin* 101:147–58.

Bryk, A., Raudenbush, S., and Congdon, R. 1996. *Hierarchical Linear and Nonlinear Modeling with the HLM/2L and HLM/3L Programs.* Chicago, Illinois: Scientific Software.

Chall, J. S. 1983. *Stages of Reading Development.* New York: McGraw-Hill.

DeFries, J. C. 1985. Colorado reading project. In *Biobehavioral Measures of Dyslexia*, D. Gray and J. F. Kavanaugh, eds. Parkton, MD: York Press.

Drumm, S. T. 1996. *Study Skills: Grades 2–8.* Seattle, WA: Kelley Wingate Publications.

Ehri, L. C. 1992. Reconceptualizing the development of sight word reading and its relationship to recoding. In *Reading Acquisition*, P. B. Gough, L. C. Ehri, and R. Treiman, eds. Hillsdale, NJ: Lawrence Erlbaum Associates.

Engelmann, S., Meyer, L., Johnson, G., and Carnine, L. 1988. *Corrective Reading Skill Applications (Decoding B1, B2, and C).* Chicago, Illinois: Science Research Associates, Inc.

Gough, P. B., Juel, C., and Griffith, P. L. 1992. Reading, spelling, and the orthographic cipher. In *Reading Acquisition*, P. B. Gough, L. C. Ehri, and R. Treiman, eds. Hillsdale, NJ: Lawrence Erlbaum Associates.

Hart, T. M., Berninger, V. W., and Abbott, R. D. 1997. Comparison of teaching single or multiple orthographic-phonological connections for word recognition and spelling: Implications for instructional consultation. *School Psychology Review* 26:279–97.

Henry, M. 1990. *WORDS: Integrated Decoding and Spelling Instruction Based on Word Origin and Word Structure.* Austin, TX: PRO-ED.

Henry, M. K. 1988. Beyond phonics: Integrated decoding and spelling instruction based on word origin and structure. *Annals of Dyslexia* 38:258–75.

Henry, M. K., Calfee, R. C., and Avelar-LaSalle, R. 1989. Structural approach to decoding and spelling. In *Thirty Eighth Yearbook of the National Reading Conference*, S. McCormick and J. Zutell, eds. Chicago, IL: National Reading Conference.

Just, M., and Carpenter, P. 1987. *The Psychology of Reading and Language Comprehension.* Boston, MA: Allyn and Bacon.

Leslie, L., and Caldwell, J. 1990. *Qualitative Reading Inventory.* Glenview, Illinois: Scott, Foresman.

Lovett, M. W., and Steinbach, K. A. 1997. The effectiveness of remedial programs for reading disabled children of different ages: Does the benefit decrease for older children? *Learning Disabilities Quarterly* 20:189–210.

Lyon, G. R. 1995. Research initiatives in learning disabilities: Contributions from scientists supported by the National Institute of Child Health and Human Development. *Journal of Child Neurology* 10:120–26.

Moats, L. 1995. *Spelling: Development, Disability, and Instruction.* Baltimore, York Press.

O'Rourke, J. P. 1974. *Toward a Science of Vocabulary Development.* The Hague, Netherlands: Mouton.

Olson, R. K., Kliegl, R., Davidson, B. J., and Foltz, G. 1985. Individual and developmental differences in reading disability. In *Reading Research: Advances in Theory and Practice*, G. E. MacKinnnon and T. G. Waller, eds. New York: Academic Press.

Torgesen, J., Wagner, R., and Rashotte, C. 1997. Prevention and remediation of severe reading disabilities: Keeping the end in mind. *Scientific Studies of Reading* 1:217–34.

The Psychological Corporation. 1992. *Wechsler Individual Achievement Test.* San Antonio, TX: Author.

Venezky, R. 1995. From orthography to psychology in reading. In *The Varieties of Orthographic Knowledge II: Relationships to Psychology, Reading, and Writing*, V. W. Berninger, ed. Dordrecht, The Netherlands: Kluwer.

Vellutino, F., Scanlon, E., Sipay, E., Small, S., Pratt, A., Chen, R., and Denckla, M. 1996. Cognitive profiles of difficult-to-remediate and readily remediated poor readers: Early intervention as a vehicle for distinguishing between cognitive and experiential deficits as basic causes of specific reading disability. *Journal of Educational Psychology* 88:601–38.

Wagner, R., and Torgesen, J. 1999. *The Comprehensive Assessment of Phonological Skills*. Austin, TX: PRO-ED.

Wechsler, D. 1991. *Manual for the Wechsler Intelligence Scale for Children-III*. San Antonio, TX: Psychological Corporation.

Wilkinson, G. 1993. *The Wide Range Achievement Test*. (3rd ed.). Wilmington, DE: Wide Range, Inc.

Wolf, M., Bally, H., and Morris, R. 1986. Automaticity, retrieval processes and reading: A longitudinal study in average and impaired readers. *Child Development* 57:988–1005.

Woodcock, R. 1987. *Woodcock Reading Mastery Test-Revised*. Circle Pines, MN: American Guidance Service.

Speaking to Read:
The Effects of
Speech Recognition Technology
on the Reading and Spelling Performance of
Children with Learning Disabilities

Marshall H. Raskind and Eleanor L. Higgins

Frostig Center
Pasadena, California

In recent literature on persons with learning disabilities (LD), speech recognition has been discussed primarily as an assistive technology to help compensate for writing difficulties. However, prior research by the authors has suggested that in addition to helping persons to compensate for poor writing skills, speech recognition also may enhance reading and spelling; that is, what was designed as assistive technology appears to serve remedial functions as well. The present study was conducted to determine whether elementary and secondary students with LD who used the technology to write self-selected compositions and class assignments would demonstrate improvements in reading and spelling. Thirty-nine students with LD (ages 9 to 18) participated. Nineteen participants used speech recognition 50 minutes a week for sixteen weeks, and twenty students in a control group received general computer instruction. Results indicated that the speech recognition group showed significantly more improvement than the control group in word recognition ($p < .0001$), spelling ($p < .002$) and reading

Annals of Dyslexia, Vol. 49, 1999
ISSN 0736-9387

comprehension (p < .01). Pre- and posttests on five reading-related cognitive processing measures (phonological, orthographic, semantic processing, metacognitive reading strategies, and working memory) indicated that for the experimental group, only phonological processing improved significantly over the treatment period when compared to controls (p < .04). Further ANCOVA suggested that growth in phonological processing was associated with significant differences among conditions for all three academic measures: word recognition, spelling, and reading comprehension.

Interest in assistive technology for individuals with learning disabilities (LD) has grown dramatically over the last several years (Bryant and Bryant 1998; Bryant and Seay 1998; Elkind, Black, and Murray 1996; Higgins and Raskind 1995; Lewis 1998; MacArthur 1996; McNaughton, Hughes, and Clark 1993; Raskind 1994; Raskind and Higgins 1995a, 1995b). According to the Technology-Related Assistance Act of 1988 (P.L. 100-407, Stat., 1046, p.102), assistive technology refers to "any item, piece of equipment, or product system, whether acquired commercially off-the-shelf, modified, or customized, that is used to increase, maintain or improve the functional capabilities of individuals with disabilities." Assistive technology for persons with LD can further be delineated as any technology that enables an individual with LD to compensate for specific deficits. In some instances, the technology may assist or augment task performance in a given area of disability, whereas in others it is used to circumvent or bypass specific deficits entirely. Furthermore, assistive technology compensates for weaknesses by "playing to" an individual's area(s) of strength. It is not intended to "fix" or remediate LD, nor to teach or instruct (as is computer-aided instruction).

Elsewhere, we have stressed that educators must have a clear understanding of the differences between assistive and remedial technologies in order to ensure that they are employing the proper technological interventions to reach their specified educational goals (Raskind and Scott 1993), and to implement technology in an ethical manner (Raskind and Higgins 1995b). Despite the necessity of distinguishing between the two approaches, they need not be considered mutually exclusive. There is no reason why technologically based compensatory strategies cannot be provided while attempts are being made to remediate specific skill deficits. For example, providing a child with training in phonological awareness should not preclude using speech synthesis to increase access to text in a particular subject area such as history.

In fact, as suggested by research (Kerchner and Kistenger 1984; Raskind, Higgins, and Herman 1997), using technology for a compensatory purpose also might result in remedial benefits. Of particular interest is our study (Higgins and Raskind 1995) that evaluated the compensatory effectiveness of speech recognition on the writing performance of university students with LD and found that essays written using assistive technology were superior to those generated through handwriting or dictating to a transcriber. Most students continued to use the technology for writing activities (essays, letters, stories) over the next two years following training, and many reported "improved reading abilities" such as enhanced word recognition and comprehension. Participants believed that these improvements were attributable to use of the speech recognition system. These anecdotal reports of improvement by participants were consistent with objective measures such as increases in standardized test scores and course grades, and decreased drop-out rates over the three-year study period (Higgins and Zvi 1995; Raskind and Higgins 1998).

The findings suggested to us the possibility that writing with speech recognition technology also might serve to remediate deficits, and led us to generate hypotheses concerning the mechanism by which speech recognition might affect reading. However, before proceeding with this discussion, it is necessary to provide an overview of how speech recognition systems operate. Speech recognition systems work in conjunction with word processing programs to enable the user to produce written text on a computer through speech. The user dictates into a head-mounted microphone and the speech recognition system (hardware and software) converts the spoken word into electronic text displayed on the computer monitor. "Discrete" speech systems (like the one used in the Higgins and Raskind 1995 study) require a pause of approximately one tenth of a second between words. As words are spoken, they appear on the monitor virtually simultaneously.[1] The system develops a phonetic model of each user's voice that is paired with an English vocabulary file. The identification of words improves over time so that the system becomes more accurate with progressive

---

[1]Several versions of continuous speech recognition have since become available which do not require one-tenth second pause between words. The text is not presented simultaneously upon speaking, but rather appears on the screen at the end of a sentence or phrase. Detecting speech recognition errors must be done at the end of the phrase or sentence, causing the task to be more like typical proofreading without the word-for-word correspondence of phonemes and graphemes present in discrete speech.

word utterances. Speech recognition programs also utilize statistical information, based on the frequency of the use of word combinations, to predict words.

The first idea to consider in conceptualizing possible links between writing by means of speech recognition and improved reading ability is to recognize that generating accurate text with this technology involves actual reading. As words are spoken into a microphone, the speaker reads/checks the word on the computer monitor to ensure that it is the correct word (the word that was spoken). If it is not, the speaker must choose the correct word from a list of words displayed in a window (choice box), again requiring the user to read. Selecting the correct word requires the user to attend to the specific/unique characteristics (phonemic, graphemic, morphemic) of the word among other, often similar sounding and looking words. Therefore, the mere process of writing with this technology requires users to read/decode words in order to monitor their own written language production. In this regard, perhaps the technology helps to improve reading skills by simply providing an additional opportunity to practice reading. As Lundberg (1995) has stressed, individuals with reading disabilities need greater exposure to print in order to develop adequate word recognition.

Another possibility for explaining how speech recognition technology might enhance reading ability results from the fact that words are presented bimodally: auditorially through speech, and visually through the computer display (virtually simultaneously as they are spoken.) Additionally, a proprioceptive/ kinesthetic component is present since the individual has to utilize the appropriate oral mechanisms to speak/articulate words. Although research on the efficacy of multisensory literacy approaches is equivocal (Myers and Hammill 1982), these approaches have a long history in the field as a strategy for improving the academic difficulties of students with LD (Fernald 1943; Gillingham and Stillman 1968; Heckelman 1969).

Furthermore, it is possible that speech recognition technology enhances grapheme-phoneme correspondence. Difficulties with recognizing the relations between the phonological segments in spoken language and their alphabetic counterparts may make reading instruction incomprehensible (Torgesen 1995; Liberman, Shankweiler, and Liberman 1989)[2] and as

---

[2]See also Ball and Blachman (1991); Berninger et.al. (1998); Bradley and Bryant (1985); Foorman, Francis, Novy, and Liberman (1991); and Swanson and Ramaglia (1992) for evidence of the importance of spelling to recognizing the relation between phonological segments and their alphabetic counterparts.

Torgesen (1995) states, "most children with reading disabilities have great difficulty learning to apply the 'alphabetic principle' to take advantage of grapheme-phoneme regularities in reading unfamiliar words. . . ." (p.77). Perhaps speech recognition technology might improve reading by promoting an awareness of the relation between the phonological segments and alphabetic codes, since the words spoken by the speaker (phonemic segments) are virtually simultaneously translated to their corresponding grapheme representations.

Finally, the notion that reading and spelling can be improved through the use of speech recognition is also consistent with literature dealing with the psychological and motivational aspects of learning. Several authorities in LD (Heshusius 1989, Poplin 1988) contend that the instruction of children with LD is enhanced through interest-driven, and self-paced experiences that can be accomplished independently.[3] Speech recognition technology can provide such a writing experience.

The improvements in reading ability reported by participants in the Higgins and Raskind (1995) study on speech recognition and writing, coupled with the above theoretical and empirical indications, provided the impetus to conduct the present study, a formal investigation of the effects of speech recognition on the reading and spelling performance of students with LD. Both a speech recognition experimental group and a control group were pre- and posttested on academic (dependent) measures of word recognition, reading comprehension, and spelling. In addition, participants in both groups were tested in specific underlying cognitive processes associated with reading, including phonological awareness, orthographic processing, semantic processing, metacognition, and working memory (Swanson and Alexander 1997). It was hoped that potential changes in these cognitive processes might serve to explain concomitant changes in dependent, academic measures. It was predicted that first, the speech recognition group would illustrate significantly higher scores on word recognition, reading comprehension, and spelling at posttesting as compared to the control, and second, these higher scores would show corresponding gains in one or more process measures.

---

[3]Several strategy-based approaches to spelling instruction for LD students have stressed many of the same principles (Fulk 1997; Graham and Voth 1990; Gerber and Hall 1989).

METHOD

PARTICIPANTS

Thirty-nine students (13 females, 26 males) enrolled at the Frostig School participated in the study. The Frostig School (part of the Frostig Center) is a K–12 private school for children with LD located in Pasadena, California. Students came from predominantly middle- and upper middle-class families. Five children were Hispanic, four African American, one Asian American, and twenty-nine Caucasian. Average age at the beginning of the study was 12.9, and ranged from 9.3 to 17.7.

All participants had been previously identified as LD by their public school district or through diagnostic assessment by Frostig Center staff and allied professionals, and were further screened to meet the criteria agreed upon by the National Joint Committee on Learning Disabilities (1994). Full scale IQ scores ranged from 74 to 137 with a mean of 92.1 and *SD* of 15.0 as measured by *Wechsler Intelligence Scale for Children-III* (Wechsler 1991) or *Wechsler Intelligence Scale for Children-Revised* (Wechsler 1974). Additionally, all students showed deficits of two years or more (below expectation for chronological age) in reading comprehension, phonological analysis, and/or spelling on the *Stanford Diagnostic Reading Inventory-III* (Karlsen, Madden, and Gardner, 1984), with an average discrepancy of 3.3 years in reading comprehension, 4.5 years in phonological analysis, and 3.0 years in spelling.

PROCEDURES

TESTING

Students were pretested on three academic tasks: (1) reading comprehension using the silent reading portion of the *Formal Reading Inventory (FRI)*, Form A (Wiederholt 1986);[4] (2) word recognition using the *Wide Range Achievement Test-3 (WRAT-3)*, Tan Form (Wilkinson 1993);[5] and (3) spelling using the *WRAT-3*. In addition, a battery of tests was administered to assess skills in five cognitive processes identified in previous literature to be related to reading (see Swanson and Alexander [1997] for addi-

---

[4]Internal consistency coefficients ranged from .92 to .97 across age groups; alternate form reliability was .75 for all of the four alternate forms ($p < .001$).
[5]Item reliability ranged from .98 to .99; alternate form correlations across age groups ranged from .88 to .96.

tional discussion of the development of the individual measures employed).[6] Although the battery is not standardized, the authors were anxious to assess changes in these measures to shed further light on exactly how the technology may have accomplished changes in dependent measures. The battery consisted of the following tasks:

1. *The Phonological Deletion Task*, formulated by Cunningham and Stanovich (1990) and modified by Swanson and Alexander (1997). Children listened to a word, deleted only the first sound, and said the remainder of the word. For example, "spark" should elicit the response "park" (10 items). We included this task because of a long line of research literature in LD that points to phonological awareness as a component directly related to improvements in reading achievement. Given the nature of the task, which requires detecting and especially correcting errors to be described below, we reasoned that it might provide additional practice in distinguishing phonologically similar words, which in turn might assist children in increasing phonological awareness.

2. *The Orthographic Choice Task*, devised by Olson, Kliegl, Davidson, and Flotz (1985) and modified for children by Cunningham and Stanovich (1990). Children were asked to look at cards with two phonologically identical words printed on them, one spelled correctly and one spelled incorrectly. Participants were asked to indicate which was a "real word." For example, for with a card containing "(a) room (b) rume," the correct response was, "a" (25 items). Similarly, given the task of correcting errors, we reasoned that additional practice with distinguishing graphically similar words may have assisted the children in recognizing correctly and incorrectly spelled words, one measure of orthographic processing.

3. *The Semantic Choice Task*, developed by Chabot, Miller, and Juola (1976). Children were shown cards with two words on them. The cards were read aloud and participants were asked if the two words belonged to the same category. For example, one card read, "minute, hour," to

---

[6]Swanson and Alexander (1997) report reliability coefficients as follows: phonemic deletion, .82; orthographic choice, .77; semantic choice, .78; sentence span (working memory), .76; and metacognitive questionairre, .86.

which the child should respond "same" (30 items). We reasoned that since focus was placed on the content and process of writing (see the Writing Sessions section later in this paper), and since previous research had shown that the development of more mature and complex vocabulary resulted from the use of speech recognition technology (Higgins and Raskind 1995), gains in the semantic organization of vocabulary may have resulted from the experimental condition.

4. *The Metacognitive Questionnaire*, adapted by Swanson and Trahan (1992) from Paris, and Cross and Lipson (1984). Twenty multiple choice questions were read aloud to students. They were asked to circle the answer that best described their attitudes, habits, and strategies concerning reading. For example, one item read,

    A good reader
    a. is also good in all other school subjects (2 points)
    b. may not be good in other subjects such as math (4 points)
    c. has lots of books at home (1 point)
    d. enjoys reading to himself or herself (3 points)

    Each choice within an item had a different value attached to it (calibrated by the originators of the task), as indicated above, so that by adding the values of choices for each item, a total could be obtained for each participant (20 items). This task was included because our group reasoned that exploratory discussions about the writing process and the emphasis on developing a positive attitude toward the writing experience may have altered attitudes and behaviors concerning reading as well as writing.

5. *The Sentence Span Task*, a common test of working memory, developed by Danemann and Carpenter (1980) and adapted for children by Swanson, Cochran, and Ewers (1989). Researchers read a set of sentences aloud, asking participants to memorize the last word of each sentence, in order. After reading the set of sentences, a comprehension question about one of the sentences was asked. The students were to answer the comprehension question, then repeat the last words of each sentence in order. The first set contained two sentences, the second contained three, the third four, and the last contained five sentences (four sets of sentences). The task was in-

cluded because we reasoned that dictation of sentences may provide additional opportunities to develop sentence comprehension, memory, or both.

We were interested to discover whether gains occurred evenly (if at all) over the entire treatment period or whether learning was concentrated at the beginning (or end). During the eighth week of the study, the Blue Form of the *WRAT-3* was administered for word recognition and spelling to all participants. Finally, all three achievement tests, spelling (*WRAT-3*, Tan Form), word recognition, (*WRAT-3*, Tan Form), and reading comprehension (*FRI*, Form B), were readministered at sixteen weeks, along with five of the psychological processing assessments.

APPARATUS

Students were randomly assigned to one IBM® VoiceType (version 3.0) and four DragonDictate® (version 2.5) discrete speech recognition systems. Fourteen participants utilized DragonDictate® and five used VoiceType. The speech recognition programs were installed in Pentium® 133 computers with 16 MB RAM, running Windows™ '95. WordPerfect 6.0 was used as the word processing program. Participants in the control condition utilized 486-66, 8MB computers with WordPerfect 6.0 running Windows™ 3.1.

TRAINING CONDITIONS

Participants were randomly assigned to either the control or the experimental condition (control $n = 20$, experimental $n = 19$). All students received computer instruction, at an individual terminal, for 50 minutes a week for 16 weeks. In both conditions, small group instruction was given and one-on-one assistance was offered when students requested it. Average teacher-student ratios were 2:4 for both conditions (ranges were 2 to 7 students, 1 to 4 teachers).

Control Condition. A computer control group was used to reduce the likelihood that differences in academic and process measures were due to technology use (novelty, attractiveness, and the like) rather than the use of speech recognition itself. The control participants were assigned to a class entitled "keyboarding" which involved such tasks as typing, writing, and using mouse and keyboard manipulations to create art, do research, write compositions, work on math and science projects, play computer games, and operate various instructional programs. Approximately 60 percent of each 50-minute session involved engagement with text (reading, writing, typing, spelling). Approximately 20 minutes of this time was spent writing.

Experimental Condition. These students used speech recognition technology to do writing exercises.

TRAINING FOR THE SPEECH RECOGNITION CONDITION

The first session was spent learning to log on and training their systems to recognize the user's voice. DragonDictate® users read single words aloud from the screen into the system. IBM users, on the other hand, read complete sentences, word-by-word, from the screen into the system. Students were told that if they did not recognize a word from the screen, the researcher or writing facilitator would whisper it for them to repeat into the microphone.

The second session was devoted to mastering techniques of correcting errors in speech recognition. Figure 1 illustrates the DragonDictate® screen as it would appear as a user was dictating the sentence fragment, "This is an example of text being"

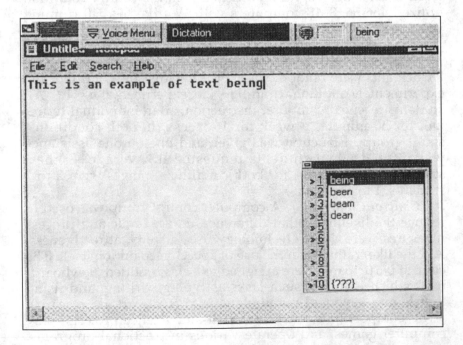

Figure 1. *Screen during dictation*

The last word dictated, "being," appears in the choice box in the lower right-hand corner of the screen. Notice that the choice box lists several words that are phonetically and orthographically similar to the last word dictated. Students were prompted to watch carefully as each word uttered appeared in text to make sure that it was, in fact, the right word. If a recognition error was made by the system, students were trained in a number of methods to use the choice box to correct the error. One method was to find the correct word among the similar words in the box, and select it by saying, for example, "Choose 4." Another method of selection was to cursor down the list to "4" and hit the enter key. Still another method was to use the mouse to click on "4." Participants were free to choose the correction method they preferred.

Sometimes when a speech recognition error had been made, the correct response was not listed in the correction box. In the example below, the last word dictated, "used," was guessed incorrectly as "acted." Two ways of correcting the recognition error were possible. The first involved spelling the word aloud using the International Alphabet ("alpha, bravo," and so on). Although offered this method, none of the participants ever chose to use it to correct errors. The preferred method of correction involved typing the first letter of the desired word from the keyboard, as in the example in figure 2.

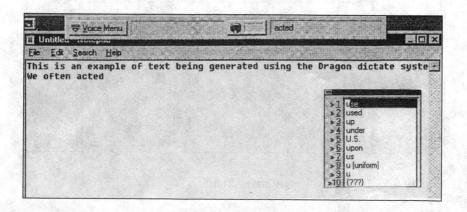

Figure 2.   Correction using typing

Typing "u" resulted in the list of words in the correction box in figure 2. Selection 2 is the correct word and could be chosen using cursor keys, the mouse, or the voice command, "Choose 2."[7]

As dictation proficiency increased, the user would sometimes jump ahead of the system's ability to print the words on the screen, so that a recognition error might not be detected until after a few words had already been dictated, as in the example in figure 3. The error, "taxed" for "text," has been passed in dictation.

Using the command "Oops" caused a history of the last six dictated words to appear. Using voice commands or cursor keys, the word to be corrected could be highlighted. The correct selection, in this case number "2," would then be chosen.

WRITING SESSIONS

The above correction procedures were mastered during the first two sessions and the remaining sessions were devoted to using the system for writing. Topics were self-selected in order to max-

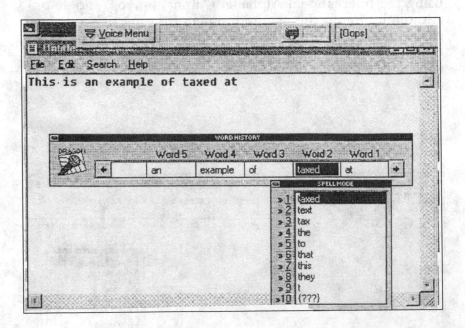

Figure 3.   Correction using word history

---

[7]Correction procedures on the IBM system were similar, except that several corrections were done at once, usually at the end of a dictated sentence.

imize the "meaningfulness" of the text, and to enhance motivation and encourage language production. A portion of the class time in the control condition was also devoted to self-selected activities. Participants could bring in homework and classroom assignments, as long as the assignment involved the dictation of sentences using the systems. Students who did not bring assignments could choose a topic or premise for writing, or were offered a variety of writing motivations designed to stimulate both fiction and nonfiction composition (Schwartz and Armstrong 1989; Senn 1992; Wilmes and Wilmes 1983). See Appendix A for examples of writing motivations from each source.

No formal instruction was given in reading, spelling, or writing. However, writing facilitators did spend five minutes at the beginning of each session to get some students started by helping the student choose a topic or generate the first sentence. A very general approach that encouraged a high volume of language output was adopted. Our reasoning was that if the systems did, in fact, remediate reading and spelling deficits, then the more the children wrote/spoke using the system, the greater the resulting benefit. It should be noted that instructors in the control condition also employed the strategies listed below, as appropriate to that setting. The following recommended strategies were used to facilitate output:

1. Students were, of course, verbally encouraged to write as much as possible.
2. Students were encouraged to discuss the process and content of their writing with facilitators (in most cases a relative strength) rather than the mistakes in the mechanics of their written products (usually a relative weakness).
3. Students were told that the technology was designed to help them utilize their strengths in oral language, and that they should allow the system, as far as possible, to contend with weaknesses such as spelling, punctuation, and the like.
4. One way that positive affective responses to the writing process were encouraged in students was by enlisting only those writing facilitators who were enthusiastic, appreciative, and vocal about the joys and benefits of writing that they themselves had experienced.
5. Writing facilitators were asked to limit heavy editing and criticism of student's work to further ensure that a nonthreatening, noncritical writing environment was provided.

6. Instruction was provided only in the form of information concerning tasks and assignments, the operation of the computer, and the correction of speech recognition errors. Other content was volunteered only when requested by the student.

7. Independent use of the equipment was encouraged in two ways. First, the necessity of correcting recognition errors made by the system was explained to the student, and, although in the beginning he or she was prompted to correct each recognition error as it occurred, facilitators gradually decreased prompts until the student was able to catch most errors himself or herself. Second, students were explicitly and repeatedly reassured that they would be able to, and expected, to use the system without assistance before the project was completed.

As writing sessions progressed, all facilitators were instructed to decrease the amount of assistance extended to the students with regard to preplanning activities and prompting students to catch speech recognition errors. Independent use of the system and percentages of speech recognition errors caught by the participants were monitored regularly during two-minute observation periods. These ranged from 87 percent to 100 percent over the last four writing sessions.

RESULTS

Pretest, midpoint, and posttest scores on the dependent measures of word recognition and spelling, as well as pre- and posttest scores for reading comprehension and for the cognitive processing measures (for both the experimental and control groups) appear in the first two columns of table I. Since alternate forms of the spelling and word recognition tests were administered, absolute scores are reported. The absolute scale combines raw scores from forms A and B of the tests so that they can be compared. To give the reader an idea of the magnitude of change, grade equivalents are also reported, although they were not used in the analysis. Similarly, for reading comprehension, standard scores are also reported in addition to the raw scores upon which the analysis was done to give the reader an estimate of the magnitude of change. Effect sizes are included in the last column of table I.

Table I.   Results of repeated measures ANOVA on differences in post-test gains between control and experimental groups.*

| Measure | Experimental | | | Control | | | F | | Effect |
	Mean	SD	Grade Level	Mean	SD	Grade Level	Value	p of F	Size
Word Recognition**									
pretest	497.1	13.94	5.2	501.0	14.82	5.9			
midpoint	500.5	15.51	6.0	498.9	14.03	5.6	6.00	.019	
posttest	503.2	13.49	6.5	501.8	13.66	6.2	16.65	.000	1.125
Spelling**									
pretest	494.1	14.25	4.4	496.0	13.62	4.8			
midpoint	498.3	13.36	4.8	498.2	13.08	5.0	4.68	.037	
posttest	500.1	12.36	5.3	498.1	12.71	5.1	10.79	.002	.72
Reading Comprehension									
pretest	9.3	9.90	77.00^2	16.6	12.45	79.6^2			
posttest	20.0	13.98	87.05^2	17.5	13.18	81.6^2	7.15	.011	.76
Phonological Deletion									
pretest	6.5	3.31		7.9	2.54				
posttest	8.3	2.16		8.3	2.13		4.62	.038	.77
Orthographic Choice									
pretest	23.1	2.90		23.9	2.43				
posttest	24.1	2.50		23.8	2.73		2.12	.154	.35
Semantic Choice									
pretest	27.6	1.54		27.1	2.59				
posttest	28.4	1.80		28.3	2.54		1.14	.294	.54
Metacognitive Choice									
pretest	56.9	10.53		56.4	12.30				
posttest	57.1	9.67		60.4	7.68		1.01	.321	.36
Working Memory									
pretest	.54	.96		.95	.69				
posttest	.68	.75		1.15	.88		.36	.550	.19

*Raw scores are reported with the exception of Word Recognition and Spelling
**Absolute scores are reported

Pretest, midpoint, and posttest gains scores on word recognition and spelling were analyzed separately using MANOVA (Word recognition Wilks' $F = 8.374$, $p = .001$; Spelling Wilks'

($F = 5.931$, $p = .02$). Since significant effects were detected, repeated measures ANOVAs were conducted to determine the direction of effects. A repeated measures ANOVA was also conducted on reading comprehension gains scores (at posttest only) as well. On all ANOVAs, the effects of the covariates of age and entry level performance on the measure have been partitioned out.

Both the control and experimental group made significant progress in word recognition and spelling as measured by posttest scores. Effect sizes were very high for word recognition and high for spelling. However, it should be noted that the experimental group had made significant gains over students in the control group even at midpoint testing, and that these significant differences in gains were even more pronounced at posttest. Similarly, the repeated measures ANOVA revealed that there was also a significant difference in gains in reading comprehension between control and experimental groups over the entire treatment period as measured by the posttest, and it should be noted effect size was high as well.

Pre- and posttest scores on the five cognitive process measures also were analyzed using repeated measures ANOVA. Again, the effects of the covariates of age and entry level performance (beginning score on each measure) have been partitioned out. As can be seen in table I, the use of speech recognition technology appears to have had differential effects on the five cognitive processes measured. Posttest scores for phonological deletion showed significant differences in gains between the groups and a high effect size, whereas the other four measures did not.

Since these findings suggest that changes in phonological processing skill may have occurred as a result of treatment, and further, may have influenced changes in some or all of the outcome measures, additional covariance analyses (using repeated measures ANCOVAs) were employed.[8] Results of the ANCOVAs of phonological gains on the three achievement measures demonstrate that when the covariate (the gains in phonological awareness) is subtracted from the treatment effect, the significance of the differences in gains between the control and experimental conditions disappears. This was shown to be true for all three of the achievement measures of word recognition, spelling, and reading comprehension. F ratios for word

---

[8]Since little or no difference in gains between groups was shown for the other four measures, ANCOVAs were not conducted.

recognition with and without the covariate were 12.38 ($p < .001$) and 1.56 ($p < .22$), respectively; 6.00 ($p < .019$) and .53 ($p < .47$) for spelling; and 18.0 ($p < .0001$) and .57 ($p < .46$) for reading comprehension.

Since we were interested in determining whether growth was uniform across the treatment periods or whether most change occurred at the beginning (or end) of the treatment period, three data points were measured in word recognition and spelling. Individual differences in the trajectories of change in these dependent measures in response to treatment condition could be calculated using individual growth-curve methodology, which addresses intraindividual change more directly (Bryk and Raudenbush 1987; Foorman et al. 1997; Francis, Fletcher, Stuebing, Davidson, and Thompson 1991; Rogosa, Brandt, and Zimowski 1982; Willet 1988). A two-stage process was employed. First, mean rates of change were determined and estimates made of the extent to which individuals differed across treatment conditions using the SAS Proc Mixed Procedure (SAS Institute 1992). Next, growth-curve parameters for both students in the control and experimental groups were evaluated as to their correlations with the five pretested cognitive processes in order to identify predictors of growth trajectories. Statistics concerning the mean of individual estimates for students in the control and experimental conditions are presented in table II.

As Table II indicates, both control and experimental groups showed a rate of change significantly greater than can be attributed to chance in word recognition, with control participants' slopes indicating 0.69 per unit of time (eight-week intervals), and experimental participants 2.91 per unit, four times the rate of controls. In spelling, students in the control

Table II. Mean individual growth curve estimates for word recognition and spelling.

Measure	Estimate	S. E.	T*	p
Word Recognition				
Control	0.69	0.34	2.03	.0440
Experimental	2.91	0.35	8.31	.0001
Spelling				
Control	1.08	0.48	2.23	.0290
Experimental	2.89	0.50	5.84	.0001

*Test statistic for rejection of null hypothesis estimate > 0

and experimental conditions showed change significantly greater than chance, with experimental participants demonstrating almost three times the growth rate.

Although pretest scores on dependent measures were controlled in the ANOVA, many researchers have noted the relation of entering performance on the various cognitive measures on subsequent growth in reading as well (Foorman, Francis, Novy, and Liberman 1991; Swanson and Alexander 1997). The correlations of pretests on cognitive process measures, with individual growth-curve estimates of combined experimental and control group participants, are presented in table III.[9]

All correlations proved significant, with the exception of working memory and spelling, supporting the hypothesis that all measures are good predictors of individual change trajectories in word recognition, and that all but working memory are good predictors of individual change rates for spelling. It also should be noted that most of the significant coefficients are similar to one another in magnitude, indicating that all are somewhat equal in their ability to predict growth.

DISCUSSION

Results of the growth curve analysis and the analyses of variance strongly indicate that the intervention "worked", that is, improved word recognition and spelling in students diagnosed with LD, and the analysis of variance indicates that the positive

TABLE III.   Correlations of pretest scores on cognitive measures with individual growth-curve estimate slopes
(Includes both experimental and control participants, $n = 39$).

Pretest Measure	Word Recognition Growth-Curve Estimate	Spelling Growth-Curve Estimate
Phonological Deletion	.61	.56
Orthographic Choice	.58	.62
Semantic Choice	.67	.56
Metacognitive Choice	.62	.57
Working Memory	.32	.18

$p < .05$

---

[9]Groups were collapsed due to the small sample size as well as the fact that both treatments showed change greater than chance.

effects also extended or transferred to reading comprehension. The study supports previous research that indicated remedial effects resulted from the use of speech recognition technology with postsecondary students. Our previous three-year longitudinal follow up of postsecondary users who employed the technology assistively showed long-term gains in reading, as measured by passage rates on standarized tests, in overall academic achievement as evidenced by better grades in courses requiring extensive reading, and in improved graduation, retention, and drop-out rates (Higgins and Zvi 1995; Raskind and Higgins 1998).

The findings are also concordant with those of other researchers who have utilized assistive computer technologies to enhance reading performance. Elkind, Black, and Murray (1996) and Elkind, Cohen, and Murray (1992, 1993), for example, showed improved reading speed and comprehension using speech synthesis/optical character recognition systems, although those studies did not find a remedial effect for reading, a transfer to written text when not using the technology. The present study compares favorably as well, however, with previous research on computer interventions that *did* find a remedial effect for reading (and in some cases spelling) (Foster, Erickson, Foster, Brinkman, and Torgesen 1994; Olson and Wise 1992; Torgesen 1993; Torgesen, Waters, Cohen, and Torgesen 1988), even though the speech recognition program used in the current study was not designed specifically to remediate reading difficulties. The referenced computer interventions in this study are phonologically based so that research on them has frequently measured phonological awareness, and has confirmed that improvement along this measure can be accomplished by explicit phonological instruction/practice. Other phonologically based remedial interventions that do *not* involve the use of a computer have demonstrated similar findings for reading (Alexander, Anderson, Heilman, Voeller, and Torgesen 1991; Foorman, Francis, Novy, and Liberman 1991; Lindamood and Lindamood 1979, 1984; Lie 1991; Olofsson and Lundberg 1983; Torgesen, Morgan, and Davis 1992), and spelling (Ball and Blachman 1991; Bradley and Bryant 1985; Foorman, Francis, Novy, and Liberman 1991).

Although the research reported here replicates and confirms the work of others in the field, in many respects, as indicated above, certain findings are unique to the study and deserve mention. Many previous researchers have suggested that phonological awareness is linked to reading acquisition (Felton and

Wood 1989; Juel, Griffith, and Gough 1986; Mann 1993; Perfetti, Beck, Bell, and Hughes 1987; Stanovich, Cunningham, and Cramer 1984; Wagner, Torgesen, and Rashotte 1994). Several studies also have demonstrated that children with LD can show increases in various phonological tasks as a result of explicit training in phoneme awareness (Alexander, Anderson, Heilman, Voeller, and Torgesen 1991; Ball and Blachman 1991; Fox and Routh 1984; Lie 1991; Torgesen, Morgan, and Davis 1992). A few have provided evidence, using growth curve analysis, that beginning scores in various phonological tasks can predict subsequent success of phonological training (Foorman et al. 1997; Torgesen and Davis 1996).[10] A small number of researchers have demonstrated growth in word reading in older elementary students with reading disabilities (Lovett and Steinbach 1997; Oakland, Black, Stanford, Nussbaum, and Balise 1998), and one study (Guyer and Sabatino 1989) has shown success using a "multisensory, alphabetic phonetic" approach with college students. The present research employed the growth curve analysis, and analyses of variance and covariance to extend the above findings by: (1) demonstrating directly the relation, not only between beginning score in phonological awareness (aptitude) and outcome measures (word recognition, reading comprehension and spelling) but also between growth in phonological awareness and growth in outcome measures; (2) utilizing a broad range of ages and grade levels to further demonstrate that older, disabled readers can also benefit from reading intervention; (3) pinning down even further the relation of phonological processing to reading comprehension, typically either not measured or not elaborated extensively in measurement instruments targeting the very young children who are the subjects of early acquisition studies; and (4) enhancing our understanding of spelling outcomes by demonstrating that phonological growth was strongly associated with spelling growth.

HOW DID SPEECH RECOGNITION IMPROVE PHONOLOGICAL AWARENESS?

As stated above, this study showed that gains in reading and spelling were strongly associated with growth in phonological awareness. However, the specific mechanisms that led to increased phonological awareness are not known. Although this

---

[10]Swanson (1992) has suggested, however, that a more general factor composed of measures of working memory outperforms single congnitive processing components as predictors.

study was not designed to determine how the use of speech recognition improved phonological awareness, there are several possibilities.

First, it is conceivable that speech recognition technology, through the process of converting the spoken word to electronic text, provided specific practice in acquiring rule-based phoneme/ grapheme correspondences. Lundberg (1995) stressed that many children with reading disabilities have difficulty extracting phonemic units from spoken language and mapping them "on to the grapheme units of written language" (p. 91). Furthermore, Lundberg (1978, 1995) has emphasized that when words are spoken, there is little conscious awareness as to the phonological segments used by the speaker, in contrast to reading (decoding) text (Lundberg 1984; Lundberg, Frost, and Petersen 1988), which requires specific awareness of phonemic segments. Similarly, Share (1995) has stressed that practice in phonological recoding (print-to-sound translation) functions as a self-teaching mechanism that leads to skilled word recognition. It is possible that speech recognition technology promoted an awareness of the relation between the phonological segments and alphabetic codes (and also functioned as a self-teaching mechanism) since the words spoken (phonemic segments) are simultaneously translated to their corresponding grapheme representations.

Second, correcting speech recognition errors by use of the choice box may have provided necessary practice in phonological awareness. As previously discussed, if the word displayed on the computer screen was incorrect (different from the one spoken by the user), the user needed to refer to the choice box and select the correct word from a list of similar sounding and looking words. In so doing, the user may have increased attention to specific internal characteristics, including phonemic units/phonological segments.

Third, perhaps the bimodal presentation of words—hearing them through the speaker's own voice, and seeing them simultaneously displayed on the computer screen—served to improve phonological awareness. This idea is consistent with research by Olson and Wise (1992) who reported that reading disabled children who had read stories on a computer with synthetic speech support made significant gains in phonological decoding and word recognition as compared to a control group who received reading instruction without computerized speech support. In addition to the auditory and visual components, the use of a speech recognition system also involves a proprioceptive/ kinesthetic component since the individual has to utilize the appropriate oral mechanisms to speak/articulate words. Along these lines, Oakland, Black, Stanford, Nussbaum, and Balise (1998) also have shown such multisensory training to be effective in enhancing phonological abilities.

Finally, speech recognition may have provided a meaningful and motivating context for interacting with text and increased opportunities for phonological exploration and play, such as rhyming, alliteration, and other formal devices. Lundberg (1995) has emphasized that reading is best developed . . . "by reading material that has personal significance and meaning to the reader" (p.92). Regarding phonological awareness, he states: "What children at risk for dyslexia may need is specialized practice with meaningful materials that allow them to abstract phonological segmentation skills, which can then be applied to learning grapheme-phoneme correspondence" (p. 92).

In accordance with other studies (Ball and Blachman 1991; Blachman, Ball, Black, and Tangel 1994, Wagner and Torgesen 1987), the present research suggests a strong association between improved phonological skills and enhanced reading abilities. However, unlike these studies, the present intervention did not provide explicit phonological training. In fact, it did not include any formal instruction in either reading or writing, aside from perhaps modeling the preplanning activities of choosing a topic and jotting down brief notes about major points. Again, students in the experimental group simply wrote (by means of speech recognition) anything they felt inclined to write; the writing activity was carried out independently and in a nonstructured, interest-driven context. The only instruction given to the participants was regarding the operation of the speech recognition system. Despite the fact that no explicit phonological training was given, students in the experimental group showed significant gains over the control group in phonological awareness (phonological deletion). Although it is difficult to determine the precise mechanisms that led to these gains, evidently the interaction between the user and the speech recognition system provided implicit phonological instruction/training embedded in an authentic and realistic academic context. This finding contradicts the suggestion by other researchers (Lovett and Steinbach 1997; Wagner, Torgesen, and Rashotte 1994) that it is necessary to provide systematic, intense, isolated, and explicit phonological training to enhance the phonological skills necessary for proficient reading in this population.

In support of our view, a few researchers such as Olson and Wise (1992) have speculated that it is possible for the correspondence of subword letter patterns and their speech sounds to be implicitly learned from whole-word feedback without attention to subword segments (p. 178). Similarly, Leong (1991), citing work by Perfetti, Beck, Bell, and Hughes (1987) and Ehri (1984), suggests that reading by itself, by means of exposure to orthographic representations, can lead to enhanced phonological knowledge.

Perhaps it could be argued that what we have termed implicit instruction is in actuality explicit. While using speech recognition technology, participants may have been forced to attend to, or make explicit, the phonological characteristics of words in both the process of monitoring the match between the words spoken and its grapheme representation, and in the process of correcting words from the list of similar sounding and looking words. However, the nonstructured nature of writing activities through speech recognition appears, in itself, to be a far cry from what might be considered explicit and systematic instruction in phonological awareness.

CONCLUSIONS/IMPLICATIONS

Over the past few years, in an attempt to provide assistive technology to persons with LD, our research group has consciously developed a line of research that has stressed using computers to accomplish authentic academic tasks, which, in turn, serve real educational, social, and recreational goals for persons with LD (Higgins and Raskind 1995, Raskind and Higgins 1995b, 1998). We wish to offer the suggestion that task-analyzing these authentic experiences mechanistically, or removing them too far from the social, educational, and recreational settings in which they occur, while appropriate for some purposes, could quite possibly invite the loss of transfer back to those very targeted authentic tasks. We believe that we have been able to demonstrate transfer to reading comprehension because the focus on and practice with phonological segments has occurred as a natural outcome of the desire to generate comprehensible language in the context of real sentences and paragraphs that have inherent personal meaning for the students. Our group cautions that attempts to replicate the positive results obtained in training that deviates too far from the reading and speaking/writing experience as it occurs in the natural settings in which students interact, may not succeed. Of course, only empirical research can clarify this issue.

In a related issue, we wish to stress again that instruction and adult supervision in learning to operate the technology during the first few sessions is critical to the successful use of the equipment for writing purposes, and that intermittent monitoring will be required to ensure that word recognition errors continue to be corrected by the user. If this is not done, voice files will become filled with incorrect linkages of spoken words with text and the system will no longer recognize the user's utterances accurately. Additionally, we found it necessary to have an abundant supply of stimulating activities at hand to ensure that participants were motivated to continue using the system (see examples in Appendix A). Finally, it was also important to spend three to five minutes, at the beginning of the early sessions with each student individually, to help in getting started; choosing a topic, listing two or more details or elaborations on the topic, and perhaps rehearsing the first sentence to be dictated. This is an especially important point when considering that some students did not have a positive emotional reaction to the systems and, in fact, several found the technology tedious, demanding, and frustrating to operate. Without this scaffolding activity, it is doubtful that students, even the most mature, would have continued to use the system effectively. We have conducted other research (Raskind, Higgins, Slaff, and Shaw, 1998) that further confirms that speech recognition technology is particularly vulnerable to underuse or misuse when inadequate support is offered.

In this regard, the argument could be made that similar results may have been obtainable with an intervention that required 50 additional minutes of writing, but that used pencil and paper and/or a word processor. We respond first that all students, both control and experimental participants, already received four hours of writing per week in class (separate from time spent in control and experimental conditions). In addition, part of the control students' time in the keyboarding class was spent writing as well (approximately 20 minutes), and 60 percent of their computer time involved text-related activities. In fact, total time writing for the control group was 4 hours, 20 minutes per week, whereas the experimental group received 4 hours, 50 minutes per week, a difference of only 30 minutes. Although possible, it seems unlikely that this 30 minute difference in writing activities per week (6 minutes more per day) accounted for such significantly greater gains in reading and spelling.

Another case could be made that writing on a computer (word processing) *without* speech recognition would also yield gains in reading and spelling. However, the extensive body of research on the IBM *Writing to Read* software program, designed to support such a notion, yielded equivocal findings (Jones 1993; Singh 1991). We believe that perhaps these results are equivocal because writing with a word processor—or pencil and paper—does not involve three of the components present in the speech recognition experience that have already been enumerated to be associated with reading improvement: (1) simultaneous, multi-sensory presentation of text (visually) and its auditory counterpart; (2) the necessity for monitoring the match between the visual output and its (intended) phonological representation; and (3) practice in reading *correctly spelled* text.

Additionally, we fully acknowledge that there is considerable research to support improvements in reading as a result of spelling and writing interventions with students with learning disabilities (see Ehri 1992 for a current review of such literature), as they have similarly acknowledged that a variety of reading and language-related interventions are effective. The researchers obviously cannot claim to have found the best method of teaching reading to children; only that the assistive use of speech recognition to generate written text can have a remedial effect.

THE RELATION BETWEEN REMEDIAL AND ASSISTIVE TECHNOLOGY

As previously discussed, Raskind and Scott (1993), emphasized the need to have a clear understanding of the differences between assistive and remedial technologies in order to ensure the attainment of specified educational goals. Interestingly, this study illustrated that speech recognition, an assistive writing technology, actually served to remediate/improve reading and spelling abilities. Although it is critical for an educator to know the primary purpose in providing an assistive technology, and to identify specific learning goals and the technology necessary to reach them, it is also important to understand that it is possible to accomplish both purposes with one technology. Some educators have expressed concerns that technologies designed to compensate for LD merely provide crutches for individuals with LD and do not serve to improve basic skill deficits, tending, rather, to make people dependent rather than independent. However, even without arguing the validity of such a notion from philosophical, theoretical, or research standpoints, we can now allay such concerns by adding the current research to the list of other studies (Kerchner and Kistenger 1984; Raskind, Higgins, and

Herman 1997) suggest that assistive technologies may have remedial value. This is not to say that all technologies will have remedial value. However, in some instances, the educator may be lucky enough to have access to a technology that provides the best of both worlds.

APPENDIX A
EXAMPLES OF WRITING MOTIVATIONS

"Many public libraries set aside one week each year for encouraging people to return overdue books. Write a humorous story about a library book that is ten years overdue. Describe the unusual circumstances that have prevented its return for so long a time."

—Schwartz and Armstrong

"Trees stay in one place their entire lives. What would it be like to be stuck in one place all your life like a tree? What would you see, hear, feel?

—Wilmes and Wilmes

"List the reasons why you would like to be covered with fur like an animal instead of wearing clothes."

—Senn

ACKNOWLEDGMENTS

The authors would like to express their gratitude and sincere appreciation to the Mufasa Trust for their generous support of this research.

A special thanks is extended to Dr. Lee Swanson of the University of California, Riverside, for his guidance in the selection of testing materials and for his analyses of the data as to growth curve parameters.

A thank you also needs to be given to Tobey Shaw, Dr. Ken Herman, Bob Goldhamer, Deborah Hori, Barbara Lundsten, Reid Schenck, Dr. Patty Finn, and Nancy Emolo of the Frostig Center for their assistance with testing and technology training.

Address correspondence to 971 N. Altadena Drive, Pasadena, CA 91107. E-mail center@frostig.org.

References

Alexander, A., Anderson, H., Heilman, P. C., Voeller, K. S., and Torgesen, J. K. 1991. Phonological awareness training and remediation of analytic decoding deficits in a group of severe dyslexics. *Annals of Dyslexia* 41:193–206.

Ball, E. W., and Blachman, B. A. 1991. Does phoneme awareness training in kindergarten make a difference in early word recogniiton and developmental spelling? *Reading Research Quarterly* 26:49–66.

Berninger, V., Abbot, R., Rogan, L., Reed, E., Abbot, S., Brooks, A., Vaughan, K., and Graham, S. 1998. Teaching spelling to children with specific learning disabilities: The mind's ear and eye beat the computer or pencil. *Learning Disabilities Quarterly* 21:106–22.

Blachman, B., Ball, E., Black, S., and Tangel D. 1994. Kindergarten teachers develop phoneme awareness in low-income, inner-city classrooms: Does it make a difference? *Reading and Writing: An Interdisciplinary Journal* 6:1–17.

Bradley, L., and Bryant, P. 1985. *Rhyme and Reason in Reading and Spelling*. Ann Arbor: University of Michigan Press.

Bryant, B. R., and Bryant, D. P. 1998. Using assistive technology adaptations to include students with learning disabilities in cooperative learning activities. *Journal of Learning Disabilities* 31:41–54.

Bryant, B. R., and Seay, P. C. 1998. The technology-related assistance to individuals with disabilities act: Relevance to individuals with learning disabilities and their advocates. *Journal of Learning Disabilities* 31:4–15.

Bryk, A. S., and Raudenbush, S. W. 1987. Application of hierarchical linear models to assessing change. *Psychological Bulletin* 101:147–58.

Chabot, R. J., Miller, T. J., and Juola, J. F. 1976. The relation between repetitions and depth of processing. *Memory and Cognition* 4:677–82.

Cunningham, A. E., and Stanovich, K. E. 1990. Assessing print exposure and orthographic processing skills in children: A quick measure of reading experience. *Journal of Educational Psychology* 82:733–40.

Danneman, M., and Carpenter, P. A. 1980. Individual differences in working memory and reading. *Journal of Verbal Learning and Verbal Behavior* 19:450–66.

DragonDictate® 2.5. Computer software. 1997. Newton, MA: Dragon Systems.

Ehri, L. C. 1984. How orthography alters spoken language competencies in children learning to read and spell. In *Language Awareness and Learning to Read*. J. Downing and R. Valtin, eds. New York: Springer-Verlag.

Ehri, L. C. 1992. Reconceptualizing the development of sight word reading and its relation to recoding. In *Reading Acquisition*. P. B. Gough, L. C. Ehri, and R. Treiman, eds. Hillsdale, NJ: Lawrence Erlbaum Associates.

Elkind, J., Black, M. S., and Murray, C. 1996. Computer-based compensation of adult reading disabilities. *Annals of Dyslexia* 46:159–86.

Elkind, J., Cohen, K., and Murray, C. 1992. *Using Computer-based Readers to Improve Reading Comprehension of Students with Dyslexia*. Palo Alto, CA: The Lexia Institute, Report 921.

Elkind, J., Cohen, K., and Murray, C. 1993. Using computer-based readers to improve reading comprehension of students with dyslexia. *Annals of Dyslexia* 43:238–59.

Felton, R. H., and Wood, F. B. 1989. Cognitive deficits in reading disability and attention deficit disorder. *Journal of Learning Disabilities* 22:3–13.

Fernald, G. 1943. *Remedial Techniques in Basic School Subjects*. New York: McGraw-Hill.

Foorman, B. R., Francis, D. J., Novy, D. M., and Liberman, D. 1991. How letter-sound instruction mediates progress in first grade reading and spelling. *Journal of Educational Psychology* 83:456–69.

Foorman, B. R., Francis, D. J., Winikates, D., Mehta, P., Schatschneider, C., and Fletcher, J. M. 1997. Early interventions for children with reading disabilities. *Scientific Studies of Reading* 1:255–76.

Foster, K. C., Erickson, G. C., Foster, D. F., Brinkman, D., and Torgesen, J. K. 1994. Computer administered instruction in phonological awareness: Evaluation of the Daisy Quest program. *Journal of Research and Development in Education* 27:126–37.

Fox, B., and Routh, D. K. 1984. Phonemic analysis and synthesis as word attack skills: Revised. *Journal of Educational Psychology* 16:1056–64.

Francis, D. J., Fletcher, J. M., Stuebing, K. K., Davidson, K. C., and Thompson, N. M. 1991. Analysis of change: Modeling individual growth. *Journal of Consulting and Clinical Psychology* 59:27–37.

Fulk, B. M. 1997. Think while you spell: A cognitive motivational approach to spelling instruction. *Teaching Exceptional Children* 29:70–71.

Gerber, M. M., and Hall, R. J. 1989. Cognitive-behavioral training in spelling for learning handicapped students. *Learning Disability Quarterly* 12:159–71.

Gillingham, A., and Stillman, B. 1968. *Remedial Training for Children with Specific Disability in Reading, Spelling and Penmanship.* Cambridge, MA: Educators Publishing Service.

Graham, S., and Voth, V. P. 1990. Spelling instruction: Making modifications for students with learning disabilities. *Academic Therapy* 4:447–57.

Guyer, B. P., and Sabatino, D. S. 1989. The effectiveness of a multisensory alphabetic phonetic approach with college students who are learning disabled. *Journal of Learning Disabilities* 22:430–33.

Heckelman, R. C. 1969. A neurological impress method of remedial reading. *Academic Therapy* 4:277–82.

Heshusius, L. 1989. The Newtonian mechanistic paradigm, special education, and contours of alternatives: An overview. *Journal of Learning Disabilities* 22:403–15.

Higgins, E. L., and Raskind, M. H. 1995. An investigation of the compensatory effectiveness of speech recognition on the written composition performance of postsecondary students with learning disabilities. *Learning Disability Quarterly* 18:159–74.

Higgins, E. L., and Zvi, J. C. 1995. Assistive technology for postsecondary students with learning disabilities: From research to practice. *Annals of Dyslexia* 45:123–42.

IBM® Voice Type 3.0. Computer software. 1997. Austin, TX: International Business Machines Corp., Special Needs Systems.

Jones, Z. 1993. Writing to read: Computer-assisted instruction and reading achievement. ERIC Document Reproduction Service No. ED365980.

Juel, C., Griffith, P., and Gough, P. 1986. Decoding, reading and reading disability. *Reading and Special Education* 78:243–55.

Karlsen, B., Madden, R., and Gardner, E. F. 1984. *Stanford Diagnostic Reading Inventory-III.* New York: Psychological Corporation.

Kerchner, L. B., and Kistenger, B. J. 1984. Language processing/word processing: Written expression, computers, and learning disabled students. *Learning Disability Quarterly* 7:329–35.

Leong, C. K. 1991. From phonemic awareness to phonological processing to language access in children developing reading proficiency. In *Phonological Awareness in Reading: The Evolution of Current Perspectives.* O. J. Sawyer and B. J. Fox, eds. New York: Springer-Verlag.

Lewis, R. B. 1998. Assistive technology and learning disabilities: Today's realities and tomorrow's promises. *Journal of Learning Disabilities* 31:16–26, 54.

Liberman, I. Y., Shankweiler, D., and Liberman, A. M. 1989. The alphabetic principal and learning to read. In *Phonology and Reading Disability.* D. Shankweiler and I. Y. Liberman, eds. Ann Arbor, MI: The University of Michigan Press.

Lie, A. 1991. Effects of a training program for stimulating skills in word analysis in first-grade children. *Reading Research Quarterly* 26:234–50.

Lindamood, C. H., and Lindamood, P. C. 1979. *Lindamood Auditory Conceptualization Test.* Austin, TX: PRO-ED, Inc.

Lindamood, C., and Lindamood, P. 1984. *Auditory Discrimination in Depth.* Columbus, OH: Science Research Associates/McGraw-Hill.

Lovett, M. W., and Steinbach, K. A. 1997. The effectiveness of remedial programs for reading disabled children of different ages: Does the benefit decrease for older children? *Learning Disability Quarterly* 20:189–210.

Lundberg, I. 1978. Aspects of linguistic awareness related to reading. In *The Child's Conception of Language.* A. Sinclair, R. J. Jarvella, and W. J. M. Levelt, eds. New York: Springer-Verlag.

Lundberg, I. 1984. *Språk och läsning.* Malmö: Liber Förlag.

Lundberg, I. 1995. The computer as a tool of remediation in the education of students with reading disabilities—a theory-based approach. *Learning Disability Quarterly* 18:89–99.

Lundberg, I., Frost, J., and Petersen, O. P. 1988. Effects of an extensive program for stimulating phonological awareness in preschool children. *Reading Research Quarterly,* 23: 263–84.

MacArthur, C. A. 1996. Using technology to enhance the writing processes of students with learning disabilities. *Journal of Learning Disabilities* 29:344–54.

Mann, V. A. 1993. Phoneme awareness and future reading ability. *Journal of Learning Disabilities* 26:256–69.

McNaughton, D., Hughes, C., and Clark, K. 1993, February. "An Investigation of the Effect of Five Writing Conditions on the Spelling Performance of College Students with Learning Disabilities." Paper presented at the 30th International Conference of the Learning Disabilities Association of America, San Francisco.

Myers, P. I., and Hammill, D. D. 1982. *Learning Disabilities: Basic Concepts, Assessment Practices and Instructional Strategies.* Austin, TX: PRO-ED.

National Joint Committee on Learning Disabilities. 1994. *Collective Perspectives on Issues Affecting Learning Disabilities.* Austin, TX: PRO-ED.

Oakland, T., Black, J. L., Stanford, G., Nussbaum, N. L., and Balise, R. 1998. An evaluation of the dyslexia training program: A multisensory method for promoting reading in students with reading disabilities. *Journal of Learning Disabilities* 31:140–47.

Olofsson, A. and Lundberg, I. 1983. Can phonemic awareness be trained in kindergarten? *Scandinavian Journal of Psychology* 24:35–44.

Olson, R., Kliegl, R., Davidson, B., and Foltz, G. 1985. Individual and developmental differences in reading disability. In *Reading Research: Advances in Theory and Practice,* 4. G. E. MacKinnon and T. Waller, eds. San Diego, CA: Academic Press.

Olson, R. K., and Wise, B. W. 1992. Reading on the computer with orthographic and speech feedback. *Reading and Writing. An Interdisciplinary Journal* 4:107–44.

Paris, S. G., Cross, D. R., and Lipson, M. Y. 1984. Informed strategies for teaching: A program to improve children's reading awareness and comprehension. *Journal of Educational Psychology* 76:1239–52.

Perfetti, C. A., Beck, I., Bell, L., and Hughes, C. 1987. Phonemic knowledge and learning to read are reciprocal: A longitudinal study of first grade children. *Merrill-Palmer Quarterly* 33:283–319.

Poplin, M. 1988. The reductionist fallacy in learning disabilities: Replicating the past by reducing the present. *Learning Disability Quarterly* 7:389–400.

Raskind, M. H. 1994. Assistive technology for adults with learning disabilities: A rationale for use. In *Adults with Learning Disabilities.* P. J. Gerber and H. B. Reiff, eds. Austin, TX: PRO-ED.

Raskind, M. H., and Higgins, E. L. 1995a. The effects of speech synthesis on proofreading efficiency of postsecondary students with learning disabilities. *Learning Disability Quarterly* 18:141–58.

Raskind, M. H., and Higgins, E. L. 1995b. Reflections on ethics, technology and learning disabilities: Avoiding the consequences of ill-considered action. *Journal of Learning Disabilities* 28:425–38.

Raskind, M. H., and Higgins, E. L. 1998. Assistive technology for postsecondary students with learning disabilities: An overview. *Journal of Learning Disabilities* 31:27–40.

Raskind, M. H., Higgins, E. L., and Herman, K. L. 1997. Technology in the workplace for persons with learning disabilities: Views from the inside. In *Learning Disabilities and Employment*. P. J. Gerber and D. S. Brown, eds. Austin, TX: PRO-ED.

Raskind, M. H., Higgins, E. L., Slaff, N. B., and Shaw, T. K. 1998. Assistive technology in the homes of children with learning disabilities: An exploratory study. *Learning Disabilities: A Multidisciplinary Journal* 9:47–56.

Raskind, M. H., and Scott, N. 1993. Technology for postsecondary students with learning disabilities. In *Success for Postsecondary Students with Learning Disabilities*. S. A. Vogel and P. B. Adelman, eds. New York: Springer-Verlag.

Rogosa, D. R., Brandt, D., and Zimowski, M. 1982. A growth curve approach to the measurement of change. *Psychological Bulletin* 90:726–48.

SAS Institute, Inc. 1992. *SAS Technical Report P-229, SAS/SAT Software: Changes and Enhancement. Release 6.07.* Cary, NC: Author.

Schwartz, L., and Armstrong, B. 1989. *Select a Story: Instant Ideas for Creative Writing*. Santa Barbara, CA: The Learning Works.

Senn, J. A. 1992. *325 Creative Prompts for Personal Journals*. New York: Scholastic Professional Books.

Share, D. L. 1995. Phonological recoding and self-teaching: *sine qua non* of reading acquisition. *Cognition* 55:151–218.

Singh, B. 1991. "IBM's Writing to Read Program: The Right Stuff or Just High Tech Fluff?" Paper presented at the Annual Meeting of the Florida Educational Research Association, November.

Stanovich, K. E., Cunningham, A. E., and Cramer, B. B. 1984. Assessing phonological awareness in kindergarten children: Issues of task comparability. *Journal of Experimental Child Psychology* 38:175–90.

Swanson, H. L. 1992. Generality and modifiability of working memory among skilled and less skilled readers. *Journal of Educational Psychology* 65:473–88.

Swanson, H. L., and Alexander, J. E. 1997. Cognitive processes as predictors of word recognition and reading comprehension in learning-disabled and skilled readers: Revisiting the specificity hypothesis. *Journal of Educational Psychology* 89:128–58.

Swanson, H. L., Cochran, K. F., and Ewers, C. A. 1989. Working memory in skilled and less skilled readers. *Journal of Abnormal Psychology* 17:145–56.

Swanson, L. H., and Ramalgia, J. M. 1992. The relation between phonological codes on memory and spelling tasks for students with and without learning disabilities. *Journal of Learning Disabilites* 25:396–407.

Swanson, L. H., and Trahan, M. F. 1992. Learning disabled readers' comprehension of computer mediated text: The influence of working memory, metacognition and attribution. *Learning Disabilities Research and Practice* 7:74–86.

Technology-Related Assistance for Individuals with Disabilities, Act of. 1988. P.L. 100-47, 29 U.S.C. 2201, 2202.

Torgesen, J. K. 1993. "Computers as Aids in the Prevention and Remediation of Reading Disabilities." Paper presented at the Fourth International Symposium on Learning Disabilities, Missillac, France, July.

Torgesen, J. K. 1995. A model of memory from an information processing perspective: The special case of phonological memory. In *Attention, Memory, and Executive Function: Issues in Conceptualization and Measurement.* G. R. Lyon and N. A. Krasnegor, eds. Baltimore, MD: Paul H. Brooks Publishing.

Torgesen, J. K., and Davis, C. 1996. Individual difference variables that predict response to training in phonological awareness. *Journal of Experimental Child Psychology* 63:1–21.

Torgesen, J. K., Morgan, S., and Davis, C. 1992. The effects of two types of phonological awareness training on word learning in kindergarten children. *Journal of Educational Psychology* 84:364–70.

Torgesen, J. K., Waters, M. D., Cohen, A. L., and Torgesen, J. L. 1988. Improving sight recognition skills in LD children: An evalauation of three computer program variations. *Learning Disabilities Quarterly* 11:125–30.

Wagner, R. K., and Torgesen, J. K. 1987. The nature of phonological processing and its causal role in the acquisition of reading skills. *Psychological Bulletin* 101:192–212.

Wagner, R. K., Torgesen, J. K., and Rashotte, C. A. 1994. The development of reading-related phonological processing ability: New evidence of bi-direcitonal causality from a latent variable longitudinal study. *Developmental Psychology* 30:78–87.

Wechsler, D. 1974. *Wechsler Intelligence Scale for Children-Revised.* New York: Psychological Corporation.

Wechsler, D. 1991. *Wechsler Intelligence Scale for Children-III.* New York: Psychological Corporation.

Wiederholt, J. L. 1986. *Formal Reading Inventory.* Austin, TX: PRO-ED.

Wilkinson, G. S. 1993. *Wide Range Achievement Test-3.* Wilmington, DE: Wide Range, Inc.

Willett, J. B. 1988. Questions and answers in the measurement of change. *Review of Research in Education* 15:345–422.

Wilmes, L., and Wilmes, D. 1983. *Everyday Circle Times.* Elgin, Illinois: Building Blocks Publication.

Repeated Reading to Enhance Fluency: Old Approaches and New Directions

Marianne S. Meyer

Wake Forest University School of Medicine
Bowman-Gray Campus

and

Rebecca H. Felton

Educational Consultant

As phoneme awareness deficits and resulting decoding weaknesses are increasingly addressed, there is heightened awareness of the role of fluency in reading. This paper reviews the history of fluency training, discusses the theoretical bases of such training, and summarizes the current knowledge about the efficacy of training procedures. We focus on Repeated Reading (RR), the most familiar and researched approach to fluency training. Outcome data on Repeated Reading, presented in the form of questions, is meant to answer practitioners' questions about implementation and efficacy and to provide a starting point for researchers interested in the topic. Although some answers are straightforward, others indicate the subtleties involved in answering the broad question, "Does Repeated Reading work?" In addition to a list of practical suggestions based on Repeated Readings findings, three new approaches to fluency training are introduced.

Annals of Dyslexia, Vol. 49, 1999
Copyright© 1999 by The International Dyslexia Association®
ISSN 0736-9387

INTRODUCTION

Recent intervention research (Torgesen, Rashotte, and Wagner 1997; Foorman et al. 1997; Foorman et al. 1997; Scanlon and Vellutino 1996) demonstrates that direct, intensive instruction in phoneme awareness and phonics improves decoding and word identification in poor readers, but yields only minimal gains in reading fluency. These findings attest to the need to turn our attention to fluency, defined here as the ability to read connected text rapidly, smoothly, effortlessly, and automatically with little conscious attention to the mechanics of reading, such as decoding. A major reason for focusing on the development of fluent reading is the theoretical relationship between fluency and comprehension. In theory, fluent reading allows the reader to attend to the meaning of text rather than to the mechanics of reading (Samuels 1979; Adams 1990). This hypothesis is supported by empirical research demonstrating strong correlations between reading fluency and comprehension (Dowhower 1987; Shinn et al. 1992; Tan and Nicholson 1997).

Dysfluent reading can also adversely affect the reader's motivation to engage in reading. Students with learning disabilities, in contrast to their normally achieving peers, often believe their academic performance is determined by their ability rather than their effort (Renick and Harter 1989). Therefore, pessimism about their ability to read, coupled with the experience of reading as an effortful and frustrating task, may lead dysfluent readers to avoid reading. Research douments that poor readers spend significantly less time reading than do skilled readers (Allington 1980, 1983; Biedmiller 1977; Lyon 1998), and Stanovich (1986) has hypothesized that reduced exposure to text leads to restricted vocabulary development which, in turn, has a negative impact on comprehension. Given the escalating demands for reading skills in our technological society, it is critical that researchers and practitioners focus on fluency as an important component of reading instruction.

THEORETICAL EXPLANATIONS FOR NONFLUENT READING

Three theoretical explanations posited for nonfluent reading are slow recognition of individual words, lack of sensitivity to prosodic cues, and failure to make higher order semantic connections between words, meanings, and ideas. Each theory has its own particular instructional implications.

SLOW RECOGNITION OF INDIVIDUAL WORDS

The earliest explanation for dysfluent reading focused on dysfluent readers' slow recognition of individual words (LaBerge and Samuels 1974; Samuels 1979). Research has confirmed that poor readers take much longer and require more exposures to recognize individual words than do normally reading children (Ehri and Wilce 1983; Reitsma 1983). Furthermore, the more complex the word, the longer it takes individuals with reading disabilities to learn it (Manis, Custodio, and Szeszulski 1993).

Two models have been proposed to account for the impact of slow word recognition on reading comprehension. LaBerge and Samuel's (1974) information processing model postulated that word recognition and comprehension cannot be performed simultaneously if a reader must focus disproportionately on word recognition. In this model, practice and overlearning lead to a high level of automaticity in word recognition, leaving attention free for comprehension. The verbal efficiency model proposed by Perfetti (1977, 1985) also assumes that through learning and practice, a reader can become more efficient and free cognitive resources to focus on higher level demands in reading. Perfetti's theory, which others have described as a sequential processing model, or "bottleneck" theory, posits that slow rate of word recognition obstructs the individual's ability to hold large units of text in working memory. This deficit makes reading less efficient. Shankweiler and Crain's (1986) hierarchical conceptualization extended Perfetti's theory by hypothesizing that the demands of orthographic decoding, in combination with limited working memory capacity, contribute to the reading comprehension difficulties of poor readers.

In the past twenty years, researchers have identified two major factors affecting speed and accuracy of single word recognition. Word recognition relies heavily on decoding ability, which, in turn, is related to underlying phonological awareness and phonological processing skills (Liberman and Shankweiler 1979; Adams 1990). Individuals who are poor decoders read slowly as they attempt to match letters to sounds in unfamiliar words. A potentially separate factor is retrieval or naming speed. Individuals with a deficit in this area have difficulty rapidly and accurately retrieving the names of familiar high frequency words (of, in, the), of word families/patterns (-at, -an), or letter-sound associations, even when decoding skills are accurate. Slow speed of lexical access has been shown to be a highly stable characteristic of poor readers (Meyer et al. 1998). A double deficit hypothesis has been proposed by Wolf (1997) and Wolf and Bowers (1999) who argue that phonemic awareness and rapid naming are partially separate, independent processes which predict different specific reading subskills. By this hypothesis, individuals with deficits in phonemic awareness are likely to have poor decoding accuracy, whereas individuals with deficits in rapid naming/retrieval are likely to have poor sight word recognition, especially in terms of speed. Individuals with deficits in both areas, the so-called double deficit, are considered to be at even greater risk for dysfluent reading than are individuals with only a single problem, either a rapid naming/retrieval problem or one involving phonology/decoding. The instructional implications of the double deficit hypothesis are clear. Effective instruction must focus specifically on an individual's area(s) of weakness.

LACK OF SENSITIVITY TO PROSODIC CUES

Schreiber (1980) proposed that dysfluency in poor readers occurs because they cannot grasp the prosodic and rhythmic characteristics of language in written text. Schreiber posits that it is the readers' ability to grasp the underlying syntactic structure of the language that leads to automaticity. He points out that young children often rely on prosodic and rhythmic characteristics of oral language to derive meaning before they acquire true linguistic competence. However, for beginning readers with poor word identification skills who do not understand how the sounds of oral language are represented in written text, such prosodic cues are not available. In this framework, fluency instruction should focus on recognition of phrases within sentences using techniques such as parsing exercises (separating noun and predicate phrases) and modeling prosody (listening to a fluent reader produce the appropriate phrasing in sentences).

FAILURE TO MAKE HIGHER ORDER ORTHOGRAPHIC AND SEMANTIC CONNECTIONS

Theorists propose that rapid single word identification and phrasal knowledge are necessary, but not sufficient, conditions for fluent reading. Adam's (1990) "connectionist" approach posits that skillful word reading is the consequence of rapid, coordinated, and highly interactive processing. She identifies four key processes—orthography, phonology, meaning, and context—and proposes that the stronger the connections among them, the more rapidly the word is recognized. As an example, Adams proposes that both orthographic and meaning processors are critical for learning morpheme patterns or units making up compound words with Greek, Latin, and Anglo-Saxon roots. Learning morpheme patterns enhances vocabulary acquisition and fluency because it makes word parts familiar and provides rich associations arising from lexical and semantic knowledge. Adams views the four processes as both complementary and compensatory to one another, and as a necessary component for comprehension.

The connectionist theory of fluent reading suggests that students should be taught to recognize common letter patterns, to map sounds onto letters and patterns within words, to understand the meanings of words, and to use context to construct meaning from text.

REPEATED READING METHODS

Recent research indicates that decoding instruction improves word attack and word identification, but does not correspondingly improve fluency (Torgesen, Rashotte, and Wagner 1997). How, then, are educators and clinicians to promote reading fluency? Because RR of connected text is the oldest, most frequently cited, and most researched method for improving fluency, we will focus primarily on this methodology. As originally conceptualized by Dahl (1974) and Samuels (1979), Repeated Reading is based on the information processing model which suggests that fluent readers are those who decode text automatically, leaving attention free for comprehension. The goals of RR as stated by Samuels were threefold: to increase reading speed; to transfer that improvement in speed to subsequent material; and to enhance comprehension with each successive rereading of the text.

The basic RR method is simple and straightforward. The student reads a passage at the appropriate instructional level aloud several times until the desired rate of reading, measured in words per minute, is achieved. After reaching the criterion rate, the student reads another passage at the same level of reading difficulty until that rate is attained again. In some cases, the child is given feedback on word recognition errors, as well as on the number of words correct. Results are graphed.

There are several variations of the RR technique in addition to the standard oral reading described above. One involves *unassisted* repeated reading where the child silently reads and rereads the same passage to himself with no adult supervision (text rereading). Another model involves *assisted* repeated reading where the child reads aloud and along with a fluent reader (spoken or modeled text) (Young, Bowers, and MacKinnon 1996). The third variation—*prosodic* reading—directs the attention of the reader to syntactic and rhythmic cues of the passage. Prosodic reading can include simply listening to the same passage read aloud several times by an adult, or be a variation on assisted repeated reading where the reader reads aloud with the person modeling. The critical factors are that the model reads in an expressive manner, using correct intonation, and reads at a rate slightly faster than that of the child (Schreiber 1980).

OUTCOME DATA:
ANSWERS TO PRACTICAL QUESTIONS

To consider the outcome data, we pose questions of practical consequence and indicate current findings in each area.

Descriptions of studies used to answer the practical questions posed below are listed in chronological order in Table I. Herman's early (1985) study serves to illustrate the methodology of RR research. Herman selected intermediate-grade students whose reading ranged from the 2nd to the 17th percentile on a group test, and whose reading rate was between 35 and 50 words per minute (wpm). Each student's reading level was subsequently assessed using an individual reading test, and the level for the repeated reading texts were chosen on that basis. After practicing their stories until they reached the criterion of 85 wpm (which took an average of four days), students chose another story at the same reading level. Students remained in the experiment for an average of 21 days. Using a repeated measures design, data on reading rate, accuracy, and number of speech pauses (analyzed by a microprocessing computer program) were collected four times during the study. Data were analyzed using a within-subjects and between-story analysis. Although Herman did not measure comprehension or prosody, other early studies, such as Dowhower's (1987), did. It seems, therefore, that early researchers anticipated many of the major questions about the efficacy of the RR method.

How fluent is fluent?

The most common way to assess fluency is by measuring oral reading rate per minute. Use of a sliding scale based on age and skill level is appropriate. In first graders, 30 to 50 words per minute is satisfactory (Mercer and Campbell 1998). For students

Table I.   Repeated Reading-Fluency Training Research.

Study	Participants	Sample Size	Length of Intervention
Spring, Blunden, and Gatheral 1981	Average readers grade 3	48	1 session
Herman 1985	Nonfluent readers grades 4–6	8	21 sessions
Rashotte and Torgensen 1985	Nonfluent reading disabled readers grades 2–5	12	7 sessions
O'Shea, Sindelar, and O'Shea 1985	Average or above readers grade 3	30	3 sessions
Dowhower 1987	Transitional readers grade 2	17	30 sessions
Rasinski 1990	Average and above readers grade 3	20	4 sessions
Stoddard, Valconte, Sindelar, O'Shea, and Algozzine 1993	Reading disabled grade 3–5	30	15 sessions
Faulkner and Levy 1994	1. good and poor readers grade 6	48	2 sessions
	2. good and poor readers grade 3	56	2 sessions
	3. good readers grade 2	48	2 sessions
	4. average readers grade 4	32	2 sessions
Varden, Bosh, VonBon, and Schreider 1995	Reading disabled grades 2–6	41	16 sessions
Young and Bowers 1995	1/2 average readers 1/2 reading disabled grade 5	85	1 session
Young, Bowers, and MacKinnon 1996	poor readers grade 5	40	1 session
Tan & Nicholson 1997	poor readers grades 2-5	42	5 sessions
Levy, Abello, and Lysynchuk 1997	poor readers grade 4	28	4 sessions (6 training sessions per day)
Flynn, Talbar, and Deering, 1998	reading disabled grades 2–7	44	54 sessions
Levy 1999	good and poor readers, grade 4	48	4 sessions

reading at approximately a mid-second grade level, rates considered acceptable range from 85 to 120 wpm with most hovering around 100 wpm ± 15 (Herman 1985; Dowhower 1987; Mercer and Campbell 1998). Oral reading rates improve slowly and incrementally over time (Hasbrouck and Tindal 1992; Hintze et al. 1997) and by 5th grade and above, desirable rates range from 120 to 150 wpm (Campbell and Mercer). Silent rates also improve incrementally (at least through high school) at a constant rate of about 10-20 words per minute/per year when reading material is at or below instructional levels (Carver 1989). In high school, the mean silent rate, based on the Nelson-Denny Reading Test revision (1993), is around 200 wpm (± 20).

A second way of assessing fluency involves counting the number and length of pauses. However, the issue of whether "fluent" reading is to be defined as virtually pause-free has never been addressed directly, and studies have produced conflicting results. Dowhower (1987) found that pauses decreased once second graders achieved a certain degree of reading facility, whereas Herman (1985) found no such decrease in length of pauses.

The third method of assessing fluency requires rating the prosodic quality (phrasing, fluency, and expression) of oral reading (Young, Bowers, and MacKinnon 1996). The Fluency Scale developed by Allington and Brown (1979) rates students on a scale from 1 to 6, with 6 defined as optimally fluent. This technique requires two independent raters and is more complex than other methods.

Can reading speed be increased by Repeated Reading?

Many researchers have convincingly shown that for a wide variety of readers, RR improves reading speed as measured by the number of words read per minute. This is true for normal third grade readers (Rasinski 1990; O'Shea, Sindelar, and O'Shea 1985; Faulkner and Levy 1994), for second grade readers with normal decoding skills but slow reading rate (Dowhower 1987), and for older elementary school students who are poor readers (Herman 1985; Rashotte and Torgesen 1985; Stoddard, et al. 1993; Faulkner and Levy 1994; Flynn, Rahbar, and Deering 1998). Note that most studies of Repeated Reading focus on elementary school students, which limits our ability to generalize the results to older students.

Do reader characteristics influence the amount of improvement?

Two reader characteristics, naming speed and degree of reliance on decoding for word recognition, have been found to be related to reading rate. Bowers (1993) studied a sample of average and poor readers, and found that those students with faster naming speeds showed greater increases in fluency after repeated reading training (reading passages four times). When accuracy of word identification was controlled statistically, slower readers' gains in fluency were predicted by naming speed. The results of this study suggest that poor readers with deficits in naming speed show improvements in reading speed more slowly than do poor readers without deficits in naming.

In direct contrast, two recent studies utilizing longer periods of training have found greater improvement in fluency among slow namers than among average namers following training. In a study by Levy, Abello, and Lysynchuk (1997), fourth grade poor readers read sets of 72 single words 20 times before reading stories containing those words. In results that contradicted those of Bowers'(1993) earlier study, slow namers gained relatively more than their faster naming peers. The 1997 results did, however, support the earlier finding that rapid naming rates did predict reading rate both before and after practice. Flynn, Rahbar, and Deering (1998) provided 54 hours of individual instruction over seven months to students categorized as either dysorthographic (overly reliant on decoding) or dysphonetic (rapid but inaccurate decoders) readers. Dysorthographic readers showed greater increases in fluency than did the dysphonetic readers when fluency training was emphasized. That study used a repeated oral-assisted reading format first with teacher modeling, then duo reading followed by student solo reading. Midway through the intervention, dysorthographic readers' rate had increased 61 wpm from baseline compared to a 43-wpm increase for dysphonetic readers.

Given that accuracy is another measure of fluency, can reading accuracy be increased by Repeated Reading?

A number of investigators report improvement in word recognition accuracy in a range of readers, including poor or disabled readers (Herman 1985; Young, Bowers, and MacKinnon 1996; van Bon et al. 1991; Flynn, Rahbar, and Deering 1998), transitional second grade readers (Dowhower 1987), and normal readers (Rasinski 1990).

How many rereadings are needed to improve reading rate?

O'Shea et al. (1985) report that in normal reading third graders who reread passages 7 times, 83 percent of the improvement occurred after four rereadings. Consistent with this, researchers typically have both disabled (Young, Bowers, and MacKinnon 1996) and normal readers (Bowers 1993) reread passages three to four times.

What is the average duration of fluency training during a single session?

In general, the length of the sessions described by various researchers averages about 15 minutes daily (range 10–20 minutes). Note that this time may include not only fluency training but also the test time for outcome measures (including rate, fluency, accuracy and comprehension) and correction of errors.

What level of instructor training is needed to implement Repeated Reading?

Although instructor training level is not addressed directly in most of the research, RR has been implemented by teachers, paraprofessionals, and volunteers (Mercer and Campbell 1998). Students at risk for reading failure can profit from reading with an adequately trained, higher-functioning peer (Simmons et al. 1990). Clinical practitioners have also provided simple, straightforward directions for parents who wish to do repeated reading exercises at home.

Which types of repeated readings are most effective: assisted, unassisted, or prosody?

Research findings suggest that variation in the students' level of reading skill prior to practice with RR techniques may produce differential results. For readers with average skills, researchers (Dowhower 1987; Rasinski 1990) found that all types of RR techniques produced gains in reading speed and accuracy. However, Dowhower concluded that the "read along" approach (prosodic reading) may be especially helpful for beginning readers who read accurately but slowly (reading rate less than 45 wpm). Young, Bowers, and MacKinnon (1996) evaluated the influence of prosodic modeling within a Repeated Readings instructional procedure on the development of fluency in fifth grade disabled readers. Whereas both assisted repeated readings (students read text in unison with a fluent oral model) and unassisted repeated readings (students read text independently) improved reading performance, it was the actual rereading of the text, not the prosodic modeling, that accounted for the most improvement.

What is the role of text difficulty in reading fluency?

Young and Bowers (1995) evaluated the impact of text difficulty on oral reading fluency in fifth grade average and poor readers. Differences in reading fluency between average and poor readers were evident on even the easiest stories; that is, poor readers were significantly slower than average readers, even when accuracy of word identification was not a factor. Poor readers showed significant declines in reading rate, accuracy, and fluency (phrasing, oral expressiveness) with each increase in text difficulty. In this study, naming speed (not phonemic awareness) contributed significant and unique variance to reading rate and fluency. This provides support for the double deficit hypothesis and suggests that accuracy of reading cannot be equated with oral reading rate or fluency in poor readers with naming deficits. These results seem to support the instructional practice of using materials that can be read accurately as the basis for fluency training with poor readers.

What factors in Repeated Readings increase the likelihood that the effects will transfer to novel text?

This is a complicated issue. Rashotte and Torgesen (1985) and Dowhower (1987) report it is the number of shared words in the text that increases transfer. Rashotte and Torgesen found that if one half of the words are shared between texts, reading speed of subsequent text improves. However, Faulkner and Levy (1994) found that for sixth graders (good and poor readers), it was only on more difficult stories that words shared between texts improved fluency; on easier stories, it was the shared content of the stories that improved fluency.

In a sample of fifth grade disabled readers, Young, Bowers, and MacKinnon (1996) studied transfer effects under four different types of fluency training conditions: repeated reading of lists of words from the text; repeated listening to the text read aloud; unassisted repeated reading with error correction; and assisted repeated reading with the students and teacher reading text together. Texts were used that contained a large number of shared words. All training conditions produced some transfer in oral reading fluency (expressiveness) and comprehension, but only the assisted repeated reading condition resulted in improved *accuracy* of word identification on the unpracticed material. The repeated reading conditions, but not repeated listening, resulted in a transfer of reading speed.

And the ultimate question: Does Repeated Reading improve comprehension?

This question is prompted by the theoretical relationship between fluent reading and comprehension and by studies indicating strong correlations between these two factors (Shinn et al. 1992; Dowhower 1994). Unfortunately, this is a very difficult question to answer since the methods of measuring comprehension—for example, cloze method (Spring, Blunden, and Gatheral 1981), unaided literal recall questions (Dowhower 1987), story-retelling (Young, Bowers, and MacKinnon 1996; O'Shea, Sindelar, and O'Shea 1985), and comprehension questions and recall (Tan and Nicholson 1997)—and subject samples vary considerably and results are not consistent across studies.

In second grade readers, Dowhower (1987) found that the assisted reading group, using the prosodic model, showed significant gains in comprehension in comparison to the unassisted group who read alone. However, in a study of poor readers, Young, Bowers, and MacKinnon (1996) came to a different conclusion. These researchers found that comprehension was improved by repeated reading of intact text, not by prosodic modeling or listening to text. They hypothesize that repeated reading practice allowed the poor readers to become more efficient readers, which, in turn, enabled them to shift their processing resources to comprehension.

O'Shea, Sindelar, and O'Shea (1985) found that the type of cueing such as directing students' attention to either fluency or comprehension is critical. Students cued to attend to fluency showed significant improvement in fluency but not as much improvement in comprehension, whereas students cued to pay attention to meaning showed better comprehension and were better able to retell the story. O'Shea et al. (1985) suggest that a combination of cueing for fluency and comprehension using materials at the student's instructional level may be ideal.

These findings indicate the complexity involved in assessing comprehension gains from fluency instruction, and suggest some factors that need to be considered such as student age, reading level, instructional method type (types of repeated reading or rapid decoding of single words), and cueing. Furthermore, the question of whether fluency and comprehension reciprocally influence one another is unanswered. Clearly, more carefully defined research is necessary to determine which approach—with which students, under what conditions, and for how long—will have the greatest impact.

SINGLE WORD AND PHRASE FLUENCY TRAINING

The efficacy of single word reading practice was cast into doubt by an early study by Dahl (1979) that reported second grade students given practice on reading single words, as opposed to repeated reading of connected text, did not make gains in reading rates. Dahl concluded that practice with reading words in context was necessary to increase reading speed. However, recent research questions Dahl's conclusion, making it important to reconsider the efficacy of single word training. Several proponents (Levy et al. 1997 and Tan and Nicholson 1997) ascribe to versions of Perfetti's "bottleneck" theory. For example, Levy et al. (1997) states that the "bottleneck" is " a disabling problem whose correction enables, but does not necessarily cause, comprehension to improve" (p. 186).

There are several techniques for single word training. *Flashcard* practice consists of printing a word on an index card, with the goal of recognizing it within a specific time period (often one second). Training continues either until the child reaches a specified criterion level or until the child has had enough practice to assure automaticity. After training, the student should be able to read the practiced words from a list of words on one page. Fleisher et al. (1979) set the goal of 90 wpm with 95 percent accuracy. Words (or sometimes phrases) selected are those frequently missed or judged to be difficult. The words selected may or may not be related to the content of the material to be presented. Time spent in flash card practice is approximately 20 minutes per session.

Computer practice, a variation of flashcard practice, presents words one at a time on a computer monitor, and the child reads the word aloud as rapidly as possible. If the child does not respond within a specified number of seconds, the word is removed automatically from the screen. The word then may be pronounced for the child.

Page speed drills such as those advocated by Fischer (1995, 1999) involves reading pages of alternating word sequences as fast as possible in one minute. For beginning readers, this may involve only three or four words repeated randomly in rows on one page. With increasing reader skill, the number of randomly repeating words on the page increases from five to seven.

Words are phonetically similar (fat, cat, sat) or contrasting (hat, hate, rat, rate). For beginning six- to seven-year-old students, Fischer recommends a goal of reading correctly 30 wpm, gradually increasing to 60 wpm by the middle of grade three.

Two questions related to single word and phrase fluency training have been addressed:

Does rate of reading text improve after practice with single words or phrases?

Recent studies of elementary students by van den Bosch, van Bon, and Schreuder (1995), Tan and Nicholson (1997), and Levy, Abello, and Lysynchuk (1997) indicate that flash card training is valuable. Training students to read words or phrases within strict time limits (defined as one or two seconds per word) resulted in improved speed and accuracy of text containing those words (Tan and Nicholson 1997; Levy et al.1997), and in reading rate of nonpracticed lists of similar words (van den Bosch et al 1995).

In a direct comparison of the benefits of practicing words in context (looking at the transfer of the same words to a different context) versus practicing lists of single words contained in the text, Levy (1999) found that use of connected text (contextual training) did not result in either greater fluency or greater comprehension. These researchers concluded that "young readers (fourth graders) appear to consolidate word recognition gains equally in or out of context." Given equal amounts of practice time, Levy (personal communication) hypothesizes that the greater number of repetitions afforded when reading the list of target words (13 trials) versus reading the stories containing the target words (4 trials) accounts for the findings. This result indicates the practice of single word reading may be a useful component of fluency instruction.

Does single word or phrase reading practice improve comprehension, and, if so, under what conditions?

Similar to the findings on repeated reading of connected text, the findings here are mixed. In a sample of third grade average readers, Spring et al. (1981) found that practice in reading lists of words did not improve comprehension when comprehension was assessed using a cloze procedure. In contrast, in a sample of poor readers, Tan and Nicholson (1997) found that training students to read rapidly a limited number of words (7 to 8 percent of the words in a passage) or phrases significantly improved comprehension. They note that the difference between their findings and those of others may have been due to several factors, including use of systematic decoding to teach single words, gearing difficulty level of passages presented to the child's reading level, and explaining unfamiliar meanings of words in the training set. Levy, Abello, and Lysynchuk (1997) found no gains in comprehension when no time limits were used. However, when demands for speed increased during the training period, comprehension improved.

GENERAL PRINCIPLES OF FLUENCY TRAINING FOR STUDENTS WITH READING DISABILITIES

Although the findings from the studies referenced above do not provide as definitive and clear cut guidelines for fluency training as would be ideal, in our opinion there is a sufficient knowledge base to support a few general principles for practitioners. These principles, presented in table II, are offered with the full realization that not all strategies are appropriate for all students, and that clinical judgments must be made appropriately. In addition to results of research, we have drawn on our own clinical experience with poor readers in preparing these principles.

NEW APPROACHES TO FLUENCY TRAINING

In spite of many limitations such as length of intervention, early studies provided positive evidence for the efficacy of fluency training. Later research helped define variables such as reader skill level and characteristics, type of RR technique, number of passages read, and length of practice to be considered. It can be said, therefore, that prior studies have prepared the way for the more comprehensive approaches currently being evaluated. Although we are aware of other approaches (Speed Drills for Decoding Automaticity by Fisher 1995, DIBELS by Kaminski and Good 1998; Continuum of Modeling Methods by Carbo 1997, Read Naturally by Inhot 1998, and an adaptation of the initial teaching alphabet by Flynn, Rahbar, and Deering 1998), we will highlight only three.

Before presenting these three approaches (RAVE-O, Great Leaps, and Decoding Pilot Program), it is important to place each in its theoretical context, to highlight their common elements, and to show how they incorporate RR techniques (including sin-

---

Table II.   General Principles of Fluency Training for Students with Reading Disabilities.

• In addition to instruction in decoding and word identification, fluency training is an important component of reading instruction for many students.

• Multiple reading of *continuous text* (Repeated Reading) can lead to improve ments in reading speed, accuracy, comprehension, and expression.

• Students should read text that can be read *accurately* (no more than 5 percent to 10 percent error rate). Material should be carefully selected so that the student is not frustrated by reading text that is too difficult.

• Material should be read *three to four times* for optimal benefit.

• Measures of *rate and accuracy* are both important benchmarks of improvement in reading fluency.

• Multiple readings of *single words and phrases* may improve fluency.

• Fluency training can be combined with strategies to enhance comprehension such as vocabulary development.

• Specific strategies for multiple readings should take individual student charac teristics into account. For *more impaired readers*: provide more adult guidance during reading; use more decodable texts as reading materials; practice on words and phrases from the text before reading the text; practice reading short passages; and model expressive reading.

• *Short, frequent periods* of fluency practice should be scheduled on a regular basis.

• *Incentives* for reading practice as well as concrete *measures of progress*—graphs of changes in rate and accuracy; records of number of stories/passages read— should be provided.

---

gle word speed drills) in addressing reading fluency. Consistent with the first causal hypothesis presented, all three approaches implicitly acknowledge that slow single word reading is a (but not *the*) main source of dysfluency. Furthermore, all three refer to research indicating that both decoding and lexical access are important to improving reading acquisition and reading fluency. Citing the role of phonemic awareness and decoding in reading acquisition, and the efficacy of code instruction for disabled readers, RAVE-O and Decoding Pilot Program use systematic code instruction as a basis for direct reading instruction. In addition, they both use decodable text for fluency practice. Although Great Leaps advocates such instruction, it does not include decoding as a formal aspect of its program. In all three approaches, retrieval or lexical access weaknesses are addressed by direct fluency training: it is the emphasis of this training which varies. Specifically, Great Leaps and Decoding Pilot Program use standard RR techniques for practicing text passages (although for shorter amounts of time than the standard

10–20 minutes), and both RAVE-O and Great Leaps place significant emphasis on single word speed drills. Great Leaps, in particular, incorporates single word speed drills that recent findings indicate to be an effective training exercise. Taking advantage of advances in computer technology, RAVE-O and Decoding Pilot Program use software with adjustable speed controls to vary rates of presentation and gradually increase reading rate.

None of the approaches specifically highlight Schreiber's prosody theory, but both RAVE-O and Decoding Pilot Program devote a significant portion of instructional time to activities consistent with Adams' connectionist theory. Briefly, the connectionist theory posits that weaknesses in orthographic and semantic knowledge account for a portion of the difficulties in fluency. Both RAVE-O and Decoding Pilot Program provide considerable instruction on "chunking," or sublexical pattern recognition, using patterns ranging from onset rimes for early readers to morphological patterns from Greek and Latin bases for adult readers. Based on the logical assumption that words with rich associations are more easily retrieved when encountered in text, both programs use vocabulary development exercises to enhance semantic knowledge.

Despite the assumption that improved fluency may be a prerequisite for better comprehension, none of these three approaches includes a complete and intensive comprehension component, although two have some elements. Although research on comprehension is not as well developed as the research base in beginning reading, we would argue that comprehension strategies should be taught directly, as part of a balanced reading program (Williams 1998).

Finally, each of these approaches provide daily fluency training over a substantial period of time (often one year). This extended length of intervention is, in itself, an important difference from the traditional repeated reading approach.

RAVE-O (RETRIEVAL, ACCURACY, VOCABULARY, ELABORATION-ORTHOGRAPHY)

RAVE-O is a direct outgrowth of the double deficit hypothesis of Wolf and Bowers (1999) and is the focus of an ongoing National Institute of Child and Human Development (NICHD) project. RAVE-O differs from earlier fluency techniques by attempting to provide a more comprehensive approach to

fluency in underlying perceptual, phonological, and lexical retrieval skills, as well as to fluency in overt reading skills (word
identification, word attack, orthographic patterns, and recognition and comprehension). RAVE-O is coordinated with Lovett et
al.'s phonological analysis and blending (PHAB) program
(1994) on the premise that there must be a systematic phonological basis for reading.

RAVE-O has two semi-independent parts: RAVE and O. The
RAVE component focuses on helping students understand the
meaning of words through awareness of common meaning
components and how the word changes in different contexts.
Wolf and Bowers propose that fast, accurate retrieval of both
oral and written words is easiest when words are familiar and
possess rich associations that arise from lexical and semantic
knowledge. The O component—orthographic fluency—is at the
heart of the program and emphasizes "the systematic development of automaticity in orthographic pattern recognition."
Consequently, teaching children to "chunk" word parts (such as
rimes, affixes, and consonant blends) is a key component since
chunking or sublexical pattern recognition allows for more
rapid recognition.

RAVE-O is taught by trained research teachers to small
groups of early elementary students whose reading level falls
below the tenth percentile. The first half hour of instruction uses
systematic, sequential code materials that emphasize phoneme
analysis and blending. The next half hour (the RAVE-O component) follows scripted lesson plans devised by the researchers
and focuses on learning a list of decodable "core" words, all of
which have multiple meanings. (An example is the decodable
CVC word, "jam", which could mean "jam on toast," "traffic
jam," or "jam an object into a box.") Specific materials and programs, many of which impart a game-like quality to lessons,
have been developed to accompany RAVE-O, with the intent of
making learning fun for readers. For example, since overlearning of orthographic patterns is critical, a computer program
called Speed Wizard has been designed. This program includes a
set of systematically controlled games that reinforce previously
taught phonological skills and emphasize rapid, automatic word
recognition. Other materials include Minute Mysteries (stories to
develop fluent reading of controlled text), manipulatives (such
as word webs to associate other words, ideas, and phrases with
the word in the middle of the web), and props (such as sand and
sandpaper to illustrate word meanings). Comprehension activities incorporate words that have been taught previously.

GREAT LEAPS

Great Leaps is a remedial program originally developed by Kenneth Campbell (1995) and supplemented at the K–2 level by Cecil Mercer, serves a broad range of ages (kindergarten through adult) and uses a wide range of tutors (community volunteers, paraprofessionals, peers and parents, in addition to regular classroom teachers). It requires a minimum of five to seven minutes daily. This fluency program is meant to supplement an existing reading curriculum, which the authors recommend should provide systematic code instruction for poor readers. For the youngest students, K–2, Campbell and Mercer have developed fluency tasks, hierarchically arranged from phonemic awareness skills to sound-symbol correspondence to systematic decoding. Materials for older students are designed to be age appropriate, that is, high interest and low vocabulary. Initial fluency levels are established by having the student read for three minutes in a basal text.

Taught for a minimum of five to seven minutes daily in a one-on-one tutorial setting, students read in one-minute segments, first from a list of learned decodable words, next from a list of phrases, and finally from a story geared to the student's instructional level. Tutors pause as needed to review skills and/or model fluent reading. After each portion of instruction (decodable word reading, phrase reading, and text reading), the student's performance is graphed. Errors are pointed out immediately following each minute segment and the student is commended for effort. This graphing—a means of visually demonstrating progress to the student and specifically calling attention to the need for speed and accuracy—is an important component of Great Leaps and encourages the student to work toward rate-per-minute goals. The student reads the same passage each day until he or she can read a page in one minute with less than two errors. The student then "leaps up" to a higher level passage.

DECODING PILOT PROGRAM

Decoding Pilot Program is Landmark College's newly devised experimental program begun by Linda Hecker and Rob Gunter-Mohr and shares a number of characteristics with the RAVE-O program. Developed for eight college students with low decoding skills (elementary level), relatively stronger oral language skills, and at least average intellectual ability, the program's general goal is to provide a sequence of courses with an intensive focus on improving reading and writing skills while providing intellectual challenge. The specific goals of this year-long program are to increase decoding skills, fluency, vocabulary, metalinguistic knowledge, and the quality and quantity of written output. Four days a week students receive individual tutoring in decoding using systematic, sequential, multisensory methods. All take a daily class on the structure of language which emphasizes the morphology (or meaningful word parts) and the structure of words in order to increase vocabulary knowledge. In addition, students take a written composition class that uses voice recognition software designed to help them overcome the obstacles of weak encoding as a supplement to the more traditional approaches of teaching paragraph and essay structure. Finally, students take a daily class which reinforces decoding skills and adds a comprehension and fluency component to the program.

Landmark's fluency training component was developed by Mary Doherty and uses computers and software to enhance a Repeated Reading approach. Using the Kurzweil Ultimate Reader-3000, a PC-based reading system with its own software program and scanner, the student wears headphones and reads along silently as the computer reads the text aloud at a chosen speed. The rate can be adjusted from 50 to 390 wpm and text can be highlighted either by single words, phrases, sentences, or lines. Pronunciation and dictionary functions can be accessed by highlighting a specific word. Passages read are from high-interest low-vocabulary material, geared to approximately a fifth grade level. After this solo exercise, students are paired and asked to read the same passage aloud to a partner, obtaining feedback about errors. Students read the passage several times to the partner, measuring subsequent improvements in rate.

RESEARCH DIRECTIONS

The good news is that the reading community is now sufficiently focused on fluency training that funding sources are allocating monies for research that explicitly incorporates fluency training in the treatment component. The critical question is not whether fluency training is effective. Rather, the question is "With what groups of children, at what stage of development, and using which methods, can fluency—and ultimately comprehension—be significantly improved?" Among the specific research questions to be addressed are:

1. What is the relationship between the intensity and type of fluency training and characteristics of individual students (subtypes)?
2. Does a code approach plus fluency training significantly improve outcome for double deficit students?
3. Are there students who can profit especially from single word and phrase reading training, and if so, is there a certain stage of fluency training at which it can be best incorporated ?
4. Are four rereadings, the standard number now used, sufficient for dysfluent readers?
5. How long do fluency gains last, and do individuals with fluency problems need "boosters" throughout their academic career?
6. What is the specific interaction between decoding, lexical access, and working memory in comprehension and fluency?
7. What comprehension approaches need to be a part of a balanced reading program?

If fluency studies are able to incorporate good research methodology—carefully chosen and defined samples, balanced and explicitly taught treatments, adequate control groups, sufficient length of intervention, awareness of teacher variables and generalization effects, etc.— as recommended by Lyon and Moats (1997), then we are on the way to helping even more children become good readers.

Address correspondence to: Marianne S. Meyer, Section of Neuropsychology, Wake Forest University School of Medicine, Medical Center Boulevard, Winston-Salem, North Carolina 27151-1043. e-mail: mmeyer@wfubmc.edu.

References

Adams, M. J. 1990. *Beginning to Read: Thinking and Learning About Print.* Cambridge, MA: MIT Press.

Allington, R. L. 1980. Poor readers don't get to read much in reading groups. *Language Arts* 57:872–76.

Allington, R. L. 1983. Fluency: The neglected reading goal *The Reading Teacher* 36:556–60.

Allington, R. L., and Brown, S. 1979. *FACT: A MultiMedia Reading Program.* Milwaukee, WI: Raintree Press.

Beidmiller, A. 1977. Relations between oral reading rates for letters, words and simple text in the development of reading achievement. *Reading Research Quarterly* 13:223–53.

Bowers, P. G. 1993. Text reading and rereading: Determinants of fluency beyond word recognition. *Journal of Reading Behavior* 25(2):133–53.

Campbell, K. 1995. *Great Leaps Reading Program*. Micanopy, FL: Diarmuid, Inc.

Carbo, M. 1997. *Continuum of Modeling Methods: Release Your Students' Learning Power*. Syosset, NY: National Reading Styles Institute.

Carver, R. 1989. Silent reading rates in grade equivalents. *Journal of Reading Behavior* 21:155–66.

Dahl, P. R. 1974. An experimental program for teaching high speed word recognition and comprehension skills. (Final report project #3-1154) Washington, DC: National Institute of Education.

Dahl, P. R. 1979. An experimental program for teaching high speed word recognition and comprehension skills. In *Communications Research in Learning Disabilities and Mental Retardation*, J. E. Button, T. C. Lovitt, and T. D. Rowland, eds. Baltimore: University Park Press.

Dowhower, S. 1987. Aspects of repeated reading on second-grade transitional readers fluency and comprehension. *Reading Research Quarterly* 22:389–406.

Dowhower, S. 1994. Repeated reading revisited: Research into practice *Reading and Writing Quarterly: Overcoming Learning Difficulties* 10:343–58.

Ehri, L. C., and Wilce, L. S. 1983. Development of word identification speed in skilled and less skilled beginning readers. *Journal of Educational Psychology* 75:3–18.

Faulkner, H. J., and Levy, B. A. 1994. How text difficulty and reader skill interact to produce differential reliance on word and content overlap in reading transfer. *Journal of Experimental Child Psychology* 58:1–24.

Fishco, V. V., and Hanna, G. S. 1993. *Nelson-Denny Reading Test*. Chicago: Riverside Publishing Co.

Fisher, P. 1995. *Speed Drills for Decoding Automaticity*. Farmington, ME: Oxton House Publishers.

Fisher, P. 1999. Getting up to speed. *Perspectives* 25(2):12–13.

Fleisher, L. S., Jenkins, J. R., and Pandy, D. 1979. Effects on poor readers' comprehension of training in rapid decoding. *Reading Research Quarterly* 15:30–48.

Flynn, J., Rahbar, M., and Deering, W. 1998. Manuscript submitted. Dysphonetic and dysorthographic readers: Response to treatments using the initial teaching alphabet.

Foorman, B. R., Francis, D. J., Beeler, T., Winikates, D., and Fletcher, J. M. 1997. Early interventions for children with reading problems: Study designs and preliminary findings. *Learning Disabilities: A Multidisciplinary Journal* 8:63–72.

Foorman, B. R., Francis, K. J., Winidates, D., Mehta, P., Schatschneider, C., and Fletcher, J. M. 1997. Early interventions for children with reading disabilities. *Scientific Studies in Reading* 1:255–76.

Hasbrouck, J., and Tindal, G. 1992. Curriculum-based oral reading fluency norms for students in grades 2 through 5. *Teaching Exceptional Children:*41–44.

Herman, P. 1985. The effect of repeated readings on reading rate, speech pauses and word recognition accuracy. *Reading Research Quarterly* 20:553–65.

Hintze, J., Shapiro, E., Conte, K., and Basile, I. 1997. Oral reading fluency and authentic reading material: Criterion validity on the technical features of CBM survey-level assessment. *School Psychology Review* 26:535–53.

Inhot, C. 1998. *Read Naturally*. St. Paul, MN: Read Naturally, Inc.

Kaminski, R. A., and Good, R. H., 1998. Use of curriculum based measurement to assess early literacy: Dynamic indicators of basic early literacy skills. In *Advances in Curriculum Based Measurement: Use in a Problem Solving Model*, M. Shinn, ed. New York: Guilford Press.

LaBerge, D., and Samuels, J. 1974. Toward a theory of automatic information processing in reading. *Cognitive Psychology* 6:293–323.

Levy, B.A. April 1999. Learning to read: Context doesn't matter. Paper presented at the Society for the Scientific Study of Reading, Montreal.

Levy, B.A., Abello, B., and Lysynchuk, L. 1997. Transfer from word training to reading in context: Gains in reading fluency and comprehension. *Learning Disability Quarterly* 20:173–88.

Liberman, I. Y., and Shankweiler, D. 1979. Speech, the alphabet, and teaching to read. In *Theory and Practice in Early Reading* (Vol. 2), L. B. Resnick and P. A. Weaver, eds. Hillsdale, NJ: Lawrence Erlbaum Associates.

Lovett, M., Borden, S., DeLuca, T., Lacerenza, L., Bensen, N., and Brackstone, D. 1994. Treating the core deficits of developmental dyslexia: Evidence of transfer of learning after phonologically and strategy-based reading training programs. *Developmental Psychology* 30:803–22.

Lyon, G. R., and Moats, L. C. 1997. Critical conceptual and methodological considerations in reading intervention research. *Journal of Learning Disabilities* 30(6):578–88.

Lyon, G. R. 1998. Critical advances in understanding reading acquisition and reading difficulty. Paper read at North Carolina Branch of the International Dyslexia Association, November 1998, Boone, NC.

Manis, F. R., Custodio, R., and Szeszulski, P. A. 1993. Development of phonological and orthographic skill: A 2-year longitudinal study of dyslexic children. *Journal of Experimental Child Psychology* 56:64–86.

Mercer, C., and Campbell, K 1998. *Great Leaps Reading Program*. Micanopy, FL: K-2 Diarmuid, Inc.

Meyer, M. S., Wood, F. B., Hart, L. A., and Felton, R. H. 1998. Selective predictive value of rapid automatized naming in poor readers. *Journal of Learning Disabilities* 31:106–17.

O'Shea, L., Sindelar, P., and O'Shea, D. 1985. The effects of repeated readings and attentional cues on reading fluency and comprehension. *Journal of Reading Behavior* 17:129–42.

Perfetti, C. A. 1985. *Reading Ability*. New York: Oxford University Press.

Perfetti, C. A. 1977. Language comprehension and fast decoding: Some psycholinguistic prerequisites for skilled reading comprehension. In *Cognition, Curriculum and Comprehension*, J. T. Guthrie, ed. Newark, DE: International Reading Association.

Rasinski, T. 1990. Effects of repeated reading and listening-while-reading on reading fluency. *Journal of Educational Research* 83:147–50.

Rashotte, C., and Torgesen, J. 1985. Repeated reading and reading fluency in learning disabled children. *Reading Research Quarterly* 20:180–88.

Reitsma, P. 1983. Printed word learning in beginning readers. *Journal of Experimental Child Psychology* 36:321–29.

Renick, M. J., and Harter, S. 1989. Impact of social comparisons on the developing self-perceptions of learning disabled students. *Journal of Educational Psychology* 81:631–38.

Samuels, S. J. 1979. The method of repeated readings. *The Reading Teacher* 32(4):403–08.

Scanlon, D. M., and Vellutino, F. R. 1996. Prerequisite skills, early instruction, and success in first-grade reading: Selected results from a longitudinal study. *Mental Retardation and Developmental Research Reviews* 2:54–63.

Schreiber, P. 1980. On the acquisition of reading fluency. *Journal of Reading Behavior* 12:177–86.

Shankweiler, D., and Crain, S. 1986. Language mechanisms and reading disorder: A modular approach. *Cognition* 24:139–68.

Shinn, M. R., Good, R. H., Knutson, N., Tilly, W. D., and Collins, V. L. 1992. Curriculum-based measurement of oral reading fluency: A confirmatory analysis of its relation to reading. *School Psychology Review* 21:459–79.

Simmons, D. C., Fuchs, L. S., Fuchs, D., Mathes, P. G., and Page, M. J. 1990. The effects of explicit teaching and peer-mediated instruction on low performing and mildly handicapped students' reading achievement. Paper presented at the American Educational Research Association's Annual Meeting. Boston, MA.

Spring, C., Bluden, D., and Gatheral, M. 1981. Effect on reading comprehension of training to automaticity in word-reading. *Perceptual and Motor Skills* 53:779–86.

Stanovich, K. 1986. Matthew effects in reading: Some consequences of individual differences in the acquisition of literacy. *Reading Research Quarterly* 21:360–406.

Stoddard, K., Valcante, G., Sindelar, P., and Algozzine, B. 1993. Increasing reading rate and comprehension: The effects of repeated readings, sentence segmentation and intonation training. *Reading Research and Instruction* 32:53-65.

Tan, A., and Nicholson, T. 1997. Flashcards revisited: Training poor readers to read words faster improves their comprehension of text. *Journal of Educational Psychology* 59:276–88.

Torgesen, J., Rashotte, C., and Wagner, R. November 1997. Research on instructional interventions for children with reading disabilities. Paper delivered at International Dyslexia Association, Minneapolis, MN.

van Bon, W. H. J., Boksebeld, L. M., Font Freide, T. A. M., and van den Hurk, A. J. M. 1991. A comparison of three methods of reading-while-listening. *Journal of Learning Disabilities* 24(8):471–76.

van den Bosch, K., van Bon, W., and Schreuder, R. 1995. Poor readers' decoding skills: Effects of training with limited exposure duration. *Reading Research Quarterly* 30:110–25.

Williams, J. 1998. Improving the comprehension of disabled readers. *Annals of Dyslexia* 48:213–38.

Wolf, M. 1997. A provisional, integrative account of phonological and naming-speed deficits in dyslexia: Implications for diagnosis and intervention. In *Cognitive and Linguistic Foundations of Reading Acquisition: Implications for Intervention* Research, B. Blachman, ed. Hillsdale, NJ: Lawrence Erlbaum Associates.

Wolf, M., and Bowers, P. 1999. The double deficit hypothesis for the developmental dyslexias. *Journal of Educational Psychology* 91:415–38.

Young, A., and Bowers, P. 1995. Individual differences and text difficulty determinants of reading fluency and expressiveness. *Journal of Experimental Child Psychology* 60:428–54.

Young, A., Bowers, P., and MacKinnon, G. 1996. Effects of prosodic modeling and repeated reading on poor readers' fluency and comprehension. *Applied Psycholinguistics* 17:59–84.

Transforming Engagement in Literacy Instruction: The Role of Student Genuine Interest and Ability

Joanne Marttila Pierson

University of Michigan
Ann Arbor

In this case study paper, I describe my work with Bill, a first grade boy with dyslexia. My goals were to identify his interests and abilities and create contexts in which these interests and abilities supported his literacy learning. A theoretical foundation that merged current understandings of highly effective pedagogical practices for individuals with dyslexia with Dewey's (1913) theory of genuine interest within a social-constructivist perspective (Vygotsky 1987, 1993) was utilized. A noticeable improvement in Bill's willingness to engage in activities of reading, writing, and phonological awareness occurred when he was given a voice in the activities. Within contexts of literacy learning that allowed him to demonstrate his interests and talents, Bill became increasingly engaged in activities surrounding the reading and writing of text. Ultimately, this project was successful in creating a context, for this six-year-old boy with dyslexia, in which meaningful learning took place and motivation was provided for future literacy learning.

Annals of Dyslexia, Vol. 49, 1999
Copyright© 1999 by The International Dyslexia Association®
ISSN 0736-9387

"But we still know nothing about positive characteristics, about the children's uniqueness: such is the research of the future."

—Vygotsky 1993, p. 48

THEORETICAL FOUNDATION

Historically, special pedagogical practices for those children who experience specific learning disabilities (including dyslexia) have typically employed a reductionist approach to instruction (Heshusius 1989; McPhail 1995; Poplin 1988). This approach stems, in large part, from a theoretical undergirding framed within a medical model of deficits. Recently, there has been a call for alternative research and instructional methodologies based on sociocultural and cognitive perspectives. In an attempt to move away from a reductionist conceptualization of disability toward a more holistic approach, a number of researchers have pursued alternative forms of inquiry in which assessment and intervention occur within natural contexts and through natural interactions (Adams 1990; Klenk 1994; Lipson and Wixson 1991; Palincsar and Klenk 1992; Palincsar and Perry 1995; Schneider and Watkins 1996).

Embedded within these inquiries is a revisionist view of disability. Rather than holding strictly to the belief that the deficit lies solely within the child, supporters of the revisionist view acknowledge that occurrence of the child's deficit depends on interactions between the child's learning profile and contexts of interaction. In an effort to move away from the "deficit within the child" premise, Coles (1987) called for an interactivity theory of learning disability that considers the interdependence of the ". . . individual (including neurology), groups, and institutions, and social, economic, and cultural forces . . . [as] . . . they all combine to create the processes and products of learning and disabled learning" (p. 209). Writing under the philosophical rubric of interpretivism and phenomenology, some scholars call for a new conceptualization of disability in which researchers work to understand it in light of the social forces that create it, the child's perceptions of these social forces, and the disability's impact on the child's self-understanding (Coles 1987; Ferguson, Ferguson, and Taylor 1992; McPhail 1995; Wansart 1995). Such a shift requires a conceptual frame that privileges the voice of the individual with the disability and his or her social context of learning.

In an attempt to incorporate the tenets of assessment and instruction within natural contexts, and allow for the students' voices to be represented, educators and researchers have turned to the seminal work of Vygotsky (1987, 1993) and his theory of social constructivism in learning and development. Vygotsky (1993) stressed the role of social forces in the creation of a child's perceptions of his or her own disability: "What decides the fate of a personality is not the defect itself, but its social consequences, its socio-psychological realization" (p. 36). The child's social interactions shape development and perceptions of the self. For Vygotsky, this occurs in two ways: (1) through the resultant inferiority complex due to an abated social position from the handicap; and (2) through the child's attempt to develop within a sociocultural milieu constructed for the individual without disabilities. For Vygotsky, "what was taken to be a physical handicap or illness, is, in fact, a complex of symptoms with a specific psychological orientation found in children who have been completely derailed socially; it is a socio and psychogenic phenomenon. . . . " (1993, p. 37). Therefore, the child's perception of his disability is heightened by social experiences that call attention to the deviation.

Dewey's (1913) theory of genuine interest additionally illuminates ways to privilege student voices and create learning contexts of interest for students with specific learning disabilities. Dewey stated, "Interest marks the annihilation of the distance between the person and materials and results of his action; it is the sign of their organic union" (p. 17). It is this notion of a *union* between student and materials that seems to be lacking in traditional pedagogy. A distance is created between the student and subject matter when the chosen curriculum falls outside the student's genuine interests. When a subject to be learned has no personal meaning for the student, the child quickly loses motivation to learn. On the other hand, within curricula that cultivate genuine interest, there is no separation between the self, the material, and the learning activity in which the individual is engaged. This synthesis is viewed as essential to proper growth and development. According to Dewey, it is information within the domain of interest that contributes to the developing self and enables the individual to persevere when faced with challenges.

Dewey's theory of genuine interest can be advantageously combined with social constructivist principles. Dewey stated that interest is an active, propulsive state. The pursuit of interest is personal and the outcome is of utmost importance to the individual.

Unsatisfied with teaching methodology in which the student is a passive recipient of information, Dewey mandated student participation in learning. Vygotsky (1987) agrees that it is through social activity that concepts are learned and development enhanced. Social constructivism calls, similarly, for authentic learning that encompasses real-world experiences. Dewey believed that interest ". . . is embodied in an object of regard" (p. 16). Together, these theories suggest that in order to be most beneficial, the learning experience should have meaning for the individual. The divorce of school curriculum and methodologies from authentic life activities risks failure to cultivate student interest. According to Neumann, Marks, and Gamoran (1995), when students are allowed to pursue learning through active techniques with real objects or problems (for example, hands-on experiences, community-based projects, cooperative learning groups, and the like), increased ". . . enthusiasm and engagement" (p. 3) result.

Empirical evidence that genuine interest plays a critical role in students' learning derives from a study of sixth graders over the course of one school year (McPhail et al. 1996; McPhail et al. 1997). In that project, students who were given their first choice of subject matter evidenced higher levels of affect—student report of being "happy, cheerful, sociable and friendly"—and activation—student report of being "alert, active, strong, and excited"—when engaged in the self-chosen activity settings than those students who did not receive their first choice (McPhail et al. 1997). This was true for both achieving and underachieving students. Affect and activation were rated using the experience sampling methodology to measure the ". . . ongoing reality of people's lives" (Csikszentmihalyi and Larson 1984; McPhail 1993). Our students were asked to respond to bipolar scales—happy/sad, active/passive, cheerful/irritable—about their experiences while in the activity. We posited that higher levels of affect and activation indicated the achievement of a learning environment in which positive feelings (affect) and engagement (active participation in the learning activity) were likely to occur. Our work demonstrated that sixth-grade students reliably identified their individual content interests and described ways of learning that advanced their understanding of interest areas. From our work, it would appear that the incorporation of student interest into learning contexts has the potential to elicit optimal engagement and, thus, improved learning from all students, even those identified as underachieving by their teachers.

Other evidence also suggests that contexts that incorporate genuine interest do facilitate intellectual development for individuals with dyslexia. Fink (1995, 1998) found that many adults with dyslexia (selected for being professionally "successful") reported that pursuing topics of interest helped them to learn to read as children. These adults claimed that it was personal interest in specific subject matter such as science, cooking, biographies, auto mechanics, and the like, that had motivated them to tackle and conquer their greatest enemy, reading. In apparent agreement with Dewey's theories, these successful adults with dyslexia had persevered in their efforts to read text because specific information contained therein held real and personal significance to the developing self. The enduring nature of individual interests was also evident among the individuals in Fink's inquiries. In some cases, these interests led to a lifelong hobby, in others to a future career choice. Regardless of outcome, the individuals whom Fink interviewed demonstrated many successful compensatory strategies, seemingly as a direct result of their personal interest reading. They ". . . developed deep background knowledge and became conversant with domain-specific vocabulary, concepts, themes, questions, and typical text structures" (Fink 1995, p. 276). Such studies of individual interest are compelling as we consider the possibilities for compensation in individuals with specific learning disabilities when engaged in interest-based learning contexts.

Finally, critical to the questions underlying the present inquiry is the manner in which knowledge is constructed and represented in the classroom. In general, classroom pedagogy privileges verbal-linguistic forms of construction and representation of knowledge. In other words, the student is required to learn material and demonstrate understanding in ways that rely primarily on oral and written language. Conceptually, many scholars (Eisner 1994; Gardner 1993; Neumann, Marks, and Gamoran 1995) acknowledge that one may represent one's knowledge through myriad forms such as words in a report or poem, symbols in a mathematical equation, composition of a musical score, dance, or visual art, and performance in dance or athletics. Such a conceptual view places value not only in verbal-linguistic representations of knowledge but also in alternative forms. Included in a redefinition of valued representational forms of knowledge is the understanding that not all individuals will construct or represent knowledge in similar ways (Gardner 1993).

Within the curriculum, educators need to allow for uniqueness among individuals. For example, Dalton et al. (1995) reported that a fourth-grade boy, "Joseph," received special education services for deficits in reading, spelling, math, and verbal expression, demonstrated sophisticated understanding of electricity concepts when allowed to do so through hands-on assessment. The incorporation of alternative forms of knowledge dissemination and representation, including visual-spatial and hands-on activities, allowed Joseph to access and represent information in ways that relied less on traditional verbal-linguistic forms. Such alternative methodology to teaching a curriculum may be essential, especially when we consider that many individuals with dyslexia evidence strong visual-spatial skills (Siegel, Share, and Geva 1995; West 1991).

Intervention to enhance literacy abilities that unites the above theoretical tenets of socioconstructivist learning in contexts of student genuine interest, and that allow for alternative representations of understanding and knowledge, may yield fruitful results for individuals with dyslexia. This work has the potential to discover ways for the child with dyslexia to demonstrate capabilities that lie outside of the customary verbal-linguistic, while at the same time help the child to overcome and compensate for areas of relative weakness.

THE PROJECT

This paper describes the initial twelve-week period of my work with Bill (a first-grade boy with dyslexia). During the first five weeks, Bill and I met on a weekly basis for an hour-long session and worked together to identify his interests and abilities, and create contexts in which these interests and abilities supported his literacy learning. After five weeks, the session length was increased to approximately one-and-one-half hours. All sessions were audiotaped. Through this inquiry, I hoped to understand how Bill makes meaning of the literacy events in his life, the nature of Bill's phonological processing and language skills, the nature of Bill's challenges in accessing and using print, how to create contexts of learning that incorporate Bill's genuine interest and abilities and that foster his identity as a competent learner, and how to assist Bill with developing his emergent literacy skills to experience success.

THE PARTICIPANTS

Bill is the younger of two boys of a white, middle-class family. When we began our work together, Bill was six years seven months of age. He was enrolled in first grade in a Catholic school in a small, ex-urban community, approximately 50 miles from a major city. In October, Bill's first-grade teacher mentioned the possibility of sending Bill back to kindergarten. His teacher expressed concern that Bill was not ready for first grade because he was having problems with phonics and learning letter names.

Bill's mother sought my counsel and we decided to begin tutoring. At the time, I had 14 years of experience working in the public schools, held a Masters degree in speech-language pathology, and was pursuing a doctorate in learning disabilities. Bill's mother described her son as a "social" boy with many friends in the classroom. She noted that Bill ". . . never wanted to be read to" as a young child, but preferred to play, fish, or build things. Bill's mother also reported that he became easily frustrated when asked to complete tasks of reading and writing. Bill's comments to his mother indicated that he did not enjoy school. He frequently complained in the mornings of being ill and not wanting to go to school. One night he asked his mother, "Why did you sign me up for school? I don't want to go."

SETTING THE CONTEXT: WEEKS 1–3

Bill's Language and Literacy Abilities on Initial Assessment. During the initial assessment, Bill evidenced some of the underlying language difficulties that are characteristic of dyslexia. Auditory discrimination abilities, as measured by the *Wepman Auditory Discrimination Test* (1973), fell into the range of "average ability," indicating satisfactory discrimination of phonemes in paired words (e.g., "Are these the same or different?—tub/tug, pat/pet, lack/lack"). Bill had difficulty, however, on all other tasks that assessed phonological processing and manipulation, including initial phoneme deletion, segmentation, rhyming, and oddity tasks. On the *Woodcock-Johnson Tests of Cognitive Ability - (WJ-R)* (1989), Bill scored an age equivalent of 6.0 (grade equivalent of K.7) on the Incomplete Words subtest (e.g., orally presented with "ba–tub", Bill must produce bathtub), and an age equivalent of 4.0 (grade equivalent of K.0) on the Sound Blending subtest (e.g., orally presented with "k—a—t", Bill must come up with cat). On nonstandardized phonological awareness assessment tasks, Bill scored 6/10 correct on a phoneme segmentation task in which he was asked to move one chip for each sound he heard in 2 to 4 phoneme words. Yet despite his moderate success on this task, Bill was unable to verbalize how he knew how many chips to move, suggesting that he may not yet have possessed a full metacognitive understanding of this task.

Further language difficulties were evidenced by Bill's failure to respond correctly to any of the items on an initial phoneme deletion task (e.g., take off the first sound of the word "cat" to give "at"). It appeared, however, that Bill did attend to the initial phoneme of the stimulus word, which he included in his responses to 5/6 items. For example, he said, "ma" for the stimulus word "man", and "not" for the stimulus "nice." Bill exhibited this same behavior on the rhyming task; although he did not correctly rhyme any words (e.g., "tell me a word that rhymes with man"), he named the initial sound in 4/5 trials. Bill was able to isolate the initial phoneme from the whole word on these tasks: to operate from whole to part. His performance suggested that he may not have understood what was required of him during these tasks. Bill's performance on a phonological oddity task provided further evidence that his phonological processing skills were below grade level. In this task, Bill correctly identified the "word that began with a different sound" from others in a group of four in only 3/10 trials.

Language samples were obtained from casual conversations with Bill about his home and school life, as well as from the tutoring sessions themselves. Bill evidenced both strengths and weaknesses in his processing and use of language. Bill's pragmatic abilities were an area of relative strength. He used language appropriately to engage in conversation with both peers and adults, and was relatively successful in these social interactions. Yet, Bill's word retrieval difficulties sometimes made it difficult to understand him fully, and Bill's conversational partner was often required to request clarification (see Appendix A).

Repeatedly, Bill demonstrated difficulty encoding and storing new vocabulary words. For example, Bill used the word "chester" when describing the game of chess (possibly a combination of checkers and chess). When referring to the compartment in his work table, he said, "I can't get into my apartment." Bill consistently demonstrated difficulties with word retrieval and naming, and frequently fell back on fillers such as "thing" and "stuff" as in "Do you have any of that bow-tying stuff?" to describe ribbon. Confusion frequently occurred with letter names as well. For example, Bill called "n," "m," but responded, "I said n," when corrected.

Bill's unique use of syntax sometimes failed to adequately express his intended meaning. For example, he noticed his name on my computer screen and said, "And that computer goes into my file. With my file is up top. That's my file is up there." When asked whether the computer went into his file, Bill recognized the error of such a statement; that his file is a part of (or in) the computer and not vice versa. His failure to self-monitor his utterances further contrbuted to the conversational breakdown.

Standardized assessments confirmed that Bill had a language deficit that affected both his receptive and expressive abilities. The school psychologist reported a verbal-performance gap of 17 points (verbal IQ 89; performance IQ 106) on the *Wechsler Intelligence Sale for Children (WISC-III)*. On the *Clinical Evaluation of Language Fundamentals (CELF-R)*, Bill's receptive language abilities fell at a standard score (SS) of 93 and expressive language at 85. Subtests of the *CELF-R* that were particularly problematic for Bill were following oral directions (SS 4; 2nd percentile) and formulating sentences (SS 4; 2nd percentile).

Bill demonstrated novice emergent literacy characteristics. Although he seemed aware of his inability to read and write conventionally (for example, answering, "I don't know how" when asked to do either), Bill possessed much knowledge about books and how to approach text. Bill effectively used what minimal strategies he had to glean information from text. Strategies that were especially helpful included the use of his prior knowledge and of the illustrations to make sense of the text. Bill demonstrated deficient knowledge about letter names as compared to the majority of his classmates who could identify and name all of the upper and lower case letters. He identified 12/26 upper case and 10/26 lower case letters, and could not name all of the letters in his name. As would be expected when asked to write, Bill produced apparently random letter strings ("AOHCHM" for "fish") with no grapheme-phoneme matches.

In summary, at the onset of intervention, Bill evidenced the language deficits in processing and use of phonological, semantic, and syntactic information characteristic of dyslexia. Also, conversational breakdown occurred as a result of his impaired processing and use of semantics and syntax, making Bill's conversational partner responsible for conversational repair. We find evidence in Bill's speech of all four deficit areas of language that Kamhi associated with reading disability: ". . . it is not possible to have a reading disability without a deficit in some aspect of phonological, syntactic, semantic, or discourse processing" (Kamhi 1989, p. 59).

Two primary characteristics limited Bill's ability to access and use print: (1) a deficit in processing and identifying the phonological components of language; and (2)difficulty learning letter symbols and subsequent sound-symbol associations (the alphabetic principle). Additionally, an area of great concern was Bill's image of himself as a learner. Bill stated, quite correctly, that he couldn't read or write, as defined conventionally, and understood, too, that the majority of his peers were successful according to this conventional standard. To compensate, Bill engaged in other behaviors in order to avoid tasks involving reading and writing. Bill was caught in a vicious cycle: to become a facile reader and writer, one must practice reading and writing; yet, since Bill was fully cognizant of his deficiencies in this area, he avoided any related activities.

Initially, I followed a lesson plan format that included the reading of little books, participation in activities designed to enhance phonemic awareness and word patterns, and writing (Hiebert 1994). At first, Bill participated in and enjoyed the lessons and activities that incorporated reading the little books and manipulating phonemes through the use of magnetic letters, write-on board, and the like, although he still refused to write. After three weeks, however, he balked at doing all the tasks in this format. If I brought out the magnetic letters, Bill would protest, "I hate this." The only way I could get him to do any work in this format was to coerce him into completing a set number of trials and promising him a reward: hardly a social constructivist approach.

According to Dewey (1913), "when things have to be made interesting, it is because interest itself is wanting" (p. 11). The transcript in Appendix B makes it abundantly clear that Bill's interest was indeed wanting. We see evidence both of Bill's aversion to the tasks and of my need to control the activity. It is obvious that there was no enjoyment in these activities for either of us.

It was also around this time that Bill's mother said he did not want to come to tutoring. When I asked why he did not want to come, Bill merely shrugged his shoulders and said that "it [the session] was long." I interpreted this to mean two things: (1) the work was hard; and (2) it was boring and not enjoyable. Keeping in mind Adams' (1990) observation that "it is not just reading to children that makes a difference, it is enjoying the books with them" (p. 46), I decided to tailor our curriculum to incorporate Bill's interests and include "dinosaurs" and "things that go" as our topics of study.

WEEKS 4–12: BILL'S VOICE, BILL'S CHOICE

Discovering Bill's Interests.   My quest to discover Bill's interests and incorporate them into literacy-learning contexts began during my initial conversation with his mother, who told me that Bill liked "fishing, dinosaurs, monster trucks, building stuff [his dad is a carpenter], and his cat and dog." From a phenomenological perspective, I hoped, in time, to understand how Bill experienced his world. Bruner (1996) states that only the person living the life can make sense of that life. I realized that, during our sessions, Bill had demonstrated interest in each of the areas that his mother had originally mentioned. Bill brought me pictures of his cat, his brother, and his dog, of fishing on his dock, and of dinosaurs in a museum. He had also drawn pictures of cars, trucks, and a cat. Bill recognized the important activities in his life and chose to represent them to me visually. I decided to explore further the areas that Bill had indicated were meaningful and of interest to him.

Given that the primary reason Bill was referred to me was to enhance his literacy abilities, I decided to incorporate books about his interests into our work. I went to the local bookseller to research trade books about the aforementioned interests. I chose two topics about which there were a multitude of trade books—dinosaurs and things that go (vehicles, heavy equipment, and so on)—and selected one book on each topic. In our next session, I presented Bill with the books and asked him to pick the one that he wanted to learn about first. Bill looked at both books, immediately grabbed the dinosaur book and said, "Dinosaurs! I like dinosaurs. Is there a T-rex?" Using his mother's reliable report of her son's interests and my observations of his actions and talk, I was successful in identifying a topic of interest for study about which there are many books. Bill fully embraced our new topic of study.

Bill's Abilities. As noted earlier, researchers have called for a reconceptualization of our approach to assessing and viewing students with disabilities, from the traditional deficit-driven approach to one which emphasizes competencies (Dalton et al. 1994; Vygotsky 1993; Wansart 1995; West 1991). One of my goals was to understand how to incorporate Bill's abilities into the instructional program. I must admit that it was rather easy to identify Bill's strengths. I merely needed to provide a range of opportunities and materials, give Bill the freedom to choose and structure activities, and then observe his actions and listen to him talk. I filled his drawer with pencils, pens, colored pencils, markers, crayons, scissors, glue, tape, stamp-making markers, and so forth. I also provided materials such as construction paper, drawing paper, oak tag, and books about drawing dinosaurs. I made a point of allowing Bill the opportunity to talk about his interests and what he liked to do.

Through the use of these items and by conversing with Bill, I learned much about his abilities. One of the first things I noticed was his inquisitiveness and his attention to visual details in his environment. For example, during one session, Bill insisted that I draw an allosaurus using a step-by-step book on how to draw dinosaurs. When I had completed the drawing, Bill exclaimed, "Hey, you didn't draw this right—he looks sad," while simultaneously slumping his shoulders. Bill grabbed my drawing along with the demonstration picture to point out that I had drawn the eye half-closed and that this minor detail changed the entire appearance of the allosaurus, from ferocious to meek. Admittedly, attending to detail in one's environment can be counterproductive if one is unable to inhibit this behavior enough to concentrate on the task at hand. Yet this ability can also be viewed as a gift if one considers the myriad professions in life that rely on attention to visual detail (artistry, architecture, design, machine repair, engineering, dentistry, and surgery) and rely on superior abilities in visual thinking, problem-solving, and spatial ability (West 1996).

Drawing is one of Bill's favorite activities and he is quite adept at it. The student teacher in Bill's classroom told his mother she had never seen a first grader who could draw like Bill. In tutoring sessions, Bill would draw any chance he could get. If I asked him to make a journal entry, he would say, "Can I draw?" He drew hot rods with lifters and rear wing foils; shocks connecting the tires to the chassis on monster trucks; skis and treads with internal wheels on snowmobiles; and dorsal, lateral, and posterior fins on fish. His drawings were easily recognizable and his attention to detail was evident in all of them.

Bill's apparent visual strengths were further evidenced in his ability to recall details in videos. Videos frequently popped up in the course of discussions. Bill recalled the details in these movies much better than I. Bill also seemed interested in music and song lyrics. He would frequently sing songs to me. He also wanted me to sing to him and often asked if I would "sing the whole thing." When left alone, he frequently hummed to himself while working.

Although Bill evidenced difficulties in some aspects of language processing and use, he demonstrated strengths in his creative use of language and in his ability to express the products of his vivid imagination. For example, during the segmentation task of the initial assessment, Bill said, "these could be a magnifying glass," referring to the transparent chips we were using.

Finally, as originally noted by his mother, Bill evidenced strengths in interpersonal skills. He was indeed a social young man. Repeatedly, the other boys in the classroom would come to look at his drawings and comment on how good they were. Both in the classroom play area and in the lunchroom, Bill interacted well with the other first-grade boys.

If, for a moment, we consider his abilities in light of Gardner's (1993) seven "frames of mind," we note that Bill evidences strengths and interests in at least three areas: visual-spatial (drawing), musical, and interpersonal. Interestingly, Bill's strengths correspond to many of the positive traits that West (1991) identified as being associated with learning difficulties: "talents in spatial, mechanical, and related right-hemisphere skills . . . ; love of construction toys, models, and craft work [Bill's love for Legos]; love of and great skill at drawing; an especially good musical ear; and an especially good ability to visualize and manipulate images in the mind" (p. 93). Bill possessed numerous abilities, some of which exceeded those of his peers. Yet his weak verbal-linguistic skills tended to override these abilities and became the primary obstacle to Bill's success in school. Because of his less sophisticated abilities in accessing and storing phonological knowledge, which in turn inhibited his understanding and use of print, Bill was marked as a child who was not succeeding in first grade.

The Renegotiation. Following my discovery of Bill's interests in learning, our sessions centered on drawing, creating artwork, reading books, and writing about dinosaurs. The incorporation into our lessons of Bill's interest in dinosaurs brought about an immediate change in his desire to come to the sessions and in his engagement and attitude during our sessions. Bill's mother reported that he repeatedly asked whether each day was the day of our tutoring session. Rarely did a session go by when he failed to bring something he had made or drawn for me. Frequently, these pictures had been drawn in school. "I made you this in the library today," he said one day, handing me a picture of a pirate ship complete with oars, masts, sails, anchor, flag, shark jumping out of the water, and a treasure chest at the bottom of the sea. When he arrived, he would head immediately into my office while I spoke with his mother. By the time I entered the office, he would have explored the new things that I had for him and he would be ready to go. He worked diligently during the sessions and did not want to leave, saying that his mother "can wait for a little bit longer." Often, I literally had to push him out the door.

Although Bill continued to dislike school and exhibit reluctance to engage in reading and writing on his own, there was a significant difference in his willingness to engage in activities surrounding text during our tutoring sessions and at home. He was quick to notice a new book on dinosaurs in our growing collection and initiated requests for me to read it to him. Bill had always complied with my suggestions to read trade books during our lessons, but after we began reading books about dinosaurs, he began to initiate requests to read. This was encouraging, especially in light of research that has demonstrated the importance of children's engagement with, and enjoyment of, text in enhancing vocabulary and skills surrounding reading (Adams 1990). We sometimes read as many as five books in Bill's area of interest during a session together, in addition to other activities. I encouraged this reading, since the amount of text children read and are exposed to has been shown to make a positive difference in their acquisition of skills required for reading (Wigfield and Asher 1984). When we were confronted with a question about dinosaurs that we could not answer, Bill would suggest we "look it up." This meant that he perused the text to find the picture of the dinosaur and then I read the text. He even suggested that I bring books to share with his friends when I visited his school. He sometimes chose to "read" books to himself (look at the pictures). I found that the best approach to working with Bill was to provide a plethora of dinosaur books and then allow him the freedom to choose whether and what we would read. Bill's interest was evidenced by the fact that he always chose to read at least two books each session. While Bill's actual conventional reading abilities remained relatively unchanged, there were qualitative improvements in the ways he approached activities surrounding text and in his enjoyment of books.

Bill's mother reported positive changes in engagement surrounding literacy at home as well. Just about the time of our twelfth session, she reported that Bill "comes home and draws all night." He had begun asking her how to spell words and to write things such as "illustrated by." At one point, he wrote the words "the end" when finishing a book in which he had drawn all of the pictures.

BILL'S CURRENT LITERACY ABILITIES

Given the ongoing nature and relatively short duration of this project, I will summarize Bill's abilities along dimensions of literacy that demonstrate salient features of change (see Table I for a summary of changes over the course of intervention). Although Bill continues to state, "I can't read" when asked to

Table I: Comparison of Bill's literacy abilities at the onset of tutoring and at 12 weeks.

Week 1	Week 12
Emergent Literacy Abilities	
• Named 12/26 upper case letters and 10/26 lower case letters	• Named 21/26 upper case and 24/26 lower case letters
• Did not name all letters in his name	• Named all letters in his name
• Rhymed 0/5 words	• Rhymed 2/10 words
• Prephonemic writing	• With support, early phonemic writing
• "I don't know how to write."	• Feels safe to attempt writing with me
• Read words from both left-right and right-left	• Consistently reads words from left-right
Strategy use	
• Possible attention to initial sound on deletion and rhyming tasks	• Creates new word to form rhyme
• Avoided the tasks	• Attends to vowels, onset-vowel, and onset
	• Provides associative words
	• Demonstrates self-monitoring and self-correction
	• Subvocalizes word beginning with letter to recall letter name
	• Asks questions for clarification
	• Will persevere when appropriate support is present
Related Behaviors	
• Does not want to go to school	• Persists in not wanting to go to school
	• Begins to attend to environmental
	• print and sounds in words
	• Understands that information is gained through text
	• Wants to "read" books on his own (although this means looking at pictures)
	• Has increased confidence toward approaching tasks of literacy such as letter naming and writing letters
	• Comes home from school and "begins to draw, and draws all night"
	• Begins to inquire how to spell words at home
	• Asked his mother to write "illustrated by" in a book he had made
	• Wrote "the end" on finishing a book

approach texts, he has evidenced growth in certain literacy skills. He understands that information is gained through texts, as demonstrated by his suggestion to "look it up" when we encounter unfamiliar words or information. He has become more confident in his willingness to approach tasks of letter naming and will attempt to spell a word to me as I look it up (in the dictionary or index) or write it down.

Another area in which I have observed growth is Bill's attention to print and sounds in his environment. During our work, he frequently associates a letter with a word or name that he knows. His mother recently reported that Bill noticed the letters on a department store marquee for the first time. Since our discussion about artists placing their signatures on their paintings, he insists that I sign my name or initials to all of our artwork.

Assessment of Bill's letter naming at Week 12 reflects a significant improvement in this area. Although deficient phonological awareness continues to plague Bill, I have noticed that his phonological awareness tends to improve when we are engaged in reading texts about dinosaurs. While we are reading or talking, he will call out a word and then give another word that rhymes with the first. In one instance, I had just read, "As the plants rotted, they made heat and . . ." when Bill interjected, "heat, Pete [a familiar name], they rhyme." This demonstrates that Bill is now attending to rhyme in words, a marked change in ability from our first session.

When left on his own, Bill continues to write words with little correct sound-symbol association. When I vocalize the consonant sounds, his success in making the grapheme-phoneme match improves. Here we see how Vygotsky's notion of the ZPD and the scaffolding provided by an "expert other" directly affects Bill's competencies in writing. Not only does my guidance assist Bill's success on, and therefore his feelings of, mastery within the task, but gives us opportunities to focus on areas of relative weakness, such as letter-sound correspondence.

A TEACHER'S CHALLENGE: IMPLICATIONS FOR PRACTICE

In much the same manner that Bill's perceptions could not be divorced from the context of our work, I also brought my own agenda and preconceptions to our interactions. To allow Bill a voice in his learning, it was necessary to constantly monitor and challenge my ideas about teaching and learning. In concert with Dewey's theory of interest, I wanted to create contexts that would engage Bill in the learning process. Even though I have witnessed personally the positive effects of such an endeavor for Bill, I have struggled with a tension during this phase of our work together. On the one hand, I have a desire for Bill to develop a healthy, positive concept of himself as a learner (Bruner 1996), a concept which I am attempting to foster by incorporating Bill's abilities and interests into contexts of literacy learning. On the other hand, I know that I need to engage him in activities that directly target areas of relative weakness, specifically tasks involving readable text, phonological awareness and letter-sound relationships, and writing in order that he possess the necessary tools to successfully approach literacy activities throughout his life. In my desire to teach Bill skills and incorporate bottom-up approaches to intervention, starting with phonological processing and making the phoneme-grapheme match, I struggled especially hard against my behaviorist training. In fact, our interest-based curriculum corresponded more directly to top-down tenets of an interactive model of reading. As Lipson and Wixson (1991) suggest, instructional practices, whether top-down or bottom-up, will vary at different times according to the needs of the reader. Based on Bill's needs at this time, it was critical to focus on reading in a holistic manner in an attempt to lessen his dislike for activities that surrounded reading and writing. We needed to make reading and writing fun before Bill would even attempt activities that focused on learning underlying skills in a more structured way. Ultimately, acting as the "expert other" (Vygotsky 1987), I was able to create a safe environment for Bill to take some risks by applying his phonological abilities to activities of reading and writing. In the future, this safe environment will provide the foundation for activities that incorporate bottom-up aspects of literacy learning. We will continue to pursue these activities using Bill's interests in dinosaurs and his expressed interest in drawing vehicles. For example, step-by-step drawing books require Bill to read text that is supported with visual diagrams. This allows him to use his strength in visual-perceptual abilities while targeting his relative weakness in decoding text within an activity of interest. After he draws a race car, letter-sound correspondence skills can be targeted as he names his car, writes "finish line," and composes a sentence about it.

Additionally, I propose that we, as educators, make different uses of standardized assessment results to inform our pedagogical practice. As a group, professionals in the field of learning disabilities have become adept at identifying students' relative cognitive strengths through the use of standardized assessment. We know that the use of psychological and achievement testing offers insight into students' individual profiles of learning strengths. Based on the results of this study, I propose that we stop focusing on the deficit areas—the valleys in the "peaks and valleys" profile of the student with LLD—which, for the most part, are related primarily to the verbal-linguistic behaviors. I propose rather, that we begin redesigning intervention approaches and curricula for students with LLD, using their cognitive strengths in contexts of their self-expressed interests. The data from this inquiry demonstrated that using such a tactic yielded positive outcomes for Bill. I found that using Bill's interests and emphasizing his processing strengths created an in-road for him to gain the literacy skills and confidence necessary to approach tasks that involved written text.

Private practitioners have an ideal setting to begin to design intervention programs using students' interests and strengths. In the schools, the continued practice of "pull-out" programs in speech-language therapy, as well as the use of learning disabilities resource rooms, provide ideal circumstances in which to begin this endeavor. Small group settings lend themselves to learning contexts that use individual student interests. The individualized mandate of the Individual Educational Plan (IEP) could support such programming. Flexibility in scheduling could allow for students to be grouped by interest rather than by grade level. This could, in turn, afford opportunities for peer tutoring, and even mentoring by members of the community.

CONCLUSIONS

The issues central to this inquiry included how Bill makes meaning of the literacy events in his life, the nature of Bill's phonological processing and language skills, the nature of Bill's challenges in accessing and using print, how to create contexts of learning that incorporated Bill's genuine interests and abilities to foster his identity as a competent learner, and how to assist Bill in successfully developing his emergent literacy skills. To ensure the success of this intervention, it was necessary not only to understand Bill's abilities and deficits in language and literacy but also to understand Bill's perceptions of himself as a learner and how he makes meaning of the literacy events in his life. Only through such understanding could Bill and I develop a shared meaning of literacy. Although quantifiable changes in

Bill's literacy abilities are modest at this point in our work together, I have witnessed some striking changes in his engagement and speech which seem largely attributable to the use of an interest-based curriculum.

As postulated by Dewey (1913), my initial pedagogical practice in which the subject matter (little book lessons) was first chosen and then made interesting, was problematic because the selection of the content was made separate from Bill's interests, and thus lacked the personal quality necessary for learning to be of interest and have meaning. Furthermore, Bill did not regard the outcome as important. The success of this intervention began when Bill was allowed a voice in the content and design of the activities and when he was given a choice.

Creating activities that employed Bill's abilities within the context of genuine interest yielded results consistent with Dewey's (1913) notion of the union between the self, the material, and the activity. For Bill, learning about dinosaurs was directly related to his personal life and to his development of self. In 1992, Schiefele summarized Herbart's proposition of a relationship between interest and learning as follows:

"In his opinion, it is first and foremost interest that allows for correct and complete recognition of an object, leads to meaningful learning, promotes long term storage of knowledge and provides motivation for future learning" (p. 151).

It appears that this twelve-week project has been successful in creating a context for learning in which three of the four tenets identified by Herbart came to be realized for Bill. Correct and complete recognition of an object is evident, for example, in Bill's response to my inaccurate drawing of the allosaurus where he noticed that my representation was not true to the fierceness of an allosaurus. Engagement in the topic of study and motivation for future learning is reflected by Bill's comment that he is "never gonna be done" studying dinosaurs. Meaningful learning (as demonstrated by increased skill) occurred for Bill when we incorporated his interest in dinosaurs into his literacy learning (see Table I). It remains to be seen whether this approach will be equally successful toward achieving long-term storage of knowledge.

Finally, this paper demonstrates the need to create learning contexts that reallocate knowledge representation from its privileged, verbal-linguistic medium to include other forms as well (visual-spatial, bodily-kinesthetic, and the like). In today's society, the ability to successfully operate within the verbal-linguistic mode remains critical. Yet for Bill, exclusive use of this method of knowledge representation and transmission was detrimental to experiencing early success in learning, thereby preventing the development of a positive self-concept as a learner. Klenk (1994) postulated that learning to read and write must involve ". . . opportunities [for students with learning disabilities] to create their own codes" (p. 55). Bill's experience in his first-grade classroom revolved around conventional aspects of print and gave him little opportunity to experiment with his own code. Allowing for alternative forms of knowledge representation could enhance opportunities for Bill to develop his own code, one which might eventually lead to his learning of the conventional code. This suggests that we must develop ways for children like Bill to demonstrate their abilities through other modalities. If every day in the classroom allows children with talents in the verbal-linguistic area (speaking, reading, and writing) to demonstrate their abilities, so should every day allow Bill to demonstrate his gifts in the visual area. If every day privileges writing, then every day should also privilege drawing, or movement, or puzzle-solving, or dance.

Ultimately, a learning context in which reading and writing activities were structured around the genuine interests of a six-year-old boy resulted in improved willingness to engage in literacy learning. This, in turn, yielded improvement in specific literacy-based skills such as phonological awareness and understanding concepts of print. Our challenge, as educators, will be to design instructional contexts that benefit larger numbers of individuals; contexts that incorporate student interest and allow students with specific learning disabilities to demonstrate their unique strengths.

ACKNOWLEDGMENTS

The author wishes to thank Jean C. McPhail, Annemarie Sullivan Palincsar, and Holly K. Craig for their guidance and comments during varying stages of this work. Additionally, she is grateful to Anne E. Fowler for the cogent comments and suggestions during the revision process. And she extends her gratitude to "Bill" and his family.

Address correspondence to: jpierson@umich.edu

APPENDIX A

(Bill was drawing a picture of a car and Joanne asked)

JP: Do you get to draw much in school?

B: No, not that much. Only, only in front of the school.

JP: Only in front of the school?

B: One second. Right in front of the school we draw. Right in front you know? When the bell doesn't, when the bell rings?

JP: You mean before school starts?

B: (Nods yes.)

JP: Are you inside or outside?

B: Inside.

JP: Oh. Are you in your classroom or . . .

B: Classroom.

JP: You're in your classroom?

B: Mhm.

JP: Before school starts?

B: Mhm.

APPENDIX B

(Bill and I have just finished reading a little book about fishing.)

JP: Do you remember what words you framed? I have to put them in here.

B: No, no, no, no, I don't.

JP: You don't?

B: I don't wanna do it.

JP: No, no, no, I just wanna know if you remember them.

B: No, no! I don't.

JP: You framed run, bite, and nibbling, right?

(Later)

JP: Okay, picture sorting [by initial phoneme], really fast.

B: Nooo!

JP: Yeesss.

B: No, no, no, no, I don't wanna . . .

JP: Yes, yes, yes.

B: No, no, no.

JP: No negotiating this, sorry buddy.

B: I'm not doin' it. I don't wanna.

JP: Or you won't get to have the treats that I have for you at the end. M, /m/ [begins the activity].

References

Adams, M. J. 1990. *Beginning to Read: Thinking and Learning About Print, a Summary*. Urbana-Champaign, IL: University of Illinois at Urbana-Champaign, Center for the Study of Reading.

Bruner, J. 1996. *The Culture of Education*. Cambridge: Harvard University Press.

Csikszentmihalyi, M., and Larson, R. 1984. *Being Adolescent*. New York: Basic Books.

Coles, G. 1987. *The Learning Mystique*. New York: Pantheon Books.

Dalton, B., Tivnan, T., Riley, M. K., Rawson, P., and Dias, D. 1995. Revealing competence: Fourth-grade students with and without learning disabilities show what they know on paper-and-pencil and hands-on performance assessments. *Learning Disabilities Research and Practice* 104:198–214.

Dewey, J. 1913. *Interest and Effort in Education*. Boston: Houghton Mifflin.

Eisner, E. W. 1994. *The Educational Imagination: On the Design and Evaluation of School Programs* 3rd ed. New York: Macmillan College Publishing.

Ferguson, P. M., Ferguson, D. L., and Taylor, S. 1992. The future of interpretivism in disability studies. In *Interpreting Disability: A Qualitative Reader*. P. M. Ferguson, D. L. Ferguson, and S. Taylor, eds. New York: Teachers College Press.

Fink, R. P. 1995. Successful dyslexics: A constructivist study of passionate interest reading. *Journal of Adolescent and Adult Literacy* 394:268–80.

Fink, R. P. 1998. Literacy development in successful men and women with dyslexia. *Annals of Dyslexia* 48.

Gardner, H. 1993. *Multiple Intelligences: The Theory in Practice*. New York: Basic Books.

Heshusius, L. 1989. The Newtonian mechanistic paradigm, special education, and contours of alternatives: An overview. *Journal of Learning Disabilities* 227:403–15.

Hiebert, E. H. 1994. A small group literacy intervention with Chapter 1 students. In *Getting Reading Right from the Start*. E. H. Hiebert and B. M. Taylor, eds. Boston: Allyn and Bacon.

Johnson, D. J., and Myklebust, H. 1967. *Learning Disabilities: Educational Principles and Practices*. New York: Grune and Stratton.

Kamhi, A. G. 1989. Reading disabilities: Terminology, definitions, and subtyping issues. In *Reading Disabilities: A Developmental Language Perspective*. A. G. Kamhi and H. W. Catts, eds. Boston: College-Hill.

Klenk, L. 1994. Case study in reading disability: An emergent literacy perspective. *Learning Disability Quarterly* 17:33–56.

Lipson, M. Y., and Wixson, K. K. 1991. *Assessment and Instruction of Reading Disability: An Interactive Approach*. New York: Harper Collins Publishers.

McPhail, J. C. 1993. Adolescents with learning disabilities: A comparative life-stream interpretation. *Journal of Learning Disabilities* 26:617–29.

McPhail, J. C. 1995. Phenomenology as philosophy and method: Applications to ways of doing special education. *Remedial and Special Education* 163:159–65.

McPhail, J. C., Ayappa, A., Freeman, J. G., Goodman, J., and Pierson, J. M. 1996. "Mind at Work in Activities of Interest." Paper read at the Second Conference for Sociocultural Research, July 1996, Geneva, Switzerland.

McPhail, J. C., Pierson, J. M., Ayappa, A., Freeman, J. G., and Goodman, J. 1997. "The Role of Interest in Fostering 6th Grade Students' Identities as Competent Learners." Paper read at the annual meeting of the American Educational Researchers Association, Chicago.

Neumann, F. M., Marks, H. M., and Gamoran, A. 1995. Authentic pedagogy: Standards that boost student performance. *Issues in Restructuring Schools*. Report No. 8. Madison: University of Wisconsin, Center on Organization and Restructuring of Schools.

Palincsar, A. S., and Klenk, L. 1992. Fostering literacy learning in supportive contexts. *Journal of Learning Disabilities* 254:211–29.

Palincsar, A. S., and Perry, N. E. 1995. Developmental, cognitive, and sociocultural perspectives on assessing and instructing reading. *School Psychology Review* 243:331–44.

Poplin, M. S. 1988. The reductionistic fallacy in learning disabilities: Replicating the past by reducing the present. *Journal of Learning Disabilities* 217:389–400.

Schiefele, U. 1992. Topic interest and levels of text comprehension. *In The Role of Interest in Learning and Development*. K. A. Renninger, S. Hidi, and A. Krapp, eds. Hillsdale, NJ: Lawrence Erlbaum Associates.

Schneider, P., and Watkins, R. V. 1996. Applying Vygotskian developmental theory to language intervention. *Language, Speech, and Hearing Services in Schools* 272:157–70.

Semel, E., Wiig, E. H., and Secord, W. 1987. *Clinical Evaluation of Language Fundamentals —Revised:* The Psychological Corporation.

Siegel, L. S., Share, D., and Geva, E. 1995. Evidence for superior orthographic skills in dyslexics. *Psychological Science* 64:250–54.

Vygotsky, L. S. 1987. *The Collected Works of L. S. Vygotsky: Problems of General Psychology*, Vol. 1. New York: Plenum.

Vygotsky, L. S. 1993. *The Collected Works of L. S. Vygotsky: The Fundamentals of Defectology*, Vol. 2. New York: Plenum.

Wansart, W. L. 1995. Teaching as a way of knowing: Observing and responding to students' abilities. *Remedial and Special Education* 16:166–77.

Wepman, J. M. 1973. *Auditory Discrimination Test*. Palm Springs, CA: Language Research Associates, Inc.

West, T. G. 1991. *In the Mind's Eye*. Buffalo, NY: Prometheus Books.

Wigfield, A., and Asher, S. R. 1984. Social and motivational influences on reading. In *Handbook of Research on Reading*. P. D. Pearson, R. Barr, M. L. Kamil, and P. Mosenthal, eds. New York: Longman.

Woodcock, R. W., and Johnson, M. B. 1989. *Woodcock-Johnson Tests of Cognitive Ability*. Itasca, IL: The Riverside Publishing Co.

Annals of Dyslexia
Information for Contributors

The Annals of Dyslexia is a peer-reviewed interdisciplinary journal dedicated to the understanding and remediation of reading disability. Primary consideration is given to original research papers; we also publish significant reviews and well-documented reports of effective practices. Each manuscript will be evaluated with regard to 1) its general significance for the Annals readership; 2) the specific contribution within the paradigm adopted; 3) the soundness of methodology and interpretation of results; and 4) the clarity and organization of writing. Only papers not previously published will be considered for publication; papers cannot be simultaneously submitted to Annals and other journals. **Please limit manuscript *text* to 20 pages not including reference lists, tables, and figures.**

Manuscripts must be submitted by December 15 in order to receive full consideration for publication in the following year. Papers submitted after that time (until January 15) will be considered only if space is available. Manuscripts will be reviewed by the Editor and two other reviewers with expertise in the area to which the topic pertains; the initial review process seldom requires more than 3 months. It is our policy to provide authors such editorial assistance as is necessary to achieve conciseness and clarity in presenting their work; most accepted papers will require some revision. The editorial decision letter will communicate suggestions to the author that should facilitate the preparation of the revision. Strict deadlines must be met in order to meet the once-a-year publication schedule.

The 1982 edition of the *Chicago Manual of Style* is the primary authority used in editing *Annals of Dyslexia*. We recommend that writers refer to it, scrutinizing language, usage, and mechanics in their manuscripts prior to submitting them. The author-date system of text reference and the reference list style should be followed. (Examples are provided in these instructions.) **NOTE: Reference lists, in particular, submitted in APA style will be returned to be resubmitted in the form shown on pages 3 and 4 of this guide.** Tables, figures, and statistical information should follow conventions outlined in Publication Manual of the APA, 4th Edition.

Submit the **original manuscript plus three copies** and retain a copy for your files. Do not staple manuscripts or copies. We also require an **abstract of the paper not to exceed 200 words**. If your paper is accepted, we will ask at a later point for a copy of the computer disk containing the word processing version of your manuscript, including an unformatted ASCII file. Details will be provided at that point.

List your name on the title page, followed by applicable affiliations, exactly as the publication should read. Except for medical doctors, no degrees are used in *Annals*. Please include work and home addresses for correspondence with the author and co-authors (designating the primary address to use), also including phone numbers, fax numbers, and e-mail addresses for each author and co-author as available.

Preparation of Manuscript

Manuscripts should be double-spaced for text, footnotes, tables, and figure legends. Reference lists should be triple-spaced throughout. All margins, left, right, top and bottom, should be at least one inch wide. Each page should have the author's name and abbreviated title at the left-hand top of the page. *Make the title of the article concise and to the point.* We suggest a three- or four-word running head to facilitate indexing and information retrieval.

A and B headings should be typed on separate lines and should not run into the paragraphs or be italicized (underscored). "A" headings should be centered, and "B" headings should be placed at the left margin. "C" headings should begin at the appropriate paragraph, using capitals and lower case and should be italicized (underscored).

Footnotes should be numbered consecutively in the text, indicated by superscript numbers, and then typed on a separate page labeled *Footnotes*.

References cited in the text should be followed, in parenthesis, by the author's surname (unless it is given in the text of the sentence, as in *a* and *d* below) and the date of the reference. If there are two or more references cited by the same author with the same year of publication, use lowercase letters after the date to distinguish them. Do not use commas preceding publication dates.

Examples:
a. The work of Victor Denenberg and his colleagues (1978) is important in this regard.
b. The brain of the rat has been altered as a result of hormone treatments (Diamond, Dowling, and Johnson 1981).
c. In recent years psychologists have referred extensively to metacognition (Brown 1978).
d. Orton provided several case studies which support this position (1928c, 1928e).
e. Satz and his colleagues (Satz and Friel 1973, 1974; Fletcher et al. 1982) undertook a series of studies to investigate the predictive value of kindergarten screening tests.

Note: Citations, including the first, of works by more than three authors use the name of the first followed by *et al*.

Illustrations should be original inked drawings in a form suitable for reduction without retouching or redrawing. Suggested size is 8½ x 11 inches. Lettering numerals, and symbols should be large enough so that they will be completely legible after reduction. Photographs should be the original and on glossy paper. Place overlays on all photographs to avoid damage. If only part of the photograph is to be used, indicate that part with penciled lines on the overlay. (Permission must be obtained for any illustrative material previously published in a book or journal.) Legends for illustrations should not be attached, but typed in double space on a separate page and clearly keyed to the illustrations.

Tables should be numbered with Roman numerals and in the order of their mention in the text. Citations in the text to the tables should also be in

Roman numerals. A brief title should be typed directly above each table. Explanatory material for the table should be placed in a footnote.

Figures should be numbered in sequence with Arabic numerals and in the order of their mention in the text. Their citations should be in Arabic numerals in the text. A note in the margin of the text where the figure is mentioned should indicate where the figure is to be placed. Each figure should be identified, either on the back or in the margin, with its number, author's name, and title of manuscript. The legends should be typed in double space and in sequence on a separate page of the manuscript labeled *Figures*; they should not be on the figures.

For all illustrative material—photographs, tables, figures, drawings— place a note in the margin of the text to indicate the approximate placement desired. All typing on or for such material—title, column heading, body of table, etc.—should be double-spaced.

Computer-generated figures must be saved in a PICT, TIFF, or EPS file. Computer-generated tables should be created in a word processing program rather than in a spreadsheet.

The reference list should include only those references cited in the text.

Entries in the list should be arranged alphabetically by the author's surname and should not be numbered. If there is more than one publication by a given author in the same year, the letters a, b, etc. should be added after the date. Please triple-space all entries and follow the style of the examples given below. (DO NOT, however, separate your references into these categories.)

Book

Bakker, D. J. 1972. *Temporal Order in Disturbed Reading*. Rotterdam: University Press.

More Than One Publication by a Given Author in the Same Year

Bakker, D.J. 1979a. Perceptual asymmetries and reading proficiency. In *Cognitive Growth and Development*, M. Bortner, ed. New York: Brunner/ Mazel.

Bakker, D.J. 1976b. A set of brains for learning to read. In *Individual Differences and Universals in Language Learning Aptitude*, K. C. Diller, ed. Boston: Newbury House Publishers.

Edited Book

Benton, A.L., and Pearl, D. eds. 1978. *Dyslexia: An Appraisal of Current Knowledge*. New York: Oxford University Press.

Chapter in a Book

Elkonin, D. B. 1973. U.S.S.R. In *Comparative Reading*, J. Downing, ed. New York: MacMillan.

Treiman, R., and Zukowski, A. 1991. Levels of phonological awareness. In *Phonological Processes in Literacy*, S. A. Brady and D. P. Shankweiler, eds. Hillsdale, NJ: Lawrence Erlbaum Associates.

Buffery, A.W.H., and Gray, J.A. 1972. Sex differences in the development of spatial and linguistic skills. In *Gender Differences: Their Ontogeny and Significance*, C. Ounsted and D.C. Taylor, eds. London: Churchill Livingstone.

Journal

Geschwind, N. 1979. Asymmetries of the brain: New developments. *Bulletin of the Orton Society* 29:67–73.

Heir, D.B., LeMay, M., Rosenberger, P.B., and Perlo, V.P., 1978. Developmental dyslexia: Evidence for a sub-group with reversal of cerebral asymmetry. *Archives of Neurology* 35:90–92.

Volume Numbers: Book

Kleuber, R. 1971. Mental abilities and disorders of learning. In *Progress in Learning Disabilities*, Vol. II, H. R. Myklebust, ed. New York: Grune and Stratton.

Torgesen, J.K. 1977. Memorization processes in reading-disabled children. *Journal of Educational Psychology* 69(5):571–578.

Dissertation or Thesis

Jones, A. J. 1947. Laterality and dominance in preschool deaf children. Ph.D. diss., Northeastern University, Boston.

Paper Read at a Meeting

Halpern, E. 1970. Reading success with children with visual-perceptual immaturity. Paper read at 47th Annual Meeting of the American Orthopsychiatric Association, November 1969, San Francisco.

COMMUNICATIONS AND MANUSCRIPTS

All communications and manuscripts should be sent to:
Annals of Dyslexia
The International Dyslexia Association®
8600 LaSalle Road
Chester Bldg./Suite 382
Baltimore, MD 21286-2044
(410) 296-0232, ext. 23

Index

(Page numbers in italics indicate material in figures or tables.)